THE SOUL
and Graves
of
YUGOSLAVIA
1941 - 1946
A National Tragedy

PART 1

*Drawing Yugoslavia
Into The War*

MARKO PIVAC

Copyright © 2013 by Marko Pivac

All rights reserved

No part of this book may be reproduced or utilized in any form or by any means, mechanical or electronic, photocopying, or by any storage and retrieval system, without prior written permission by the author or his designated beneficiary. Inquiries should be addressed to K. W. Olsen, kwolsen@gmail.com.

Library of Congress Cataloguing-in-Publication Data
Pivac, Marko
The Soul and Graves of Yugoslavia, 1941-1946 A National Tragedy
Marko Pivac – 1st ed.

Cover Design: Kathy Olsen

1	British plan for the Balkan Front (Greece-Turkey-Yugoslavia) and responses to the plan
2	Pre-war activities of Section D of MI6 and of Special Operations Executive and their domestic co-operatives in Yugoslavia
3	Drawing Yugoslavia into the Second World War
4	Mission of Foreign Minister Sir Anthony Eden and General Sir John Dill in Greece and the Middle East
5	The role of US Colonel William J. "Wild Bill" Donovan
6	Mission of SOE's George Taylor in Yugoslavia
7	Yugoslavia's adherence to the Tripartite Pact without military clauses and obligations, 25 March 1941
8	Military *coup d'état* in Belgrade, 27 March 1941
9	British Expeditionary Force in Greece
10	Germany's attack on Yugoslavia and Greece
11	Assessment of the British intervention

Printed in the United States of America

ISBN-13 978-0-972-02461-7

Second Printing 2015

IN MEMORY

OF THE VICTIMS

OF

THE SECOND WORLD WAR

Table of Contents

TABLE OF CONTENTS iii
   ACKNOWLEDGEMENTS 11
   NOTES ON THE STRUCTURE OF THE TEXT 12
   NOTES ON PRONUNCIATION OF SOUTH-SLAVIC (YUGO-SLAV) NAMES 12
   THE UNION OF THE SOVIET SOCIALIST REPUBLICS WAS NOT RUSSIA 13
   SHAPERS OF EVENTS 15

INTRODUCTION 17
   REST IN PEACE 25
   A GRAVE 28
   A LETTER 29
   A REPORT 30

CHAPTER 1 32
   "A war in the Balkans was not what Hitler wanted." 32
   Importance of the Mediterranean for the British Empire 32
   The impact of Italy's conquest of Albania 33
      * On Greece 33
      * On Turkey and Yugoslavia 34
   "Should Italy become hostile ..." 34
   Churchill's attitude toward the neutrals 35
   "British slowness in supplying arms" 36
   17 September 1940: *"... the end of Sea Lion ..."* 36
      * German troops in Rumania – an unforeseen impact on Yugoslavia 37
   The Tripartite Pact 38
   Italy's attack on Greece, 28 October 1940 38
   Consequences of Italy's attack on Greece 39
      * Immediate reactions of the British military 39
   To help or not to help Greece 40
      * Initially, the British military leaders were opposed to the aid 40
      * The Prime Minister was in favor of aid 41
   "A crucial difference" between Britain and Greece on Salonika 43
   Hitler was prepared to help Mussolini in Greece 43

CHAPTER 2 44
   *** Feelers for German-Yugoslav negotiations 44
   The idea of the Balkan front in 1941 – *"wishfully minded"* 44
   Hitler's *Directive No. 18*: Occupation of the northern Greek mainland 45
      *** German-Yugoslav negotiations 45
      *** More on the German-Yugoslav negotiations: Hitler and Ciano, 18 November 46
   Churchill to Halifax: *"... firm up Turkey and Yugoslavia ..."* 46
   "Subversive Activities in Relation to Strategy". 47
   Churchill to Halifax: *"We want Turkey to come into the war as soon as possible"* 48

    ***The start of the German-Yugoslav negotiations: Hitler and Cincar-Marković, 28 November 1940 48

CHAPTER 3 50
The British shaped Yugoslavia's role to fit their goals 50
Greek King's appeal for American aid to Greece 50
Churchill to Dalton: the Balkans – "SOE's acid test" 51
Hitler was firming up his plan to help Italy. 51
    *** German-Yugoslav negotiations continued 52
    * Examination of the situation by the Joint Planning Staff in Cairo 54
Hitler to Mussolini: a non-aggression pact with Yugoslavia 55

CHAPTER 4 56
Roosevelt-Churchill contacts 56
Harry Hopkins in London, January 1941 56
Colonel Donovan's missions 57
    * Lunch with Churchill, 18 December 1940 58

CHAPTER 5 59
Shift from the Middle East to the Balkans 59
Germany's "… ultimate descent upon Greece …" 59
    *** German-Yugoslav negotiations: the meeting on 14 February 1941 61

CHAPTER 6 63
The issue of assisting Greece 63
Succor to Greece 63
General Wavell's meeting with the Greek leaders in Athens, 14-15 January 1941 64
    * General Ioannis Metaxas refused the proposal for British troops 64
Anglo-Turkish negotiations, 15-22 January 65
Churchill's support for SOE operations 66
Change in Greece's leadership 67
Churchill's letter to Turkey's President 67
Beginning of George Taylor's activities in the Balkans 68
The US Minister in Belgrade: "We are not pushing you into the war." 68
Eden and Dill to go to Greece 69
The Turko-Bulgarian Non-Aggression Pact, 17 February 1941 71
Churchill – General John Kennedy meeting, 16 February 1941 71
Eden – Donovan meeting in Cairo, 19/20 February 72
The Greeks accept Eden's and Dill's visit 73
The Tatoi Conference: the Anglo-Greek agreement, 22/23 February 1941 74
    * Inflating the figures of aid to Greece 77
Doubts about the Aliakmon Line defense 77
    * "… attempt to persuade the Yugoslav Government to play their part" 78
"The real service" of Donovan for the British cause 79
"Full steam ahead" with the enterprise in Greece, 24 February 1941 80
SOE's mission in the Balkans: to help British operations in Greece 80
Pro-British Serb public opinion … SOE's best hope 81

Failure of Eden's mission in Turkey, 26 February – 1 March, and pressure on Yugoslavia 81
Churchill to Eden: *"Your main appeal should now be made to Yugoslavia"*, 1 March 1941 82
"Rumors about a possible Italo-Greek peace"..83

CHAPTER 7 84
Unexpected change in Greece's decision..84
Churchill thoroughly approved SOE's support for the coup d'état in Yugoslavia, 2 March 1941 85
Eden's letter to Prince Paul, 3 March..86
Hitler's letter to the Turkish President, 4 March 1941..86
  *** German-Yugoslav negotiations: Prince Paul's meeting with Hitler, 4 March 1941...............87
Arrival of the British Expeditionary Force into Greece...88
Early planning for evacuation of BEF from Greece 89
"changed and disturbing situation" in Greece. 5 March..90
"... the right decision was taken in Athens."..91
Churchill to Eden: *"... Cabinet accepts for itself the full responsibility,"* 7 March 1941 93
"A bait for the Croats and Slovenes" 94
Campbell's visit to Zagreb, early March 1941 95

CHAPTER 8 96
Urging Prince Paul *"in the sense desired"* 96
Major Milisav Perišić's talks with the British in Athens, 9-12 March 1941 96
Eden's gross misunderstanding...98
  *** German-Yugoslav negotiations: positive reply to the Yugoslav demands 98
Churchill expected a change in Yugoslavia...98
  *** German-Yugoslav negotiations: all Yugoslavia's demands accepted, 12 March 98
Churchill instructed Eden to stay in Cairo, 14 March 99
London was convinced, *"Hitler had decided to attack Russia"* 100
  * *"... there was no sound answer"* to the questions by the Joint Planning Staff 100
18-20 January 1941, Hitler informed Mussolini about his intended attack on Greece................101
In March 1941 London knew of Hitler's plan to attack the Soviet Union 102
Until mid-March, Germany *"made no preparations to attack Yugoslavia"* 102
Outflanking the British and Greek defense line 103
Eden's pressure on Prince Paul: letter of 17 March 1941 103
17 March: Hitler's decision to occupy the whole of Greece; Crown Council decided in principle to join the Tripartite Pact 104

CHAPTER 9 106
Eden's second round of unsuccessful talks with the Turks, 18 March.......................................106
"... urging the necessity of action for a coup d'état ...", 18 March..106
Eden's memorandum to the Yugoslav Government, 18 March...107
Delivery of Eden's letter to Prince Paul, 18 March..107
The Crown Council meeting on March 19 107
All-British conference, 19 March 1941...108
20 March: Crown Council meeting, *"no way to avoid keeping a humiliating rendezvous in Vienna"* 110

20 March: Resignation of three Ministers, *"the work of SOE …"* 110
Shone's attempt to influence Maček, 20 March 111
Urging American support for British policies 112
20 March: *"… use all means to raise a revolution"*... 112
20 March, Prince Paul – Slobodan Jovanović meeting 113
21 March, Campbell: *"Would it be preferable to delay the coup …"*... 113
21 March: Eden's instruction to Campbell on the timing of the coup 114
Eden *"would stop at nothing to ensure …Yugoslavs fight to deny passage to Monastir Gap …"* 115
21 March: *"… ensuring vehement reaction in Serbia …"*.. 115
22 March: *"a crushing telegram to Tsvetkovitch"*... 116
22 March, Campbell: Feeling in Serbia ready, *"if led"*... 116
Mirković - Mapplebeck - Legation connection 116
Churchill's directive: *" …get Yugoslavia in to the war anyhow… "* 22 March 1941................ 117
Recalling President Roosevelt's letter to Hitler.. 117
Prince Paul – Terence Shone meeting, 22 March... 118
23 March: SOE made contribution to prevent signature of the Pact; Macdonald – Mirković meeting 118

CHAPTER 10 120

on 24 march Eden authorized Campbell to inform the Putschists of British support secretly 120
Prospective leaders quietly apprised of British full support 120
24 March: *"Nothing is to be hoped for from the present military chiefs, with one possible exception"* … General Dušan Simović.. 121
The question of the timing of the coup... 122
"Put full steam on … after consulting the Minister".. 122
The idea of blowing up the train with the Yugoslav representatives..................................... 123
Eden to Campbell: There are no weapons to supply the Yugoslav army. 25 March 124
*** Protocol of adhesion of Yugoslavia to Tripartite Pact, Vienna, March 25, 1941 124
German radio report on the signing of the Pact, 25 March, 5 p.m.. 126
Macdonald – Mirković meeting, afternoon of 25 March 126
Macdonald – Simović first meetings, morning of 26 March, 1941... 127
Dalton: Macdonald went to Simović *"and finally persuaded him to act"*, 26 March 1941 127
26 March: Publication of first two Notes of the Protocol 128
Churchill to Campbell, 26 March: *"… do not neglect any alternative … "*............................... 128
Macdonald – Simović second meetings, late afternoon of 26 March 1941.......................... 128
26 March: Leo Amery exhorting … without supporting 129
27 March 1941: The coup d'état in Belgrade 129

CHAPTER 11 131

Churchill: *" … the Yugoslav nation found its soul"*. The coup d'état – *"one tangible result"* of British desperate efforts 131
Churchill to Dalton: *"…patient work of your people had reaped such a rich reward"* 132
Preparing Serb political and popular opinion; Dalton was delighted..................................... 133
"Fullest possible measure of aid" … which Britain did not have 134
Coup d'état … magnificent news for Eden, warmest congratulations for Campbell 135

Dalton: *"Our chaps have done their part well"* 136

Julian Amery: *"… climate of opinion in which the coup became inevitable"* 136

John Colville: *"The Prime Minister is overjoyed"* 137

SOE and Legation worked together 137

"The triumph of hope over reality"; "wild rejoicing in the streets of Belgrade" 138

George Taylor's letter to Dalton, 27 March 1941: *"Trifunovich had kept us informed of conspiracy …"* 138

Thomas Masterson's report, 27 March 1941: misled about the role of the Knežević brothers 139

Report by *"Daddy"*, Ilija Trifunović Birčanin, ...141

Dalton's letter to Churchill, 28 March 1941: *"… the coup d'état itself was largely the work of Trifunovich …"* 142

Churchill's reply to Dalton: Destroy the railroad lines 143

In Dalton's opinion, the chief organizer of the coup was George Taylor 143

John Bennett: Trifunović and Đonović pushed and planned 143

CHAPTER 12 145

The coup raised Churchill's hope 145

First shocks of cruel awakening 145

Conference of Hitler and the German High Command on the situation in Yugoslavia, Berlin, 27 March 1941, at 1300 hours 146

"Directive No. 25" – excerpts 148

Vauhnik informed American colleagues of Hitler's plan 149

Hitler's letter to Mussolini 149

Hitler asked Hungary and Bulgaria to cooperate 150

The coup in Belgrade, a part of a *"large design"* – Churchill claimed 150

General Dill's secret visit to Belgrade, 31 March – 1 April: Simović *" quite unwilling to sign anything that would commit the Yugoslav Government."* 151

The conference in Greece, 3-4 April 1941 *"… in Belgrade Dill had said that Britain would ultimately have 150,000 men on the Aliakmon line …"* 153

The coup and Turkey 155

Instead of the promised attack on the Italians in Albania … negotiations 155

CHAPTER 13 157

Sunday, 6 April 1941: Germany attacked Yugoslavia 157

* The air bombardment of Belgrade 157

The Simović Government were fleeing, too 158

Human losses from the bombings of Belgrade 159

On 9 April Churchill spoke in the House of Commons 159

The disastrous end of the Eden – Dill mission 160

The Independent State of Croatia on the 10th, the fall of Belgrade on the 12th of April 161

From *"The triumph of hope over reality"* to the death-bringing reality … 161

CHAPTER 14 165

"Misplaced optimism" for the British enterprise in Greece 165

Assessment of the Balkan Front idea and of the British Expedition in Greece 166

CHAPTER 15 174

    "A revolutionary stroke" … with Britain's complicity 174
    British policies towards Greece and Yugoslavia 176

CHAPTER 16 181
    The July 1973 Conference 181
    On Churchill's Greek expedition: 181

APPENDIX A - WILLIAM DONOVAN'S MISSIONS 183
    Donovan's first trip to Britain (14 July to 4 August 1940) 183
    Donovan's second trip to Britain (6 December 1940 to 18 March 1941) 185
        * More on Donovan's lunch with Churchill, 18 December 1940 186
    Donovan's tour of the Mediterranean 186
        * Churchill's confidential agent 187
        * Donovan's message: the USA is solidly behind Great Britain 187
    Donovan in Cairo 188
    Donovan in Greece 189
    Trip to Sofia and Belgrade 190
    Donovan's visit in Belgrade 191
        * Donovan – Cvetković meeting 192
        * Donovan – Prince Paul meeting 192
        * Donovan – Maček meeting 193
        * Donovan - General Simović meeting (24 January 1941) 194
        * General Simović's own account of the meeting with Donovan, written in exile 197
        * Simović's account of the meeting with Donovan, as given in Belgrade, in July 1951, ... 199
    Alleged *"White Russian Prince"* was a British Knight of the Garter 201
    British arrangements for Donovan's mission 201
    Assessments of Donovan's visit in Belgrade 202
    After Donovan's trip to Sofia and Belgrade 203
    Donovan-Eden meeting in Cairo 204
    Back in London: *"… an extremely interesting visitor …"* 207
    "… increasing co-ordination of policy and diplomatic activity …" 208
    An assessment of Donovan's role in the Balkans and Middle East 208

APPENDIX B - BLACK PROPAGANDA ABOUT THE BRITISH EXPEDITIONARY FORCE IN GREECE 209
    …a hundred…two hundred…three hundred thousand troops…and they believed every word …... 210
    "… there had been not three thousand British troops in Greece." 211

APPENDIX C - THE IDEA OF SEPARATION OF SOUTHERN SERBIA 212
    To defend the Vardar and Monastir gaps 212

APPENDIX D – IDEAS FOR A MILITARY COUP 215
    The Đonović - Trifunović group 215
        * "D"-men's report to Minister Campbell 217
        * Foreign Office's reaction to a coup proposal : Eventual success must not be endangered by premature action 218

The Serbian Peasant Party's proposals *219*
  * The Serbian Peasant Party's idea of a military coup in 1938 220
Rumors of the substitution of the Government in Yugoslavia *221*

APPENDIX E - THE ISSUE OF RESISTANCE IN OLD SERBIA 222

APPENDIX F - YUGOSLAVIA'S LACK OF MILITARY SUPPLIES.. 224

SOURCES 226
  * Notes regarding General Simović's and General Mirković's documents 226
  Sources and selected bibliography.. 227

INDEX **233**

Acknowledgements

Judy Bultman, Richard Meyerring, Marc Olsen, Michael Olsen, and Janet Taylor assisted me generously by reviews, editing, and suggestions during the writing of the book. Ivan Jakić and Paul Taylor provided me with source data widely used to establish activities of several influential persons who shaped events affecting Yugoslavia. Professor Emeritus Andrejs Plakans very kindly gave me valuable advice, and Professor Zora Devrnja Zimmerman steadily encouraged me in my work. Copy-editing by Gina Dragutinovich was truly valuable and appreciated. To all of them I am deeply indebted and sincerely grateful.

I respectfully manifest my gratitude to all authors of sources from which I quoted and used information to present relevant events.

Mihailo – Miša Kostich very gladly engaged his efforts by preparing the Index – a very highly appreciated contribution.

My deepest gratitude is expressed to Kathleen – Kathy Kelly Olsen for her unending patience in giving me technical assistance, inspiring encouragement, and wise council throughout long years of my research.

Information and quotations from The National Archives at Kew, Richmond, Great Britain, and The Hoover Institution Archives, Stanford University, USA, appear with the permission of their respective authorities.

Special gratitude is expressed to the Office of SPAN at the University of Minnesota for making available to me the study of John D. Scanlan.

Notes on the structure of the text

For the sake of documentation, and to relay to the reader information as found in the sources, lengthier excerpts are often quoted – very respectfully and gratefully to the authors - rather than paraphrased or summarized.

Except in the case of short sentences, translated text is not put in quotation marks "...".
   The reason: *Translation* is not an exact process, and text translated from the original may vary from one translator to another.
   Therefore, the translated text is put into double parentheses marks ((...)) .
   Geographical names are written as found in the sources; personal Slavic names likewise are also given in their Slavic spelling.
   This story is generally presented chronologically. However, some themes and parts of the overall story are described in the Appendices.

Notes on pronunciation of South-Slavic (Yugo-Slav) names

In this book, the Latin alphabet ("Latinica") is used in what is now "politically correctly" called the "Bosnian / Croatian / Montenegrin / Serbian" language(s).

Latinica alphabet letters:	Pronounced as in the English word:
a, A	**a**rt
c, C	**ts**e**ts**e fly
č, Č	**ch**ur**ch**
ć, Ć	soft **ch**, as in future, (or Italian ciao)
dž, DŽ	**j**am
đ, Đ	soft **j**, as in job
e, E	p**e**t
I, I	**i**t **i**s
j, J	**y**ou
lj, LJ	wi**ll y**ou
nj, NJ	**kn**ew
o, O	**o**ld
š, Š	**sh**e
u, U	f**oo**d
ž. Ž	vi**s**ion

In Slovenian, pronunciation is identical to the other South-Slav language(s).
In the course of the war, military personnel advanced in ranks and so many persons mentioned in this story were, - after the war - honored for their services, decorated, knighted... It was not easy, and it was not essential, to follow promotions and to use correct ranks, as they applied at the given times. Therefore, with all due respect to each individual, ranks and titles used are as found in the identified sources.

A qualifying note on political terminology:

The Union of the Soviet Socialist Republics was not Russia

Stated very briefly, to give an understanding of what is included under that name is used:

(A) The Communist International (Comintern) was organized in Moscow between 2 and 6 March 1919. (*)
At its first Congress it had 28 voting delegates, including one from the Communist Party of Yugoslavia. (**)
Financed by the Comintern, "The array of the national communist parties saw themselves in a very real sense as national subdivisions of a single world party and they accepted centralization as a matter of principle, and direction in revolutionary strategy and tactics from Moscow, the home of the only successful proletarian revolution, was logical and natural." (*)

> Subordination of national Communist Parties to the Communist International was complete. ... The decisions of the ECCI [Executive Committee of the Communist International] were obligatory for all Sections of the Communist International. And although the Sections had the right to appeal against decisions of the ECCI to the World Congress, they had to execute them. ... (*)

(*) (Executive Committee of the Communist International,
http://en.wikipedia.org/wiki/Executive_Committee_of_the_Communist_International   6/1/10)

(**) (List of members of the Comintern,
http://en.wikipedia.org/wiki/List_of_members_of_the_Comintern   5/31/10)

Accepting direction and tactics from Moscow, and complete subordination to the Comintern, the individual Parties subsequently acted as agents of the Power centered in Moscow, the Union of the Soviet Socialist Republics (USSR). (This is shown in the case of the Communist Party of Yugoslavia, CPY. The Party was ordered by the Comintern to initiate resistance against Germany only after Germany invaded the USSR on 22 June 1941, ... *but not after Germany attacked Yugoslavia on 6 April 1941*. At that time the USSR was still honoring the pact with Germany and was supporting Germany with supplies of oil and other materiel.)

Russia did not have a similar world-wide organization to use in her international affairs. *Russia* had her own national anthem; the USSR had *The International.*

(B) The USSR was formed on 30 December 1922. On that occasion, Stalin said, *inter alia*, that Soviet power was not concerned only with its preservation, "but with developing into an important international force, capable of influencing the international situation and of modifying it in the interest of the working people"; that the new state "created the dictatorship of the proletariat, awakened peoples of the East, inspires the workers of the West, transformed the Red Flag from a Party banner into a State banner, and rallied around that banner the peoples of the Soviet republics in order to unite them into a single state, the Union of the Soviet Socialist Republics, the prototype of the future World Soviet Socialist Republic."
The assembled delegates, approving the formation of the USSR, declared that "the admission to the union is open to all Socialist Soviet Republics, whether now existing or hereafter to rise."
(The formation of the Union of the Soviet Republics,
http://www.marx2mao.com/Stalin/FUSR22.html   5/31/10)

It is not known that the leaders of *Russia* ever desired a worldwide expansion of their state. The leaders of *the USRR,* to the contrary, never stopped desiring it ... even when they dissolved the Comintern in May 1943 ... for tactical reasons.

The Western Allies' leaders did not factor the USSR's expansion plans into their own war aims ... until it was too late to stop the Soviets. Sir Winston Churchill himself had to acknowledge this fact in his speech at Fulton, Missouri, on 5 March 1946, stating that an iron curtain had descended on Europe from Stettin in the Baltic to Trieste in the Adriatic. "A Soviet curtain" was a more appropriate description. It existed long before 1945. As Sir Ian Jacob, Military Assistant Secretary to the British War Cabinet 1939-45, wrote,

> Stalin ruled Russia in a manner which could not be examined in detail. No one in the outside world could tell how the power was distributed, or what the machinery of control consisted of. None of the officers of our Military Mission ever had more than the briefest glimpse of their natural opposite numbers in Moscow. They had to deal solely through a single channel. Stalin was never seen touring Russia, or driving about in Moscow. His life was entirely concealed. ... None of us ever penetrated into a private house. (Wheeler-Bennett(ed), 214)

A skillful practitioner of remorseless *Realpolitik,* Stalin never denounced expansionistic plans of the Soviet State. Professor Hugh Seton-Watson observed that the generation raised between the Bolshevik revolution of 1917 and the beginning of the Second World War in 1939 "did not read the signs", did not read the works of Lenin and Stalin, and the early history of the Comintern.

> The whole program is there in the speeches and articles of the prominent Soviet and Comintern figures of the 1920's. Organisation, methods of political warfare, political alliances and tactics, short-term and long-term aims - all are explained no less frankly and much more clearly than in [Hitler's] *Mein Kampf.* The enemies and dupes are named. But no one seems to have read or listened but the faithful. For those outside the fold, uncritical praise or uncritical abuse, or ostrich-headed optimism took place of Knowledge. (Seton-Watson(ER), ix)

The organization, methods, alliances, tactics, aims ... were of **the USSR,** not of ***Russia.***
While aware of the substantive differences, in this book the name of that state is used as it is found in the sources.

Charles C. Bohlen, Roosevelt's interpreter at the Teheran and Yalta Conferences, wrote in his *Witness to History* ,"Stalin's enmity was based on profound ideological convictions." (Loewenheim *et al*[eds], 48-9n.9)

Not an ethnic Russian, Stalin held profound Marxist-internationalist ideological convictions and strove to establish a new world order based on Marxist and his own teaching. That order meant a denial of every *"national"* expression of a people, their history, culture, symbols, specificity. The Bolsheviks suppressed *Russia* from their 1917 Revolution – until they were forced to invoke *old Russia and her symbols, Russian history and patriotism* in the *Great Patriotic War* to stop the German invaders.

In dealings with Western Allies during the Second World War, Stalin and his *Commissars* acted as representatives of **the USSR,** not of *Russia.* Calling them *the Russians,* or the state they ruled *Russia,* or *Soviet Russia,* was not what they called themselves and the state they ruled; it was wrong, a complete misrepresentation of reality .

Shapers of events

Germany :
Dr. Jacob ALTMAIER - Journalist (code-name A/H 9)
Viktor von HEEREN - Minister in Belgrade
Adolf HITLER - Leader of the National Socialist German Workers' Party (the Nazi Party), the Chancellor after 30 January 1933, *Der Führer* after 19 August 1934
Joachim von RIBBENTROP - Foreign Minister

Great Britain :
Julian AMERY – Son of Leopold (Leo) Amery, Secretary for India. Section D / SOE agent (code-name A/HA); Assistant Press Attaché in Belgrade
W. S. (Bill) BAILEY – A metallurgist at the Trepča mine. Section D / SOE agent; later Liaison officer with General Dragoljub-Draža Mihailović.
John BENNETT - Section D /SOE agent. One of Taylor's "chief lieutenants in Yugoslavia", who "discovered" Trifunović Birčanin.
BOUGHEY Peter – Section D / SOE agent (code-name D/H 70)
Sir Alexander CADOGAN - Permanent Under-Secretary at the Foreign Office
Ronald Ian CAMPBELL - Minister in Belgrade
Winston Spenser CHURCHILL - Prime Minister and Secretary of State for Defence (10 May 1940 - 26 July 1945)
Colonel Charles S. CLARKE – Military Attaché in Belgrade
Dr. Hugh DALTON - Minister of Economic Warfare (15 May 1940 – 22 February 1942), in charge of the Special Operations Executive (SOE), from 22 July 1940 to 22 February 1942 (code-name, SO)
General Sir John DILL - Chief of Imperial General Staff   (CIGS)
Anthony EDEN - Secretary of State for War (10 May - 22 December 1940); Secretary of State for Foreign Affairs (22 December 1940 - 26 July 1945)
Alexander GLEN – Arctic explorer. Section D / SOE agent (code name A/H 10); Assistant Naval Attaché in Belgrade
Duane T. (Bill) HUDSON – A mining engineer. Section D agent – (code-names D/HZ). ; later the first British officer sent to Yugoslavia (known as Fred Smith, Marko)
Gladwyn JEBB - Chief Executive Officer of SOE, formerly Private Secretary to Sir Alexander Cadogan
Julius HANAU – Businessman. Section D agent (code-name *Caesar*). He originally "picked winner in Tupanjanin".
Hugh H. MACDONALD – Wing Commander, Air Attaché in Belgrade
Thomas G. MAPPLEBECK - Businessman. Honorary Air Attaché in Belgrade
Thomas MASTERSON - Businessman connected with oil companies. The head of SOE in Belgrade from November 1940 (code-name DHY). Another of Taylor's "chief lieutenants in Yugoslavia".
Sir Frank NELSON - Businessman in India and Britain, and former Conservative Member of Parliament. Executive Director of SOE, from July 1940 to May 1942 (code-name CD)
Terence C. RAPP – General Consul in Zagreb
Roundell Palmer, 3rd Earl of SELBORNE - Minister of Economic Warfare, in charge of SOE (22 February 1942 – 23 May 1945)
Hugh SETON-WATSON - Section D / SOE agent (code-name D-H 72)
Terence A. SHONE – Former Secretary of the British Legation in Belgrade
George Francis TAYLOR - A businessman from Australia. Chief of Staff of the Executive Director of SOE (code-name, AD)
General Sir Archibald WAVELL - Commander-in-Chief, Middle East

Greece :

Alexandros KORYZIS - Prime Minister (after 29 January 1941)
General Ioannis METAXAS - Prime Minister and Minister for Foreign Affairs (until 29 January 1941)
General Alexandros PAPAGOS - Commander-in-Chief of the Greek Army
……….. PAPPAS - journalist and propagandist in Belgrade, March 1941

Italy :
Benito MUSSOLINI - Leader of the National Fascist Party; Prime Minister (31 October 1922 – 25 July 1943); *Il Duce* since 1925; "His Excellency Benito Mussolini, Head of Government, Duce of Fascism, and Founder of the Empire" after the victorious war against Abyssinia in 1936
Galeazzo CIANO - Foreign Minister

The Soviet Union :
Vyacheslav Mikhailovich MOLOTOV – the Commissar for Foreign Affairs of the Soviet Union
Joseph Vissarionovich Dzhugashvili STALIN – a leader of the Bolshevik October Revolution in 1917, the first General Secretary of the Central Committee of the Communist Party of the Soviet Union (1922 – 1953), the Premier of the Soviet Union (6 May 1941 – 5 March 1953)
Andrei Yanuarievich VISHINSKY - the Deputy Commissar for Foreign Affairs

Turkey:
Ismet INÖNÜ - President of Turkey
Sükrü SARACOGLU – Foreign Minister

USA :
Colonel William J. "Wild Bill" DONOVAN - Special emissary for the President
Arthur Bliss LANE - Minister in Belgrade
Franklin Delano ROOSEVELT – The President (4 March 1933 - 12 April 1945)

Yugoslavia :
Aleksandar CINCAR-MARKOVIĆ - Minister for Foreign Affairs (until 27 March 1941)
Dragiša CVETKOVIĆ - The Premier (until 27 March 1941)
Jovan ĐONOVIĆ – Former Minister in Tirana, Albania (code-name "Monkey")
Dr. Milan GAVRILOVIĆ - President of *Zemljoradnička stranka,* the Agrarian Party; Ambassador in Moscow from August 1940
Ilija JUKIĆ – Assistant Foreign Minister
Knez Pavle KARAĐORĐEVIĆ (Prince Paul) - The Regent (9 October 1934 - 27 March 1941) (code-name "F")
Major Živan-Žika KNEŽEVIĆ – Battalion Commander, Royal Guards
Radoje KNEŽEVIĆ – member of the Main Committee of the Democratic Party
Dr. Fran KULOVEC - Slovenian representative, Minister without portfolio (until 27 March 1941)
Dr. Vladko MAČEK - The Vice-Premier in Cvetković and Simović Government; President of *Hrvatska seljačka stranka* (the Croatian Peasant Party)
Brigadier General Borivoje-Bora MIRKOVIĆ – Assistant to the Commander of the Air Force
Momčilo NINČIĆ – Foreign Minister in Simović's Government
Colonel Žarko POPOVIĆ – Military Attaché in Moscow
Captain Dragiša RISTIĆ – General Simović's *aide-de-camp*
Army General Dušan SIMOVIĆ - The Commander of the Air Force; the Premier after 27 March 1941
Vojvoda Ilija TRIFUNOVIĆ BIRČANIN - President of *Narodna odbrana* (The National Defense League). (*Vojvoda* – Highest military rank, obtained in war). (Code-name "Daddy")
Dr. Miloš TUPANJANIN - Deputy President of the Serbian Peasant Party (code-name "Uncle")
Colonel Vladimir VAUHNIK – Military Attaché in Berlin
Zemljoradnička stranka - The Agrarian Party, usually called the Serbian Peasant Party (SPP)

Introduction

In the early 1930s, Yugoslavia was bordered by seven states: Austria, Hungary, Rumania, Bulgaria, Greece, Albania and Italy.

> The frontiers of the new state had been recognized by all big powers except the USSR, but Yugoslavia was still surrounded by irredentist claimants: the Italians for Dalmatia; the Hungarians for territories inhabited by Hungarians in Croatia and Vojvodina; the Bulgarians for the Yugoslav part of Macedonia and the Albanians for the mainly Albanian regions of Kosovo. All these threats were more menacing since Hitler and Mussolini were now repudiating as "scrap of paper" the postwar settlements. (Beloff, 50)

In March 1938, Austria was annexed by Germany and so, at the outbreak of the Second World War in September 1939, Yugoslavia was bordered by two Great Powers ruled by two dictators scheming grandiose plans, Benito Mussolini and Adolf Hitler, for whom the supreme values were the State and the Race, respectively. The agenda of each dictator contained threats to Yugoslavia and her people. Mussolini's was real and imminent, Hitler's potential and in the future.

Italy harbored the leadership of the Croatian separatists, the Ustaše. Their terrorist acts within pre-war Yugoslavia were not insignificant, and their participation in the assassination of King Aleksandar I in Marseille, France, in October of 1934, was more than symbolic. Mussolini's vision of a restored Roman Empire, coupled with irredentist Italian aspirations for Dalmatia and with expected "payment for services rendered" to the Ustaše – were real threats that a responsible Government of Yugoslavia could not ignore.

> With the Italian invasion of Albania [7 April 1939], and German infiltration into Hungary, Yugoslavia faced potential enemies on five of her seven borders. Italy's declaration of war on Britain and France in June 1940 turned the Adriatic into an Italian lake. (Onslow, 6n15)

The Italian conquest of Albania in 1939 – just three weeks after Germany's occupation of Prague - was, simultaneously, the Axis' first direct step of encircling Yugoslavia. Italy's declaration of war on Britain and France prevented an eventual British intervention in the Adriatic, as the British Foreign Minister, Lord Halifax, later explained. As for the conditions in Yugoslavia, at this time,

> ...the UK did not suffer from lack of information about Yugoslavia: she possessed sound intelligence and good links with ruling circles and the Yugoslav service departments. The Section D/SOE [Special Operations Executive] and SIS [Secret Intelligence Service] networks were more extensive than historians have charted. (Onslow, 7)

Hitler's threat was not imminent: it was conditioned on the realization of his vision of a Thousand-Year-German-*Reich* in which the people of Yugoslavia – being of Slavic origin – would be treated as an inferior race. Aware of this and simultaneously aware of Yugoslavia's grossly inferior military strength compared to Germany's, and mindful of the British armament shortages at that time, which rendered Britain unable to effectively bolster Yugoslavia's military strength, on 5 September 1939 the Yugoslav Government declared strict neutrality. (www.hungarian-history.hu/lib/montgo/montgo23.htm 11/16/09) Yugoslavia's declaration was not unique. On the same day the US Government also proclaimed neutrality in the European war. (www.indiana.edu/-league/1939.htm 11/16/2009)

The British welcomed Yugoslavia's neutrality until late in 1940, when His Majesty's Government decided that Yugoslavia should "come into the war" in order to implement the British plan for forming the Balkan Front against the Axis. Describing this decision of the British Government, as well as its consequences for Yugoslavia and her people, is the subject of the story that follows. The defining event was the military *coup d'état* executed in Belgrade on 27 March 1941, to "resist" Germany.

**

The Belgrade coup was arguably the most fateful event in the brief history of the state of Yugoslavia. Following the British Prime Minister's instruction to his Foreign Minister on 22 March *"to get Yugoslavia in to the war anyhow"*, on 24 March the Foreign Minister authorized and supported the coup. And indeed, it was executed during the night of the 26th and 27th.

> The events in Belgrade were seen as, and presented as, a remarkable propaganda victory for the British cause. ... Prime Minister Churchill, above all, understood the value of gesture, and the coup was perceived as giving Nazism a bloody nose. (Onslow, 2)

This *"remarkable propaganda victory"* and *a bloody nose,* however, set in motion events which ultimately took the lives of at least 6.67% of Yugoslavia's population, while the United Kingdom lost 0.94%.

Truly remarkable !

This "propaganda victory" insulted and infuriated Germany's *Führer* Adolf Hitler so intensely that within the same day, in an utmost rage, he decided to brutally punish the people of the open city of Belgrade and *"to destroy Yugoslavia militarily and as a national unit."* In the afternoon of March 27th, he told the German High Command:

> ... An attempt will be made to let the neighboring states participate in a suitable way. An actual military support against Yugoslavia is to be requested of Italy, Hungary, and in certain aspect of Bulgaria too. ... The Hungarian and the Bulgarian ambassador have already been notified. During the day a message will still be addressed to the Duce. ... The war against Yugoslavia will be very popular in Italy, Hungary and Bulgaria, as territorial acquisitions are to be promised to these states; the Adriatic coast to Italy, the Banat to Hungary, and Macedonia to Bulgaria."
> (http://www.nizkor.org/hweb/imt/nca/nca-01-09-aggression-11-05.html 8/31/05)

Mercilessly, within a few weeks after the coup Hitler realized his intentions.

Northern Slovenia was annexed to Germany and the Southern part to Italy. Thousands of Slovenes were uprooted and shipped away, mostly to occupied Serbia.

An "Independent State of Croatia" (ISC) was formed; it included the regions of *Banovina* Croatia, Bosnia and Herzegovina. Its leader, Dr. Ante Pavelić, *Poglavnik* (the leader, head man), and a group of his Ustaše adherents, were transported from Italy to the ISC by Italian soldiers, and entered Zagreb under the cover of night. Soon after, Pavelić acknowledged and formally approved Italy's annexation of part of the coastal region and some Adriatic islands of Dalmatia. During the summer of 1941 he began the genocidal implementation of the "final solution" for the Serbs, Jews and Gypsies within the ISC. Concentration camps were erected, and the people began to perish by the thousands.

Serbia proper and Banat were occupied by the Germans. "The Germans took some 254,000 prisoners, excluding a considerable number of Croat, German, Hungarian, and Bulgarian nationals who had been inducted into the Yugoslav Army and who were quickly released after screening." (Blau, 62) These imprisoned Serbs were sent to the Prisoners of War camps in Germany.

Serbia's historic regions Kosovo and Metohija were annexed to Italian-occupied Albania, along with the western part of Macedonia. The Albanians from poorer mountainous regions moved into the more fertile, newly-acquired areas. Persecuted Serbs fled to occupied Serbia. Thus, occupied Serbia - without a sizeable portion of her own working population - had to provide for hundreds of thousands of endangered refugees, under conditions of a cruel occupation, and exposed to the harshest reprisals in occupied Europe.

Southeastern Serbia and eastern Macedonia were annexed to Bulgaria. The regions of Bačka and Baranja, and small areas of Slovenia and Croatia, were annexed to Hungary. Montenegro was occupied by Italy.

Not much would be written later by the Serb and British coup-wisher-and--plotters about these and other coup-related consequences. The reasons are obvious. But, to justify the coup, its admirers boasted about the coup *"giving Nazism and Hitler a bloody nose".*

> According to the conspirators, the March coup not only saved Yugoslavia's honor but had far-reaching political and military consequences. It forced Germany to revise its military plans against Greece and the Soviet Union. Those responsible for the coup can thus say with good reason that their deed represented a major political defeat for Hitler and that it contributed immeasurably to the ultimate defeat of Germany. (Professor Wayne S. Vucinich, in the "Preface" to D.N. Ristić's book)

That assertion is debatable. Evidence found in the German and Soviet archives contradicts these claims. In either case, this subject is outside the scope of this book.

However, it does seem pertinent and, not merely for the sake of an argument, to consider what would have happened **had the coup not been executed when it was**, but possibly at a later date – or even not at all. The consideration of such development is relevant to discussions about Yugoslavia and requires a few brief notes about the events preceding the coup.

On 10 May 1940, Germany invaded France. On 28 of May, British forces began their evacuation from Dunkirk, in France. The evacuation was completed on 4 June, but almost all British military equipment was lost. This, in turn, negatively affected British capability to supply at least some military equipment to Yugoslavia later on. With Franco-German armistice signed on 22 June 1940, Yugoslavia lost her principal political supporter within Europe, and thus had to face the unfolding events politically and militarily weakened.

However, even before Germany started her victorious advance through the Western countries, a tide began to form which would immensely contribute to her final defeat. First, German Enigma messages were decoded by the British on 17 January 1940. Then the German Air Force code was broken on 22 May 1940. As shown in Chapter 1, on 17 September 1940 the British accurately concluded that the German plan for the invasion of Great Britain (*Operation Sea Lion*) had been postponed. This most welcome news was made known to only a few British war leaders.

The Soviet personnel in Belgrade knew that huge German forces were at their borders, and told that to Professor Slobodan Jovanović. He thought that Yugoslavia's strategy should take that fact into consideration. (Petranović & Žutić, 239) German troops began entering Rumania on 7 October 1940. Intelligence about the Balkans (the German Enigma traffic) began on 23 October 1940. After the middle of January 1941, this traffic became more voluminous. The railway administration code (Railway Enigma) was broken at the end of January 1941. (Hinsley *et al*, 350, 356, 359) The German Navy code was deciphered in the spring of 1941 and their Army code in the spring of 1942. Understandably, the British kept this breakthrough under utmost secrecy. In October 1940 Churchill told senior commanders that Germany would inevitably attack Russia in 1941. (F.H. Hinsley in Blake & Louis(eds), 421) On 18 December 1940 he was more specific: he told Col. Donovan that the attack would happen in May 1941. (Dunlop, 239)

Expecting Germany's attack in May, why did the British war leaders not wait with the coup in Belgrade until **after** Germany's attack, when her war machine was engaged on a massive scale?

**

"The intelligence about the Balkans" dealt with movements and operations of the German military units in Rumania and Bulgaria. From the intercepted and decoded German messages it was clear to the British that Germany was going to attack Greece *through Bulgaria, not through Yugoslavia*. On 2 March 1941, German troops started crossing from Rumania into Bulgaria.

While they were ominously advancing through Bulgaria, on 25 March Yugoslavia joined the Tripartite Pact with Germany, Italy, and Japan, which was formed on 27 September 1940. After some four months of tenacious negotiations, Yugoslavia succeeded in becoming the only signatory to the Pact who did not accept its military clauses and obligations, "a non-belligerent member of the Axis pact" (Beloff, 63). In the first two of four Notes attached to the Protocol of Adhesion, the Axis Powers obligated themselves "to respect the sovereignty and territorial integrity of

Yugoslavia at all times", and they stated that "the Axis Power governments during this war will not demand of Yugoslavia to permit the march or transportation of troops through the Yugoslav state or territory". These Notes were published in both Berlin and Belgrade on 26 March 1941. In the third Note, Italy and Germany assured the Government of Yugoslavia that *they do not wish to advance, on their part, any request whatsoever regarding military assistance."*

Most of those who participated in or sanctioned the coup in Belgrade justified their actions by dismissing the Pact's non-military clauses / obligations for Yugoslavia, and by pointing to Hitler's record of breach of solemnly-given promises and to his disrespect for international treaties. Therefore, they claimed, sooner or later Hitler would have reneged on the non-belligerent clauses of the Pact, and demanded that Yugoslavia provide support the Axis' war efforts, and would have enforced her doing so, if she refused. Indeed, history had repeatedly shown that Hitler could not be trusted. However, in case of Yugoslavia, a fair question would be: **when and under what conditions** would such a scenario have taken place?

One can not answer this question with certainty. But one can draw likely conclusions based on these facts:

The evidence points out that – before attacking the Soviet Union – Hitler wanted to preclude a possible attack from Yugoslavia while he would be engaged in the Soviet Union. Indeed, that was the reason why he accepted Yugoslavia's exceptions to the military clauses of the Tripartite Pact.

Without the coup in Belgrade, there would have been no hasty meeting between Hitler and his top military commanders in the afternoon of 27 March, and Hitler would not have been "determined, without waiting for possible loyalty declarations of the new government, to make all preparations to destroy Yugoslavia militarily and as a national unit."German troops would have continued their advances through Bulgaria only, and would have had to attack Greece through the Metaxas fortified defensive line. This would have resulted in more German losses. One can only guess how much would that have slowed Germany's capture of Salonika and Athens, and how that would have affected operations of the British Expeditionary Force in Greece. In any case, it seems probable that Germany would not have initiated the invasion of the Soviet Union before capturing the Island of Crete – which they did on 1 June 1941.

As it was, on 22 June 1941 "Russia had been treacherously and ignominiously attacked [by Germany], and for more than a year had moved rapidly backwards, suffering immense losses of men and material. Only in the Moscow and Leningrad areas had innate patriotic tenacity of individuals held the line." (Dodds-Parker, 102)

During the first several months of the campaign there was a "rapid advance of the German forces into Russia."(de Guingand, 86) The Germans were so successful, conquering such vast territories in quick succession and with minimal losses, that a victory must have seemed to Hitler within quick reach. A significant part of these initial successes lay in the pre-existing and unsettled relations between the Russians and the Ukrainians, i.e., the "Katzapi" and the "Khokli", respectively, as they contemptuously called each other. (Krylov, 144) How these relations contributed to Germany's rapid advancement is mentioned briefly here just to show that until King Peter's coming of age (on 6 September 1941), Yugoslavia would probably not have been forced to side militarily with the Axis.

When the invasion of the Soviet Union began, the 2nd Infantry Division ("they are all khokli") made an attempt to murder their commanders and political commissars and surrender to the Germans. The "khokli" and the men from Northern Caucasia expected the Germans to proclaim the independence of their republics. (Krylov, 112)

Also troublesome were the 56th Regiment and two battalions of the 23rd and the 29th. "Ukrainians every time." (Krylov, 115)

On July 6th Stalin delivered a speech. "He had not addressed his listeners as 'citizens' or 'comrades', but as brothers and sisters, like a preacher". Captain Ivan Nikitch Krylov, the bearer of the Order of Lenin, who had access to and moved in high circles of the armed forces, commented:

It was odd, almost disagreeable, to hear him adopt that tone. I knew his 'Machiavellism', his inclination to 'play a part', his conviction that he could keep on deceiving the whole world. It had occurred to me that this new tone was due to exceptional danger. He was afraid. For the first time in his life the old revolutionary, the organizer of the armed raid on the Bank of Tiflis, the organizer of the Baku-Batum insurrection, the leader of the Red Guards in Petrograd, the man who had crushed all opposition plots, was afraid. He was doubtful of the people in face of German attack; he was afraid of a revolt against the regime, against his international dogma which turned Russia into an instrument of a Communist plot against the whole world instead of giving the country a really popular government. (Krylov, 119)

On July 10th, a German communiqué announced 323,000 Soviet soldiers had been taken prisoner. By contrast, the Soviet confidential bulletin reported: "Our troops have suffered heavy losses, but the number of prisoners did not exceed 150,000. The Germans counted mobilized civilians captured in the neighborhood of the fighting amongst their prisoners of war." (Krylov, 118-19) In a counter-offensive in the neighborhood of Mohilev and Rogatchev, that July, the official Soviet bulletin reported the loss of 120,000 prisoners, whereas the Germans claimed 300,000. (Krylov, 120-21)

During a debate in the Council of War, in the Kremlin, on 21 August 1941, the Chief of the General Staff, Marshal Shaposhnikov, stated that two of their divisions, "in the neighborhood of Uman [a small town in the Ukraine] killed their political commissars and refused to fight." "That's those blasted Khokli. The sons of bitches cling to the Germans like whores to their pimps", commented Marshal Budionny. (Krylov, 128)

On their march to Moscow, "The Germans claimed their "Victory of Smolensk" on August 7th together with allegedly 300,000 prisoners. ..." (Krylov, 141)

Toward the end of August 1941, the Ukrainian intellectuals in Kharkov – the former capital of rural Ukraine – formed "a big clandestine organization attached to the Lvov organization known by its initials U.V.O. (Ukrainian Military Organization). A section of the Ukrainian officers of the Kharkov garrison had decided to surrender with their troops as soon as the *Wehrmacht* appeared before the town. ... The authorities were now hastily evacuating purely Ukrainian regiments to Siberia and the Far East and replacing them by regiments from Central Asia and Siberia." (Krylov, 142-3)

There were Ukrainian conspiratorial officers, party and government officials, journalists, writers and others who supported 'national liberation' "at all costs, even at the price of alliance with Hitler's Third Reich. All these people hoped that the German High Command would bring them along a Ukrainian national government in a *Wehrmacht* knapsack, liberating them from the oppression of the Katzapi." (Krylov, 143-4)

After the battle of Kiev in August-September 1941 – in which the Soviets lost more than 600,000 dead or captured, "a certain number of the inhabitants (always Ukrainians) had given the Germans a triumphal reception, bombarding them with flowers and delivering speeches of welcome. A number of priests had joined the collaborators. ..." (Krylov, 185)

Why did the Ukrainians not initially oppose the German troops? Mostly, because they had not forgotten the waves of Soviet oppression in the early 1930s, nor the atrocious liquidations in 1937. In the "Great Purge" of 1937-1938, millions were sent to labor camps and victimized.

The German troops, however, were not coming to liberate Ukraine from the Soviet regime after all, but to conquer her land for Germany's *Lebensraum,* as envisioned by Hitler for his Third Reich that was to last a thousand years. In the Nazis' views, the Ukrainians - being of the Slavic "inferior" race - were not to be a free and independent people to rule their own land, but rather to serve the "superior" Aryan race. Hundreds of thousands of Ukrainian soldiers unwilling to fight and readily surrendering during the first few months of the war, very likely influenced Hitler's imagination of a speedy victory. This, in turn, made it unnecessary for him to consider involving Yugoslavia in the war while Germany was wining.

Later on, when it became clear that Hitler was coming as a conqueror, not as a liberator, the Ukrainians as well as the Russians found **their Country** (*Patria*) to be the cause worth fighting for against the would-be enslavers – for their country... not for an ideology. That turned the war into their *Great Patriotic War.* It was at this time that Germany began losing the war. Under such conditions, it is reasonable to consider that Hitler could have been tempted to abrogate the Notes of the Protocol of Adhesion to the Tripartite Pact of 25 March 1941, in order to try to engage Yugoslavia in the war on his side.

However, abrogating those four Notes would make the Pact null and void, and Yugoslavia's Government – now under King Peter !! – would be free to make their own decisions.

And **how** would have Hitler forced Yugoslavia into the war on his side? By the force of German armies from Bulgaria and Greece? Even Prince Paul's Government - including their Croatian and Slovenian members – had repeatedly stated that Yugoslavia would defend herself if attacked by the Axis (*"if only with sporting rifles"*, as the Vice Premier Maček told the British Minister Campbell in March 1941, in Zagreb. (Ostović, 160))

With more support available from the Allies, and Germany's deepening engagement on the Eastern Front, chances of Yugoslavia's successful defense operations against Germany would have been incomparably better than they were in March 1941.

Given all new circumstances - the weakening of Germany's war potential and that of the Allies' increasing, it is probable that the Yugoslav Government would have decided to enter the war on the Allies' side, against the Axis. That would have given the Allies a very desirable chance to weaken the German war machine even more by strengthening Yugoslavia with armament which had not been available in the spring of 1941.

Creating the Balkan front while losing on the Eastern – and fearing the Allies' landing in the West – would have been a self-defeating proposition for Germany.

Therefore, one might reasonably conclude: had the military coup of 27 March **not** been executed, Hitler would have had no need and would not have tried to compel Yugoslavia to fight on his side **while he was winning** the war on the Eastern Front. Moreover, one could argue, as noted above, that while **he was losing the war**, it would also have been a self-defeating proposition to force an unwilling Yugoslavia into the war on his side – and thus possibly open another front.

Most likely, just the opposite could have happened, with Yugoslavia getting into the war **against** the Axis on the Allies' side. Yugoslavia's engagement on the Allies' side under such circumstances and at such time would have hurt Germany's war efforts much more than the coup of 27 March did in April 1941. As Sir Winston wrote years later, Hitler himself implied that possibility: *"… He [Hitler] deemed it fortunate that the Yugoslavs had revealed their temper before "Barbarossa" [invasion of the Soviet Union] was launched.* (Churchill(GA), 163. Italics added.)

*****

However, the British war leaders had their own plans and timetable, their own immediate goals and interests on their minds – and certainly not those of Yugoslavia. Their domestic "friends" and "contacts" uncritically assisted them, their "Allies". The British knew **before the coup of 27 March** that Hitler was planning to attack the Soviet Union – but were still "encouraging" and "stimulating" the coup – without waiting for Hitler's engagement in the USSR.

> Even before the Yugoslavs signed the Tripartite Pact [on 25 March] the GAF [German Air Force] Enigma showed that some German Army formations had been ordered to leave the Balkans for Poland. (This order was in fact a consequence of Hitler's decision on 17 March to transfer the armour from Army Group South to Cracow preparatory to *Barbarossa* [Invasion of the Soviet Union].) On 26 March, the day after the signing, the Enigma revealed that these formations included three armoured divisions, SS Division Adolf Hitler, the HQs [Headquarters] of Panzergruppe Kleist and of XIV Corps, and some troops of 12 Army. This was a powerful pointer to the German intention to attack Russia. (Hinsley *et al*, 370-71)

It was "*a powerful pointer to the German intention*" to attack the Soviet Union, Prime Minister Churchill understood it as such, and intended to warn Stalin about it on 3 April 1941. (Churchill(GA), 358) Still the Prime Minister did not want to modify his own plans for Yugoslavia:

On 22 March he directed his Foreign Minister, Anthony Eden, "to get Yugoslavia in to the war anyhow". (PREM 3/510/11, no. 369)

On 24 March Eden instructed his Minister in Belgrade, Ronald Campbell:

> You have my full authority for any measures that you may think it right to take to further change of Government or regime, even by *coup d'état*.

Any new Government formed as a result of these events and prepared to resist German demands would have our full support. **You may secretly so inform any prospective leaders in whom you have confidence.** (Eden, 227. Emphasis added.)

Campbell had to do as ordered, and on 27 March the military coup was executed.

Had the Belgrade coup of 27 March **not** been executed, how would events have developed within Yugoslavia, until King Peter II came of age on 6 September 1941? No one could foresee future developments, but it is reasonable to conclude that the following events would **not** have happened – assuming the absence of British "encouragement" and support for the coup:

* The State of Yugoslavia would not have been dismembered, and her territories neither annexed by other states, nor occupied.
* The city of Belgrade would not have been bombed on 6 April 1941, at the cost of up to 10,000 human lives, and the city would not have been badly burned and destroyed, and the treasure of the National Library irretrievably lost.
* Some 254,000 Serb men would not have been sent to POW camps (Blau, 62).
* The Independent State of Croatia (ISC) would not have been formed, concentration camps not organized, and there would have been no "final solution" for the Serbs, Jews, and Gypsies in ISC; no concentration camp "Jasenovac", and all it has symbolized ever since; the still uncertain (but indeed huge) number of human lives would not have been terminated in those camps, nor some of that camp's prisoners shipped to German concentration camps;
* Yugoslavia's military and internal security forces would have been left intact, continuing their normal services of protecting the state and her citizens, respectively. Probably, even more troops could have been mobilized for eventual future use;
* "Engineer Tomanek" [Josip Broz Tito, the Secretary General of the Communist Party of Yugoslavia (CPY), who returned from Moscow late in 1939 (Shoup, 47n8)], "elegantly – almost too elegantly dressed", with his "carefully manicured" hands "and a large diamond ring glittering on his finger", (Clissold, 9-10), would not have a need to move from Zagreb to Belgrade, because there would not have existed post-coup Communist activities in Belgrade. (The Communists had no part in the preparation and/or execution of the coup of 27 March, but took advantage of it to promote their own and the Soviets' causes.)

Until Germany's invasion of the Soviet Union – following *Operation Marita* (conquest of Greece) and *Operation Merkur* (conquest of Crete) – the Communists would have probably continued doing what they were doing before the coup: obediently following the Communist International's (Comintern's) line of supporting the Nazi-Soviet Non-Aggression Pact of 23 August 1939, blaming England and France for "imperialistic war", and clamoring for Yugoslavia's "Alliance with Russia".

After Germany's invasion of the Soviet Union, the Communists would have been obligated to follow the Comintern's orders to help the Soviet Union, their "glorious model" – to use Tito's own words. What form their actions would have taken, and how effective they would have been, is uncertain. With the then-existing state's apparatus intact, directed by a not pro-Communist "bourgeois" Government, it seems probable that the Communists would not have been very effective.

What would have happened after King Peter would have taken power – is uncertain. With Prince Paul gone from the political scene, political opposition to his policies would have faced an altered situation. There is no evidence that the "bourgeois" political parties and institutions, and "nationalistic" military and internal security leaders, were in favor of a Soviet-type political, social and economic model for Yugoslavia; it is very probable that they would not have followed the Communist Party's lead after Germany's attack on the Soviet Union.

Without the coup-provoked order to destroy Yugoslavia by a furious Hitler, there would have been no "resistance to the occupation", and no "national liberation" movements because there would have been no occupation. Although there existed unresolved issues within Yugoslav internal affairs, there is no evidence that the "bourgeois" political parties and institutions were considering civil war to be their proper means of resolution. Therefore, there would have been no three-way civil war and no blood spilled to poison the relations among the Southern Slavs for generations to come.

Based on Prince Paul's life in the pre-Regent-era, it is very probable that this British Knight of the Garter, "an impenitent anglophile" (Beloff, 60), would not have been interested in furthering his political career after September 6, 1941, and would have spent more of his time in London than in Belgrade. Sir Cecil Parrott - tutor to young King Peter from April 1934 to spring 1939 – knew Prince Paul well and wrote about him:

> ... He had been educated at Oxford and before becoming Prince Regent had spent much time in England, ... , where he had many friends. His two sons were born in this country and he always spoke English at home with his wife and family. His children had English nurses and went to school in England. His wife's sister was the Duchess of Kent. Even the palace he had reconstructed for his official use was built in Adam style. Excellent French speaker and scholar tough he was, he seemed most at home in our own language which he spoke and wrote faultlessly, and with a style and polish I envied. (Parrott, 95)

**

Most tragically, the coup was executed and the state of Yugoslavia was destroyed. Differently-motivated and instigated resistance movements were formed, in pursuit of diverging (and irreconcilable) post-war goals. Bloody civil wars ensued. Enormous numbers of human lives were lost. How huge those numbers were is shown below. To understand the meaning of, and the reaction to, the losses in the Second World War, it is helpful to keep in mind the losses in the First as well – because the losses in both wars had to be taken into account when "resistance" to the occupiers in Yugoslavia was demanded by "our Allies".

REST IN PEACE

Estimates of **casualties in the First World War:**

| | Mobilized forces | |
Country	Killed and died	Wounded
Russia	1,700,000	4,950,000
France	1,357,800	4,266,000
British Empire	908,371	2,090,212
Italy	650,000	947,000
United States	116,516	204,002
Japan	300	907
Rumania	335,706	120,000
Serbia	45,000	133,148
Belgium	13,716	44,686
Greece	5,000	21,000
Portugal	7,222	13,751
Montenegro	3,000	10,000
Germany	1,773,700	4,216,058
Austria-Hungary	1,200,000	3,620,000
Turkey	325,000	400,000
Bulgaria	87,500	152,390
Total	8.528,831	21,189,154

(*Encyclopaedia Britannica, 1973*, page 759)

It was hoped that World War One would be "the war to end all wars". It was not.

"The Serbs had been allies from 1914 to 1918, incurring fantastically high casualties". (G.H.N. Seton-Watson, in Auty & Clogg(ed) p. 283)

In the course of the First World War, "Serbia lost one quarter of its adult male population: casualties proportionately even heavier than in the whole of the Second World War." (Beloff, 38)
    The losses in Montenegro (on the Allies' side), and those in Slovenia, Croatia and Bosnia-Herzegovina (on Austria-Hungary's) should be included in order to estimate the total losses of people in the former Yugoslavia.
    Add losses of births during the war years ...

Those losses, and the enemies who inflicted them, were not forgotten, and were evoked when needed for propaganda purposes.

Before the outbreak of and throughout the Second World War, for many people in the former Yugoslavia - and particularly in Serbia - the enemies in WWI still remained "Our Enemies", and the former Allies still "Our Allies". That attitude was purposefully cultivated and used by those who wanted to *influence and stimulate Serb public opinion* in order to draw Yugoslavia into the Second World war on the side of "Our Allies" – against "Our Enemies". That feeling was fertile soil for the pro-British and anti-German propaganda. Unfortunately, not much thought was given to potential losses if the country was to be engaged in a new war. Not enough attention was paid to terrorist acts committed by centrifugal forces within the country and abroad. The meaning of those acts was not heeded.

Estimates of **casualties in the Second World War** for the British Commonwealth, United States and Yugoslavia:

Country	Military			Civilian deaths due to war	Estimated total deaths
	Killed, died of wounds, in prison	Wounded	Prisoners or missing		
British Commonwealth	373,372	475,047	251,724 (*)	92,673	466,000
Australia	23,365	39,803	32,393	-	24,000
Canada	37,476	53,174	10,888	-	38,000
India	24,338	64,354	91,243	-	-
New Zealand	10,033	19,314	10,582	-	10,000
South Africa	6,840	14,363	16,430	-	7,000
United Kingdom	264,443	277,077	213,919	92,673 (**)	357,000
Colonies	6,877	6,972	22,323	-	7,000
United States	292,131	671,801	139,709	6,000	298,000 (^)
Yugoslavia	305,000	425,000	-	1,200,000	1,505,000

(*) Figures for all Commonwealth nations include those still missing in 1946, some of whom may be presumed dead.
(**) This figure comprises 60,595 killed in aerial bombardment, 30,248 in the merchant marine service, 624 in women's auxiliary services, and 1,206 in the Home Guard.
(^) There were an additional 115,187 deaths of U.S. servicemen from non-battle causes, making the estimated total of U.S. deaths to 413,187. (##)
(*Encyclopaedia Britannica 1973*, page 802J)

(##) Most American sources put this total at 405,399 deaths for 1941-1946.

∗∗

The exact number of the dead in Yugoslavia in WWII may never be known. Editors of the *1973 Encyclopaedia Britannica* estimated the number to be 1,505,000. Some were executed by the occupiers, others killed in the civil wars – some murdered even after the WWII ended; others were killed by bombs – first by the Axis forces, then by those of the Allies' in 1944.

The Communist government of Yugoslavia operated with a figure of 1,700,000 – a number exaggerated to gain the world's sympathy and higher reparation compensation. The government officials were very skilled with numbers, always to their advantage – whether claimed as the numbers they had suffered from their enemies, or they had inflicted on them. Responsible and knowledgeable statisticians claim the total to be significantly lower. "The number of actual victims may vary between 900,000 and 1,150,000." (Kočević, 47)

In a 1954 report, the US Census Bureau estimated 1,067,000 deaths.

To get a better feel for the enormity of the casualties Yugoslavia suffered, one can compare her losses with those of the British Commonwealth and the USA:

Combined losses:
    British Commonwealth   373,372
    The United States   <u>405,399</u>
    Combined losses of the British
    Commonwealth and the USA   778,771

Rounding the numbers: 779,000 vs. 900,000-1,150,000.

One can make another comparison – losses in Yugoslavia and the USA:

US losses -	in the Civil War:	Union	364,511	
		Confederate	133,821	
		Total		498,332
	in WWI			116,516
	in WWII			405,399
	Combined USA losses in these three wars			1,020,247

The US Census Bureau's number of casualties for Yugoslavia is greater than the combined number of deaths for the British Commonwealth and the USA in WWII. It is comparable to the combined losses the US suffered in the Civil War and the First and Second World Wars.

Whatever the exact number of dead in Yugoslavia, however, did they all *have* to die?

I do not think so.

A grave

My wife Dragojla and I visited Great Britain for the first time in the summer of 1982. One morning our tour-bus stopped near an inn in a small place. "Bladon," announced our lady tour-guide, in a low voice.

"Wouldn't you want a cup of hot tea or coffee," she asked us, "because it's rather chilly and a bit damp outside?"

"Yes, we would." And we did.

Then she led us into a churchyard.

Silently, respectfully, we approached a gravesite and positioned ourselves around it: Churchill's grave.

Dragojla and I looked at each other. Emotions ... deep, powerful.

A heart-felt gratitude and respect for what he had done on a grand scale in the Second World War.

A sorrow for his contribution to the suffering and loss of human lives in our native land, Yugoslavia.

A letter

You realize, I am sure, that throughout the world hundreds of millions of human beings are living today in constant fear of a new war or even a series of wars. ...

On a previous occasion I have addressed you in behalf of the settlement of political, economic and social problems by peaceful methods and without resort to arms.....

Three nations in Europe and one in Africa have seen their independent existence terminated. A vast territory in another independent Nation of the Far East has been occupied by a neighboring State. Reports, which we trust are not true, insist that further acts of aggression are contemplated against still other independent nations. Plainly the world is moving toward the moment when this situation must end in catastrophe unless a more rational way of guiding events is found. ...

Nothing can persuade the peoples of the earth that any governing power has any right or need to inflict the consequences of war on its own or any other people *save in the cause of self-evident home defense. ...*

Are you willing to give assurance that your armed forces will not attack or invade the territory or possessions of the following independent nations: Finland, Estonia, Latvia, Lithuania, Sweden, Norway, Denmark, The Netherlands, Belgium, Great Britain and Ireland, France, Portugal, Spain, Switzerland, Liechtenstein, Luxembourg, Poland, Hungary, Rumania, Yugoslavia, Russia, Bulgaria, Greece, Turkey, Iraq, the Arabias, Syria, Palestine, Egypt and Iran. ...

I think you will not misunderstand the spirit of frankness in which I send you this message. Heads of great Governments in this hour are literally responsible for the fate of humanity in coming years ....

A similar message is being addressed to the Chief of the Italian Government.

(Excerpts from President Roosevelt's letter to Hitler, 14 April 1939, one week after Italy's occupation of Albania.   -   www.ibiblio.org/pha/7-2-188/188-12.html   7/11/07) (Italics added.)

**

It will be shown how actions taken by the heads of the Great Powers' Governments have forever altered the fate of Yugoslavia.

A report

The Archives of the Hoover Institution (Stanford University, Palo Alto, California) contain a document – entitled PRESENT SITUATION IN YUGOSLAVIA – which recorded a conversation held after Italy's occupation of Albania (7 April 1939). Neither the interlocutors nor the reporter are identified. However, the identity of the informant is important because of his social and political standing in the country and relations he had with the Regent of Yugoslavia, Prince Paul Karađorđević. Therefore here are some pertinent excerpts which will help to identify the 'informant':

> Informant, whose reliability is beyond question, and whose social and business standing is the highest in the country, is a Yugoslav belonging to the Roman Catholic church but in no way bigoted.
>
> Informant has himself, for the last three years, resolutely refused ever even to visit Belgrade from his own country seat, as his dislike and mistrust of the late premier STOYADINOVITCH were so intense and he told Prince Paul that this was the reason which prevented him even going to stay with the Prince; further that if Prince Paul wanted to see him, ie informant, he must go and see him. This Prince Paul has frequently done; he also informed the Duke and Duchess of Kent that he could not visit them in Belgrade and so they stayed with him.
>
> 1. He [the informant] states that Prince Paul's one concern at the present moment is to play for time until the moment when Great Britain is herself strong enough and, with her allies and countries with whom she has made unilateral pacts, is in a sufficiently preponderating position to enable Yugoslavia openly to side against the Axis powers. ...
>
> 3. Informant states that the unsuccess of the recent attempt to reach an agreement between the Croats and Serbs was really due to the Croats' dislike and mistrust of Prince Paul's apparently pro-Axis policy; the Croats of course did not realise that this is merely Prince Paul's attempt to gain time. He says that undoubtedly an agreement will be reached and that the driving force in the matter is Father KOROSHATZ, the Slovene Catholic, who is much more able man that either MATCHEK of the Croats or the present premier SVETKOVITCH. The latter really is more or less of a dummy.

In the event of war in the near future, informant

> was anxious regarding the attitude of Hungary and Bulgaria. Their adhesion to the Axis powers would of course enormously increase Yugoslavia's difficulties and extend the frontiers which she would have to guard. He placed primary importance on the speedy conclusion of a pact between Great Britain and Turkey and said this would have an overwhelming influence in the Balkans. ...
>
> He was questioned by X ..., an Englishman present at the meeting, about the possibility and desirability of Great Britain providing military assistance to Yugoslavia in the Adriatic, but naturally replied that the Adriatic in war would be a "mare clausum" owing to Italy's possession of Albania, ...
>
> He said that the greatest support that Great Britain could give to Yugoslavia would be military assistance sent via the Aegean and Salonika. ...   (Great Britain, Special Operations Executive, 91087 10.V)

**

The above description of the "Informant" compares very favorably with the information found in Professor Vodušek Starič's book, *Slovenski špijoni in SOE 1938-1942*, about the internationally famous sculptor Ivan Meštrović.

* The sculptor certainly was *"A Yugoslav belonging to the Roman Catholic church but in no way bigoted"* - Some of Meštrović's masterpieces graced – and still do – Serbia and Montenegro.
* *"Informant's reliability beyond question"* - The British General Consulate in Zagreb was located in Ilica No. 12, in a house owned by Ivan Meštrović. The second floor was rented to the British. One area of the Consulate was rented to the British firm, "Hanau, Burr &Co".

(Vodušek Starič, 78) Meštrović was one of the most prominent members of the *Association of the Friends of Great Britain*. (*Ibid.*, 82) In his reminiscences Meštrović recorded that in the afternoon of 12 April 1941 the British Consul in Zagreb, [Terence Cecil] Rapp, reached to him [in Split, where the sculptor had a residence, a country home]. (*Ibid.*, 251)

On 18 April 1941, the Foreign Office informed their Ministers in Belgrade and Athens about a need for additional evacuations of prominent people out of Yugoslavia: for the sake of future British influence in Yugoslavia, it would be necessary – if still possible – to evacuate several people, including Ivan Meštrović. (*Ibid.*, 227)

All this would put Ivan Meštrović's "*reliability beyond question*"

> * For political reasons, for three years "the informant" did not go to Belgrade to stay with Prince Paul so the Prince had frequently come to see 'the informant' in his country home. "This Prince Paul has frequently done; he also informed the Duke and Duchess of Kent that he could not visit them in Belgrade and so they stayed with him.
>
> These visits also imply 'the informant's' "highest social and business standing in the country".

During their frequent meetings, Meštrović had opportunities to assess Prince Paul's policies. The statement that

> Prince Paul's one concern at the present moment is to play for time until the moment when Great Britain is herself strong enough and, with her allies and countries with whom she has made unilateral pacts, is in a sufficiently preponderating position to enable Yugoslavia openly to side against the Axis powers. ...

is based on the knowledge of the Prince's policy. It is reasonable to assume that he talked about it with the sculptor, a well known Anglophile. Therefore, all these elements point to Meštrović as the 'informant'. His opinion of Prince Paul's policy underscores the Regent's pro-British attitude.

Chapter 1

"A war in the Balkans was not what Hitler wanted."

"The form which this war has taken, and seems likely to hold, does not enable us to match the immense armies of Germany in any theatre where their main power can be brought to bear. We can, however, by the use of sea-power and air-power, meet the German armies in regions where only comparatively small forces can be brought into action. We must do our best to prevent the German domination of Europe spreading into Africa and into Southern Asia."
(Excerpt from the letter by the British Prime Minister Winston S. Churchill to the American President Franklin D. Roosevelt, dated December 8, 1940.)   (Churchill, *Their Finest Hour*, p.559)

"A war in Balkans was not what Hitler wanted." (*The Eden Memoirs - The Reckoning,* p, 242)

"The reasons why the British insisted so strongly that Prince Paul should abandon his benevolent neutrality and that Yugoslavia should go to war, whatever the cost, why they in fact forced Hitler to undertake an operation against Yugoslavia which he had not intended, at any rate at that time, can be understood only in the light of their doubts and fears about the outcome of the Balkan campaign of 1941." (Elisabeth Barker, *British Policy in South-East Europe in the Second World War,* 96)

In his article, "SOE and British Involvement in the Belgrade Coup d'état of March 1941", Professor David A. T. Stafford stated: "British policy toward Yugoslavia early in 1941 became a function of the British desire to save Greece." (Stafford(cp), 401) British "doubts and fears about the outcome of the Balkan campaign of 1941", " the failure of Britain's attempts to construct a Balkan front to withstand Axis encroachment", "a function of the British desire to save Greece" – determined British plans for Yugoslavia.

In her article, "Britain and the Belgrade Coup of 27 March 1941 Revisited", Professor Sue Onslow concluded that "the British endorsement of the *coup* was born of the failure of Britain's attempts to construct a Balkan front to withstand Axis encroachment." (Onslow, 3)

If Hitler did not want a war in the Balkans in the spring of 1941, then who wanted it and why? Why was Hitler forced to undertake an operation against Yugoslavia? Why had the British wanted to save Greece? Had the British just *endorsed* the Belgrade military coup of 27 March 1941, or had they actively *approved, encouraged and contributed* to it? The answers to these and related questions come primarily from British sources. They also reveal how *"saving Greece"* first and foremost exposed Yugoslavia to the *coup d'état* which, then, led directly into the war.

Importance of the Mediterranean for the British Empire

Greece was pivotal to Great Britain's interests. Why? The one who controls Greece and her islands is in a position to control and dominate the Eastern Mediterranean. The Mediterranean was Britain's most important seaway to her Empire's eastern possessions. "A vital artery" (Eden, 171) This sea had been "for two hundred years Britain's principal foothold outside its island base". (Keegan. 131)

British admirals and generals had campaigned in the eastern Mediterranean for 150 years; Nelson's reputation had been made by his victory at the Nile in 1798. The British had ruled the Ionian islands from 1809 to 1863, had possessed Malta since 1800, Cyprus since 1878, and maintained a fleet and an army in Egypt since 1882. In 1915 a British army had almost captured the Black Sea straits, and between 1916 and 1918 sustained an offensive front against Bulgaria on Greek soil (the Salonika campaign). (Keegan, 146)

Between the First and the Second World Wars, Britain's interests in the Mediterranean remained undiminished. Because Italy is also a Mediterranean country, maintaining good relations with her was also important for Britain, whatever Italy's internal regime – Fascism or not. The ideology was not the deciding element in Britain's foreign policies; the usefulness was. Sir Alexander Cadogan, Permanent Undersecretary for Foreign Affairs, wrote on 14 October

1938 – two weeks after the signing of the Munich Agreement - that the Mediterranean, a highway to Britain's eastern possessions and Dominions, was an area of direct interest to the British and that, therefore, "we should do everything we can to maintain the best relations with, and give such assistance as may be possible to, Turkey and Greece. It follows, of course that we should spare no reasonable effort to resume our former friendly relations with Italy." (Dilks(ed), 117) "Italy was treated by the British Government as a genuine neutral until the eve of Mussolini's declaration of war in June 1940." (Hensley et al, 224)

Why give assistance to Turkey? Britain was "a historic protector of the Turks against Russia, in which cause she had fought the Crimean war of 1854-6, and a sponsor of Islamic nationalism by her foundation of the States of Iraq and Trans-Jordan." (Keegan, 146)

Therefore, when in early 1941 the British Government were implementing their policy of safeguarding the Mediterranean, providing the assistance to both Greece and Turkey was vigorously debated.

As Historian Alan John Percival Taylor observed, in the previous war Britain had kept the Mediterranean open to her shipping. "But when Italy entered the war and France fell out [in June 1940], the Mediterranean could no longer be used by British ships and it remained closed until May 1943. ("The Statesman", *Churchill: Four Faces and the Man,* p.42)

Therefore, keeping the Mediterranean open to British ships – not only during the war, but also in the future - was one of British strategic goals. " ... Because Greece was seen to have become central to Britain's strategic and political position, inclusion of Greece in Britain's sphere of interest in the ultimate settlement of Europe was paramount – even at the cost of having to cede Poland or its eastern European neighbours to the Soviet Union." (Lawlor, 1-2) "In the eyes of British strategists, then [in May 1940] as now [in 1968], Greece was an essential part of the defensive complex of the Eastern Mediterranean, a Levantine rather than a Balkan state." (Howard, 10-11)

According to Churchill's physician, Lord Moran, the Mediterranean was always on Churchill's mind. "The control of the Mediterranean meant in his eyes the control of the Western world." (Moran, 86)

When, on 28 October 1940, Italy attacked Greece from Albania, British control of the Mediterranean became tenuous. Therefore, a way had to be found to avert the danger which had continued after Italy's earlier invasion of Albania on 7 April 1939.

The impact of Italy's conquest of Albania

On 13 April 1939, Italy's invasion led Britain and France to pledge assistance to Greece and Rumania should they consider a threat to their independence. "In April 1939, in place of something more concrete and binding, the British government publicly guaranteed Greece's independence; it was a solemn and face-saving gesture, but empty of any substantive commitments." (Koliopoulos, 28)

* **On Greece**

    ... in October 1938, the British government had turned down a proposal by Ioannis Metaxas, the Greek dictator, for an Anglo-Greek alliance. Britain needed a friendly, not an allied, Greece, ... British planners were interested in Greece mainly as an air and naval base from which air attacks could be launched against Italy and communications in the Aegean Sea controlled. Greek strategy and war preparations, ... , had been directed toward covering a static defensive war against Bulgaria; so much so that, until April 1939,when Italy occupied Albania and posed a direct threat to Greece, Greek war planning was concerned exclusively with defense against Bulgaria. In April 1939, the Greek General Staff was caught off-guard and facing the wrong enemy. ... coastal defenses were non-existent. Considerable funds – and pride - had been invested on the elaborate fortifications sealing of Bulgaria, the line which was named after Metaxas. (Koliopoulos, 28-9)

    Greece even lacked a plan covering the Italian danger. As was to be expected, the Italian occupation of Albania sounded the alarm, and, on May 4, 1939, the General Staff produced the first war plan covering both Italy and Bulgaria, Plan IB. (Koliopoulos, 29)

    The guarantee to Greece was a panic response by Britain to the Italian invasion of Albania on 8 April [7 April]; it was more understandable than the guarantee to Rumania since it could be seen as serving the requirements of traditional naval strategy in the Mediterranean. (Barker, 4)

* On Turkey and Yugoslavia

Italy's invasion of Albania "led to an Anglo-Turkish Declaration of friendship signed on May 12, 1939. ... A month later the Anglo-Turkish Declaration became tripartite when France joined as soon as the negotiations for the return of the Hatay to Turkey were completed." (Scanlan, 4)

> On October 19, 1939, the Tripartite Treaty of Mutual Assistance was signed [in Ankara] by Turkey, France and England. It was to be of 15 years' duration and provided:
> 1. The Allies agreed to assist Turkey in case of aggression by a European power. Turkey agreed to assist Great Britain and France:
>   a. in case Britain and France became engaged in hostilities on account of the guarantees given to Greece and Rumania in April, 1939;
>   b. in case of an act of aggression by a European Power leading to war in the Mediterranean. (Scanlan, 6-7)

"The pact was followed immediately by military consultation and extension of large credits to Turkey." (Scanlan, 7)

When Italy entered the war against the Allies on 10 June 1940, the French and British Ambassadors asked the Turkish Foreign Minister to act in accordance with provisions of item 1.b. of the Treaty. However,

> The fall of France, a few days later, prompted the Turks not to honor her obligation. Since the Treaty was Tripartite and France had now surrendered, the necessity of Turkey's entry, according to the nature of the Treaty, was questionable and, at any rate, England, realizing the hopelessness of the situation, did not press for such entry. (Scanlan, 9)

Turkey's "non-belligerent" status proved to be an impediment to Britain's plans for the Balkans in the winter of 1941. Although this lack of Turkish support, in turn, increased Britain's pressure on Yugoslavia, no treaty of alliance was concluded between Great Britain and Yugoslavia. "*Yugoslavia lies outside or rather on the edge of our major interests.*" (Eden, 523-4. Italics added.) Therefore: without British guarantees, there would be no British assistance. On the contrary: Yugoslavia was expected to assist Britain.

Italy's conquest of Albania was also the first step of encirclement by the Axis which Yugoslavia had to face without help from outside.

"Should Italy become hostile ..."

Winston Spencer Churchill became Britain's Prime Minister and the Defense Minister on 10 May 1940. Having in mind Mussolini's "waiting upon events" to develop, Churchill wrote:

> Should Italy become hostile, our first battlefield must be the Mediterranean. I was entirely opposed, except as temporary convenience, to all plans for quitting the centre and merely sealing up the ends of the great inland sea. ...
> The British domination of the Mediterranean would inflict injuries upon an enemy Italy which might be fatal to her power of continuing the war. ... Not to hold the Central Mediterranean would be to expose Egypt and the [Suez] Canal, as well as the French possessions, to invasion by Italian troops with German leadership. Moreover, a series of swift and striking victories in this theatre, which might be obtainable in the early weeks of a war, would have a most healthy and helpful bearing upon the main struggle with Germany. ... (Churchill(GS), 415-16)

Ever conscious of the importance of the Eastern Mediterranean, on 31 May 1940 Churchill suggested, if Italy attacked Greece, then Britain and France should be responsible for Crete. When General Ioannis Metaxas (Greek Prime Minister and the Minister for Foreign Affairs), "on 22 August [1940] asked what assistance he could expect, he was told that until Egypt was secure no land or sea forces were available for service in the Balkans." This did not mean that Britain intended to desert Greece; it just meant that at that time her forces were hopelessly inadequate. (McClymont, 87) It did not at all mean that Britain would desert the Balkans.

So the British domination of the Mediterranean became a guiding strategic policy, with Greece holding a key position. As Greece shared borders with Bulgaria, Turkey and Yugoslavia, therefore, the policies of these countries were also meaningful and important. From Yugoslavia's point of view, without a major ally after the fall of France in June 1940, and without an alliance with Britain, it was in her own best interest to maintain a benevolent neutrality.

Churchill's attitude toward the neutrals

But Churchill viewed the neutrality of others from his own angle. He was convinced that neutrality was a form of delinquency and that concessions to Hitler were a sin against a higher morality. (Barker, 9)   In 1939 he wrote that Great Britain "had the duty and the right to abrogate for a time some of the conventions the democracies were seeking to reaffirm. Small nations, like Yugoslavia, must not tie the hands of great powers who were fighting for the rights and freedom of small powers." A technical infringement of international law, when not accompanied by acts of inhumanity, "would not deprive Britain of the good wishes of the neutral countries." (Hoptner, 234) "He regarded the British cause as the cause of freedom and national independence all over the world and therefore dismissed those who failed to support it as traitors. He supposed that this view was universally held and that in every country an indignant majority of eager patriots was held down by German agents." (Alan John Percival Taylor, "The Statesman", *Churchill: Four Faces and the Man,* p. 38)

Some might argue that a just and durable international order cannot be founded on a selective and temporary abrogation of conventions, or on the infringement of international law - even when Great Powers claim to be fighting for the rights and freedom of the small ones. The painful experience of small countries tells them that the Great Powers pursue their own interests at the expense of smaller countries and above international laws and conventions when it suits them. Churchill's *Iron Curtain Speech* at Fulton, Missouri, USA, on 5 March 1946, is testimony to the fact that in the Second World War, the Western Great Powers did not guard the rights and freedom of small powers, as they had claimed to have been fighting for.

**

In his essay, *Principles and Compromises: Churchill, Roosevelt and Eastern Europe,* presented at the Annual Churchill Conference, Boston, 28 October 1995, Professor Warren F. Kimball stated, *inter alia:*

> Winston Churchill was a British statesman whose goal was to advance the interests of Great Britain. When in office, that was the principle fundamental to his actions. If other principles came into conflict with that bedrock commitment, they automatically took second place. And there were times when what individuals might consider immutable rights – political freedom, for example – came into conflict with what Churchill considered British interests. He understood that conflict and tried to reconcile the two – but when that failed, his interpretation of British interests prevailed. The political fate of Eastern Europe after the Second World War, particularly Poland, is one such case.
> (http://www.winstonchurchill.org/i4a/pages/index.cfm?pageid=62   12/10/03)

Dr. Hugh Dalton, Minister of Economic Warfare who in July 1940 was appointed head of the Special Operations Executive (SOE), on 17 August told his Cabinet colleagues: "... we must learn, for the duration of this war at least, to shed many inhibitions and to act on the assumption that the end justifies the means ...We must beat the Nazis at their own game." (Stafford(so), 29)
   In the case of Yugoslavia, many inhibitions and scruples were dropped or disregarded.

"British slowness in supplying arms"

To abandon neutrality and provide serious opposition to Hitler's war machine – as Churchill wanted Yugoslavia to do – Yugoslavia desperately needed arms. Unfortunately, in 1940, Great Britain could not supply them.

> In May 1940 [Alexander] Cadogan [Permanent Undersecretary for Foreign Affairs] received a report that all the Balkan Ministers in London were complaining of British slowness in supplying arms, and that a Yugoslav Military Mission had left England "with nothing accomplished and worst possible impression". "If we had any goods to sell," Cadogan wrote, .."the transactions would go through quick enough. But we have to haver and procrastinate to hide the emptiness of the shop." (Barker, 29; 273n8)

On the subject of supplying arms to Yugoslavia, Lord Edward Halifax, then Foreign Minister, recorded on 17 May 1940 a conversation he had with Prince Paul's wife Princess Olga, who was visiting London. When she asked him what Britain would do if Italy attacked Yugoslavia, he told her that "We should naturally wish to do anything in our power to help but ... we must recognize that if Italians, as .... was likely, mined the entrance of the Adriatic, the navy would presumably not be able to do too much". When she asked about the Yugoslav order for aircraft, the answer came that the British were throwing everything they could into the Western battle, and that it was very difficult to spare military aircraft which the British needed for themselves. (Barker, 78; 280n2)

The inability of Britain to provide needed armament for Yugoslavia in 1940 extended well into 1941, and the Yugoslav Government was acutely aware of it. Additionally, after the conquest of Albania Italy could mine at will the entrance to the Adriatic, the Strait of Otranto – and *the British Navy could not prevent it.* The situation for Yugoslavia worsened with Italy's attack on Greece in October 1940.

17 September 1940: "... the end of Sea Lion ..."

The worsening situation turned out to be a consequence of the then-developing combination of some of the most critical decisions of WWII, which took place by mid-September of 1940. Germany's plan for the attack on the Soviet Union "had been ready since 5 August [1940]. However, Hitler's determination to launch *Sealion* [the invasion of Britain] was already wilting down when on 11 September he decided to send Army and Air Force missions into Romania..." (Hinsley *et al*, 249)

A firsthand account of the *wilting down Sealion, "the end of Sea Lion",* was provided by Group Captain, Frederick William Winterbotham of the Royal Air Force, who was in charge of security and dissemination of the most secret information obtained from the broken code of the German Air Force, the Ultra signals. Due to the tremendous importance of this event, his account is quoted here extensively.

> On September the seventh [1940] Invasion Alert No. 1 was sent out which meant that the Germans might be expected within twelve hours ... (Winterbotham, 56)
> On September the ninth we got Goering's orders at 11 a.m. for an early evening raid by two hundred-plus bombers, again on London itself, but this time our fighters were able to meet them further south and few got through to the city. That night, however, they came again. *Still the invasion barges remained in their ports;* ...
> On September the tenth came blessed rain and clouds; it lasted for four days. ... (Winterbotham, 57. Italics added.)

> To those of us scanning every [Ultra] signal of the German armed forces, the impression had been forming, ever since Goering's switch to attack away from our aerodromes, that *time had run out for Sea Lion.* Churchill I know felt this although he could not relax the mood of the nation in any way. That Hitler and his generals would not risk Sea Lion whilst the RAF [Royal Air Force] still lived was evident, and Goering's last-minute effort to break the morale of the civil population with bombs was having the opposite effect. *The odds against invasion lengthened.* (Winterbotham, 57. Italics added.)

On the fourteenth the rains lessened but the weather was not good enough for any major effort. But, Sunday, the fifteenth of September, dawned alas, an ideal day for the German planes, cloudy but with sufficient gaps to find their way. Once again the hand of Goering was guiding what he hoped would be the final knockout. By mid-day, wave upon wave of bombers were heading for London.

Dowding [Air Chief Marshal Sir Hugh Caswell Tremenhare], correctly judging his moment, ... , threw in everything we had. ... The unexpected strength of our fighters was too much for the Luftwaffe; ... they turned and fled. Goering must obviously have been getting frantic by this time. He promptly ordered a second raid, and this time it was to be pressed home. His signal was duly picked up and this was an occasion when the speed of Ultra operation and the direct line to Dowding made history. The fighters were refueled, rearmed and ready again to meet the second wave, and once again the raiders dropped their bombs wherever they could and fled. It was a tremendous day. ...(Winterbotham, 57-8.)

Invasion alert Cromwell was still operative. But one of the main features of the German invasion plans had been the vast preparations that had been made on the Belgian and Dutch aerodromes for loading and quick turn-round of the supply and troop-carrying aircraft, which were by this time supposed to have an unopposed flight to England.

On the morning of the seventeenth the officer-in-charge of these operations in Holland *received a signal from the German General Staff to say that Hitler had authorized the dismantling of the air-loading equipment at the Dutch aerodromes.* It was quite a short signal, but its significance was so great that 'Humph' [wing commander Humphreys] had telephoned it down to me the moment it had been decyphered. It was obviously a signal which required some explanation if Churchill was to be able to grasp its meaning. I, therefore, indicated its full significance on my cover headline. *If the loading equipment was being dismantled, the invasion could not take place,* and I sent it over to the underground room in its red box with another note to Winston's Principal Secretary John Martin asking him to see that the Prime Minister had it at once. I also explained the signal to [General Stewart] Menzies [Chief of the Secret Service]. ... (Winterbotham,58. Italics added.)

Churchill called the Chiefs of Staff and Menzies to a meeting at 7.30 p.m. in his underground war room.

There were controlled smiles on the faces of these men. Churchill read out the signal, his face beaming, then he rightly asked the Chief of the Air Staff Sir Cyril Newall to explain its significance. Cyril Newall had been well briefed; he gave it as his considered opinion that *this marked the end of Sea Lion, at least for this year.* Churchill asked Menzies if there was anything further to confirm the signal. He turned to me, but I was unable to give any further assurance as yet. *But the conference knew that the dismantling of the air-loading equipment meant the end of the threat, and so it was accepted.* (Winterbotham, 59. Italics added.)

**

By the time the Germans entered Rumania on 7 October 1941, "*Sealion* had further receded", and on 12 October "Hitler put off *Sealion* for the first time." (Hinsley *et al*, 250) "On 10 January 1941, except as a means of providing deception cover for the *Barbarossa* [invasion of the Soviet Union] preparations, he [Hitler] again, and for the last time, put *Sealion* off." (Hinsley *et al*, 261)

At the beginning of February 1941 the Enigma traffic revealed "that an entire GAF [German Air Force] administrative formation which had supported the *Sealion* preparations in the Antwerp area was moving to Romania. But anxiety about the renewal of the invasion threat still persisted. So did the reluctance to conclude that Germany would attack Russia." (Hinsley *et al*, 365)

Understandably, *the end of Sea Lion* became a carefully guarded secret. Whether recognized or not, at that time, Hitler's plan to attack the Soviet Union, would very shortly have a great impact on Yugoslavia.

* **German troops in Rumania – an unforeseen impact on Yugoslavia**

Information related to Germany's entering Rumania – gathered from British sources – indicates that this move was not related to Yugoslavia at all. However, subsequent events developed the way not foreseen and/or planned in the late summer of 1940, but nevertheless greatly impacting Yugoslavia in the spring of 1941.

Maurice Pearton, the author of *British Policy towards Romania, 1939-1941* and other works, wrote that

> in Romanian thinking, not only in the government but among the scattered and mutually hostile opposition groups, relations with both Germany and the western Allies turned on the country's relations with Russia. It was axiomatic that Germany was less of a threat to Romanian interests than the Soviet Union, with the corollary that, even if the western Allies defeated Germany, the Russian danger would still exists for Romania. That is fundamental to any analysis of Romania's politics at this period. (M. Pearton in Seaman(ed), 123-4)

On 11 September – when the *Sea Lion operation* to invade Britain was still on schedule – Hitler

> decided to send Army and Air Force missions into Romania. This step was taken after he had received from the new Romanian government request for help against other Balkan countries and Russia, who had occupied Bessarabia, north Bukhovina and the Baltic states in June. The missions entered Romania openly on 7 October [1940], their ostensible purpose being to train Romanian forces but their real task being to protect the Romanian oil and to prepare Romania's facilities for use in future operations. (Hinley *et al*, 249-50)

> From the last days of October 1940 the [British] intelligence authorities began to receive incontrovertible evidence that Germany was actively preparing a large scale Balkan campaign. ...
> ... But while it was an immense advance to be able to chart in detail Germany's preparations for the attack on Greece and Crete, Whitehall still failed to discern that the strategic purpose underlying these attacks was to safeguard the southern flank of Germany's invasion of Russia. (Hinsley *et al*, 259)

The Tripartite Pact

Another event in 1940 that later affected Yugoslavia was the formation of the Tripartite Pact between Germany, Italy, and Japan. Signed in Berlin on 27 September 1940, the pact was made accessible – *nolens volens* - to additional signatories. Article 3 of the pact stated:

> Japan, Germany and Italy agree to cooperate in their efforts on aforesaid lines. They further undertake to assist one another with all political, economic and military means if one of the Contracting Powers is attacked by a Power at present not involved in the European War or in the Japanese-Chinese conflict. (http://www.historyguy.com/worldwartwo/tripartite_pact_axis_treaty.htm ... 12/28/11)

Because of that clause, Germany and Italy declared war on the United States on 11 December 1941, following Japan's attack on the US naval base at Pearl Harbor on 7 December 1941. Ultimately, both of these declarations contributed tremendously to the Axis' defeat.

Italy's attack on Greece, 28 October 1940

Between May and September 1940 Germany's military superiority was evident, and Churchill had wanted the attitude of Greece and Turkey to remain benign. (Lawlor, 116) However, "From early September reports suggested that the Italians were preparing a Greek campaign, possibly in late October." (Lawlor, 115) Rumors about Italy's possible attack on Greece "had been rife since Italy's occupation, in April 1939, of Albania, and the Foreign Office had been considering its implications for the war in the Mediterranean for some time. (van Creveld(G), 66)

On 19 September, Hitler decided to send a full division to Rumania, but Italy was informed about it only on 10 October. The Italians "first learned through the press, the radio, and their own sources of information of the dispatch of German military units to Rumania." (Ristić, 39)

"As early as 24 September Sir Michael Palairet, British minister in Athens, was instructed that, in case of war, he was to *'maintain Greek determination to fight'*, a message that was repeated on the day of the invasion. (van Creveld(G), 66. Italics added.) *Maintaining Greek determination to fight* implicated Yugoslavia into the war six months later.

On 4 October, at the Brenner meeting with Hitler, Mussolini "was strengthened in his determination to occupy Greece." (Hinsley *et al*, 250)

On 12 October an indignant Mussolini declared : "Hitler always faces me with a *fait accompli*. This time I am to pay him back in his own coin. He will find out from the papers that I have occupied Greece. In this way the equilibrium will be re-established." That same day Italy's Foreign Minister, Count Galeazzo Ciano, recorded in his diary: "I believe that the military operation will be useful and easy." (Ristić, 39-40)

On 15 October, furious on account of Hitler's unilateral move into Romania he [Mussolini] fixed a date for the invasion [of Greece] without informing Germany. (Hinsley *et al*, 250)

On October 19, Mussolini wrote to Hitler telling him of the decision to which he had come. Hitler was then on his journey to Hendaye and Montoire. The letter …. seems to have followed him round. When it finally reached him, he at once proposed to Mussolini a meeting to discuss the general political situation in Europe. This meeting took place in Florence on October 28. That morning the Italian attack on Greece had begun.

… There can be no doubt that he [Hitler] did not like what had been done by his associate. … (Churchill(FH), 532)

Consequences of Italy's attack on Greece

Regardless of what Hitler wanted, on Monday, 28 October 1940, Italy attacked Greece from Albania. "The Italian declaration of war on Greece … foreordained deepening German involvement in the Balkan peninsula". (Gorodetsky, 46) It also deeply involved Great Britain into certain immediate military moves in Greece and long-term policies related to the Balkans.

> [The decrypted German signals] yielded voluminous information about the movements and order of battle of the German forces in the Balkan area from the beginning of November 1940, and left no doubt that they were massing for an attack on Greece. But it did not reveal that the attack was fundamentally a defensive operation – one which Hitler had ordered initially to safeguard the Romanian oil – which on 5 December he made dependent on the failure of Italy to reach a negotiated peace with Greece and which, in a new directive of 13 December, … he finally ordered to go forward as a means of securing the flank of the projected assault on Russia… (Hinsley *et al*, 260)

> Special intelligence, … , had meanwhile established at the end of 1940 that she [Germany] was extending her infiltration of the Balkans to Bulgaria, and the Cabinet had already authorized an attempt to bring Turkey into the war on the British side before the decrypts confirmed rumors from the embassies and the SIS [Secret Intelligence Service] that Hitler planned a considerable offensive through Bulgaria to Greece. (F.H. Hinsley in Blake & Louis(eds), 414)

The attack on Greece prompted the British to review their policy and the roles of Turkey and Greece. If Italy won, she would control the Eastern Mediterranean. To prevent this and for Britain to gain a foothold on the Continent, Greece had to be helped. The central questions then became: First – could the British effectively assist Greece with their existing resources, without weakening the position in North Africa; and Second – was it more advantageous to control the North African coast or to take a risk to help Greece, with their resources depleted? The answers would also end up determining the role the British would assign to Yugoslavia.

* Immediate reactions of the British military

The President of the Greek Council, General Ioannis Metaxas, "applied at once to Britain for help at sea and in the air, but did not ask for troops. The Cabinet regarded themselves as bound both *by self-interests and by the guarantee to Greece*, to send this assistance." (Dilks(ed), 333. Italics added.) Prime Minister Churchill responded to Metaxas' appeal: "We will give you all the help in our power. We will fight a common foe and we will share a united victory" ", wrote the Prime Minister. (Churchill(FH), 533)

How adequate and effective *all the help in the British power* really was at the time, became crucial to both Greece and Yugoslavia later on. But at that moment, according to Churchill, "One salient strategic fact leaped out upon us – CRETE! The Italians must not have it. We must get it first – and at once". On 29 October he telegraphed to Eden, who was in Cairo: "We here are all convinced an effort should be made to establish ourselves in Crete, and that risk should be run for this valuable prize." (Churchill(FH), 534)

"At the invitation of the Greek Government, Suda Bay, the best harbour in Crete, was occupied by our forces two days later." *(Churchill(FH), 534)* On 31 October 1940 "Britain occupied Crete and the Aegean island of Lemnos with troops sent from Egypt, and in the next few days transferred air units to southern Greece, thus putting Romania's Ploesti oilfields, his [Hitler's] main source of supply, in danger of bombing attack." (Keegan, 134)

The British Minister in Athens, Michael Palairet, suggested that, although Greek morale was high, the non-appearance of British air force was encouraging some criticism. "So, without waiting for instructions, the Air Commander in Chief, Middle East, Air Marshal Sir Arthur Longmore, had No. 30 Blenheim Squadron in Greece by 3 November." "Churchill considered this move to be both wise and bold. In his opinion, every effort must be made to assist the Greeks." (McClymont, 89)

> ... British air forces had moved into Greece immediately after the Italian attack, and since it was feared that they might attack the Romanian oilfields, the [German] missions in Romania were to be reinforced and preparations begun for the occupation of continental Greece with 19 divisions via Bulgaria with the object, at his stage, for attacks on such British forces as might threaten the Romanian oil. (Hinsley *et al*, 251) "These developments provoked him [Hitler] to an outburst of contingency planning. He ordered OKH [Army's High Command]... to prepare another plan for the invasion of Greece." (Keegan, 134)

**

The Ploesti oilfields were Germany's main source of petroleum supply and thus became the central strategic target, either for the British to bomb or for the Germans to keep from being bombed. So both Churchill and Hitler undertook measures aimed to achieve their respective goals.

However, destroying the Ploesti oilfields was not Britain's only objective in Rumania. Already in operation before Italy's attack on Greece, to prevent supplies of all kinds from the Balkans reaching Germany, a blockade of the Danube River was a major assignment of Section D of the Secret Intelligence Service (SIS), and of "D's" successor, Special Operations Executive (SOE). Both organizations were very secret, and their center in Belgrade was manned by a large number of operatives.

After Italy's attack on Greece, activities of Section D / SOE broadened beyond the blockade and into the political affairs of Yugoslavia. "Contacts" with domestic "friends" were sought and established in pursuit of British political objectives for the Balkans. Belgrade – with a large number of these secret agents – became the center of the "D" / SOE operations for the Balkans. (The story of this co-operation is examined in **Part Two**.)

To help or not to help Greece

* Initially, the British military leaders were opposed to the aid

Anthony Eden, then Secretary of State for War, was in Cairo when Italy announced her ultimatum to Greece. On 28 October he recorded his disapproval of aid to Greece in his diary: "As it is we are not in a position to give effective help by land or air, and another guaranteed nation looks like falling to the Axis." (Eden, 161) Eden's meetings with Wavell "had deeply impressed upon him how serious the situation was there. If the Suez Canal went so did the war." (Rhodes James, 233) "Malta was now highly vulnerable, and was essential not only for maintaining British naval strength in the Mediterranean but for protecting the shipping routes to and from the Suez Canal." (Rhodes James, 237)

> The Middle East was the only area in which the British Army, having been driven out of Europe, could attack for the foreseeable future, but all Wavell had were one very incomplete armoured division, two incomplete infantry divisions and another capable only of policing duties. As Eden well knew, he lacked tanks, vehicles, anti-tank weapons and artillery, while air position, so crucial in that area, was inadequate; ammunition was meager – but so was everything. (Rhodes James, 238)

Still opposed to the idea of aiding Greece, on 1 November, Eden telegraphed his reasons to the Prime Minister:

> We cannot, from Middle East resources, send sufficient air or land reinforcement to have any decisive influence upon course of fighting in Greece. To send such forces from here, or to divert

reinforcement now on their way or approved, would imperil our whole position in the Middle East and jeopardize plans for offensive operations now being laid in more than one theatre. (Eden, 168)

Using Eden as their mouthpiece, the Service Chiefs Middle East informed Churchill that sending aid to Greece would "imperil our whole position in the Middle East", and that " from the strategical point of view the security of Egypt is the most urgent commitment and must take precedence of attempts to prevent Greece being overrun". (van Creveld(G), 67-8) General Wavell agreed with Eden and strongly resisted the idea of diverting men, aircrafts and material from Egypt to Greece. (Rhodes James, 241)

Like the Service Chiefs Middle East, the three Chiefs of Staff and other military personnel in London also discussed a plan for aid to Greece. As Colville recorded, General Hastings Ismay – the Chief of Staff at Churchill's Ministry of Defence, "a key figure in the working of the Prime Minister's military activity" (Wheeler-Bennett(ed), 196) - "says that there is nothing we can do on a sufficiently large scale to save the Greeks and the C.O.S. [Chiefs of Staff] seem rather unenthusiastic about the P.M.'s [Prime Minister's] determination to throw considerable forces into the fray even at the expense of weakening Egypt. Ismay thinks that concentrated air-attack, with little opposition, will break Greece as it broke Poland and France." (Colville, 286)

High-ranking military generally opposed the idea of a British expedition in Greece. General John Kennedy explained why:

> ... We had not enough troops for intervention in Greece. We have calculated that at least twenty divisions, plus a considerable air force, would be needed to hold Salonika alone. The Germans could overrun Greece with the utmost ease if they wanted to do so. They would then be in a position to inflict much damage on our shipping in the Mediterranean. We, on the other hand, would be able to afford almost complete protection to that same shipping if we could win the control of the African coast line. This prize was infinitely more desirable. And we stood to gain more by winning the African coast for ourselves than by denying Greece to the Germans. On this issue we should resist political pressure for all we were worth. (Kennedy, 72)

* The Prime Minister was in favor of aid

While having no illusions about the shortages that affected British ability to help, Churchill was still in favor of giving aid. On 29 October he reminded the Cabinet that, while 'certain military measures in support of Greece were in preparation', the Cabinet should be 'under no illusion as to the extent of the assistance [they] ... could give', because they were 'severely limited by the size of [their] forces in the Middle East Theatre'. (Lawlor, 119)

On 31 October 1940, he reiterated that while the British were 'doing all [they] could to help Greece ... it would be wrong and foolish to make them promises which we could not fulfill". (Lawlor, 119-20) But within days, Churchill's assessment of the situation and his attitude changed. 'He began to advocate assistance to the Greeks. He urged both direct help, particularly the dispatch of aircraft, and indirect help in the form of attacking Italy elsewhere, despite objections from the Middle East where Eden and commanders wanted all their resources for [General] Wavell's proposed offensive [in the Western Desert]'. (Lawlor, 121) "From having at the outset considered Greece to be insignificant in the grand scheme of imperial defence, he [Churchill] now suggested that it no longer was". (Lawlor, 121)

With that in mind, on 2 November Churchill telegraphed Eden:

> The Greek situation must be held to dominate others now. We are well aware of our slender resources. Aid to Greece must be attentively studied lest the whole Turkish position is lost through proof that England never tries to keep her guarantees. (Churchill(FH), 536)

On 2 November, Eden again recorded his opposition to military support for Greece in his diary : "My main purpose in wishing to go [home] was ... above all, try to stop folly of diverting men, aeroplanes and material from here to Greece. Disturbing telegram, in all senses, arrived. It seems that Greece is now to dominate the scene. Strategic folly." (Eden, 169) Eden wrote on 2 November: "Egypt is vital, Greece is not. We are barely strong enough in Egypt as it is; weakness in the air especially dangerous." (Rhodes James, 241)

On the morning of 3 November, Eden conferred with the Middle East military commanders and the British Ambassador in Egypt, and concluded: "All were of the same opinion, Egypt was strategically vital, while Greece was not. We are barely strong enough in Egypt as it was, and our weakness in the air would speedily become dangerous." (Eden, 169) He informed Churchill "that the Commanders-in-Chief were strongly of the opinion that the defence of Egypt was the crux of our whole position in the Middle East. From the strategic point of view, they thought that the security of Egypt was the most important commitment and must take precedence of any attempt to save Greece. It was also essential if we were to retain the support of Turkey." (Eden, 170) Eden further informed Churchill:

> My anxiety is lest by dividing our limited resources we risk failure in both theatres [the Middle East and Greece]. We have always taken the line with the Greeks that we cannot help them on land or in the air. We are convinced that, however disagreeable, we should hold to that line and continue to assemble our forces here [the Middle East]. I submit that ineffective help to the Greeks may have worse effect on Turks than to withhold help on the grounds that we are collecting force here that will be really effective later. (Lawfor, 113)

On 3 November, Churchill instructed Eden about the fortification of Crete and the aid to Greece:

> ... Establishment of fueling base and airfield in Crete to be steadily developed into permanent war fortresses [is] indispensable. This is being done. But surely effort must be made to aid Greece directly, *even if only with token forces*. ... Greece, resisting vigorously with reasonable aid from Egypt and England, might check invaders. I am trying to send substantial bomber and fighter reinforcements to Crete and Greece ... (Churchill[FH], 538-9. Italics added.)

**

On 5 November, Eden noted in his diary:

> Saw Yugoslav Minister who brought me a message of thanks from Prince Paul for the information I had sent him, much of which was new to him. He did not conceal his surprise that the Greeks had fought so well, and thought that the Italians had been equally taken aback. That remains to be seen. (Eden, 171-2)

After expressing his disapproval of aid to Greece, Eden returned from Cairo to London on 8 November.

**

While the debate about aid to Greece was taking shape, a conference of Allied nations was organized in London and Greek representatives were invited to attend. On 17 November the Greek position was made clear to the British. Fearing that such participation might provide Germany with the pretext to attack, Greek Prime Minister Metaxas recorded his conversation with Sir Michael Palairet, the British minister in Athens:

> "If ... the British Government believe that it is opportune to provoke such an attack, he [Palairet] must state that categorically, aware as he is of the consequences and the responsibilities we have accepted in common. If that was the case, he must see to it that we are supplied with aircraft, not only against the Italians – inadequate in the first place – but against the Germans as well, whose air attacks against us must be given very serious consideration." Naturally, no reply was given to this inconvenient inquiry. (Koliopoulos, 33-4)

At that time Britain simply did not have weapons, an adequate number of rifles or trucks, let alone the aircraft, Metaxas was talking about.

**

At the end of 1940, His Majesty's Government were satisfied with Yugoslavia's neutrality. Pierson Dixon of the Foreign Office minuted that maintaining "benevolent neutrality" in the Italo-Greek conflict and rejecting all German and Italian demands "incompatible with Yugoslav sovereignty" - were two essentials. (Barker, 80; 281n16) By January of 1941, though, it became clear that *reasonable aid from Egypt and England* might not keep the invaders in check, and therefore Yugoslavia and Turkey had to be involved to provide additional help.

In the meantime, Turkey made her position known and stuck to it persistently, in spite of subsequent efforts by Britain to engage her to check the invaders of Greece. On 1 November 1940

> President Ismet Inönü, of Turkey, reaffirmed non-belligerency and friendship with Britain and Russia. "Our attitude of non-belligerence does not need to constitute an obstacle to normal relations with all other countries which show the same good will. This attitude of non-belligerence makes it impossible without exception for belligerents to use our territory, our seas and skies, against each other, and it will continue to make such use categorically and absolutely impossible so long as we take no part in the war. ... " (Events 1940, http://www.ibiblio.org/pha/events/1940.html 8/18/09)

"A crucial difference" between Britain and Greece on Salonika

In addition of forcing the Greeks to adopt a mobile strategy against Italy, her invasion of Albania necessitated decisive consultations between Britain and Greece. According to Greek historian Ioannis Koliopoulos,

> Pre-January [1941] consultations had made it clear that, although policy toward Germany did not differ as yet, there existed a crucial difference of approach with respect to a possible British base at Salonika. As far as the British were concerned, the establishment of a base at Salonika, from which air attacks could be launched against the Rumanian oil fields, was a tempting but distant possibility for the time "when adequate forces (had) arrived in the Middle East." A British military presence at Salonika, therefore, was considered as an offensive move against the enemy, and fell within the bounds of overall strategy. The Greeks, on the other hand, although they frequently paid lip-service to the long-term Allied aims and interests, saw the problem presented by Germany mainly in the light of their own limited interests. For the Greeks, and more particularly for the government, what counted most at the time was not one more strike against the Axis, but to avoid a German attack, or at least to postpone it; ... What the Greeks essentially meant by a Balkan front was not so much a theater of offensive operations, but a deterrent to Germany. (Koliopoulos, 33)

As establishing just an air base at Salonika was a distant possibility, establishing a Salonika front was even less in Britain's plans at the time. This point is very important to keep in mind because, also in November 1940, Britain was not able to support the evacuation of Yugoslav troops through Salonika or Kavalla – when inquired about that by the Yugoslavs. (Barker 84, 281n40)

Hitler was prepared to help Mussolini in Greece

After Greece had been invaded from Albania on 28 October by some 100,000 Italian troops,

> ... By mid November [1940], they [the Greeks] had regained all lost territory and began to push into Albania. The war reached a stalemate by winter, with the Greeks controlling more than a quarter of Albania. (Leary, 1)

This affected Hitler's plans for Germany's operations in the Balkans. Eden concluded that "As early as November 4th he [Hitler] reflected that he might have to come to the rescue of the Fascist excursion against Greece, which he described as a 'regrettable blunder' ". (Eden, 184) "As soon as he heard of the failure of the Italian attack, Hitler ordered his army to prepare to enter Greece via Rumania and Bulgaria." (van Creveld(G), 68)

Via Rumania and Bulgaria – **not Yugoslavia.** This is important to keep in mind when analyzing further developments involving Yugoslavia.

Chapter 2

Note: To make it possible to follow the German-Yugoslav negotiations without interruption by other topics examined herein, the passages related to the negotiations are identified with *** , so that the reader may easily skip from one negotiation-passage to the next.

*** Feelers for German-Yugoslav negotiations

According to Professor Martin L. van Creveld, the above-described circumstances produced the German-Yugoslav negotiations which ultimately led to Yugoslavia's joining the Tripartite Pact – with Germany, Italy and Japan – but without military clauses and obligations.

> Hitler's decision to attack Greece had made it essential to win over Yugoslavia; early in November, the Germans believed that they had discovered a suitable lever to do this in form of Salonika. Both before and after World War I the city had been the subject of a bitter dispute between Yugoslavia and Greece. When it was finally awarded to the latter, Yugoslavia was granted free harbour. As her sole port not facing Italy, Salonika was naturally of the greatest importance to that country. Wouldn't it be possible to win her over by offering her the city? During the first half of November, the Yugoslavs gave every indication that it would. As soon as the Italian invasion of Greece had started the Prince Regent had summoned a conference attended by Cvetkovic, the prime minister, Cincar Markovic, the foreign minister, Nedic, the minister for war, and Antic, the commander-in-chief. **(#)** The conference seems to have resulted in Nedic instructing Colonel Vauhnik, the military attaché in Berlin, 'to put out feelers with the highest German authorities to find what steps would be appropriate to secure Yugoslavia's interest in Salonika.' Direct negotiations with Italy, the military attaché said, were 'out of the question', but in return for 'mediating in favour of Yugoslavia, Germany might perhaps be able to make certain demands on Yugoslavia'. (van Creveld, 79)

(#) The Crown council met on 28 October, and then again on 31 October and 1 November. "A partial mobilization was considered, but opinions differed: everyone agreed, however, that the Italians could not be allowed to occupy Salonika." (Ristić, 43)

The Yugoslav Government's growing concern was that Salonika might become occupied by Italy. At the time of the conferences, there was a justifiable fear in Yugoslavia that Italy might target Salonika as her principal strategic goal in Greece. Italy's possession of Salonika - in addition to the already-achieved stranglehold on the Adriatic after Italy's conquest of Albania in April 1939 - would effectively make Yugoslavia a land-locked country. That would preclude any potential supply to or retreat route from Yugoslavia by sea.

The idea of the Balkan front in 1941 – *"wishfully minded"*

"Even before Mussolini precipitated matters by his invasion of Greece in the autumn of 1940, British diplomacy had been actively seeking to build up a Balkan League of Yugoslavia, Greece and Turkey to provide a second European front." (Howard, 11)   After Italy's attack this effort was intensified.

> ... In November 1940, responding to the chiefs of staff's demand "to bring Turkey in as a belligerent at once", London subjected Ankara to considerable pressure. The Turkish government, ... , refused to be drawn into the war. It was at this point that the British cabinet came up with its more far-reaching "Balkan front" scheme. It decided to take advantage of the Greek army's success in Albania and to induce Turkey, Yugoslavia, and perhaps Bulgaria to join in a common front with Greece against German aggression. ... in view of the massing of German troops in Rumania, which accelerated in December [1940], none of the proposed members of the common front wanted to take the risks involved in siding with the British. (Petrov, 139)
> Even the Greeks were wary of the scheme. When in early January [1941] the British cabinet offered to send Greece five air squadrons to be based near Salonika (mainly in order to establish air bases within range of the Rumanian oilfields), Ioannis Metaxas, prime minister of Greece, declined the offer on the grounds that "such a reinforcement would merely provoke a German attack without being enough to repel it." (Petrov, 139)

However, Metaxas' refusal did not alter British plans.

Hitler's Directive No. 18: Occupation of the northern Greek mainland

As much as the British wanted to reach the Rumanian oilfields, Hitler was determined to deny them that capability. On 4 November 1940 the British Air Force began to operate from Greek airfields, and Hitler ordered preparations for eventual intervention in Greece. (Blau, 150) According to General Franz Halder, Chief of the General Staff of the German Army (September 1938 – September 1942):

> The Führer's first inclination was to render help [to Mussolini] neither in Albania nor Africa – "The Italians should go it alone." But the danger of British air bases on the Greek mainland and islands and air raids on the Rumanian oil fields could not be ignored, and on November 4 Hitler ordered that the Luftwaffe should be prepared to destroy any island bases. The instructions given at this time were spelled in greater detail in "Führer's Directive No. 18" signed on November 12. (Ristić, 40)

Hitler's initial plan to aid Italy's operations in Greece did not include occupation of the entire country. In early January of 1941, Eden recorded: "On November 12th he [Hitler] ordered the German Army Staff to prepare for an advance through Bulgaria in order to occupy the northern Greek mainland." (Eden, 184) *Directive No. 18* stated:

> The commanders-in-chief of the Army will make preparations for occupying Greek mainland north of the Aegean sea in case of need, entering through Bulgaria, and thus make possible the use of German air force units against targets in the Eastern Mediterranean, in particular against those English sir bases which are threatening the Rumanian oil area.
>
> In order to be able to face all eventualities and keep Turkey in check, the use of an army group of approximate strength of ten divisions is to be the basis for the planning and the calculation of development. It will not be possible to count on the railway, leading through Yugoslavia, for moving these forces into position.
> (11. Aggression against Greece and Yugoslavia
>   http://fungamentalbass.home.midspring.com/x6989.htm   9/19/04)
>
> ... it is now known that until he learned that British forces were arriving, Hitler had intended to occupy Greece only down to Salonika, in an operation taking only a week, to guard his flank while he turned to Russia. (F.H. Hinsley, in Blake & Louis(eds), 415)

Again: through Bulgaria – not Yugoslavia. As early as 12 November 1940, it was clear to Hitler that it would **not be possible** to move his armed forces through Yugoslavia; that proviso would be formally confirmed in the Notes to the Protocol of adhesion of Yugoslavia to the Tripartite Pact, on 25 March 1941.

*** German-Yugoslav negotiations

As for the negotiations, on 12 November – the day of signing the *Directive No. 18* – there was another semi-official Yugoslav approach.

> A well known pro-German journalist, Danilo Gregoric, visited Berlin – presumably on the instructions of Cincar Markovic himself - and had a long talk with Dr. Paul Schmidt, the head of the press department at the German foreign ministry. Yugoslavia, he said, wanted *rapprochement* with Germany; behind their wish loomed the question of Salonika. ... Though Schmidt stated that Ribbentrop was too busy to receive the journalist ... the Reich minister thought the matter sufficiently important to receive Gregoric later on. The meeting between the two, of which no record had been found in the archives of the German foreign ministry, took place on the 23rd. According to Gregoric's own account, Ribbentrop undertook to send a telegram to Heeren [German minister in Belgrade] and to invite Cincar-Markovic to Berlin. (van Creveld, 79-80)

**

In the meantime, when the initial Italian offensive against Greece stalled, on 14 November, Churchill instructed General Wavell, his Army Commander-in-Chief, Middle East:

> It is unlikely that Germany will leave her flagging ally unsupported indefinitely. Consequently, it seems that now is the time to take risks and strike the Italians by land, sea and air. You should act accordingly in concert with other Commanders-in-Chief. (Churchill[FH], 546)

Churchill correctly assumed that Hitler would intervene in Albania. A few weeks later he would attempt to push Yugoslavia into the war in Albania, and would even ask President Roosevelt to support his idea.

*** More on the German-Yugoslav negotiations:
Hitler and Ciano, 18 November

> While expecting the Yugoslav foreign minister, Hitler – who correctly recognized the Salonika question for what it was, i.e. an effective lever to apply to Yugoslavia – deemed the matter sufficiently important to raise it with Ciano on 18 November. Would Mussolini, he asked the Italian foreign minister, consent to an accord with Yugoslavia on the following basis: 1. An Axis guarantee for Yugoslavia's frontiers. 2. Demilitarization of the Dalmatian Coast. 3. In return, the transfer of Salonika to Yugoslavia. Ciano expressed his personal agreement and undertook to raise the matter with the Duce, who, he said, was sure to agree. Mussolini, indeed, had already received a somewhat similar Yugoslav offer for an Italian-Yugoslav agreement, and had been receptive to the idea; to him, it was a heaven-sent opportunity to secure his rear in Albania, while Ciano thought a new Yugoslav-Italian accord might be useful if Rome should at any time decide on an anti-German line … (van Creveld, 80)

In his November 22 letter to Hitler, Mussolini gave his consent to the nonaggression pact. (Jukić, 29)

Churchill to Halifax: "… firm up Turkey and Yugoslavia …"

Greatly concerned with a German attack through Bulgaria, on 24 November Churchill minuted to the Foreign Secretary, Lord Edward Halifax: " Every effort should be made to firm up Turkey and Yugoslavia against this [attack]. The impending fortnight is momentous." (Colville, 300)

Thus, while the Prime Minister wanted to *firm up Yugoslavia* against Hitler's intervention in Greece, Hitler planned his intervention by bypassing Yugoslavia.

A part of "firming up Yugoslavia" was related to Yugoslavia's defense plan. In a conversation about this subject, on 28 November, Prince Paul told the British Minister in Belgrade, Ronald Campbell, that for obvious political reasons it was impossible to leave Croatia defenseless. (Barker, 83-4) On 30November, Pierson Dixon of the Foreign Office minuted: "… this conversation confirms our supposition that political considerations will militate against the adoption of the right strategic plan … i.e. abandonment of Croatia and withdrawal to old Serbia." (Barker, 84; 281n37)

So, one month after the attack on Greece, the British and Yugoslav Governments took opposite stands. For the British, the right defense plan for Yugoslavia was *withdrawal to old Serbia,* which bordered Greece – and thus really amounted to the defense of Greece. The political consequences of leaving Slovenia and Croatia defenseless were of no concern to the Government of His Majesty. Actually, the British and Greeks subsequently attempted to do something about "the right plan".

**

The Axis' encirclement of Yugoslavia, which began with Italy's invasion of Albania, continued in November 1940. Hungary adhered to the Tripartite Pact on the 20th, and Rumania on the 23rd. Stating that Yugoslavia was exposed to "the immediate possibility of most severe Axis pressure", on the 23rd Campbell urged a formal British communication that would

> 'strengthen the hands of the Prince Regent and other staunch elements'; 'in particular Prince Regent would then have justification before history for the decision to expose his small and in materials weakly armed country to the armed might of the Axis. This is especially important in view of his position as trustee for young King.' (Barker, 81)

On 24 November, the Permanent Under-Secretary for Foreign Affairs, Alexander Cadogan, reflected on Campbell's suggestion:

> Telegrams from Belgrade asking for a communication encouraging them to think we shall help them to resist. Sent these to P.M. [Prime Minister] with draft (acquiescent) reply ... P.M. wanted to put off consideration until Cabinet tomorrow, but H. [Lord Halifax, the Foreign Minister] got on the phone to him and we got off the right telegram. (Dilks(ed), 337)

For that *right telegram* Churchill minuted, *inter alia*: "... If we cannot promise any effective material aid, we can at any rate assure them that, just as we did last time, we will see their wrongs are righted in the eventual victory." (Barker, 81) The Chiefs of Staff said, 'it is not possible for us to assist Yugoslavia with land forces.' (Barker, 81)

The Foreign Office replied to Campbell on 24 November:

> ... if the Yugoslav government and people should be called upon to defend again their freedom and independence, they may rest assured that H.M.G. will make the common cause with them ... Yugoslavia will be fighting side by side with us and our allies, and we could look forward once again to achieving a victory by our joint effort that would secure Yugoslavia all her rights and interests. (Barker, 81)

**

E. Barker thought that this reply was nebulous, and concluded: "In giving this assurance, the British were in fact demanding a supreme act of faith in British victory: they could promise nothing before then." (Barker, 81)

However, the "Victory" card was purposefully and systematically played by the British with the domestic "friends" and "contacts" in Yugoslavia. Bickham Sweet-Escott – a very important and influential Section D / SOE operative – wrote on this subject in his acclaimed book, *Baker Street Irregular:* " And if we were to work through such bodies it was necessary first of all to convince them that *a British victory would help them to achieve their political objectives.*" (Sweet-Escott, 29. Italics added.)

"A British victory" was an expected future reward for which "such bodies", i.e. most of the Prince Regent's opponents, were ready to make national sacrifices in war. (See **Appendix D**.) Remembering his spring-1940 talks with Jovan Đonović – a major opponent and coup-wisher - Baron Julian Amery wrote in 1973:

> The right course for the Serbs, he [Đonović] went on, was to stand up to the Germans even if this meant war. In a war they could give a good account of themselves and, though military defeat might follow, they would have a place of honour at the Conference table and would share in the fruits of victory." (Amery, 175)

At the end, the victory was won – but not the way Đonović expected and wished it. The Serbs did not stand a chance at all *to give a good accounts of themselves* in the war. The Serbs, including Đonović and his like-minded political and military friends, did not have *a place of honor at the Conference table*, and *did not share in the fruits of victory*. Only the Communists shared *in fruits of victory*: a Soviet-type regime, imposed in part through the political and military support given to them by the Prime Minister.

**

On 25 November the British Chiefs of Staff (CoS) issued their first directive to the secret Special Operations Executive (SOE),

"Subversive Activities in Relation to Strategy".

By this directive, CoS wanted to invigorate the blocking of oil and foodstuff supplies to Germany via the Danube River, in which the SOE agents had already been engaged for some time.

Concerned with Germany's plan and with the eventual defense of Salonika, on 26 November, Churchill telegraphed Wavell:

> It seems difficult to believe that Hitler will not be forced to come to the rescue of his partner, and obviously German plans may be far advanced for a drive through Bulgaria at Salonika. (Churchill(FH), 546)

Then practical considerations arose: how to defend Salonika? Already engaged against the Italians in Albania, the Greek troops could not be expected to stop the German invasion from Bulgaria at the Metaxas line. Once that line was broken, the Greeks alone could not stop the German troops from taking Salonika. Therefore, Yugoslavia had to be drawn into the war in order to defend Salonika. If Turkey could "join in" as well, so much the better.

Churchill to Halifax:
"We want Turkey to come into the war as soon as possible"

With those considerations in mind, on 26 November Churchill wrote to the Foreign Secretary, Lord Halifax:

> We want Turkey to come into the war as soon as possible. We are not pressing her to take any special steps to help the Greeks, except to make it clear to Bulgaria that any move by Germany through Bulgaria to attack Greece, or any hostile movement by Bulgaria against Greece, will be followed by immediate Turkish declaration of war. We should like Turkey and Yugoslavia now to consult together so as, if possible, to have a joint warning ready to offer Bulgaria and Germany at the first sign of a German movement towards Bulgaria. In the event of German troops traversing Bulgaria with or without Bulgarian assistance, it is vital that Turkey should fight there and then. (Churchill(FH), 547)

It will be shown that Turkey – not honoring the Treaty of 19 October, 1939, after the fall of France in June 1940 - refused to comply. Her self-interest made Churchill's requests wishful. Turkey's refusal made the British concentration on drawing Yugoslavia into the war an even more pressing matter.

***The start of the German-Yugoslav negotiations:
Hitler and Cincar-Marković, 28 November 1940

The Yugoslav Foreign Minister, Aleksandar Cincar-Marković, was invited to visit the German Foreign Minister, Joachim von Ribbentrop. "Prince Paul at once told Campbell and said that he had given very strict instructions that the Foreign Minister was not to commit Yugoslavia to anything." (Barker, 81) Responding to this information on 27 November, the Foreign Office (FO) told Campbell that the Yugoslavs should make it clear that they would "stand four-square against any Axis demands designed either to assist Italy in her difficulties or to advance German military aims in the Balkans". (Barker, 81-2)

> Cincar-Marković had a conversation with Hitler on November 28. The Führer opened the talk by expounding his plan for a world coalition from Yokohama to Spain. He said that countries like Yugoslavia were essentially within the sphere of Italy, since they were Mediterranean countries. Germany had no territorial claims in the Balkans, but he would make certain that any agreements Italy and Germany made with Yugoslavia were faithfully upheld. He was now in the position to persuade Mussolini to adopt the policy toward Yugoslavia he had always urged but had never been able to force upon him. A unique situation had arisen, and his views on the consolidation of the Balkans would prevail. He was not asking permission for his troops to pass through Yugoslavia, he said; he wanted to get the situation in the Balkans settled only because of Russia. ... He believed that Yugoslavia's relation with Germany and Italy could be put on a satisfactory basis by a non-aggression pact. Since Yugoslavia was going to get Salonika, she could make a nice gesture and consent to the demilitarization of the Dalmatian coast, which amounted to little more than a courtesy. (Jukić, 27-8)

> On 22 November the Duce ... agreed to [Hitler's] idea [of 18 November] with some enthusiasm. By then, however, it was too late. On 28 November the Führer exercised all his powers of persuasion on Cincar Markovic, trying to convince him that Yugoslavia should sign *a non-aggression treaty* with Germany and Italy. He promised in return to give her Salonika and, explicitly declared that *he did not require right of transit.* (van Creveld, 80. Italics added.)

Here van Creveld observed:

> However, the series of Italian defeats in Albania, which had now begun in earnest, spoke even more loudly. Having no reason to fear Salonika would ever fall into Italian hands, the Yugoslavs saw no reason to commit themselves irrevocably to the Axis, and lost interest in the matter.
>
> Hitler did the same, and at approximately the same time. ... However, an accord with Yugoslavia that would give her Salonika made sense only as long as a German attack on Greece was planned, that is, as long as the 'peripheral' strategy was alive; In this context, his offer of Salonika to the Yugoslavs is an excellent 'external barometer' to gauge his intentions towards Greece. By the beginning of December, however, the eastern Mediterranean had ceased to be the focus of Hitler's attention. (van Creveld, 80)

But not of Mussolini's.

> As the defeats of his troops in Albania multiplied, it seemed to Mussolini that there was only one way out short of a humiliating armistice; an agreement with Yugoslavia that would allow him to transport reinforcements and material, particularly lorries, by way of the latter's territory. The Duce, ... had agreed with the Führer's plans for an accord with Yugoslavia, and even consented to scrapping one of his original prerequisites for such an accord. During the first days of December, however, it began to look as if this gesture was not appreciated in Berlin, where people seemed to have lost interest in the matter. To remind them, Mussolini – who had no idea that Hitler had in the meantime lost interest in the Mediterranean – on 5 December dispatched Alfieri [the Ambassador in Germany], who had been convalescing in Rome, to Berlin 'with the real, specific mission to request the Führer to bring about a speedy accession of Yugoslavia to the Tripartite Pact'. (van Creveld, 85-6)

> Mussolini was out for disappointment. When Yugoslavia had first been discussed by Hitler and Ciano on 18 November the German dictator was reported to have grown 'warm, almost friendly'; this time, his reaction was decidedly less enthusiastic. Instead of warming to the subject, he merely replied that 'Yugoslavia ... was very cool in her attitude'. (van Creveld, 86)

> On December 5, Hitler informed Mussolini of his conversation with Cincar-Marković without mentioning the German guarantee that Italy would honor the provisions of any agreement reached. He did report his proposal for a nonaggression pact, which, he stressed, would be psychologically easier to explain to Hungary and Bulgaria. (Jukić, 28)

**

In Belgrade,

> The same day, Prince Paul held a conference with the three chief members of his government – Dragiša Cvetković, the premier, Vladko Maček, the vice-premier, and Anton Korošec, the minister of education - to inform them of the conversation between Cincar-Marković and Hitler. Maček told me that they all agreed that Paul should keep the dialog going so that Yugoslavia could avoid having to be in either of the belligerent camps. (Jukić, 28)

> In its reply to Hitler, sent on December 7, the Yugoslav government declared itself ready to open talks on a nonaggression pact with Berlin and Rome on the basis of the existing Italo-Yugoslav Friendship Pact. (Jukić, 28)

Chapter 3

The British shaped Yugoslavia's role to fit their goals

The Yugoslav Foreign Minister, Aleksandar Cincar-Marković, was invited to visit the German Foreign Minister, Joachim von Ribbentrop. "Prince Paul at once told Campbell and said that he had given very strict instructions that the Foreign Minister was not to commit Yugoslavia to anything." (Barker, 81) Responding to this information on 27 November, the Foreign Office (FO) told Campbell that the Yugoslavs should make it clear that they would "stand four-square against any Axis demands designed either to assist Italy in her difficulties or to advance German military aims in the Balkans". (Barker, 81-2)

The FO's demand that Yugoslavia should "stand four-square against any Axis demands", noted E. Barker, " was the first time that this precise British demand, which became so insistent in the following months, was made to Yugoslavia". (Barker, 82) She succinctly described this period, "British demands: no British aid". (Barker, 78) "Yugoslavia therefore had to face the Balkan crisis of early 1941 *without arms supplies from any quarter.*" (Barker, 82. Italics added.)

At the same time, aid to Greece to withstand a German attack, with its ensuing ramifications, was not the only policy under consideration in London. Some British leaders had broader strategic goals which would affect Yugoslavia directly. Thus, on 1st December Leopold-Leo Amery – Secretary of State for India and a close friend of Churchill - of whom Churchill once said that Leo Amery seemed to think the British Empire was his private property (Howarth, 99) - made a speech at Newmarket in which he said:

> If we can enable Greece to hold her own until we have disposed of the Italians in Egypt, we shall have secured for our armies a foothold from which we might threaten the flank of any German attack upon Turkey. Last but not least, from that foothold we might eventually, with our own armies and with the new allies whom our growing strength will gather, deal a mortal thrust at the German dragon, not against the scaly armor of the Siegfried line, but against his soft under-side. (Barker, 101)

"This 'soft under-belly' concept was typically Churchillian, ... The concept won a new and potentially influential supporter in January 1941 in Col. William Donovan, who was touring South-East Europe on a special mission on President Roosevelt's behalf" (Barker, 101)

Colonel Donovan's tour included a visit to Belgrade. (**See Appendix A**)

Greek King's appeal for American aid to Greece

While British leaders were considering the pros and cons of giving aid to Greece, on 3 December 1940 Greek King George personally appealed to President Roosevelt requesting moral and material assistance, "which General Metaxas spelled out as a loan to buy munitions and planes." On 5 December the President replied to the King that "steps were being taken" to extend assistance. A reply to Metaxas emphasized that lending money to Greece for the purchase of munitions was impracticable because of existing legislation, related to the Neutrality Act, but that "special consideration" would nevertheless be given to facilitate the acquisition of the needed materiel. Unfortunately for Greece, this turned out to be a case in which "the President first resolved to send aid to Greece and only then began to consider the pros and cons of his decision". (Langer & Gleason, 116-17)

> What the President meant by "special consideration" soon became painfully apparent to his harassed advisers. Peremptory instructions were given Assistant Secretary of State [Adolf] Berle to make available to the Greeks immediately thirty of the new P-40 pursuit planes. This gesture was to mark only the first step in a tragicomedy of attempted aid to Greece which ended only when the German invasion of the spring of 1941 mercifully rescued the Administration from its embarrassment. In effect, there were no P-40 planes not already earmarked, ... To give such planes to Greece would have meant to take them from U.S. Army and Navy stores, or from the British. ... The Greeks never secured any P-40's. (Langer & Gleason, 117-18)

> ... Finally, in mid February [1941] the Navy Department was induced or ordered to provide the modern planes. At the same time, however, it was decided to delay shipment until the Lend-Lease bill had been approved by the Congress. As a result, Greece was overrun by the Germans before this important item of American aid arrived. (Langer & Gleason, 401)

Meanwhile, on 5 December 1940 the German Army plans for the campaigns against Greece and the Soviet Union were presented at a conference with Hitler. (Blau, 151)

Churchill to Dalton: the Balkans – *"SOE's acid test"*

"The precise British demand", that Yugoslavia should "stand four-square against any Axis demands", was not pressed on Yugoslavia only through normal diplomatic channels. Increasing pressure was also exerted through the secret SOE agents and their Yugoslav co-operatives. In December 1940, Churchill personally told Dr. Hugh Dalton – the Minister of Economic Warfare and the head of SOE - that the Balkan situation "was the acid test for SOE". George Taylor, Chief of Staff to the SOE's Executive Director, Sir Frank Nelson, later considered that this had been the direct origin of his subsequent mission to the Balkans and the Middle East. (Stafford(so), 52)

This two-pronged pressure was applied simultaneously. It will be shown that Taylor's mission to the Middle East and the Balkans, in January-March 1941, coincided with the Eden-Dill mission to Greece and the Middle East, and was in the service of the latter. Just a brief note here about the pressure from SOE:

According to Bickham Sweet-Escott, the part SOE played in the Yugoslav *coup d'état* of 27th March 1941 was one of three successful operations, but in this one SOE "could not take all the credit" – i.e., could take a partial one. In 1940, SOE activities in the Balkans had been limited to small-scale sabotage against the Axis and to "black propaganda disseminated by local political parties or organizations with which we were in touch. Now [in early 1941] that a campaign in the Balkans was impending, it was George Taylor's main task to draw all the strings together so that the best possible use might be made of our contacts *by those who were to direct it."* (Sweet-Escott, 59-60. Italics added.) (See **Part Two**.)

It is important to note that many of those SOE "contacts" were "subsidized" by the British. (This topic is examined in **Part Two**.) Taylor came to prepare them for activities by those who were to direct them.

In the meantime

Hitler was firming up his plan to help Italy.

When the Italians attacked Greece from Albania, the Greeks stood firm near the frontier and launched a temporarily successful counterattack. Their offensive began on 14 November 1940, lost its impetus by early December, and came to an end on January 6, 1941. (Koliopoulos, 31)

On 5 December, while reviewing his army's plan for an attack on the Soviet Union, Hitler stated:

> If the Greeks do not drive out the English of their own accord, it is possible that action against them through Bulgaria will become necessary. However, the Greeks too may have realized this; particularly if the Italians retreat from Albania. Should the Greeks drive out the English, no attack by us will be necessary. (van Creveld(G), 69)

As his assumptions that the Greeks would drive out the British had not materialized,

> On December 13th Hitler issued his orders for the attack on Greece through Bulgaria and, ... [on December 18th] for the campaign which broke his power, the attack on Russia. There remained the problem of the Yugoslavs. If possible they must be coaxed; the carrot of Salonika was therefore dangled before them, but pressure was also applied to make them join the Tripartite Pact. (Eden, 185)

On 13 December 1940, Hitler issued *Directive No. 20* for *Operation Marita,* the campaign against Greece. (Blau, 151) One should emphasize this point: Hitler was deciding to go through Bulgaria - not Yugoslavia – from the very start of his planning to attack Greece. The Yugoslav Government insisted all along on not allowing the passage of German troops through Yugoslavia. This requirement was formally accepted by the Axis when Yugoslavia joined the Tripartite Pact.

Hitler insisted on bypassing Yugoslavia in spite of contrary advice by his Generals.

> During the planning for Operation MARITA, German military leaders pointed repeatedly to Yugoslavia's crucial position and asked that diplomatic pressure be used to induce that country to join the Axis Powers. Because of the lack of direct rail lines between Bulgaria and Greece, the use of the Belgrade-Nis-Salonika rail lines was essential for the rapid execution of Operation MARITA and the speedy redeployment of forces for Operation BARBAROSSA. (Blau, 20)

However, even when Yugoslavia eventually joined the Axis Powers, German troops were prohibited the passage through Yugoslavia.

**

At the same time the British had their own plans for Greece. In mid-December, they

> expressed the wish to send a small reconnaissance party to report on airfields in northern Greece, with a view of operations in the spring. Churchill and the Chiefs of Staff were excited by the prospect of large-scale air attacks launched from Greek bases. In addition to the possibility of hitting Germany in the Rumanian oil fields, the presence of British forces in northern Greece would greatly facilitate the dispatch of help to Turkey, if the need arose. Moreover, airfields in that area would be of considerable value in the event of a German invasion of the Balkans. (Koliopoulos, 34)

In late December, the question was referred to the Foreign Office, now headed by Anthony Eden. Ultimately, "the plans and preparations stumbled on Greek reluctance to risk incurring a German attack." (Koliopoulos, 34)

**

In one view of Hitler's intervention in Greece:

> Just as the British plan to support Greece rested on hidden as well as ostensible motives, so Hitler's determination to carry the war into the Balkans was based on diverse considerations. Naturally he felt that he had to uphold the prestige of the Axis by wiping out the presumptuous little Greek state. But he appears to have been even more concerned over the deployment of British forces in Greece and the establishment of airfields for modern bombers, which he rightly looked upon as a grave menace to the Rumanian oil fields. His objective of crushing Greece, therefore, was primarily to expel the British from the continent. There could be no argument about this and the Fuehrer was prepared to incur even the ill will of his Soviet partner in order to attain this end. (Langer & Gleason, 394-5)

Among other motives to support Greece was the British desire to dissipate German forces.

> ...the British were doing everything to extend it [the war], because it was only by forcing the Germans to dissipate their forces and fight a growing number of opponents that they [the British] could hope to win the war at all. (van Creveld(G), 71)

*** German-Yugoslav negotiations continued

> Early in December [1940] German-Yugoslav negotiations aimed at obtaining Yugoslav cooperation, or at least connivance, in the liquidation of Greece had reached deadlock. The Hitler – Cincar Markovic conversation of 28 November resulted, nine days later, in a statement from Belgrade that 'Yugoslavia is willing to discuss with the Reich government and the Italian government the possibilities of signing a *non aggression pact.*' At that time, however, Hitler had already launched his attempt to end the Italo-Greek war, and the Yugoslav note was therefore left unanswered. It was only on 21 December – that is, on the very day when negotiations with Turkey

were also resumed – that the Wilhelmstrasse shook off its two-week lethargy and renewed contact. (van Creveld, 124. Italics added.)

By then, circumstances had changed. On 28 November Hitler had pressed for a *non-aggression pact*; he was willing to grant Salonika to Yugoslavia, and emphasized that 'Germany did not ask for anything, *not even the right of passage of troops.*' By the end of December, on the other hand, 'Barbarossa' [a plan to attack the Soviet Union] was a settled matter; and further, the relation between it and 'Marita' [attack on Greece] had been thoroughly clarified by OKH [Oberkommando des Heeres]. Though 'directive No. 20' of 13 December prudently advised that the use of the Yugoslav railways was not to be reckoned with, the possibility of shortening the build-up for 'Marita' from ten (as originally planned) to six weeks was too tempting to be discarded. On 21 December, therefore, Ribbentrop answered Cincar Markovic that:

> The Führer and I ... gave consideration to the proposal ... that a non-aggression pact be concluded between Germany, Italy and Yugoslavia ... the conclusion of such pact would of course not meet the specifications for the strengthening of Yugoslavia's relations with the Axis powers that we had envisaged in the conversations with Cincar Markovic at the Berghof and Fuschl. (van Creveld, 124. Italics added.)

Because of 'Barbarossa', a non-aggression pact was not simply insufficient; it was positively dangerous, as it would allow Yugoslavia to close her frontiers with impunity to the passage of German troops and war material. The Yugoslavs, on the other hand, knew nothing of 'Barbarossa' and were – or pretended to be – surprised. After all, Cincar Markovic politely reminded Ribbentrop, the proposal for a non-aggression pact had come from Hitler himself. (van Creveld, 124)

Again deadlock followed, and Hitler did not renew the contacts.   (van Creveld, 124)

On 18 December 1940, *Directive No. 21* was issued, ordering preparations for the *Operation Barbarossa*, the campaign against the Soviet Union. (Blau, 151)

Eden's change of mind to support Greece

On 22 December 1940, Anthony Eden replaced Lord Edward Halifax as the Foreign Secretary, and 'became an eager protagonist of Balkan intervention'. (Lawlor, 143) "The change of guard at the Foreign Office was not exactly calculated to fortify him [General Metaxas, the Greek Premier], and he wondered with apprehension about his relations with Eden." (Koliopoulos, 32)

Eden's biographer David Carlton provided the following explanation for the change:

> In the early months of 1941 Greece was indeed to become a dominant concern for Eden. For signs began to appear that Hitler might decide to come to the rescue of his embarrassed ally. This in turn might open the way to a total German victory in the Balkans and even possibly permit a thrust through Asia Minor into the heart of the Middle East. For all his lofty rhetoric in support of a country guaranteed by Great Britain in 1939, Eden was bound to view the German threat to Greece in this wider context. He was in any case undoubtedly more sympathetic to and concerned about the fate of Turkey. Hence the suspicion must remain that he was not particularly scrupulous in his handling of Athens. For example, he did nothing to encourage proposals for a compromise settlement between Greece and Italy and refrained from passing on to the Greeks hints from neutral sources that, provided she behaved with prudence, Hitler might by-pass Athens in any *Drang nach Osten*. Eden's aim seems to have been to use Greeks to draw both Yugoslavia and Turkey into collective resistance to Hitler. (Carlton, 170)

Elisabeth Barker observed:

> After more bickering between Churchill and Eden over strategy in the Middle East and Greece, the changeover took place in December. Eden welcomed it in his heart, feeling that 'my responsibility must be greater as Churchill's colleague at the Foreign Office, than as his subordinate with the army'. (Barker(CE), 21)

As deliberations about aid to Greece progressed, the situation in the Balkans was changing and the military commanders, cooperating with Eden, also began changing their views. "But now Dill changed his mind, and Wavell's was a dominant voice in his conversion. Yet Wavell too had originally been opposed to intervention, on the ground that it entailed too much risk; he seems to have come round to the opposite view, for reasons that are not clear, about the middle of February, and at once to have become an ardent supporter of the expedition." (Bennett, 31)

* Examination of the situation by the Joint Planning Staff in Cairo

"From the moment that this strategic switch was heralded, intensive planning went on in Cairo", wrote Major General Francis de Guingand, a member of the Joint Planning Staff in Cairo, later Director of Military Intelligence in the Middle East, and finally Field Marshal Bernard Montgomery's Chief of Staff for more than two and a half years:

> The examination of the situation in the Balkans became of paramount importance. We concentrated on the German capabilities in this area, ... The part that Turkey might play was naturally all important. ... But Turkey's attitude was extremely difficult to assess. Common sense dictated that we should never count upon her active support until we showed ourselves capable of defeating Germany, ... It always appeared extraordinary to me how during this period the politician was so optimistic, as to Turkey's attitude. ...
> Besides the strategical examinations being undertaken, a vast amount of detailed planning took place. ...
> The more we examined the problem, the more unsound the venture appeared. ... (de Guingand, 43-4)

As for the attitude of the Greeks, the General stated:

> I don't know what the Greek attitude to our intervention was at that time. ... I had an impression at that time that Metaxas foresaw certain disadvantages. The gallant Greek Army was fighting a heroic campaign against the Italians in Albania, fighting with an ill-equipped army in appalling conditions. In spite of this, it had achieved great successes. But the German Army was a different proposition. The crux of the matter appeared to be – would the arrival of Allied forces precipitate a German attack, with the result that the Greek Army would be swamped long before sufficient forces had arrived to remedy the situation? I may be wrong, but I think this vital factor weighed heavily with Metaxas. But Metaxas died [on 29 January 1941] at this momentous hour in his country's fortunes. (de Guingand, 44)

> The Greek Army had suffered tremendous losses in men and equipment. Their successes had not been won cheaply. ... Morale against the Italians was high, but the results of the long winter campaign might well affect the Army's spirit if suddenly required to face the German Army as well. Equipment and munitions were anything but plentiful as far as we were concerned, ... (de Guingand, 45)

On the basis of the above examinations and observations, de Guingard came to the conclusion:

> Without a strong Greek Army with full fighting powers, any force that we could afford to send was doomed to disaster. It would not be lack of spirit, but lack of *materiel* that would prevent the Greek Army from playing its part.
> The forces which we could muster were not numerous; neither were they well provided with the most modern implements of war. We were particularly short of such items as tanks, aircraft, transport and anti-aircraft guns. Compare this with the colossal weight of equipment that the Germans could muster. They had many and better tanks and an enormous air force which could swamp anything we could produce. In addition, they had a number of troops and leaders who had great experience of modern war in Europe. (de Guingand, 45. Italics in the source..)

> Of the many military problems I have studied during this war, I never came across one which appeared so unattractive. A planner is often apt to foresee too many difficulties, but with this problem the military advantages appeared to be nil. The one factor which might weight the scales in our favour was intervention of Turkey and/or Yugo-Slavia. But these were long shots – both most uncertain quantities. (de Guingand, 46)

Such were the observations and conclusions of the Planning Staff in Cairo. They were in consonance with the presentation and warning Gen. John Kennedy, Director of Military Operations, gave to the Prime Minister on 16 February. Have they been taken into consideration when the final decision was made to send aid to Greece? No.

**

Meanwhile, Hitler's intentions were becoming clearer to the British:

> On 24 December MI [Military Intelligence], … , repeated the view that Germany would wish to avoid fighting on two fronts, and on 28 December it quoted approvingly AI [Air Force Intelligence] appreciation which found GAF [German Air Force] dispositions in Romania to be consistent with defence of oilfields rather than with plans for a Balkan offensive during the winter. (Hensley *et all* (1), 351)

London was also getting more information about the Yugoslav army. In a report dated 30 December 1940, the British military attaché, Colonel Charles S. Clarke, forecast that the Yugoslav army would "prove itself in every way worthy of the great Serbian fighting tradition". (Barker, 83; 281n35) This assessment may have been influenced by their fighting spirit and tradition and personal contacts. At that time he was maintaining close relations with some ranking Serb officers in the Army, reserve officers in their associations, and Air Force Brigadier Borivoje-Bora Mirković - who became the main executor of the *coup d'état* on 27 March 1941.

Hitler to Mussolini: a non-aggression pact with Yugoslavia

In a letter to Mussolini, dated 31 December 1940, Hitler wrote the following about Yugoslavia's position:

> 6. *Yugoslavia*. Yugoslavia is prudently gaining time. If circumstances are favorable it may be that she will conclude a non-aggression pact with us, but it seems now that she will not adhere in any case to the Tripartite Pact. I do not count on trying to obtain anything more until our military successes have improved the psychological climate. (Churchill[GA], 11,13)

So: at the end of 1940, Hitler was considering a non-aggression pact with Yugoslavia. As the situation in the Balkans changed, he abandoned this idea and pressed for adhesion to the Tripartite Pact. However – as it will be shown - even then he ultimately agreed to make an exemption for Yugoslavia: a Pact **without** military clauses and obligations.

Chapter 4

The Foreign Office's instruction to Campbell on 27 November 1940, that Yugoslavia should reject "any Axis demands designed either to assist Italy in her difficulties or to advance German military aims in the Balkans" (Barker, 81-2), got an assistance from the US Government. The American Minister in Belgrade, Arthur Bliss Lane, was on friendly relations with Prince Paul while performing his limited duties. His activities were expanded after the visit to Belgrade - in January 1941 – by William J.Donovan, who was on a special mission for both, President Roosevelt and Prime Minister Churchill. To better understand that mission, a short background information follows.

Roosevelt-Churchill contacts

On September 1, 1939, Hitler's forces invaded Poland.

On September 3, Great Britain and France declared war on Germany, thus effectively turning the invasion into a world war.

On September 5, Franklin D. Roosevelt declared American neutrality. But only six days later, in an extraordinary and virtually unprecedented move, the President of the neutral United States invited Winston Churchill, recently appointed First Lord of the Admiralty and thus a subordinate official of a foreign belligerent, to enter into direct correspondence with him. (Loewenheim *et al* (ed), 79)

In these letters the basis for Anglo-American cooperation was established and the means for implementing it devised long before the United States actually entered the war. (Loewenheim *et al* (ed), 4)

To find the means to implement cooperation,

... in the summer of 1940, a steady flow of special observers and official representatives from the United States descended on London. ... Col. William Donovan was sent over by Secretary of the Navy [Frank] Knox and the president on a special mission... While Donovan was still in England, a high-level joint army-navy-army air corps investigatory team ... was organized and sent to London, arriving within two weeks of Donovan's departure. In the fall of 1940, the president also sent Harry Hopkins to confer with Churchill, while Donovan returned for a second British survey during the same period. (Smith, 27-8)

The most illustrative of Roosevelt's ultimate intentions was revealed in Harry Hopkins' mission.

Harry Hopkins in London, January 1941

While Colonel Donovan was sent on a thorough investigative mission to the Mediterranean and Middle East region, President Roosevelt was deciding on an even more important mission to London. In his fire-side speech on 29 December 1940, he told the American people: "We must be the great arsenal of democracy. For us this is an emergency as serious as war itself. We must apply ourselves to our task with the same resolution, the same urgency, the same spirit of patriotism and sacrifice as we would show were we at war." (http://www.presidency.ucsb.edu/ws/index.php?pid=15917 1/4/12) A week later he sent to London Harry Hopkins, one of his closest advisers, who "played an enormously important role in shaping Roosevelt's decisions." (Loewenheim *et al* (ed), 26)

Hopkins' mission aimed at reassuring Churchill that the US *would indeed* help Britain. Here is Churchill's account of the meeting with Hopkins:

On January 10 [1941] a gentleman arrived to see me at Downing Street with the highest credentials. Telegrams had been received from Washington stating that he was the closest confidant and personal agent of the President. I therefore arranged ... that we should lunch together alone ... Thus I met Harry Hopkins, that extraordinary man, who played, and was to play, a sometimes decisive part in the whole movement of the war. ...

At our first meeting we were about three hours together, and I soon comprehended his personal dynamism and the outstanding importance of his mission. ... it was evident to me that advisor, considered Hopkins' visit as "his epoch-making visit to England" here was an envoy from the President of supreme importance to our life. With gleaming eye and quiet, constrained passion he said:

> "The President is determined that we shall win the war together. Make no mistake about it.
> "He has sent me here to tell you that at all costs and by all means he will carry you through, no matter what happens to him – there is nothing that he will not do so far as he has human power." ... (Churchill(GA), 22-3)

> There he sat, slim, frail, ill, but absolutely glowing with refined comprehension of the Cause. It was to be the defeat, ruin, and slaughter of Hitler, to the exclusion of all other purposes, loyalties, or aims. ... (Churchill(GA), 24)

How significant was Hopkins' mission? Lord William Strang, a British diplomat and Government advisor, considered Hopkins' visit in January 1941 to be "his epoch-making visit to England". (Dilks2(ed), 71) In the opinion of John Colville, Churchill's Assistant Private Secretary: "His [Churchill's] confidence in victory, even in the darkest days, was at least partly based on his certainty that Roosevelt would not desert us." (Wheeler-Bennett(ed), 95) "... Harry Hopkins, has paid his visit to England and had also become closely bound to Churchill. Throughout the difficult year that had followed the fall of France it was the support of the President, ... , that had sustained Churchill." (Sir John Jacob, Military Assistant Secretary to the War Cabinet, in Wheeler-Bennett(ed), 205-6) Roosevelt's support meant that at this time Britain did not really stand alone, without another great power to be consulted – as is often claimed.

Professor David Dilks, the editor of Cadogan's *Diaries,* added this about the Churchill-Hopkins meetings in January 1941:

> A few days later, ... ,Churchill and Hopkins dined in Glasgow, with Tom Johnston, Secretary of State for Scotland. Churchill wept when Hopkins said:
>
>> I suppose you wish to know what I am going to say to President Roosevelt on my return. Well, I am going to quote you one verse from that Book of Books in the truth of which Mr. Johnston's mother and my own Scottish mother were brought up: 'Whither thou goest I will go; and where thou lodgest. I will lodge; thy people shall be my people, and thy God my God.'
>
> And then, very quietly, 'Even to the end'. (Dilks(ed), 348)

American General Albert C. Wedemeyer, a war planner in Washington from 1940 into 1943, wrote about the President's support of Britain: Roosevelt had been "determined to get the United States into the war by one means or another in spite of the reluctance or positive refusal of the American people to become involved." At the Atlantic Conference in August 1941, Roosevelt told Churchill: "I may never declare war; I may make war. If I were to ask Congress to declare war, they might argue about it for three months." (Wedemeyer, 6-7)

As Colville stated: Churchill's confidence in victory, from early 1941 onward, was at least partly based on the certainty of Roosevelt's support. Donovan's mission was to serve that purpose.

Colonel Donovan's missions

Supplementing Hopkins' mission was Colonel William Donovan's second mission. By the end of November 1940 – which coincided with the FO's instruction to Campbell that Yugoslavia should "stand four-square against any Axis demands" - a plan for a new survey trip was set in motion. This time to visit Britain and the western and eastern Mediterranean theater, "to see how the United States might be of practical assistance. The most secret portion of the mission was to acquaint himself with the subversive and counterintelligence organizations that the British had been developing since the summer." (Smith, 40)

"Wild Bill" Donovan was sent on this confidential mission on behalf of both President Roosevelt and Prime Minister Churchill. The mission was completely arranged by the British. A part of his mission was to impress everyone of the USA's support for Britain. Even if he did not play a direct role in Britain's decision to send an expeditionary force to Greece, Donovan approved and encouraged it. With that goal in mind he visited Belgrade in January 1941, and talked with some Government and military leaders, including General Simović – who would become the Yugoslav Premier after the military coup of 27 March 1941. The General would later refer to their conversation frequently. It seems the meeting gave impetus to Simović's subsequent actions against Prince Paul's policies, which contributed to the military *coup d'état* of 27 March 1941.

Upon Donovan's return to Washington in March 1941, President Roosevelt received a message of thanks from Churchill for "the magnificent work done by Donovan in his prolonged tour of the Balkans and the Middle East. He has carried with him throughout an animating, heart-warming flame". (Ford, 104)

An overview of Donovan's *magnificent work* is provided in **Appendix A.** His work coincided with, and was interwoven into the mission to the Middle East by Foreign Minister Eden and General Sir Dill's, when it was being decided whether or not to aid Greece against Germany's expected assault. George Taylor, one of the highest-ranking officials of the Special Operations Executive (SOE), was simultaneously carrying out his mission in Greece and Yugoslavia – as presented in **Part Two, Appendix K.** Thus the operations of all three missions – Donovan's, Eden-Dill's, and Tailor's – pushed Yugoslavia in the same direction: In support of the polices of Great Britain.

* Lunch with Churchill, 18 December 1940

Informed of Donovan's all-out pro-British stand and activities following his first visit to London, Churchill expressed a desire to see Donovan as soon as he arrived. "On this trip Churchill was definitely anxious to see Donovan." (Smith, 428n61)   During lunch at No. 10 Downing Street on 18 December , Churchill stated that the US and the United Kingdom must together defeat Hitler. "Donovan kept to the instructions given to him by Franklin Roosevelt. He informed Churchill that the United States and Britain must help each other in this crisis in history in a "relationship of mutual selfishness". (Dunlop, 239)

> … Churchill took the colonel to his ample bosom like a long lost friend. The prime minister saw in the visiting American a loyal champion of Britain and the perfect instrument through which to increase the pressure on the Balkan governments. Without fully opening his bag of Ultra tricks, Churchill instructed Donovan on the facts and issues involved in the Mediterranean situation as the British saw them and urged him to encourage the influential personalities with whom he came in contact in the eastern Mediterranean to throw off neutrality and join a Balkan and Middle Eastern group backed by Britain. Donovan raised no objections to the British estimate of the situation and became a willing and enthusiastic instrument through which London could increase its Balkan clout. (Smith, 46)

> The prime minister told Donovan he was convinced that, the Nazi-Soviet Nonaggression Pact notwithstanding, the Germans would attack Russia in May. Donovan saw that his trip into the Mediterranean must include an effort to create a Balkan entente that would stand up to German intentions in the area and, if all went well, throw off the Nazis' timetable so they could not attack the Soviets until later. The more the Germans delayed invading Russia, the greater the chance that they would not be able to complete their conquest before the severe northern winter entrapped their armies. (Dunlop, 239)

Chapter 5

Shift from the Middle East to the Balkans

Preceding the Eden-Dill mission, General John Kennedy, Director of Military Operations, thought that the

> Military policy in the Middle East and the Balkans was our main preoccupation throughout January and February. To those in the know, the German threat to Greece was already apparent, ... On the surface everything was splendid, for [General] Wavell's offensive was in full swing. On 5th January the forces under his command took Bardia, with 2,000 officer prisoners and 40,000 other ranks. ... (Kennedy, 71-2)

From January through March, when the British leaders' attention shifted from the Middle East to the Balkans, "Greece, rather than Turkey, became central to British interests in the Mediterranean and the Middle East, so that by the end of the war Churchill seemed more ready than Chamberlain had ever been to *sacrifice relations with eastern Europe, just so long as he could preserve a sphere of influence in Greece.* " (Lawfor, 24. Italics added.)

> Those two months were used not to reconsider the precipitate decision to offer help to Greece, but to increase the diplomatic pressure on Greece to accept it and on Turkey to participate in her defence, and to increase the help offered till it comprised the bulk of the Middle East land forces. (F.H. Finley in Blake & Louis(eds), 415)

Germany's "... ultimate descent upon Greece ..."

> On 21 December Enigma, which had so far given little information about the German Army in Romania, gave the first pointer towards its area of concentration. On 24 December the decrypts gave the first reliable indication of the scale of the Army's involvement by mentioning the locations to be taken ...; these, predominantly in southern Romania, were a powerful indication that Germany's advance was to be southwards against or through Bulgaria. (Hinsley *et al*, 351)

The Bulgarian route would have bypassed Yugoslavia entirely.

On 6 January 1941, Eden called Churchill's attention to the Balkans:

> ... Germany is pressing forward her preparations in the Balkans with a view to an ultimate descent upon Greece. ... we may feel certain that Germany will seek to intervene by force to prevent complete Italian defeat in Albania. Already there are reports of increased enemy air forces operating against the Greeks, ... It would be in accordance with German methods to establish superiority in the air before making any move on land.
> ... It is essential that our victories in North Africa should not result in any decrease of watchfulness on the part of the Turks and Yugoslavs, and we are doing what we can in the political sphere to ensure this. ... (Churchill(GA), 14-15)

Thus, already early in 1941 Turkey and Yugoslavia entered into Eden's planning. While the expectations for Turkey's involvement were based on the Anglo-French-Turkish mutual assistance pact of 19 October 1939, there existed no such alliance with Yugoslavia and, therefore, there were no mutual obligations between Great Britain and Yugoslavia.

Churchill prepared for the Chiefs of Staff an appreciation about German movements and preparations for a Balkan campaign. Excerpts related to Greece and Yugoslavia follow:

> 12. ... The only aid we can give [to Greece] quickly is four or five more squadrons from the Middle East, perhaps some artillery regiments, and some or all the tanks of the 2nd Armoured Division. ...
> 14. The attitude of Yugoslavia may well be determined by the support we give to Greece ... it would be more natural for the Germans to push on through Rumania to the Black Sea and to press down through their old ally Bulgaria to Salonika, rather than to force their way through Yugoslavia. ... We must so act as to make it certain that if the enemy enters Bulgaria, Turkey will come into the

war. If Yugoslavia stays firm and is not molested, if the Greeks take Valona and maintain themselves in Albania, if Turkey becomes an active ally, the attitude of Russia may be affected favourably. [Churchill(GA), 5, 9,10)

Success of this British policy depended on many **IFS.** On 6 January Churchill wrote to Wavell, ' "It is clear to me that supporting Greece must have priority after the Western flank of Egypt has been made secure." That assurance proved – with terrible consequences – to be entirely misconceived.' (Rhodes James, 251)

That same day, Cadogan recorded in his diary: "I had talk with A. [Eden] about rumors of German move into the Balkans, which looks imminent. The Greeks are in a flap, I believe there's more to be done, now, in Albania than in Libya. A. has put this to PM who, I think, agrees." (Dilks(ed), 347)

Eden was changing his mind.

Early in 1941, the Foreign Office feared that Greece might reach a neutrality agreement with both Italy and Germany. (Carlton, 171) The reason for the Foreign Office concern was the presence of German troops in Rumania, estimated by the Greek minister in Bucharest at 80,000 men and growing. In the memorandum 'Assistance to Greece', dated 7 January 1941, Orme Sargent, Deputy Under-Secretary in the Foreign Office, stated:

> If we are unable to come effectively to the assistance to Greece, there is a real danger that she may be tempted ... to make a separate peace if reasonable terms are offered to her, and this is no doubt what Germany is trying to bring about. If that occurred Greece would naturally be compelled to resume her previous strict neutrality, which would mean that she would have to insist upon our evacuating any naval and air bases which we had occupied on Greek territory. ... We might of course defy the Greek government ... but if we did so our position would politically be an extremely invidious one. Moreover, it is likely that Germany would retaliate by ... occupying Salonika. With a German air force based upon Salonika it would ... be doubtful how far we should be able to maintain ourselves at the Greek bases which we could continue to hold. Further, the threat to our naval forces in the eastern Mediterranean would be greatly increased. (van Creveld(G), 74-5)

Professor M. van Creveld concluded: "Greece had to be kept in war at any cost, even that of supplying her with those troops and weapons which Middle East Command could so ill afford." (van Creveld(G), 75) To lower the cost and increase the chance of success – Yugoslavia had to be drawn into the war as well.

**

While the discussion about aid to Greece was proceeding within diplomatic and military circles, the role of the "ungentlemanly warfare" was not neglected. Responding to Churchill's order to prepare SOE for action in Yugoslavia, on 8 January 1941 Dalton had a conference with the SOE's top officials, Gladwyn Jebb and Sir Frank Nelson [code name CD], at which he decided to send George Taylor - Nelson's Chief of Staff - to the Balkans. "C.D. has him [Taylor] alone to explain that this is a great mission, ordered from the All Highest, and not a means of shelving him from a key job in the organization at home." (Pimlott(ed), 139) On 13 January the Cabinet's Defence Committee approved Taylor's mission. (Stafford(so), 51)

Taylor's mission to the Balkans and Middle East is described in **Part Two**. His main task was "to draw all the strings together so that the best possible use might be made of our contacts by those who were to direct it." (Sweet-Escott, 60) Or, expressed in simple, non-diplomatic language: "In January 1941 he was sent to take over operations in Belgrade to prepare the way for a coup against the country rulers."(Glen(B), 187n13)

How Taylor planned to accomplish his mission is detailed in his Report to Sir Frank Nelson, dated in Athens on 26 February 1941, and sent to London the same day by plane in a diplomatic bag. Such speedy delivery makes it probable that Hugh Dalton had been aware of Taylor's plans by the time he attended the meeting at Chequers on 2 March, presided over by Churchill. Those plans included the SOE's supporting *those elements in Yugoslavia which are ready to resist German domination,* taking matters *into their own hands.* (The Report, p. 12. Italics added.) Clearly, supporting the overthrow of the Government, if necessary.

Indeed, *drawing all the strings together* resulted in the military *coup d'état* on 27 March 1941.

*** More on the German-Yugoslav negotiations

As German troops were streaming into Rumania, a diplomatic reconnaissance by Yugoslavia seemed to be in order.

> ... Sometime after the middle of January [1941], therefore, the Prime Minister, Cvetkovic, indicated his willingness to go for talks in Germany to [journalist] Gregoric, whose services had already been utilized in a similar manner by Cincar Markovic in November. Gregoric fulfilled his task in an admirable way, ... Would the Führer agree to meet Cvetkovic in person? Not so, it seemed. Several days passed and no answer came from Berlin. ... After some obscure wrangling, the visit was arranged for 14 February. (van Creveld, 124-5)

*** German-Yugoslav negotiations: the meeting on 14 February 1941

Based on records in the *Documents on German Foreign Policy,* Professor M. van Creveld provided the following account of the meeting:

> The Yugoslavs, ... , were tough bargainers. Upon inquiries being made Prince Paul had – on approximately 20 January – assured both Metaxas and the American envoy, Colonel Donovan, that Yugoslavia would fight rather than allow German troops to cross her territory. On 14 February Cvetkovic and Cincar Markovic put up such a determined resistance that the question simply never rose at all. The Prime Minister started his conversation with Ribbentrop with a flat denial that he had ever charged Gregoric with any mission; on the contrary, his decision to travel to Germany was the result of a conversation between the journalist and Schmidt, during which 'the two gentlemen' had concluded that a visit might be useful. For the rest, Yugoslav policy aimed only at keeping the peace in the Balkans. Ribbentrop tried to counter this by saying – somewhat unconvincingly - that the Tripartite Pact to which the two Yugoslav gentlemen were asked to put their signature was aimed at 'preventing the extension of the war', and 'did not represent a treaty of alliance against England'. Germany, too, would have preferred not to fight in Greece, but British machinations there – remember the Salonika front ? – made a clash inevitable. If, Cvetkovic countered, throwing the British out of Greece was Germany's objective, Yugoslavia would be willing to assist; she could try to mediate in a diplomatic solution for the Italian-Greek war and then construct a neutral Balkan block, also including Turkey, with the aim of keeping the British out. The pre-requisite, of course, was that Germany should also stay out. What did the Reich foreign minister think of such a plan? Not much, answered a somewhat surprised Ribbentrop. Frankly, he doubted whether it was possible to drive the British out by peaceful means. (van Creveld, 126)

Then Hitler attended the second part of the meeting.

> Hitler's attempt in the afternoon of the same day to succeed where his foreign minister had failed similarly suffered defeat. The Yugoslav premier scarcely listened to the exposition of the Führer's plans; instead, he kept returning to his own scheme for a diplomatic solution and a neutral Balkan block. Hitler never even had the chance to raise the all important question of transit, or perhaps he sensed that raising it would contribute nothing to disarming the Yugoslavs. As to Cvetkovic's plan for a diplomatic solution, he was as skeptical about its prospects as his foreign minister; but he agreed to have the proposal transmitted to Rome which, for appearance's sake, was still presented to the world as the Axis-appointed arbitrator on all Balkan questions. Having dealt with the Führer's plans in such an exemplary fashion Cvetkovic, always aware of the menacing presence of the German divisions in Rumania and intent on gaining time, had the cheek to ask for a meeting between Hitler and Prince Paul. (van Creveld, 126)

Van Creveld observed:

> The Serbs have put on a brave show, but could not maintain their opposition forever. The growing concentration of German troops in Rumania spoke a stronger language than moral exhortations from England's friends, and on 24 February Prince Paul agreed to go to Germany. (van Creveld, 127)

Historian Gabriel Gorodetsky commented:

Cvetković, in the now predictable pattern, tried in vain to deter a decision on joining the Axis by pointing out the Soviet concern and exploiting the increasing Soviet-German tension. Ribbentrop not only dismissed such suggestions but assured his guests that Stalin was 'a sensible, clear-thinking man' who knew perfectly well that a conflict with Germany would 'lead to the destruction of his regime and his country'. Hitler cunningly discouraged Cvetković from playing the Russian card by disclosing to him that in Berlin Molotov had offered Bulgaria territorial change at Yugoslavia's expense. (Gorodetsky, 138-9)

Regarding *the increasing Soviet-German tension,* Professor Paul Hehn observed:

… The Yugoslavs knew through their military intelligence Hitler would attack the Soviet Union in the spring. After invading Bulgaria and Greece, they believed, he would bypass Yugoslavia then attack the USSR. Once Yugoslavia became neutralized, Hitler would launch an attack on the Soviet Union which could not be postponed for another year as the Red Army then would be too strong. … (Hehn, 370)

In turn, Hitler's plan determined his policy toward Yugoslavia.

There is no evidence that Hitler intended to attack Yugoslavia until the fateful events of March 27, 1941. Göring testified at his post-war trial that Hitler desired to bring the Yugoslavs into the Tripartite Pact in order to neutralize Yugoslavia and not to draw it into the war. Despite pressure from the Wehrmach High Command, Hitler expressly ordered that no troop transports should go through Yugoslavia after its entry into the Three Power Pact to avoid compromising its neutrality. This policy was strategic as well as economic. Göring testified at Nuremberg that the Balkans and Yugoslavia's raw materials had become extremely important for the Germans. Hitler wished to keep Yugoslavia out of the war to avoid sharing its mineral wealth and foodstuffs with Italy. This has always been Germany's policy toward Yugoslavia except on the eve of the Polish campaign when he encouraged Mussolini to attack Yugoslavia to draw Allied pressures from the Polish front. Yugoslavia, therefore, was at all times – in the words of General Jodl – treated as a kind of "prima donna" by Hitler. (Hehn, 370)

Chapter 6

The issue of assisting Greece

Gravely concerned with the front in Albania, where the Greek counter-offensive was stalling – and preoccupied with desire to secure British aid for the needs of the Albanian front - on 4 January, 1941, Metaxas impressed upon both the British Military Mission and Minister Palairet "the urgent need for transport vehicles, aircraft, and a greater effort to prevent the enemy from being reinforced in Albania: the king made a similar appeal to the British Military Attaché." (Koliopoulos, 35)

> The question of help to Greece was referred to Churchill, who in turn invited the Defence Committee to consider the matter. On January 8, the Defence Committee considered the Greek war effort anew, and decided to help the Geeks and to approach them at the same time about the possibility of sending British forces to Salonika. If the Greek government agreed, General Wavell, Commander-in-Chief, Middle East, would be instructed to proceed to Athens in order to confer with the Greeks. Metaxas's reply was prompt and in affirmative. (Koliopoulos, 35)

It is important to note that "In the Foreign Office instructions to Palairet no mention is made of the Defence Committee decision to dispatch an expeditionary force to Greece, let alone of the estimated size of that force." However, "As a result of the decision of January 8, the Chiefs of Staff instructed the Middle East Command to allocate forces for operations in Greece at the earliest possible moment. ... " (Koliopoulos, 36)

London's response to Metaxas initiated a lengthy process in which initially two stands were taken: **for** and **against** aid.. In this process Yugoslavia was ultimately pressured to help – regardless of possible consequences for her as a state and for her people.

Major participants in this decision-making process were Prime Minister Winston Churchill, War / Foreign Minister Anthony Eden, Chief of Imperial General Staff General Sir John Dill, and Commander-in-Chief for the Middle East, General Sir Archibald Wavell.

**

On 8 January – while Donovan and Dykes were meeting with General Sir Archibald Wavell and Air Vice Marshal Sir Arthur Longmore in Cairo - the FO informed the British Minister in Athens, Michael Palairet, that the Defence Committee had decided to send General Wavell to Athens at once to ask the Greeks to allow the British forces to move into Salonika. (Carlton, 171; Dilks(ed), 347)

> ... On 9th January, ... , a telegram was sent to Wavell to say that the support of Greece was now to take precedence of all operations in the Middle East. ... at mid-day we received Wavell's reply, in which he said that the new instructions filled him with dismay. ... (Kennedy, 72)

That night the Defence Committee "decided on quite adequate assistance to Greece". (Dilks(ed), 348) The Committee was of the opinion that it was of first political importance to provide Greece with the fullest possible support. (Hinsley *et al*, 353)

On 10 January, Churchill instructed General Wavell:

> 1. ... We have a mass of detail indicating that a large-scale movement through Bulgaria towards the Greek frontier, aimed presumably at Salonika, will begin before the end of the month. ...
> 2. Nothing must hamper capture of Tobruk, but thereafter all operations in Libya are subordinated to aiding Greece, and all preparations must be made from the receipt of this telegram for the immediate succour of Greece up to the limits prescribed. ... (Churchill(GA), 18-19)

Succor to Greece

On 11 January the Foreign Office instructed Campbell to inform Prince Paul that some mechanized force and additional air force units would be sent to Greece.

> ... he [Prince Paul] expressed "dismay at the British decision which he firmly believed would cause the Germans immediately to overrun the Balkans". Britain, he said, "threatened to destroy the few

remaining free countries in Europe"; he did not think it fair on the Balkan countries still at peace. *His own responsibility was to keep his country from war and destruction if possible.* Paul did however give Campbell a definite assurance that he would refuse any German demand for the passage of troops across Yugoslavia – yet partly withdrew it the next day by sending his Minister of Court to say that if the British were determined to constitute a 'Salonika front', Yugoslavia might be forced to modify its attitude. (Barker, 87. Italics added.)

The British themselves were not determined to constitute a Salonika front. They wanted Yugoslavia, Greece and Turkey to do it. And when Turkey refused, the British concentrated their whole pressure on Prince Paul and Yugoslavia.

By the 12th of January, "Eden had drafted a telegram to 'stiffen' Jugoslavia, in which he said that our offer to Greece, of certain army units and of aircraft showed 'our determination and ability to help our friends'." But the military cut out words "and ability". (Kennedy, 72-3)

After George Taylor's SOE mission was approved on the 13th, Cadogan wrote a note to Eden about SOE on 14 January. Although Cadogan did not think much of their activities (Dilks(ed), 349), it is important to note that the Foreign Office was quite aware of the SOE's operations in Yugoslavia. A few days later, Eden was set to preside over a meeting at which George Taylor – the second most-important man in the SOE – would be given instructions for his mission to the Balkans and the Middle East. (Cooperation of the British Legation in Belgrade with the SOE network in Yugoslavia is examined in **Part Two**.)

Also on 14 January, Churchill cabled Eden:

> The Cabinet today should consider these telegrams from Belgrade about Prince Paul's views. They leave me unchanged. It is for the Greeks to say whether they want Wavell to visit Athens or not. It is the Greeks who must be the judges of the German reaction.
> The evidence in our possession of the German movements seems overwhelming. In the face of it Price Paul's attitude looks like that of an unfortunate man in a cage with a tiger, hoping not to provoke him while steadily dinner-time approaches. (Churchill(GA), 158)

As it turned out, it was the British-supported coup that "provoked the tiger" who then tore Yugoslavia apart.

General Wavell's meeting with the Greek leaders in Athens, 14-15 January 1941

Following Churchill's directive of 10 January, General Wavell and Air Chief Marshal Sir Arthur Longmore went to Greece on the 13th January and conferred in Athens with the Greek King, Prime Minister Metaxas, and General Papagos on 14 and 15 January 1941. "These staff talks began immediately and continued until 13 February 1941." (McClymont, 96n4)

* General Ioannis Metaxas refused the proposal for British troops

First a conclusion by a Greek historian:

> A lengthy review of the situation on the fourteenth January led to nowhere, except of producing a conviction in Metaxas that the British had very little to spare for Greece; and the same can be said of the meeting on January 15. ... In any event, from the Greek point of view, help against German attack took second place to the war at hand. ... the more he [Metaxas] thought about it, the more convinced he became that he had done well to reject the British offer, for the British had "next to nothing". As might be expected, the needs of the Albanian front were given priority by the Greek side, which produced a formidable list of requirements, ... Wavell tried to meet Greek needs, but not to the extent the Greeks wanted. ... Essentially, the top level military consultations stumbled on the diverging views of the two sides: the Greeks were mainly concerned over their requirements for the prosecution of the war against the Italians, while the British were almost exclusively interested in preparations to anticipate a German invasion of the Balkans in the near future. Such opposite views and aims were impossible to bridge. (Koliopoulos, 36)

Now a conclusion of a British historian:

> When Mr. Churchill pressed his aid on them in mid January he received a cold douche. General Metaxas, the Greek Prime Minister, rejected the proposal, saying that the forces offered would be likely to provoke German aggression without being anything like strong enough to check it. The Greek Commander-in-Chief, General Papagos, argued that nine divisions were needed, whereas the British Government offered an immediate deposit of two regiments, to be followed by two or three divisions. He thought that the British would be wiser to complete their victory in Africa before attempting anything fresh. To split their effort would be bad strategy. (Liddell Hart, 17)

And in the view of the American authors:

> "The Greeks expressed skepticism regarding action either by the Yugoslavs or the Turks in the event of German intervention against Greece. Papagos pointed out ... that he would require the support of nine British divisions, together with large-scale air forces, and that these reinforcements would have to arrive before the Germans entered Bulgaria." (Langer & Gleason, 396)

On 15 January, Metaxas thought that ten divisions – not nine - was the minimum aid required to give a reasonable chance of withstanding a German attack:

> This [Metaxas'] refusal was accepted with relief by General Wavell, who returned to Cairo and cabled a report to London. The suggested plan had been 'a dangerous half measure'. Now that the *Luftwaffe* was operating in the Mediterranean the first task for the British was to secure Benghazi and make Egypt safe from an attack. No promise should be made to send troops to Greece, but he did think that preparations should be made for a force to defend Salonika. (McClymont, 96n3, 96)

Churchill noted the Greek refusal: "On January 15 they told us that the Greek Government were unwilling that any of our troops should land in Salonika until they could do so in sufficient numbers to act offensively." (Churchill(GA), 19) In March 1941 Eden told Cyrus L. Sulzberger, *The New York Times* foreign correspondent, that "Britain had offered the late General Metaxas an expeditionary force but the dictator had refused unless 200,000 well-equipped men were promised." (Sulzberger, 124) When the Greeks refused to accept an insufficient number of British troops, on 15 January Cadogan "devised telegram to Belgrade conveying message to Prince Regent, who has lost his head and his nerve." (Dilks(ed), 350)

**

Dykes and Donovan came to Athens on the 15th, while the British-Greek negotiations were going on. Kept informed of the negotiations, Donovan himself talked at length with the Premier John Metaxas and his Chief of Staff, Gen. Alexander Papagos, expressing his support for the British. He assured the Greeks of the USA's determination to assist Britain. Taking notes of Greek needs for military equipment - Donovan was creating the impression that the equipment could be delivered. (More detailed information about Donovan's support for the British cause is presented in **Appendix A.**)

**

Not only military, but SOE personnel were partially involved in Greece. During these Anglo-Greek negotiations, "In Greece itself there was nothing much that we [SOE] could do." It seems that at times it was difficult for the British Legation to arrange contacts between the British military and Metaxas, "then in the last days of his life". However, "we [SOE] were able to fix it up through an under-cover relationship we had established with the dictator through his Minister of the Interior, Maniadakis." (Sweet-Escott, 61) Namely, a British businessman in Athens, in the service of SOE, "could talk to Maniadakis and Maniadakis could get hold of Metaxas, which was often more than our own legation could do." (Sweet-Escott, 62)

Anglo-Turkish negotiations, 15-22 January

Immediately following the Greco-British talks in Athens, there followed talks with the Turks. When approached with an offer of British air support, during the Anglo-Turkish negotiations, 15-22 January 1941, the Turks refused it. (Langer and Gleason, 396) The report by the British Liaison Mission from Turkey, received in London on 22 January, stated that lacking the resources with which to challenge the Axis powers, the Turks preferred to remain neutral. (McClymont, 97)

> The British Government still tried to insist on the Greeks accepting the immediate deposit, but Metaxas maintained his refusal. Mr. Churchill then addressed an offer to Turkey, only to meet with another refusal, on similar grounds. Despite these rebuffs, he continued to cherish the scheme. (Liddell Hart, 18)

> Still obsessed with the desire to bomb Rumanian oilfields, the British cabinet toward the end of January offered ten British-manned air squadrons to the Turks and expressed the opinion that if the Germans should attack, the Straits might serve as "a useful anti-tank ditch." The Turks, who had no quarrel with Hitler, evasively answered that they might consider military action only if and when German troops invaded Bulgaria, although they would really prefer to limit themselves to the defense of their own territory. (Petrov, 139, n. 22)

**

On 16 January, Wavell and Longmore reported, "with obvious satisfaction, that the Greeks did not want our units for fear that their arrival might provoke the Germans to attack them." (Kennedy, 73)

Referring to this development, on 16 January, Cadogan entered into his diary:

> ... Wavell has seen Metaxas who (probably prompted by Prince P. [Paul]) refuses all aid in men. Even refuses guns, if accompanied by crews! ... Defence Committee at 6 to consider Wavell's telegram. ... Agreed, of course, that we can't force assistance down Metaxas' throat. C of S [Chiefs of Staff] drafting telegram repeating our arguments. I think these Balkan states are probably wrong. But they are all terrified. And it *may* be that the Germans are hoping to lure a small British force into the Balkans, to destroy it. (Dilks(ed), 350)

**

On 17 January, Yugoslav Premier Cvetković informed the Greek Minister in Belgrade that the occupation of Salonika was a vital question for Yugoslavia. (Petranović & Žutić, 214)

Churchill's support for SOE operations

After the approval of Taylor's mission on 13 January, on 20 January 1941, Churchill replied to Dalton's report on SOE operations:

> Pray press on with any useful scheme to cause trouble to the enemy in his own country or occupied territories. ... Local action ... and the organisation in occupied territories of passive resistance to the enemy may embarrass enemy plans out of all proportion to the energy expanded or the risk of loss incurred. ... As a result of the meeting on Monday last [the 13th of January] you are now empowered to proceed urgently with action to prevent Roumanian oil reaching Germany. If you wish for authority to pursue other major plans elsewhere I shall be glad to consider them. (Mackenzie, 92-3)

As in earlier directives, Churchill himself considered that preventing Rumanian oil from reaching Germany was an urgent priority of Taylor's mission.

**

On 21 January – while Donovan and Dykes were in Sofia - Eden informed his Minister in Athens that, according to the Greek Minister in London, Prince Paul's reaction to the British sending arms and aircraft to Greece influenced the Greeks to decline the offer of British land forces first made by Wavell in mid-January. (Barker, 87; 281n56)

**

As more than 500,000 German troops were concentrated in Rumania, (Hoptner, 203n3), on 23January – when Donovan was in Belgrade - Cadogan met with Gladwyn Jebb, the Chief Executive Officer of SOE, and Sir Frank Nelson, its Executive Director, to talk about the SOE operations in Rumania (Dilks[ed], 351), which were directed from Belgrade. "Seeing that turmoil had begun there, decided to jump in at once, even though our arrangements not complete. A. [Eden] agreed and got P.M.'s [Churchill's] concurrence." (Dilks(ed), 351)

As the German troops were concentrated in Rumania, by 24 January, the British Military Intelligence learned from diplomatic and other sources, or the Secret Intelligence Service, "that staff talks had begun between the German and the Bulgarian military authorities, as indeed they had on 22 January"... "But about the penetration of Bulgaria by the GAF [German Air Forces], and about the scale of the force the GAF planned to move to Bulgaria, the Enigma provided a great wealth of detail". (Hinsley et al, 356) The gathered information pointed out that the Germany's penetration southward would go through Bulgaria, not Yugoslavia.

Change in Greece's leadership

On 27 January, Cadogan met again with Gladwyn Jebb, Sir Frank Nelson, and some Foreign Office officials. "Agreed to go ahead with trying to 'keep the pot boiling' in Rumania, although Cadogan feared that this may be difficult." (Dilks(ed), 351) However, SOE operations in Rumania were not successful. In February 1941, "British nationals were forced to quit the country" [Rumania]. (Maurice Pearton. "SOE in Romania", in Seaman(ed), 123)

(In his report to Nelson, dated 26 February 1941, George Taylor wrote about the difficulties in Rumania.)

**

On 29 January Metaxas died suddenly and was replaced "by the much less authoritative Alexander Koryzis". For Eden, this news was "a heavy blow". (Eden, 188) In this changed situation Churchill and Eden concluded that a major effort should be made to get the Greeks to modify their stand. Eden was hoping to influence Turkey into resisting Germany. He believed that he could persuade the Turks to accept a major British presence. On 29 January he wrote in his diary: "Turkey is the key and we must intensify our efforts there. We [Eden and Churchill] discussed my going to Turkey." (Carlton, 171)

> ... Metaxas had died suddenly on January 29, and Mr. Churchill was quick to revive his cherished project. The new Greek prime Minister had sent to the British Government a note reaffirming his predecessor's *principle* of resisting the Germans if they attacked, while reiterating that the dispatch of British troops should not take place unless a German invasion threatened – through the Germans' moving into Bulgaria's intervening territory. That slight sign from the Greek Government was enough for Mr. Churchill – enough to make him abandon the advance on Tripoli in favour of a venture in Greece. (Liddell Hart, 19. Italics added.)

Churchill's letter to Turkey's President

On 31 January, it was more or less settled that Eden should go to the Middle East, noted Cadogan. (Dilks[ed], 352) Never giving up on the idea of drawing Turkey into the war, and using his fertile imagination more than realistic arguments, Churchill wrote a lengthy letter to Turkey's President, Ismet Inönü , hoping to inspire him to accept British proposals. Here are some excerpts:

> ... unless you promise the Germans not to march against Bulgaria or against their troops passing through Bulgaria, they will bomb Istanbul and Adrianople the same night, and also dive-bomb your troops in Thrace. No doubt they would hope either to reach Salonika unopposed or to compel the Greeks to make peace with Italy and yield them air bases in Greece and in the islands, thus endangering the communications between our armies in Egypt and the Turkish Army. They would deny the use of Smyrna to our Navy, they would completely control the exits from the Dardanelles, and thus complete the encirclement of Turkey in Europe on three sides. This would also facilitate their attacks upon Alexandria and Egypt generally. (Churchill(GA), 33)

> ... we shall place Turkey in a position, once our squadrons are on the Turkish airdromes, to threaten to bombard the Rumanian oilfields if any German advance is made into Bulgaria, or if the air personnel already in Bulgaria is not speedily withdrawn. We will undertake not to take such action from Turkish airfields except by agreement with you. (Churchill(GA), 34)

**

On 31 January, Churchill's Assistant Private Secretary commented in his diary:

> ... There can now be little hesitation in predicting a German move through Bulgaria, which has finally succumbed to German influence and infiltration and where heavy German concentrations are taking place. The point at issue is whether Turkey will resist and will concert measures with Yugoslavia in time. (Colville, 349)

Also on 31 January, Churchill reaffirmed to the Chiefs of Staff Committee the decision which had been conveyed to Gen. Wavell, "that once Tobruk was taken, the Greek-Turkish situation must have priority." (Churchill(GA), 35) With that in mind,

> The British Ambassador in Washington, Lord Halifax, sent a note to [the Secretary of State] Hull on February 5 requesting support for the Yugoslav-Greek talks on joint action against the threat posed by the concentration of German troops in Rumania. Four days later, Hull advised the Yugoslav government of the United States government's position as recently expressed by Roosevelt. (Jukić, 46)

That was the position of support for Britain, as emphasized by Donovan during his recent visit.

**

Until 7 February, the Foreign Office had "remained confident that Yugoslavia would resist any Italian or German demand for passage of troops through the country, and seemed content with it". (Barker, 87; 282n57) But that attitude changed when Churchill decided to send "speedy succour to Greece".

Then on 8 February, Alexandros Koryzis "sent a note to the British Government reaffirming the determination of his country to resist any German attack but repeating the statement by Metaxas that no British force should be sent into Macedonia until the Germans had entered Bulgaria. ... Koryzis now suggested that the size and composition of the British expeditionary force be determined." If the combined Greek and British forces could not resist the Germans and encourage support from Turkey and Yugoslavia, "then the premature appearance of insufficient forces in Macedonia 'would do no more than provoke German intervention'. " (McClymont, 97)

> While Churchill saw merit in giving aid to Greece in any case, he was more pessimistic about Turkish intentions – whereas Eden "was primarily anxious to aid the Greeks, if at all, as a means of bringing Turkey into the conflict." (Carlton, 171)

Beginning of George Taylor's activities in the Balkans

Also on February 8, George Taylor arrived in Istanbul. Two days later he reported from Istanbul, and sixteen days later prepared and sent his report to Sir Frank Nelson from Athens. (Mackenzie, 107n2) In the rank of full Colonel, he spent more time in Athens than intended "in discussions with the British Military Mission and with Ian Pirie ['an old Section D hand'] and the Greek SOE team." (Glen(B), 58). Well informed of the Anglo-Greek negotiations in Athens, on 27 February he moved to Belgrade, to direct activities of SOE and their local co-operatives in support of the planned British expedition in Greece, and to do everything that could be done about: the Danube blocking scheme, W/E communications, the smuggling organization from Yugoslavia into Bulgaria, and Ilija Trifunović Birčanin's (code-named "Daddy") demolition plans on the railway line Niš-Skoplje-Đevđelija – as Taylor stated in the letter to Sir Frank Nelson on 26 February 1941. (This report is described in **Part Two, Appendix K.**)

The US Minister in Belgrade: *"We are not pushing you into the war."*

Donovan's visit to Belgrade (evening of 22 – morning of 25 January, 1941) invigorated US Minister Lane. He understood and approved the President's support for the British, as explained and delivered by Donovan. On 10 February, Lane came to see Jukić, the Yugoslav Assistant Foreign Minister, who later described the meeting:

> We knew each other very well, and we were able to speak frankly. Reminding him of the Maček-Donovan talks, I pointed out that he was wrong in suggesting that Maček was in favor of appeasing

Hitler. He then gave me a complete account of the Hitler-Molotov talks, emphasizing the need to resist Hitler. I described the truly desperate position of Yugoslavia. Hitler was at the height of his power. German troops were passing through Hungary into Rumania, keeping Yugoslavia hemmed in from the north and the east. In the southeast, Yugoslavia faced Bulgaria, a country that would probably be receiving German troops very soon. On the northwest and west, we had Mussolini, who had always been ill-disposed toward us. Soviet policy was complete enigma. Turkey was unwilling to take a definite stand against Hitler. We could expect little help from Britain. "We could easily take a strong stand against Hitler," I told him, "if the Americans were already in the war. Co-operation between Yugoslavia and Turkey could be arranged, if only you Americans were to send a few hundred bombers to bases in Turkey for use against the German army,"

"We don't have hundreds of aircraft to send anywhere, " Lane cut in. "We hardly have enough to satisfy Britain's minimal needs."

"But Yugoslavia is already halfway to being gulped down the Nazi monster gorge," I exploded. "It has only to snap its jaws – and that's the end of Yugoslavia. Why are you pushing us toward its jaws?"

"But we are not pushing you into the war," Lane said with embarrassment. *Others are doing that.* You propose that we send bombers to the Turks. I wonder if that is wise. At one time you told us that foreign troops in Bulgaria would be a *casus belli* for them, whereas now they won't even think about going to war for Greece. They make everything depend on Yugoslavia." (Jukić, 46-7. Italics added.)

In view of President Roosevelt's pro-British messages, and additional Colonel Donovan's support for the British policy – as shown in **Appendix A** - it is extremely hard to justify Lane's implication that only Britain – and not the US as well - had been pushing Yugoslavia into war.

Eden and Dill to go to Greece

On 10 February, Cadogan noted the differences in opinion about support for Greece and the intention to send Eden and General Dill to the Middle East:

... Settled A. [Eden] and Dill should go out. Decided to stop at Benghazi and run over to Balkans. Dill inclined to say our first obligation is to Turkey. P.M. [Churchill], rightly, I think, said he wouldn't accept that. Greece was fighting and Turkey was doing nothing but evade rather plain obligations. We ought to do all we can to help Greece. That may encourage Turkey. Abandonment of Greece would confirm Turkey in what I believe to be their quite equivocal attitude. We will give them what's left over. (Dilks(ed), 354)

Also on 10 February Wavell informed the War Office that he might be able to capture Tripoli, which would mean the end of the Axis' presence in North Africa. (Lamb, 86)

On 11th February Greece was still refusing our offer to send a few military units. ... but Churchill now returned to the charge. He urged that Turkey should be pressed to show her hand and not wait until it was too late. He also pressed for assistance to Greece, and on a bigger scale. He put his idea into definite shape in a telegram to Wavell which suggested that he should make four Divisions available for Greece from the Middle East. (Kennedy, 74)

The Chief of the Imperial General Staff (CIGS), General Sir John Dill, also opposed giving aid to Greece at that time. General Archibald Wavell, too, originally opposed intervention in Greece because it entailed too much risk.

... Until very recently, the CIGS had been vehemently opposed to the project [of aiding Greece]: he had told the Cabinet so on 11 February, thereby provoking Churchill's wrath and an angry signal to Wavell specifically ordering aid to Greece and forbidding the attempts to reach Tripoli which he had hitherto urged. (Bennett, 30-31)

Forbidding the attack on Tripoli, on 12 February Churchill ordered Wavell to make his "major effort to aid Greece and/or Turkey. This rules out any serious effort against Tripoli ... you should therefore make yourself secure at Benghazi and concentrate all available forces in the [Nile] Delta for movement to Europe." Then he continued:

4. Both Greece and Turkey have hitherto refused our offer of technical units, because they say these are too small to solve their main problem, but conspicuous enough to provoke German intervention. ... *If Turkey and Yugoslavia would tell Bulgaria they will attack her* unless she joins them in resisting a German advance southward, this might create a barrier requiring much larger German forces than are now in Rumania. ... (Churchill(GA), 64. Italics added.)

The Prime Minister was basing this plan and hope on too many **IF'S**. Knowing the negative outcome from the Anglo-Turkish negotiations of 15-22 January, and Price Paul's critical view of inadequate help to Greece, it was clear that neither Turkey nor Yugoslavia would go to war against Bulgaria. It was unrealistic to expect them to go to war against a state supported by a mighty enemy when their national interests were not threatened.

Churchill's decision on North Africa was criticized even in London. On 12 February, Churchill's intelligence adviser, Major Desmond Morton, told John Colville, Assistant Private Secretary to Churchill,

> that there was great opposition to the P.M.'s decision not to press on Tripoli but divert our effort to Greece and Turkey. In continuing our African campaign we had the practical certainty of winning all North Africa and holding an impregnable position. In forming a bridgehead in Greece we ran a risk of another Dunkirk. The C.I.G.S. felt so strongly about it that he was almost thinking of resigning, and the military were making a determined effort to get Wavell to intervene. ... Desmond pointed out that this was the vital decision of the first stage of the war. (Colville, 356)

However, Churchill continued to believe that British aid to Greece "with all our strength" would draw both Turkey and Yugoslavia into the war. But "all British strength" at that time was not strong enough to stop the German invasion of Greece, which made his thinking wishful.

Also on 12 February, the vanguards of the German Afrikacorps – under the command of Field Marshal Erwin Rommel – began to arrive in Tripoli. (Keegan, 149)

Departure of Eden - Dill's team to the Middle East, 12 February

On 12 February, Eden and General Sir John Dill, with a small number of aides, began their journey to the Middle East. (Carlton, 171-2) Eden's mission, drafted by Churchill and approved by the Cabinet, contained the following directives related to Yugoslavia:

> 2. His principal object will be the sending of speedy succour to Greece. For this purpose he will initiate any action he may think necessary with the Commander-in-Chief of the Middle East, with the Egyptian Government, and with the Governments of Greece, Yugoslavia, and Turkey. (Churchill(GA), 66)

> 4. (h) He will communicate direct with the Governments of Turkey and Yugoslavia, duplicating his messages to the Foreign Office. The object will be to make them both fight at the same time or do the best they can. For this purpose he should summon the Minister at Belgrade or the Ambassador in Turkey to meet him as may be convenient. (Churchill(GA), 67-8)

Churchill summarized Eden's mission as follows: "In short he is to gather together all the threads, and propose continuously the best solutions for our difficulties, and not be deterred from acting upon his own authority if the urgency is too great to allow reference home." (Churchill(GA), 68)

In her study of the Belgrade coup, Professor Onslow wrote about Eden's mission:

> At the outset of his tour of the Near East, Eden was instructed by Churchill
> 'to deal directly with the Yugoslav and Turkish Governments, *with the object of making both countries fight at the same time or do the best they could*".

> The Foreign Secretary's mission was paralleled by SO2 Deputy Director George Taylor's tour of the Near East to establish post-occupational wireless networks and sabotage and resistance, to support the Commander-in-Chief, Middle East, General Wavell's plans and General Wilson's operations in Greece. In Eden's tour of the Near East from 22 February to 6 April 1941, the Foreign

Secretary attempted to bring the wider world to bear upon Yugoslavia. In this Eden adopted a four-fold approach.

Initially the War Cabinet's idea was to boost Yugoslavia's resolve by aiding Greece. Failure to help Athens would mean 'there is no hope of action by Yugoslavia'. This was Churchill's view too. However, under Eden, this policy was turned on its head, and Yugoslavia and Turkey were to save Greece.

Secondly, Eden sought to use Turkey as the means to draw Yugoslavia into regional military planning and diplomatic defiance. The Chief of Imperial General Staff, Sir John Dill, conceived Turkey as being more important strategically than Greece. 'Yugoslavia will not fight unless Turkey fights and the converse is very likely true.'

Thirdly, Eden attempted to use American, Greek and Soviet channels to bolster Yugoslav resistance.

And fourthly, Britain was to exert pressure on Prince Paul's Government to resist German pressure, and Italian enticement to join the Axis, using British diplomatic contacts, and SOE illicit network. (Onslow, 41-2.Italics added)

The Turko-Bulgarian Non-Aggression Pact, 17 February 1941

While Eden and Gen. Dill were on their hazardous trip to Cairo, by 15 February the *Wehrmacht's* 'army of observation' in Rumania reached the strength of seven divisions. After refusing to accept Churchill's offer of 31 January to put British *squadrons on the Turkish airodromes, to threaten to bombard the Rumanian oilfields if any German advance is made into Bulgaria,* on 17 February Turkey signed a non-aggression pact with Bulgaria. (Keegan, 150)

Sir H. Knatchbull-Hugesson, British Ambassador in Ankara, commented on this Pact: "From the British point of view this was a great disappointment." (Scanlan, 12)

In Cairo, the same day, Colonel Dykes recorded in his diary:

> ...In the afternoon we went to see [General] Marshall-Cornwall who said he was not discouraged by the result of recent Turkish conversations, although G.H.Q.[General Head Quarters] were disappointed that he had not been able to bring them into the war on our side right away. The Prime Minister's offer of aircraft and anti-aircraft guns came very inappropriately after Marshall-Cornwall himself had been able to promise nothing. ... They [the Turks] were sticking out for 1,300 aircraft. ... the Turkish General Staff had taken the line of asking what we wanted them to attack if they went to war, what exactly were our plans and what support we would send them. These were difficult questions to answer. ...
> ... As regards Greece he [Marshall-Cornwall] thought that the chief danger was that if no final success came within two or three months, politicians of the Opposition would work up a peace move, and there might not be sufficient resolution in the Government to withstand this. (Danchev(ed), 56-7)

Without clear answers to their "difficult questions", the Turks did not want to be drawn into the war, which made it more pressing for the British to draw Yugoslavia into it.

Churchill – General John Kennedy meeting, 16 February 1941

At the same time, back in England ...

Invited to visit the Prime Minister at Dytchley, near Oxford, on 16 February, Director of Military Operations, Gen. John Kennedy, presented to him a general review of the situation as the General Staff saw it at the time. Here are excerpts related to the Balkans:

> With regard to Greece, it seems fairly certain that the Germans have now put 20 to 25 Divisions in Rumania. It is more than likely that they will move south through Bulgaria as soon as weather permits, say about the end of March or beginning of April, perhaps even sooner.
> It may be possible to form a political front in the Balkans. But a political front is of no use unless it can be backed up by an effective military front. *It is impossible to form an effective military front because the Balkan nations are so ill-equipped and we have no sufficient forces to spare to do it ourselves.*
> Nothing we can do can make the Greek business a sound military proposition. The Greeks have not got reserves for more than a month or so of fighting against the Germans. The farther

> forward the Greeks get in Albania the worse will be their dispositions to meet German attack. If we put four divisions into Greece, a month's hard fighting there would suck the bulk of our reserves of ammunition, etc., out of the Middle East.
>
> The locomotive and the petrol engine will always beat the ship, especially when the ship has to go round the Cape. The chances of our getting four divisions into Greece are in any case extremely small. It would take a hundred ships or more to put them in one flight. And it takes time to organize bases. The prospect is that we should try to put our forces in piecemeal over a period of six weeks or two months. And it is inconceivable that the Germans would allow us to do this.
>
> It has been argued that the country round Salonika is easily defensible. So was the country in Norway. For effective defence you want not only defensible country but an adequate force to defend it. We have discussed the size of the force required for Salonika on many occasions with the French and the Turks. Everybody has agreed that we should need a force of about 20 divisions (the front is 150 miles long). And everybody wanted everybody else to provide the 20 divisions.
>
> Anything we put in Greece on account of the very important political aspect, we should be prepared to lose. We must not lose so much that our power of offensive action in the Middle East is killed, nor so much that our power of defence in the vital Egyptian centre is impaired. (Kennedy, 82-3. Italics added.)

> In the Middle East we must not throw away our power of offensive action by adopting an unsound strategy in Greece. The real bastion of our position there is Turkey. If Turkey will not enter the war and accept our support we should hold out strategic reserves for other tasks, such as the seizure of Sicily. (Kennedy, 85)

General Kennedy stated his views to the Prime Minister "frankly and forcefully", and expected that this "might provoke him into anger" but, to his surprise, the Prime Minister "argued most reasonably and even seemed to accept" Kennedy's view. That puzzled Kennedy who recalled that the Prime Minister "had pressed for a forward policy at recent meetings of the Defence Committee." (Kennedy, 78)

The Prime Minister's actions soon showed that he still was pressing for a forward policy.

Like Kennedy, "Wavell too had originally been opposed to intervention, on the ground that it entailed too much risk; he seems to have come around to the opposite view, for reasons that are not clear, about the middle of February, and at once to have become an ardent supporter of the expedition." (Bennett, 31) According to one opinion, once changed his mind, Wavell's voice was dominant in changing General Dill's views. One reason for change was a supposed Wavell's inclination to defer to superior rank and to bow to authority. (Bennett, 33-4)

> Cadogan too expressed his doubts about Middle Eastern affairs, ... He feared that *the Greeks might have to make a separate peace,* but that even that would be better than having Greece devastated to the last acre or putting in British troops and seeing them trapped. He felt sure that the Germans had been trying to entice a British force into Greece, and did not believe the Turks or Yugoslavs would move. If they would, to put British troops in Greece would be a different matter. (Dilks(ed), 357. Italics added.)

Eden – Donovan meeting in Cairo, 19/20 February

At about 11 p.m. on 19 February, Eden and Dill arrived in Cairo. Before they arrived, Wavell had written a memorandum "strongly in favor of going to the help of Greece". Although Wavell did not tell them of this memorandum, he told them: "As you were so long [in coming] I felt I had to get started, and I have begun the concentration for a move of troops to Greece." To this Eden commented: " Dill and I exchanged a glance, relieved that Wavell's mind was apparently in tune with our instructions." (Eden, 195)

By that time, Wavell already knew Donovan was in favor of sending aid to Greece, and may have rightly assumed that this was a view of the USA Government. **(See Appendix A)**

General Kennedy considered Wavell's reversal to be curious, because Churchill " had urged the Greek venture from the outset", while Wavell had not. (Kennedy, 85)

After a late arrival to Cairo, Eden dined, talked with the British Ambassador, read telegrams from London, and "finally had a discussion with Colonel William Donovan" very early on 20 February.**(See Appendix A)** Eden asked Donovan to plead with President Roosevelt to help with shipping, and Donovan promptly did. On that day, Eden wrote in his diary: "Met three Commanders-in-Chief and Dill at Wavell's office where we went into a three-hour session. There was agreement upon utmost help to Greece at earliest possible moment." (Eden, 195) Then he continued:

> Much discussion about Turkish position. ... [Members of a British mission for staff talks] gave doleful account of state of Turkish readiness. They do not know how to use technical arms and their operational efficiency in the air is very low. All this led Wavell to take the view, which Dill did not share, that Turks would be more a liability than an asset at present time. (Eden, 196)

The Greeks accept Eden's and Dill's visit

While the Turkish position was discussed and analyzed in Cairo, Churchill might have been temporarily influenced by the developing situation in Africa. When the "Ultra" decrypts revealed that the Germans were sending troops to Tripoli, Churchill became more cautious about support to Greece.

But neither Eden nor Dill felt it would be another Norwegian fiasco, and Churchill, "…. pressed ahead. [David] Margesson, who had replaced Eden at the War Office in December [1940] felt that it was not only another 'Norway', but also that 'Dunkirk and Dakar rolled into one' was looming 'threateningly before us'; he was correct. (Charmley, 442)

On 21 February, Eden entered into his diary:

> Another full discussion this morning with C-in-C's [Commanders-in-Chief] found us all agreed on line with Greeks and our plans laid. Greeks have accepted visit.
> After the meeting I sent the Prime Minister a telegram describing our interim conclusion:
> Dill and I have exhaustively reviewed situation temporarily* with Commanders-in-Chief. ...
> Gravest anxiety is not in respect to army but of air. There is no doubt that need to fight a German air force, instead of Italian, is creating a new problem for Longmore. ... We should all have liked to approach Greeks tomorrow with a suggestion that we should join with them in holding a line to defend Salonika, but both Longmore and [Admiral Sir Andrew] Cunningham are convinced that our present air resources will not allow us to do this. Dill and I are not prepared to take a final decision until we have discussed the matter with the Greeks. (Eden, 196)
> *This word may have been wrongly deciphered. (Eden, 196)

According to General de Guingand, Eden and Dill did not discuss the situation with the Planning Staff in Cairo before leaving for Greece.

> In February, 1941, a very high-powered party arrived in Cairo. ... Discussions took place behind closed doors and we on the lower level were all agog to know what was happening, and what decisions were being made. As far as I can remember the Planners were not asked to produce a paper giving their views as to the feasibility of the project. We certainly held some very decided ones.
> The D.M.I. [Director of Military Intelligence], Brigadier [Eric J.] Shearer, did produce a paper drawing attention to the great danger of this campaign in view of the German resources and methods. I remember this paper coming back from the C-in-C [Commander-in-Chief], General Wavell. There was a short note in his own hand across the top – it said:
> " 'War is an option of difficulties.' – Wolfe. A.P.W."
> We admired the spirit but questioned – in so far as junior officers are allowed to question – the judgment! (de Guingand, 48)

General de Guingand was detailed to accompany the party that left for the talks with the Greeks in Athens. (de Guingand, 48)

**

Overlooking British weaknesses in the air and at sea – flagged out by Longmore and Cunningham – on the night of 21st February Dill sent a telegram to Lieut.-Gen. [Sir Robert] Haining, the Vice-CIGS. Here are some excerpts:

> I came out here with firm idea that forces sent to Greece would inevitably be lost and that we should concentrate on help to Turkey. I have now heard views of three Commanders-in-Chief,

Marshall-Cornval and Heywood [the army member of our Military Mission in Greece]. It has been made clear to me by them:
(a) That Turkey will not fight at our bidding. ...
(d) That Yugoslavia will not fight unless Turkey fights and that the converse is very likely true. ...
I have concluded that our only chance of preventing the Balkans being devoured piecemeal is to go to Greece with all that we can find as soon as it can be done. The risks are admittedly considerable but inaction would in my mind be fatal.

It is not yet possible to see what line we should aim at holding in Greece but I doubt very much whether Salonika could be covered. If this proves to be so after our discussion with Greeks tomorrow we may still be able to hold a line covering northern Greece and giving Yugoslavia a bolt-hole through the Monastir Gap. ...

Have had a long talk with Donovan. He clearly thinks that help for Greece is urgent. (Eden, 197-8)

Eden and the military Commanders – who initially were strongly opposed to the idea of aid to Greece - now became supporters of it. Eden's biographer expressed the opinion that

... the military advice was reinforced in the political sphere by the presence in Cairo of Colonel William Donovan, ... In a brief meeting with the Foreign Secretary [on 19/20 February], Donovan urged British resistance to German encroachment upon the Mediterranean, not least on the grounds that a passive attitude would be unfavourably received by American public opinion. (Carlton, 172)

Optimistic about drawing the United States into European affairs, Eden "was only too ready to give disproportionate weight to Donovan's counsel. The British team in Cairo accordingly invited themselves to Athens for a secret meeting to be held on 22 February and privately decided to offer substantial assistance to the Greeks." (Carlton, 172)

The Tatoi Conference: the Anglo-Greek agreement, 22/23 February 1941

The Greek inquiry came at a very propitious moment: Benghazi had been captured, and Churchill and the Defence Committee were considering a fresh "employment" for the Middle East forces. Important decisions were now being taken in London, irrespective of Greek misgivings: Greece had become the focal point of British strategy with respect to the Balkans. (Koliopoulos, 38)

Once in Cairo, and before starting to Athens, Eden, Dill, and the Commanders-in-Chief, Middle East, agreed on the following line of approach in Athens: the Greeks should be persuaded to accept the British expeditionary force at the earliest possible moment, and should be asked for information about the forces which they would be able to release from Albania to form a line against the Germans. ... although the British preferred the Aliakmon line, the question of the line to be held was left to be decided in common with the Greeks. (Koliopoulos, 38-9)

The forces in Cyrenaica were already in process of being pulled back when, on February 22, Mr. Eden arrived in Athens accompanied by an imposing military staff, and pressed the new Greek Prime Minister to accept the British offer. (Liddell Hart, 19)

**

After two days of consultations in Cairo, on 22 February, Eden, Dill, Wavell and their aides flew to an airfield north of Athens, were taken to the Royal palace at Tatoi, where they were met by Greek representatives, and had "a really good English tea with the King." (de Guingand, 49)

King George of the Hellenes wanted Eden to confer with his new Prime Minister, Alexander Koryzis, who had something to say to Eden. Reluctantly, Eden agreed, and Koryzis read a statement which concluded with:

But let me repeat once again that whatever the future holds in store, and whether there is any hope of repelling the enemy in Macedonia or not, Greece will defend its national soil, even if she has to do it alone. (Eden, 199)

Martin L. van Creveld interpreted that Koryzis knew from experience that the arrival of a British mission meant that London was having doubts about Greece's willingness to fight on. "Eden, however, did not think this was sufficient, and had him [Koryzis] repeat the declaration of loyalty with the King of the Hellenes present. Only then did the two sides settle down to business." (van Creveld, 81)

The first Plenary Meeting was held at 5:30 p.m. (van Creveld, 81n64)   After he made sure that the Greeks were not going to desert, Eden told the assembled company that

> "the [British] War Cabinet had unanimously reached the conclusion, with which the Commanders in Chief in the Middle East were in full agreement, that we ought to offer the maximum possible help to Greece." He then explained what forces the British could send over, amounting in all to 100,000 men, 142 tanks, a few hundred guns of various kinds, and another five squadrons of aircraft. Since these forces, representing "the limit of what we could do at present", could hardly be expected to resist the 500 aircraft and 23 divisions which, according to Eden's estimate, the Germans had concentrated in Rumania, hope for success was based, in the final analysis, on Turkish and Yugoslav intervention. (van Creveld(G), 81)

Van Creveld continued:

> This point was immediately pounced upon by Koryzis, who dwelt on the danger lest the British force might 'precipitate' a German attack without being sufficiently strong to repel it, forcing Eden to admit that he did not really know what Turkey and Yugoslavia would do. After Koryzis had expressed his opinion that "it was of importance as a preliminary to establish whether the Greek forces in conjunction with the British forces would be sufficient to constitute an effective resistance to a German attack", the conference adjourned. (van Creveld(G), 81-2)

In his *Memoirs,* Eden did not mention 100,000 men. On the question of Turkey and Yugoslavia, Eden wrote that Koryzis wished "to draw our attention to the danger of precipitating a German attack. We should first consider whether the Greek forces and those that Great Britain could provide would be sufficient to give effective support to Greece, in view of the dubious attitude of Yugoslavia and Turkey. ... He also asked what we thought the attitude of Yugoslavia and Turkey was likely to be." (Eden, 200)

> I told M. Koryzis that we did not know what these two countries would do. Sir John Dill and I were to visit Ankara and hoped to get an indication then. ... I emphasized that it was important that we and the Greeks should take our decisions independently of the attitude of Turkey and Yugoslavia, since if we waited to find out what they would do, it might be too late to organize an effective resistance to a German attack on Greece. We then adjourned for the military to do their work. (Eden, 200)

A few hours later, General Papagos and the British military representatives met again. There are two accounts of what took place, Eden's and Papagos'. According to both:

> Papagos opened the meeting by explaining Greece's strategic position. In view of his commitments in Albania he could spare only three divisions to fight the Germans. As to the line that had to be held against them, this depended on the attitude of Yugoslavia. Should Yugoslavia come in on the Allied side, it would be necessary and possible to hold a line covering Salonika, since the city was vital to Yugoslavia as her only port outside the Adriatic. Should that not be the case, the Greek position in Thrace would become untenable, and the Greeks would withdraw to a line further south from the mouth of the river Aliakhmon to the Yugoslav border, the so-called Aliakhmon line. On this line the British, too, would have to deploy their forces, so that the combined defending armies would amount to eight divisions and one in reserve. After answering British queries as to the time he would need to withdraw his forces from Thrace to the Aliakhmon and the ports through which the British would have to disembark. Papagos asked whether everybody present "was in agreement with him on the military view he had expressed." The British answered that "from the military point of view" they "entirely agreed", and the meeting was then adjourned without having reached any decision. (van Creveld(G), 82)

**

As General Dill later informed General Kennedy, when he and Eden met the Greek Commander, General Papagos, on 22nd February,

> the plan he [Papagos] had propounded was that he should withdraw his forces from the frontier to the Aliakmon line, which was shorter and naturally strong, and that the stand should be made by

both the Greeks and the British. This was accepted by Wavell and Dill as 'a sound military plan offering a reasonable chance of stopping a German advance'. Wavell had thereupon ordered the movement of the British forces from Egypt to begin. (Kennedy, 100-101)

**

Excerpts from Eden's account of the military conference:

> [Papagos] realized the extreme importance of time, which made it impossible to wait for Yugoslavia and Turkey to declare themselves. He had therefore asked his Government for permission to begin the withdrawal [to the Aliakhmon line] as soon as possible and, in any case before a German move made the withdrawal look like a retreat. ... The time required to withdraw the troops from Thrace and Macedonia was twenty days. ...
>
> If Yugoslavia said tonight that she was going to fight, the Greeks would hold the Nestos line and ask the British to land at Salonika and Kavalla. Asked if the Greeks could cover disembarkation at Salonika, General Papagos said they would do their best: there were ten heavy and thirty-two light A.A. [Anti Aircraft] guns at Salonika. If the Aliakhmon line was held, these guns would remain at Salonika till the last phase of the withdrawal to the line ... (Eden, 200-201)

At 7:45 p.m. the British representatives met again, without the Greeks. They reached a "general agreement" :

> Unless we could be sure of Yugoslavia coming in, it was not possible to contemplate holding a line covering Salonika; in view of the doubtful attitude of Yugoslavia, the only sound plan from the military point of view was to stand on the Aliakhmon line. (van Creveld(G), 82-3)

Van Creveld said of this "general agreement" [that Yugoslavia was needed to defend Salonika] : "Since, however, this solution meant that the Allies would be virtually cut off from Yugoslavia it destroyed the hope of Yugoslav intervention, and with it the only premise under which British aid to Greece made sense at all." (van Creveld(G), 83)

> In a second plenary session that took place at 10.45 p.m., Papagos gave a resumé of the military situation as he saw it; Wavell then put forward the British point of view by saying that "in view of the uncertainty of the attitude of Yugoslavia and Turkey the only reasonable course was to make certain of the line indicated by General Papagos [i.e. the Aliakhmon]". Summing up, Eden said that "it was clear that the British and Greek representatives were in agreement on the military plans". He then enumerated the alternatives facing the Allies:
>
> 1   To withdraw the troops without waiting for Yugoslavia to declare herself.
> 2   To begin the withdrawal concurrently with an approach to the Yugoslav Government.
> 3   To wait until Yugoslavia made her intention clear. (van Creveld(G), 83)

Van Creveld then added that:

> It was decided to send a British staff officer to Yugoslavia in order to learn her intentions (subsequently the staff officer was replaced by a telegram) and also that 'PREPARATIONS [emphasis supplied] should at once be made and put into execution to withdraw the Greek advanced troops in Thrace and Macedonia to the line which we should ... hold if the Yugoslavs did not come in'. Finally, the British tried to seal Greece's commitment to fight the Germans by demanding to know 'the point at which Greece would break off relations with the German government and intern Germans in Greece'. However, the Greeks evaded the question and the matter was left to the consideration of the Greek government. (van Creveld(G), 83-4)

Eden wrote about this theme:

> We also spoke with the Greeks about how I should deal with the Turkish Government when I visited Ankara in a few days' time, and discussed how to get into touch with Prince Paul of Yugoslavia. It would have been too risky to send a staff officer to inform him of our decisions. Instead I instructed our Minister in Belgrade, Mr. Ronald Campbell, to tell Prince Paul that a German advance on Salonika seemed certain and that it was urgently necessary for us to know what Yugoslavia's attitude would be. I also suggested that the Prince Regent should send M.

> Dragiša Cvetković or M. Alexander Cincar-Marković, the two Ministers who had just been to Germany, to meet me in Athens or Istanbul. During the next two months Campbell and his small staff in Belgrade had to live and work at high pressure in an atmosphere of mounting tension. They never faltered in advice or action and the *Minister's [Campbell's] influence played a decisive part in shaping events.* (Eden, 203. Italics added.)

During the next two months Campbell and his small staff did not work alone on shaping events; they worked together with George Taylor and his SOE operatives, with personnel in the *Britanova* press agency and others, in an effort to overthrow Prince Paul's government.

* Inflating the figures of aid to Greece

General de Guingand wrote about his participation at the Tatoi conference:

> I only took my place at the table during the discussions which turned upon the purely military angle. … I was, however, present when three important items were discussed. First was the question of aid we were prepared to give the Greeks – men and weapons. Secondly, was the military opinion of what we hoped to achieve, in the event of German invasion. And thirdly, the Greek acceptance of our offer.
>   When I took my place at the table it was getting very late, and I noticed that everyone looked very grave – particularly the Greek Prime Minister. …
>   I think it was Eden who stressed and enumerated the 'formidable' resources which we were prepared to send over. It sounded pretty good, but if a real expert had carried out a more detailed investigation, I doubt whether those present would have been so satisfied. Totals of men and guns are generally impressive. In the aircraft flying over I had been asked to produce a list showing totals of items we were preparing to send. My first manpower figures excluded such categories as pioneers, and in the gun totals I only produced artillery pieces. This was nothing like good enough for one of Mr. Eden's party who was preparing the brief. He asked that the figures should be swelled into what to my mind were doubtful values. I felt that this was hardly a fair do, and bordering upon dishonesty. … (de Guingand, 49-50)

> The Greeks referred frequently to the question of Turkey and Yugo-Slavia. The danger of German advance through the latter was brought up on many occasions. If either or both of these countries came in against Germany, the whole outlook would be vastly improved. (de Guingand, 51)

After his presentation, de Guingand was asked to leave the room, while the assembly was going to draft the report to be sent to London. Remaining a few moments in the ante-room, the General noted:

> Eden came in looking buoyant. He strode over to the fire and warmed his hands, and then stood with his back to it dictating signals to his staff. They in turn looked nearly as triumphant as he did, and were positively oozing congratulations.
>   Presumably he has done his job, and accomplished what he set out to achieve. He was, therefore, no doubt entitled to be pleased with himself. But whether it was a job worth doing and in our best interests seemed to me very doubtful. (de Guingand, 51)

The *swelled figures of doubtful values* included the *100,000 men* that the British were going to send to Greece - Eden had said at Tatoi.

**

In another room, "a small meeting took place to discuss the provisions of equipment and munitions for the Greek Army. Their staff had produced a formidable list. No one could deny that the items were necessary, but it was obvious we should have great difficulty in meeting anything like their full demands." (de Guingand 49)

Doubts about the Aliakmon Line defense

After the Tatoi conference, Commander-in-Chief Wavell instructed General de Guingand to "stay behind and carry out a reconnaissance of the Aliakmon positions with the Greeks." (de Guingand 51-2) Wearing mufti, the General would go as a War Correspondent visiting the Albanian Front and other parts of Greece. With his Pressman's pass (written in Greek), accompanied by Greek officers, the General embarked on his journeys. (de Guingand, 52-3)

Their travels took them to Larissa, northwest of Athens, into Albania, to Mount Olympus, the Florina and Salonika area.

> We flew up close to Salonika and from our position we could see the great Struma and Varda [Vardar] rivers stretching away to the far horizon. The flight did not, I'm afraid, dispel my doubts about our ability to conduct a successful defence of the Aliakmon positions – in fact it increased them. The extent of the front appeared so immense. The country along the coast was by no means too difficult to make a turning movement in this area impossible. We flew over at a very low altitude and combed the various roads and tracks. (de Guingand, 60)

> The journey back to Athens on February 28th was pleasant. The sun shone and I looked at one or two potential ports on the way, arriving back late in the evening. A very few weeks later this road was to be the scene of a retreating army – an army heavily outnumbered, with little air support and short of heavy weapons. Above this army roared Stukas more or less as they pleased. Behind it was the sea, and another Dunkirk to be attempted. Poor old Army, not yet given a fair do, but despite that, these gallant soldiers from all over the Empire did not lose their morale. They were beginning, however, to lose their confidence in the higher direction of the war. (dr Guingand, 60)

**

On February 28, when General de Guingand's doubts about the defense of the Aliakmon Line were increasing, Foreign Minister Eden was in Ankara unsuccessfully attempting to draw Turkey into the Balkan Front, and SOE's George Taylor was in Belgrade, concluding that influencing the Serb public opinion was the best way to achieve British war goals.

** "... attempt to persuade the Yugoslav Government to play their part"

From Eden's diary entry for 22 February:

> I authorized Wavell to set his plans in motion and Dill and I worked until 3 a.m. preparing messages for London. ...
> Our chief anxiety is in respect of the air. Longmore is much weaker than I had thought and much weaker than he should be. Flow of aircraft out to him has been recently most disappointing. It must be speeded up at all costs, and I only pray that the Hun [the Germans] gives us time.
> In any event our decision was the only possible one. On this I have no doubt. (Eden, 203-4)

Eden sent Churchill a telegram which included references to Yugoslavia:

> From the ensuing discussion between the CIGS, Commander-in-Chief Middle East and Air Officer Commanding on the one hand, and General Papagos on the other hand, it emerged that in view of the doubtful attitude of Yugoslavia the only line that could be held and would give time for withdrawal of troops from Albania would be a line west of the Vardar-Olympus-Veria-Edessa-Kajmakcalan. If we could be sure of Yugoslav moves it should be possible to hold a line further north from the mouth of the Nestos to Beles covering Salonika. It would be impracticable, unless Yugoslavia came in, to hold a line covering Salonika in view of the exposure of the Greek left flank to German attack.
> In full agreement with the Greek Government the following detailed decisions were reached:
>
> a. In view of the importance of the Yugoslav attitude as affecting the redeployment of troops in Greece, it was agreed that I should make a further effort to attempt to persuade the Yugoslav Government *to play their part.*
> b. That the Greeks should at once make, and begin the execution of, preparations to withdraw the advance troops to the line which we should have to hold if the Yugoslavs were not willing to come in.
> c. That work should immediately be started on improving communications in Greece to facilitate the occupation of the line. (Carlton, 175-6. Italics added.)

"The existence of this telegram is not mentioned in Eden's memoirs" – noticed the biographer, Dr. David Carlton. (p. 176) Churchill, likewise, omitted the above quote in his history of the Second World War (Vol. III).

> Before the conference broke up in the early hours of 23 February, M. Kozyris, at Eden's request, stated formally that the Greek Government accepted with deep gratitude the offer of assistance made by the British Government, and that the military plan was completely acceptable. (McClymont, 103)

"On 22 February Eden and Dill had learned that Greece's reinforcement of Albania had left her with only three weak divisions on her border with Bulgaria." This information shocked Eden and Dill.(Hinsley et al, 362)

**

In a telegram reporting the agreement with the Greek Government, dated 24 February 1941, Eden stated that further efforts ought to be made to make Yugoslavia "come in". Churchill noted:

> Agreement was reached today [23] with the Greek Government on all points.
>
> 3. The President of [the Greek] Council, ... , reiterated the misgivings of the Greek Government lest insufficient British help should merely precipitate German attack, and stated that it was essential to determine whether available Greek forces and forces which we could provide would suffice to constitute efficacious resistance to the Germans, taking into account the doubtful attitude of Turkey and Yugoslavia. ... (Churchill(GA), 75)

In *The Grand Alliance* the date of this telegram is given as 24 Feb. 1941, while the date of the Tatoi agreement was the 23. This suggests that the telegram was not written immediately after the end of the conference.

**

As concluded at the meeting at Tatoi, Eden asked Prince Paul what his position would be. In the reply – which reached Eden five days later – the Prince confirmed that he would not let Axis troops pass through Yugoslavia, but refused to say precisely what Yugoslavia would do if Germany pushed through Bulgaria against Greece.

> But this was what the British wanted: *that the Yugoslavs should go to war, even if their country was by-passed.* Eden then summoned Campbell to Athens to discuss Prince Paul's position and sent him back to Belgrade with a personal letter urging the Prince to resist German demands and 'join with ourselves and the Greeks'. (Barker, 88. Italics added.)

Eden did attempt – very energetically – *to persuade the Yugoslav Government to play their part*. Understandably from his point of view, it was His Majesty's Government who would determine what *Yugoslavia's part* should be. And helping to implement that *part* were not only the Foreign Office personnel in Yugoslavia, but also various British institutions operating there, individuals engaged in various activities, overt and covert, including agents of the rarely mentioned Secret Intelligence Service and the recently formed super-secret Special Operations Executive (SOE).

"The real service" of Donovan for the British cause

Although deeply involved in decision of assisting Greece, Eden took time out on 22 February to suggest to the Prime Minister that, on Donovan's return to London, "We show him every attention and express our gratitude in anyway possible." "... it would strengthen his hand when he gets home" if Churchill agreed to send a message to the President, thanking both the President for sending Donovan, and the latter for the "judgment and energy ... the real service" he had rendered to "this country and our cause." (Smith, 87, 223n46)

**

While the Greeks at Tatoi were "reluctantly and under pressure" agreeing not to fight for Salonika and the north but to withdraw to the Aliakhmon Line, the first clash between Germany's Afrikacorps and the British also occurred on 22 February 1941 in North Africa. (Bennett, 31, 37)

In London, on 23 February, Cadogan commented on Eden's reports from Tatoi: "Telegrams in from A. who seems to have plumped for helping Greece (he is in Athens now). That is certainly respectable, *but we must eventually be beaten there.*" (Dilks(ed), 358. Italics added.)

In a lengthy meeting on 23/24 February, the Chiefs of Staff "produced a paper in which they advised that, on balance, the Greek enterprise should go forward." (Kennedy, 85) However, they also concluded that without cooperation from Yugoslavia or Turkey British support of Greece was "unlikely to have a favorable effect on the war as a whole". (Hinsley *et al*, 361)

> ... It seemed to me very wrong that the Cabinet had never asked for or received a purely military view from either the Chiefs of Staff or from Wavell. All the service advice given on this problem had been coloured by political considerations – a very dangerous procedure. The array of opinion in favour of the project was now formidable. I did my best to press my point of view without avail. (Kennedy, 85)

"Full steam ahead" with the enterprise in Greece, 24 February 1941

At the Cabinet meeting on 24 February, Churchill said that, based on the evidence presented, he was in favor of the plan. "It was then approved unanimously, ..." (Kennedy, 85) "Spread on the table were optimistic signals from Wavell and Dill, together with the COS assessment. They favoured going ahead. ... He [Churchill] also stressed the fact that Dill had changed his views and was now in favour, although he had previously doubted whether " Germany would be successfully resisted." (Lamb, 88)

> Churchill cabled to Eden on 24 February: 'while being under no illusion, we all send you order "Full steam ahead",' but although the mood had definitely changed in London the War Cabinet took Eden's advice and formally assumed responsibility for it. (Rhodes James, 251)

In Greek historian Ioannis Koliopoulos' opinion,

> The British were determined to send help to Greece mainly for political reasons: (a) to commit Greece to fight the Germans; (b) to placate world public opinion, and particularly the American opinion, since Britain had solemnly assured the independence of Greece in April 1939; and (c) to draw Yugoslavia and Turkey into the war. Moreover, British help had to be sent at the earliest possible moment both in order to prevent the possibility of Greece coming to terms with the Axis and to make resistance against the enemy worthwhile. (Koliopoulos, 44)

After the Cabinet meeting the evening of 24 February, Cadogan wrote:

> Read Chiefs of Staff report endorsing proposals for a Balkan expedition to help Greece. On all moral and sentimental (and consequently American) grounds, one is driven to the grim conclusion. But it *must*, in the end, be a failure. ... A. [Eden] has rather jumped us into this. But it is impressive that *Wavell,* and Dill endorse him. ... It's a nasty decision, but I *think,* on balance, I agree with it. P.M. [Churchill] evidently made up his mind. (Dilks(ed), 358. Italics in the source.)

SOE's mission in the Balkans: to help British operations in Greece

As shown above, SOE's George Francis Taylor was also on a special mission in Greece and Yugoslavia during the Eden-Dill mission. Eden was well informed of Taylor's mission and Taylor knew of theirs. Reporting from Athens on 26 February to his chief in London, Sir Frank Nelson, about the organization and plans of SOE in the Balkans, Taylor pointed out that his report *was written rather from the angle of what help SOE could be to General Wavell* - which was "the only possible point of view to take" "in the present situation and with the recent decision" – i.e. the Anglo-Greek agreement of 22/23 February, at Tatoi.

> The Foreign Secretary's mission was paralleled by SO2 Deputy Director George Taylor's tour of the Near East to establish post-occupational wireless networks and sabotage and resistance, to support

the Commander-in-Chief, Middle East, General Wavell's plans and General Wilson's operations in Greece. (Onslow, 41)

Taylor was going to move to Belgrade on 27 February to provide whatever help SOE could to Gen. Wavell – "to persuade the Yugoslav Government *to play their part*", i.e., to defend approaches to Salonika from the expected German invasion – by force, if necessary.

Pro-British Serb public opinion ... *SOE's best hope* ...

In accordance with the decisions reached at the Tatoi Conference,

> As for the Yugoslavs, Eden continued to press them, but there was little indication of commitment. ... And despite the fact that the plans with the Greeks had been made on the basis that they could not count on the Yugoslavs, none the less without them the prospect of successfully defending Salonika were slim. (Lawlor, 227)

It was not only Eden who pressed the Yugoslavs; in late February King George VI also pressured Prince Paul. He wrote, *inter alia:* "... My government are faced with decisions of vital importance ... which depend to a large extent on the attitude of Yugoslavia as the central factor of South-East Europe." Therefore, the King personally appealed to the Prince to make a "full statement" on the Yugoslav government's position as soon as possible. (Barker, 88)

On 26 February 1941 - while Eden was traveling to Turkey to persuade her leaders to "come "in" – George Taylor sent, from Athens, an extensive Report to the SOE London. Moving from Athens to Belgrade on 27 February, he was assessing the situation and searching for best ways and means to accomplish his mission.

"*On his arrival Taylor assessed pro-British Serb public opinion as SOE's best hope of influencing the Yugoslav government's policy.*"In addition to the contacts with the groups "subsidized" by the British, "SOE's political contacts also included the opposition parties – Radicals, Democrats and the Yugoslav National Party – which had many influential members who held sway over Serb public opinion." "SOE was in almost daily contact" with them. (Williams, 28-9) "Taylor regarded SOE's influence with the party leaders as 'undoubtedly effective in preventing this good material being led astray'." (Williams, 29. Italics added.)

> Since Dalton, spurred on by Churchill, had sent George Taylor to Belgrade early in 1941, S.O.E. had stepped up their activities, aiming, first, *by means of political agitation and propaganda* to deter Prince Paul from signing the [Tripartite] pact, and second, if that failed, *to stage a coup against him*. Agitation against the pact became vociferous from early March on. (Barker, 91. Italics added.)

With outstanding support from Thomas Masterson – the head of SOE in Belgrade, who was transferred there from Rumania in November 1940 – and with the cooperation of various British entities, with the British-subsidized disloyal domestic opposition political parties, some domestic patriotic organizations and other individuals - Taylor helped tremendously to implement HMG's idea of what *Yugoslavia's part* should be.**(See Part Two)**

Failure of Eden's mission in Turkey, 26 February – 1 March, and pressure on Yugoslavia

Following the meeting at Tatoi, Eden returned to Cairo and then proceeded on to Turkey, arriving there on 26 February. That same day he informed Churchill that he and General Dill had a discussion with the Turkish President of the Council, the Minister for Foreign Affairs and Marshal Chakmak "on extremely frank and friendly basis". The Turks reiterated their determination to fight if attacked by Germany,

> But since Turkey's forces at present had no offensive power they considered the common cause would be better served by Turkey remaining out of the war until their deficiencies had been remedied and she could be employed with the maximum effect. ...

> The upshot of these discussions is that Turkey undertakes in any event to enter the war at some stage. She will of course do so immediately she is attacked. But if she is given time by Germans to re-equip herself she will take advantage of it, and will then make war at a moment favourable to the common cause, when her weight can be used with real effect. (Churchill(GA), 97)

Prof. Dilks commented on that meeting:

> The Turkish military situation proved to be a most disappointing one. Marshal Chakmak and his officers explained that they would not declare war when Germany attacked Greece – which should have been a Turkish obligation – because, lacking modern weapons, they would be a liability. (Dilks(ed), 359)

Dr. Lawlor noted that Eden had concluded, "from the harmonious exchanges - possibly as the result of wishful thinking - that Turkey would enter war at some stage, or immediately, if attacked; that 'the frank and realistic outlook of the Turks' had been impressive. All had left 'with the feeling that they are genuinely loyal and determined to play their part'. (Lawlor, 226)

> He received a friendly reception and was congratulated on the wisdom of his decision to assist Greece. But his hosts were no more willing than before to promise any immediate aid to Greece. (Carlton, 177-8).

On 28 February, Cadogan commented on Eden's report from Ankara in his diary:

> Telegram from A. at Angora, which puzzles me. It is couched in jaunty and self-satisfied terms, talking of the 'frankness' and 'friendliness' and 'realism' of the Turks. The 'reality' is that they won't do a damned thing. Has he had his head turned by crowds of hand-clapping Turks? **(#)** And what is he now to say to the Yugoslavs and Greeks? The former will now of course curl up, *and we shall be alone with the Greeks to share their inevitable disaster. ...* (Dilks(ed), 359. Italics added.)

(#) A ball had been thrown in Eden's honor by the Turks. He left impression of having a gullible 'faith in Turkey's loyalty', creating a 'tremendous superficial clamour' while talking 'in generalities', completely oblivious to Balkan intricacies. He was obsessed with his favorite plan of forming a Balkan block with Yugoslavia. (Gorodetsky, 109)

While Eden was failing to get Turkey to "resist" Germany, on 28 February German troops were bridging the Danube from Rumania to Bulgaria. Based on Eden's telegram to Churchill of 28 February, Dr Lawlor concluded:

> Eden had failed to get anything out of the Turks who made no promises, ... They had refused to commit themselves on whether they would look on a German advance through Bulgaria and across the Greek frontier as a *casus belli*. ... they did nothing to indicate that their actions would be as Britain wanted, or that they were prepared, practically and in principle, to take the necessary steps to prevent German domination of the Middle East." (Lawlor, 226-7)

Churchill to Eden: *"Your main appeal should now be made to Yugoslavia"*, 1 March 1941

On 1 March, Churchill replied to Eden's report of 28 February, *inter alia:*

> Your main appeal should now be made to Yugoslavia. *A sudden move south by Yugoslavia would produce an Italian disaster of the first magnitude, possibly decisive on whole Balkan situation.* If at the same time Turkey declared war the enemy could not gather sufficient forces for many months, during which our air strength will grow. I am absolutely ready to go in on a serious hazard if there is reasonable chance of success, at any rate for a few months, and all preparations should go forward at fullest speed. (Churchill(GA), 97-8. Churchill subsequently added Italics.)

Then he continued with a significant consideration for Greece, never shown for Yugoslavia:

> But I should like you so to handle matters in Greece that if upon final consideration of all the factors, ... , you feel that there is not even a reasonable hope, you should still retain power to liberate

Greeks from any bargain and at the same time liberate ourselves. Evidently you and we have a few days in which to make our final decision. Meanwhile all should proceed as arranged. (Churchill(GA), 98)

On 1 March, Cadogan continued to comment on Eden's failure in Turkey:

> Glad to find P.M. [Prime Minister] sent a sobering telegram to our temperamental Secretary of State, saying 'You appear to have got nothing out of the Turks. 'And that is true. ... This stunt trip is most disastrous one. ... What the hell is A. going to say to Greeks and Yugoslavs? *It is a diplomatic and strategic blunder of the first order.* ... B.B.C. tonight announce signature of Axis Pact by Bulgaria and entry of German troops. A real answer to A.'s silly antics. (Dilks(ed), 360. Italics added.)

"Rumors about a possible Italo-Greek peace"

"Meanwhile, with Eden's back turned on Athens, rumors about a possible Italo-Greek peace again filled the air." – wrote Martin van Creveld. On pages 84-85 of his essay "Prelude to Disaster: ... " he presented information on this subject originating from Washington, Berlin, Moscow, Ankara and Bucharest. Because of particular interest, shown herein is his account of the British ambassador in Ankara, Hughe Knatchbull-Hugessen's, report to the Foreign Office of 4 March 1941:

> ... he reported a letter from Hitler to [the President of Turkey, [Ismet] Inonü, upon the delivery of which [the German ambassador Franz von] Papen had said that 'personally' he thought 'Greece could be induced by pressure to make peace with Italy and he even hoped that the British would authorize this. Greece could have an "honourable peace". ' (van Creveld, 85)

On 6 March, Field Marshal Wilhelm Keitel, Chief of the Wehrmacht High Command, told General Halder that Hitler hoped "to bring Greece to heel without force".

**

Meanwhile ...

On 1 March, Bulgaria joined the Tripartite Pact, thus completing the encirclement of Yugoslavia by the Pact signatories, and allowing Germany, the next day, to move her army – from Rumania into Bulgaria, across the Danube - for the attack on Greece. That caused multiple reactions by the British. Churchill instructed Eden: "Your main appeal should now be made to Yugoslavia." The Prime Minister also noted: "The whole defence of Salonika depended on their [Yugoslav Government's] coming in, and it was vital to know what they would do". [Churchill(GA), 98) To make the Yugoslavs "come in", both overt diplomatic and covert SOE activities were increased.

Chapter 7

Unexpected change in Greece's decision

On 2 March, the Cabinet approved Eden's and Dill's going back to Athens. (Kennedy, 86)

In one of Eden's biographer's opinion, "... Eden's return to Athens on 2 March was arranged as a public spectacle designed to boost the morale of the Greek people for the inevitable ordeal. But on arrival Eden and Dill were informed, ... , that no Greek troops had been withdrawn [from the frontier] to the Aliakmon line." (Carlton, 179) Along the same line: "I believe that on his return he [Eden] did receive a great ovation – I often wonder whether he deserved it!" (de Guingand, 53)

> When Eden returned to Athens on the same day [2 March] he found Papagos 'unaccommodating and defeatist'. Hence, there was no question of the British demanding fresh proofs of loyalty from Greece; rather, her determination to resist had to be bolstered. Here, however, the British immediately suffered a heavy blow. Eden and Dill had hardly arrived at the British legation when General Haywood informed them that the Greeks had not yet begun their withdrawal from Thrace to the Aliakhmon. Eden regarded this as a breach of the agreement of 22 February; Papagos in his memoirs has claimed that the decision had been made conditional on receiving an answer from the Yugoslavs. Since the decision to withdraw the Greek army from Thrace had been made in an exclusively *British* meeting, whereas at the plenary session it had been agreed that *preparations* should be made towards that move, it seems that, on balance, history must support Papagos' version of exactly what was agreed on at Tatoi. (van Creveld(G), 85-6)

In Martin van Creveld's opinion,

> Through the period from 22 February to 2 March Papagos seems to have been more optimistic than either the British or his own government about the prospects of Yugoslav intervention, and this must have been the real motive for his reluctance to move his troops from their exposed positions in Thrace. (van Creveld(G), 87)

In Koliopoulos' opinion,

> The second round of Anglo- Greek talks (March 2—4) came as a result of the "unfortunate misunderstanding" a week earlier. The reason given by Papagos for his failure to withdraw the Greek forces to the Aliakmon line was that he had put off the withdrawal expecting a reply from the Yugoslavs. ... For his part, Eden had returned to Athens empty-handed: both the Yugoslavs and the Turks had been evasive to the point of outright refusal to be accommodating in any way. (Koliopoulos, 44)

Gen. de Guingand provided more information. At 1 a.m. on 3 March, Lt.-Gen. Arthur Smith "told me that complications had set in and that I must fly back early that morning to Cairo and report matters to Genera Wavell. He then proceeded to dictate to me a memorandum setting out the salient difficulties that had emerged. Apparently Papagos was not happy with the military situation; he was a realist, and as the time drew near, he must have had grave doubts as to the soundness of the plan." In de Guingand's opinion, the first among the difficulties "was the prospect of fighting the Germans without any assistance from the Turks and Yugo-Slavs." A significant sentence towards the end of Gen. Smith's clear account ran something like this: "From the strictly military point of view this would provide us the opportunity of withdrawing from what appears now to be an unsound venture." De Guingand "took this to mean that the Greeks did not consider our help could save them." (de Guingand, 61)

"He [Gen. Wavell] arrived on 3 March and discussions have been practically continuous" until 5 March, when Eden reported about them to Churchill. [Churchill(GA), 99) A decision was reached to send British troops into Greece anyway.

> The decision to go ahead and take up positions alongside the three Greek divisions on the Aliakhmon was accordingly made in Athens and confirmed, not without much soul searching, by the War Cabinet in London. However, the whole case for extending British aid to Greece was based on

the assumption that Turkey, and especially Yugoslavia, would join the Allies; by their decision to deploy on the Aliakkhon, the Allies destroyed this hope, for this meant the abandonment of Salonika as the only port through which Yugoslavia could be supplied, and left Yugoslavia surrounded by a ring of Axis forces on every one of the frontiers except one running through the very difficult country of Western Macedonia. (van Creveld(G), 88)

Churchill thoroughly approved SOE's support for the *coup d'état in* Yugoslavia, 2 March 1941

After receiving an unsatisfactory reply from Prince Paul to his suggestion to send to Athens or Istanbul one of the two Ministers who had just been in Germany (Cvetković or Cincar-Marković), Eden invited Campbell to Athens. Churchill noted:

> On March 2 Mr. Campbell, our Ambassador at Belgrade, met Mr. Eden in Athens. He said that the Yugoslavs were frightened of Germany and unsettled internally by political difficulties. There was a chance, however, that if they knew our plans for aiding Greece they might be ready to help. Mr. Eden and the Greeks feared lest the enemy should find out. ... (Churchill(GA), 98)

**

In the meantime, on 1 March, Bulgaria joined the Tripartite Pact unconditionally. The German Twelfth Army was entering Bulgaria from Rumania. At the Tatoi conference it was decided that Eden would attempt *to persuade the Yugoslav Government to play their part.* What was a *"premature action"* in the summer of 1940, was a timely action now. Diplomatic pressure by the British Minister in Belgrade on persuading Prince Paul was unsuccessful so far. Other means and instruments had to be used. There was an opportunity for SOE and their domestic "contacts" and ""friends", *to take matters into their own hands,* as Taylor reported to Sir Frank Nelson from Athens on 26 February. Therefore, secret SOE operations were discussed on 2 March, at a meeting at Chequers, presided over by Churchill. Dr. Hugh Dalton presented

> a secret plan to deal with Prince Paul. If and when the Regent signed a deal with Hitler, SOE undercover agents in Belgrade would support a *coup d'état.* Already they were in contact with dissident senior Royal Yugoslav Air Force officers and secret subsidies were being fed to anti-government newspapers and politicians.
> Churchill thoroughly approved. Three weeks after the Chequers meeting Prince Paul signed Hitler's pact [25 March] and *London gave the go-ahead to SOE Belgrade.* Within forty-eight hours Army and Air Force officers launched a successful coup. ... (Stafford (C), 211-12. Italics added.)

At this meeting with Dalton "Churchill showed himself very well briefed on SOE's plans and operations, and keen to support them. The Yugoslav coup later that month undoubtedly helped, because Churchill rationed his time and energy. Until Dalton could show results, he [Churchill] was reluctant to spend time with him." (D. Stafford, "Churchill and SOE", in Mark Seaman(ed), *Special Operation Executive,* p.49)

All subsequent SOE decisions about the *coup d'état,* made later in Belgrade, were based on this fundamental decision made at Chequers.

This meeting is noteworthy because on 2 March – two days *before* Prince Paul met with Hitler, and 15 days *before* the Yugoslav Crown Council decided, in principle, to join the Tripartite Pact, but at the same time that German troops were crossing from Rumania into Bulgaria – the British war leaders had decided on the timing of the coup in Belgrade. The Serbian conspirators were not even mentioned, let alone asked for an opinion or concurrence.

Eager to be in Churchill's good graces, *to show results,* and aware that the actions in the Balkans were considered by Churchill to be the *acid test* for the SOE, Dalton was bound to alert and prepare the SOE in Belgrade to execute the SOE's secret plan. His chief covert operative, George Taylor, was already in Belgrade, assessing the situation, planning the organization of resistance once Yugoslavia was occupied by Germany.

Eden was well aware of Taylor's mission in the Balkans, and Taylor, in turn, was well informed of the Anglo-Greek agreement of 22/23 February 1941, and was doing all that was necessary and possible to assist the British expedition in Greece.

**

While new negotiations were going on in Athens, on 3 March Cadogan wrote in his diary:

> ... He [Churchill] authorized me to read [to the Cabinet] A.'s [Anthony's] raspberry from Ankara. Which I did, and left them all looking rather blue-nosed. ... Everyone's reaction is the same – how *can* one account for the jaunty tone of a recital of *complete* failure? Germans have swarmed over Bulgaria, and here we are. I confess everything looks to me as black as black. ... (Dilks[ed], 360. Italics in the source.)

On 4 March at noon, Churchill returned from Chequers, "and saw Colonel Donovan, just back from the Balkans, *where the stage is set and the curtain about to rise."* (Colville, 359. Italics added.)

Eden's letter to Prince Paul, 3 March

Upon Campbell's arrival in Athens, Eden wrote a letter that Campbell was to take to Prince Paul. Dated Athens, 3rd March, 1941, the letter was published in Eden's memoirs in its entirety – more than 40 lines. Here are a few excerpts:

> ... Germany's objective in the Balkans is to subdue Greece and to immobilize Turkey. If Germany could achieve these dual objects and in the course of so doing occupy Salonika and dominate the Straights, Yugoslavia would be at Germany's mercy. Yugoslavia's fate must then surely be like that of Roumania, ...This seems clearly to be the inevitable sequence of events unless we can take steps together to prevent it, as I am confident that we can.
> ... It has been made abundantly clear to me in my visits to Turkey and Greece that neither is prepared to be the dupe of German assurances, and I have no doubt that Turkey and Greece if attacked will resist by force.
> ...I have no hesitation in urging you most earnestly to decide to resist this evil [German methods of bleeding and disruption] and to join with us and Greece in an attempt to withstand it.
> ... In choosing the alternative to resist with us ... You will then be able to face the future with the greater courage and hope, rooted as they will be in your own splendid traditions and brave deeds. ... (Eden, 215-16)

Eden then gave Campbell additional instructions on how to approach Prince Paul, including the request to send a Yugoslav staff officer to Athens at once to, basically, discuss the defense of Salonika which, in Eden's opinion, depended largely on Yugoslavia.

**

It is shown above that Hitler's gradually expanding plans to "subdue Greece" were a function of aiding Italy, and simultaneously preventing a British foothold in Greece. Although Turkey was a formal ally of Great Britain – and therefore expected to honor her obligations - her self-interests at the moment demanded her "immobilization".

Eden was not keeping Prince Paul fairly and fully clued in on this point. He wrote that if Turkey were attacked, she would defend herself. Like the Greek and Turkish Governments, so had the Yugoslav Government repeatedly stated that Yugoslavia would defend herself if attacked. But Eden did not inform Prince Paul that Turkey did not want to "come in" and would not consider a German attack on Greece as *casus belli*.

Hitler's letter to the Turkish President, 4 March 1941

A day after Eden's letter to Prince Paul, i.e. on 4 March, the same day Hitler was meeting with Prince Paul, Hitler sent a letter to the Turkish President "informing him that German troops would not come near the Turkish frontier." The Turkish President replied that the Turks would not initiate any military action against Germany. (Jukić, 42)

"The Turks have nothing quixotic in their make-up. They are realists. They keep out of conflicts in which their interests are not directly involved. But if need be they know how to fight and how to die." – explained Turkey's Ambassador in Moscow. (Krylov, 74) They kept out of the conflict even as they had a treaty of alliance with Britain.
   Not so the Putschists in Yugoslavia – who had no alliance with Britain at all!

*** German-Yugoslav negotiations: Prince Paul's meeting with Hitler, 4 March 1941

Also on 4 March, while Eden was still in Athens, "Prince Paul left Belgrade on a secret visit to Berchtesgaden, and under dire pressure undertook verbally that Yugoslavia would follow the example of Bulgaria". (Churchill[GA}, 159)   He went "with his government's approval but without telling the British"; "secretly met with Hitler, who demanded that Yugoslavia should sign the Tripartite Pact. Since German troops were pouring into Bulgaria, so that Yugoslavia was militarily hemmed in by the Axis on three sides, it must have required some courage for Prince Paul to refuse an answer." (Barker, 88)

According to van Creveld:

> The meeting between him [Prince Paul] and Hitler took place on 4 March, and we know its details from a summary Ribbentrop sent Heeren [his Minister in Belgrade] two days later. After his usual harangue about the inevitability of Germany's victory, Hitler cleverly argued that after the liquidation of the British in Greece the German troops would not stay in the Balkans indefinitely; if Yugoslavia failed to stake her claim to Salonika, the city might fall to the Bulgarians or to the Italians. 'Visibly impressed' by these remarks, Prince Paul said that, although his personal sympathies were for England, Yugoslavia had no choice but to consider the course offered by Germany. He expressed the fear that agreement on his part would lead to revolution in Yugoslavia, then took his leave. (van Creveld, 127)

According to the German archives, Ribbentrop wrote:

> The Prince Regent was visibly impressed by these remarks, but he explained frankly how difficult for him the decision was which the Führer advised him to take; and he said plainly that, as far as he personally was concerned, the Greek descent of his wife, his personal sympathies for England, and his attitude toward Italy as well were opposed to it. Nevertheless, the Price Regent termed a further agreement with Italy a possible first step along the course counseled by us. (Ristić, 56)

**

On 30 March 1941, the American Minister in Belgrade, Arthur Bliss Lane, reported to the Secretary of State:

> With regards to Prince Paul's meeting with Hitler at Berchtesgaden on March 4 or 5 (not 11) I am informed by reliable source that Hitler said to Prince during 2-hour interview Yugoslavia must sign Tripartite Pact in own interest *as in June or July he was going to attack Russia.*
> British Minister says foregoing fits in with information he has. (FRUS1, 973. Italics added.)

Therefore: according to the American Minister in Belgrade, both he and the British Minister were informed about the meeting and Hitler's intention to attack the Soviet Union.

> Hitler invites Yugoslavia's Prince Paul to take his share in the "New World Order". Prince Paul gathers from Hitler's comments that Germany will invade the Soviet Union. He will tell his brother-in-law, the King of Greece, who will tell the British.
> (1941 Timeline   http://www.fsmitha.com/time/1941.htm   7/26/12)

**

The developments after the Hitler – Prince Paul meeting are outlined as follows:

> Immediately after his return from Berghof Prince Paul summoned a crown council to discuss the German demands. A thorough examination of courses open to Yugoslavia resulted in the conclusion that accession to the pact, however distasteful, was the least unpalatable course – provided some conditions could be fulfilled. Two days later a list of these conditions was presented to Heeren. If Yugoslavia signed, would Germany and Italy guarantee in writing that:
>
> 1. The sovereignty and territorial integrity of Yugoslavia will be respected.
> 2. No military assistance will be requested of Yugoslavia and also no passage or transportation of troops through the country during the war.

3. Yugoslavia's interest in a free outlet to the Aegean Sea through Salonika will be taken into account in the reorganization of Europe. (van Creveld, 128)

An affirmative answer, Cincar Markovic claimed, would 'make it much easier for the government to agree to the desired policy'. By now, German troops had already entered Bulgaria and were rapidly marching southward. Although [the German] Twelfth army headquarters was complaining about the congestion in Bulgaria and continually pointing at the Yugoslav railways as the only possible solution, Heeren, in his comments on the Yugoslav demands, expressed the opinion that they presented a *condicio sine qua non*. Unless they were granted, further talks would be necessary, and by the time these got under way the entire question of passage was outdated. What was more, the Yugoslavs were clearly determined to resist the demand for transit; they were even reported to be mining their railways. Under the circumstances, it must have seemed to Hitler that partial success securing his flank and linking Yugoslavia to the Axis was better than no success at all, and on 8 March he wrote to Mussolini that he on his part was ready to agree to the Yugoslav demands. (van Creveld, 128)

It seems that the content of Prince Paul's talks in Berghof were not kept in confidence. "Stalin had been informed about the guarantees which Hitler was offering Yugoslavia in return for joining the Axis." (Gorodetsky, 139)

... Stalin was briefed by 'Sophocles', the military attaché in Belgrade, about Prince Paul's agreement to join the Axis during his meeting with Hitler in early March. Reliable sources in the palace revealed that, in an attempt to discourage the Yugoslavs from playing the Russian card, Hitler had disclosed to the Prince his intentions of abandoning the plans for war against England in favour of seizing the Ukraine and Baku in April-May. (Gorodetsky, 139-40)

Ilija Jukić provided the following information on this subject:
From the end of January 1941 on, the Yugoslav Government was getting the information of Hitler's preparation for an attack on Russia from various sources. The most important was the report by the Yugoslav Ambassador in Moscow, Milan Gavrilović, sent by a courier in mid-February, that Hitler had decided to attack Russia between 15 May and 22 June – the date depending on the weather conditions. This report was confirmed from Slovakia, where the road-signs for the German army were pointing toward the Russian border. In addition, Prince Paul was getting more information from the Yugoslav Military Attaché in Berlin, Colonel [Vladimir] Vauhnik **(#)**, which he then shared with the Vice-Premier Maček.
Before Maček went to the first Crown Council's meeting, on 6 March, to hear Prince Paul's report about his talks with Hitler, Jukić informed him of the Gavrilović's report; Maček, in turn, relayed this information to [Fran] Kulovec [the Slovene representative in the Government]. "Svi učesnici na tom Vijeću bili su upoznati s tim Hitlerovim planovima ovako ili onako." ((All participant on that Council had been acquainted with those Hitler's plans one way or another.))
Information of Hitler's pending attack on Russia was bound to influence the reasoning and subsequent decision of the Council on adhesion to the Tripartite Pact: there was a need to endure Hitler's pressure, at any price, until at least Russia was involved in the war with Hitler. (Jukić(65), 134-5)

(#) On 15/16 March Col. Vauhnik obtained information that the Soviet Union would be attacked by the end of May, with 200 divisions, divided into three army groups, with support from the satellite countries. He relayed this information immediately to the Yugoslav main General Staff, with a request to keep it in the strictest secrecy. He sent a similar information to the court-adjutant of Prince Paul, but never received a confirmation of the reception. (Vauhnik, 130-1)

Arrival of the British Expeditionary Force into Greece

Meanwhile, in Greece, the advance guards of the British Expeditionary Force - "withdrawn from the desert army, which was thereby dangerously depleted – began to disembark on 4 March. It was the start of an ill-fated venture." (Keegan, 149) Also on 4 March, Admiral of the Fleet, Sir Andrew Cunningham, warned Churchill of "the considerable naval risks" in the Mediterranean, involved in moving the Army, Royal Air Force, stores and vehicles to Greece. "If the Germans started an air offensive from Bulgaria we must expect losses in the convoys both at sea and at their ports of disembarkation". (Churchill(GA), 97-8)

**

British troops were disembarking in Greece in the first week of March in accordance with the schedule. However,

> The effect of the Greek commitment had by this time begun to be felt in Libya. Our forces there had been so weakened, to provide for Greece, that they were unable to maintain their positions in face of German attacks. As our troops began to arrive in Greece the Desert Army was in full retreat from Benghazi to the Egyptian front. (Kennedy, 86)

"The expedition, under the command of General [Henry Maitland (Jumbo)] Wilson, started to move to Greece on the 4 March." (Ismay, 201)

> In view of Britain's deployment of the four divisions to Greece, Hitler now decided that [Operation] Marita's [invasion of Greece] objects would not be limited to securing a strategic position in Greece from which the Luftwaffe might dominate the Aegean and eastern Mediterranean; they were to comprehend the occupation of Greece outright. (Keegan, 150)

Whether four full divisions or fewer landed, the British Foreign Secretary considered their arrival a very important event. "The presence of British and Dominion forces in Greece had directly influenced events in Yugoslavia." (Eden, 229) It was indeed important on military grounds, but even more so for its "black-propaganda" effects in Belgrade. Propaganda played a substantial part in the British intent to "influence Serb public opinion" in favor of British policies, examined in **Part Two.** An illustration of how the propaganda was spread, and of its effects on "the Serbian oppositionists" and "the Simović crowd", is shown in **Appendix B.**

When *"the curtain rose",* and the stage was revealed, it was evident that there were no three hundred thousand British troops in Greece, no mighty air armada and war ships – as the black propaganda claimed, and as the *"Serbian oppositionists"* and *"the Simović crowd"* believed. "In actual fact, on April 6, the day the Germans invaded Greece, the British had about 62,000 men there, most of them landed after mid-March. They also had about 80 aircraft and some tanks and artillery against an enemy force at least ten times as powerful." (Petrov, 176n55)

Early planning for evacuation of BEF from Greece

Serving on the Joint Planning Staff, where he also served as the secretary of the Commanders-in-Chief Committee, de Guingand "was involved in controversy when it was discovered he had on his own initiative been planning from an early date the evacuation of the expeditionary force to Greece. However, with the support of the naval and air C-in-Cs he was allowed to continue with his prescient plans." (http://en.wikipedia.org/wiki/Freddie_de_Guingand 8/16/12)

Naval C-in-C, Admiral Andrew Cunningham, wrote: "Indeed, when the decision to send troops was finally taken, we started at once to think of how we should bring them out." (McClymont, 117n2) General de Guingand himself wrote about it:

> In spite of this firm decision [of sending troops to Greece], many of us felt extremely unhappy. In the J.P.S. we considered we should be failing in our duty if we did not start writing a paper dealing with an evacuation. We started this in the utmost secrecy very soon after my return from Greece [on 3 March], i.e. whilst our forces were in the process of being transported over to that country. (de Guingand, 61-2)

> ... General Wavell realised very rightly that no mention of such a course should reach the fighting soldiers, and the study was therefore kept strictly within the orbit of the planners. Later, however, when the troops came under the full weight of the German attack [the 2nd week of April], and it became patently clear that the Aliakmon Line could never be held for very long, the planners asked their respective chiefs to be allowed to set certain preparatory arrangements for evacuation in action. (de Guingand, 65)

> ... The Navy and the R.A.F. [Royal Air Force] decided that the time had now come to set certain machinery for evacuation in motion, but the Army's hands were tied. (de Guingand, 66)

De Guingand was assigned to go to Greece as the member of the Joint Planning Staff "to start clewing up inter-Service plans". General Wavell allowed him to go "- but only upon pain of death if I mentioned anything to the Army in Greece." (de Guingand, 66)

> The end of story is well known; how the evacuation took place, and all our valuable equipment and transport was left behind in Greece. How a gallant attempt was made to hold Crete; how we lost most things other than our honour. ... (de Guingand, 66)

The realism, foresight and advice of military planners in Cairo and London were dismissed for political reasons. How did the C-in-C of the Middle East feel when confronted with evacuation plans when the Germans just began attacking Greece?

**

Unexpectedly, as the British troops began moving to Greece, Eden and Dill visited Athens again and found a

"changed and disturbing situation" in Greece.   5 March

Lord Hastings Ismay, Churchill's former Chief of Staff, wrote in his memoirs:

> On 5 March a bombshell reached London in the shape of a report from Eden that he and Dill had visited Athens again, and found 'a changed and disturbing situation and an atmosphere quite different' from that of their last visit. General Papagos now offered only sixteen to twenty-three battalions for the defence of the Aliakmon line, instead of the thirty-five that we had been led to expect; and he was no longer prepared to order any withdrawals from the Albanian front. Nevertheless, the military advisers on the spot still 'did not consider it by any means a hopeless proposition to check and hold the German advance.' (Ismay, 199)

On 5 March, Eden and Dill reported to the Prime Minister :

> On arrival here we found a changed and disturbing situation and the atmosphere quite different from that of our last visit. ... We had expected that this withdrawal [of all troops in Macedonia] to the Alikhmon line had already begun. Instead we found that no movement had in fact commenced. ... (Churchill(GA), 99)

The British agreed to "Accept three Greek divisions offered for the Alikhmon line, the equivalent of about sixteen to twenty-three battalions, instead of thirty-five we had been led to expect on our previous visit, and to build our concentration behind this." [Churchill(GA), 100]

Also on 5 March Colville wrote into his diary:

> ... an alarming telegram arrived from Eden. It showed the Greek situation in a somber light. Eden, Dill and Wavell have found General Papagos discouraged and obviously weakened by the loss of Metaxas. They have accepted a strategic position which will mean that our troops will find themselves in a dangerous plight. Yugoslavia is weak and vacillating; Turkey is in no position to do anything but remain on the defensive. Eden says: "This is as tough a proposition as ever I have known." (Colville, 360)

Colville then added the following significant observation:

> Last night David Margesson [Eden's successor as Secretary of State for War since December 1940] told me how much he disliked the whole venture upon which we are about to embark. Many others felt the same. It was thrust upon us partly because, in the first place, the P.M. felt that our prestige in France, in Spain and in the US, could not stand our desertion of Greece; partly because Eden, Dill, Wavell **(1)** and Cunningham (who has now telegraphed to point out the extreme length to which his resources are stretched) recommended it so strongly. *But the danger of another Norway, Dunkirk and Dakar rolled into one, looms threateningly before us.* (Colville, 361, 756. Italics added.)

(1) "Wavell, having been opposed to the whole scheme of intervention on behalf of Greece, veered round and became its warm exponent." (Colville, 362n1)

On 5 March, Cadogan commented on Eden's action:

> "He has really run ahead of his instructions and *agreed* to things which the Greeks will take as commitments and on which they may make decisions as to their policy in a critical moment. He may have had to do it to prevent an immediate collapse. But really I think his head is turned a little." (Dilks(ed), 361. Eden's Italic.)

Professor Dilks explained:

> Eden telegraphed that he had found in Athens 'a changed and disturbing situation and the atmosphere quite different from that of our last visit'. The retirement from Thrace and Macedonia to the Aliakhmon line, which the British had thought to be agreed on 22 February, had not even begun. Papagos wished to 'dribble our forces piecemeal up to the Macedonian frontier'. This the British refused. They thought it equally disastrous to withdraw the offer of British military support; and therefore finally accepted three Greek divisions, little more than half the force earlier expected, for the Aliakhmon line. (Dilks(ed), 361)

**

Facing a *"changed and disturbing situation,"* on 5 March, Eden sent Campbell back to Belgrade. (Churchill(GA), 98) The Cabinet discussed Eden's telegram from Athens, but ultimately accepted three Greek divisions. Although the risks in the new plan were now greater, still, in Dill's and Wavell's opinion,

> 'on the Aliakmon position good troops under a capable and resolute commander should have a reasonable chance of checking and holding a German advance. At worst it should be possible to conduct a fighting withdrawal through country eminently suitable for rearguard action.' (Kennedy, 101)

> Through his own personal contacts and persuasion, the Legation staff in Belgrade, and the Washington and Moscow Embassies, Eden tried to draw the threads together. Prince Paul had already made abundantly clear his opposition to the idea of reinforcing Greece. Yet Eden was convinced that he could pull it off: 'that Greece, Turkey and Yugoslavia would all eventually come into the fight, but there would be a lot of slipping before that happens.' At the critical meeting at Tatoi on 23 February 1941 between Greece and British personnel, Yugoslavia inadvertently became the strategic epicentre of British plans in the Balkans. However, the importance General Papagos attached to the Yugoslav response to Greek and British overtures, combined with the Greek determination to defend Salonika, escaped both Eden and Dill. Only in the final stages did Yugoslavia become the prime focus of British attentions – that is, after the failure of Eden's mission to Turkey [at the end of February], Bulgaria's accession to the Tripartite Pact on 1 March, and the awful realisation on 5 March 1941 that the Greeks had not withdrawn to the Aliakhmon line as Eden and Dill had anticipated.
> Thereafter, British policy became a desperate race [to] prevent Yugoslavia's signature of the Tripartite pact to protect Britain's exposed flank in Greece, comprising Commonwealth troops (from Australia and New Zealand, which was politically very sensitive in itself, given the theatre of war.) (Onslow, 42-3)

**

On 11 March, in this changed situation, the Greek Minister in Belgrade submitted an aide-mémoire to the Yugoslav Government, pointing out that Germany could hardly undertake an action against Greece if the flanks of German troops in Bulgaria would be attacked by Yugoslav and Turkish armed forces. (Petranović & Žutić, 214) This was a hopeless attempt: Turkey never considered going to war, and even if Yugoslavia had, her entry could not have prevented an overwhelmingly superior Germany from attacking Greece.

"... the right decision was taken in Athens."

However, even with the changed situation, "Eden also stuck to his guns". On 6 March, he wrote to the Prime Minister:

> The Chief of Imperial General Staff and I, in consultation with the three Commanders-in-Chief, have this afternoon re-examined the situation. We are unanimously agreed that, despite the heavy commitments and grave risks which are undoubtedly involved, the right decision was taken in Athens. (Ismay, 200)

After three days' discussion in Athens, without even inspecting the area, Wavell and Dill reached a compromise with General Papagos . "British forces would concentrate on the Aliakmon Line and be joined there by three Greek divisions, while the rest of the Greek army would have to remain in more exposed positions." (Carlton, 179)

After Eden and Dill found a *"changed and disturbing situation"* in Greece, London became concerned, and on 6 March, Churchill telegraphed Eden, now in Cairo:

> Situation has indeed changed for worse. ... Failure of Papagos to act as agreed with you on February 22, ... , make it difficult for Cabinet to believe that we now have any power to avert fate of Greece unless Turkey and/or Yugoslavia come in, which seems most improbable. We have done our best to promote Balkan combination against Germany. *We must be careful not to urge Greece against her better judgment into a hopeless resistance alone when we have only handfuls of troops which can reach scene in time.* ...
>
> We must liberate Greeks from feeling bound to reject a German ultimatum. If on their own they resolve to fight, we must *to some extent* share their ordeal. But rapid German advance will probably prevent any appreciable British Imperial forces from being engaged.
>
> Loss of Greece and Balkans is by no means a major catastrophe for us, provided Turkey remains honestly neutral. ... We are advised from many quarters that an ignominious ejection from Greece would do us more harm in Spain and Vichy than the fact of submission of Balkans, which with our scanty forces alone we have never been expected to prevent. ... (Churchill(GA), 101-2. Italics added.)

Since the end of February, the Prime Minster knew that Turkey did not want to be involved in the war. Although the loss of Greece and the Balkans would not have meant a major catastrophe for Britain, Churchill still wanted British forces deployed in Greece, thus preventing any Greek-German arrangement. Aware that the British forces were scant, he insisted on strengthening them with Yugoslavia's. Therefore, the British *continued urging* Yugoslavia against *her better judgment* into a hopeless resistance – although Britain had no troops or armaments to support Yugoslavia, and Britain's scant's scant *forces have never been expected to prevent* Germany's attack on Greece.

Churchill would not tolerate any Yugoslav-German arrangement which would not strengthen the British forces. It also turned out that his attitude towards a possible Greek arrangement with the Axis was short-lived.

On 6 March, Cadogan recorded:

> A. [Anthony] has evidently committed us up to the hilt. Telegram this morning gives text of agreement signed with Greeks. ... Finally decided to defer decision till we get A.'s answer to telegram which P.M. sent him last night. (Dilks(ed), 361-2)

Following a full review with the Commanders-in-Chief and General Jan Christian Smuts, the Prime Minister of South Africa, on 7 March, Eden telegraphed Churchill, *inter alia:*

> ...While we are all conscious of the gravity of the decision, we can find no reason to vary our previous judgment. ...
>
> 4. Collapse of Greece without further effort on our part to save her by intervention on land, after the Libyan victories, as all world knows, made forces available, would be the greatest calamity. Yugoslavia would then certainly be lost; nor can we feel confident that even Turkey would have the strength to remain steadfast if the Germans and Italians were established in Greece without effort on our part to resist them. No doubt our prestige will suffer if we are ignominiously ejected, but in any event to have fought and suffered in Greece would be less damaging to us than to have left Greece to her fate. ... (Churchill(GA), 105-6)

Eden defended his earlier decision. If he personally did not realize – which is doubtful – Churchill told him that he had gotten nothing out of the Turks, and that his main appeal should now be made to Yugoslavia ... not to save *her* from the *greatest calamity,* but to save what was left of the idea of a Balkan Front.

Churchill to Eden: *"... Cabinet accepts for itself the full responsibility,"* 7 March 1941

The Former Assistant Foreign Minister of Yugoslavia, Ilija Jukić, concluded:

> On March 7 [1941], Eden repeated to Churchill a view he had expressed before, that, as he later wrote,
> "If we withdrew from the operation now, we would have lost the last chance of bringing Yugoslavia into the war."
> Their observations show clearly that Churchill and Eden were defending the decision to assist Greece primarily on political grounds, and foremost among these was their fervent desire to turn Yugoslavia against Hitler. (Jukić, 37)

On 7 March - while British troops were landing in Greece - Churchill telegraphed Eden, *inter alia,* that a precise military appreciation of the situation was indispensable. However, the "precise military appreciation" never materialized. Instead, Eden's reply testified to the unshaken unanimity on the spot:

> Whole position again fully reviewed with the Commanders-in-Chief and Smuts ... We can find no reason to vary our previous judgment. There has been no urging Greece against her better judgment ...We are all agreed that the course advocated should be followed and help given to Greece. (Ismay, 201)

Also on 7 March, Cadogan noted briefly: "Cabinet at 12, which practically decided to go ahead in Balkans. On a nice balance, I think this is right." However, the editor of his Diaries, Professor D. Dilks, added: "Churchill assured Eden immediately that by this decision the Cabinet had taken upon itself 'the fullest responsibility'. The fact that Cadogan's views on the Balkans shifted several times in a matter of weeks .... testifies to the complexity of the issues." (Diks(ed), 362)

That same day, Churchill informed Eden, who was still in Cairo:

> ... Cabinet decided to authorise you to proceed with the operation, *and by so doing Cabinet accepts for itself the fullest responsibility.* (Churchill(GA), 107. Italics subsequently added by Churchill.)

Colville noted: "The P.M. was much happier. His mind is relieved now that a great decision has been irrevocably taken. He was witty and entertaining." (Colville, 362)

> ... In one way this was a surprising decision for no detailed military appreciation had been received. On the other hand, the definite attitude of the once hesitant commanders-in-chief was very convincing and the Government itself was anxious to support Greece if it was administratively possible. (McClymont, 113)

**

While the British expeditionary force was moving into Greece, it suited the British that Prince Paul should keep the Germans in play, because they wanted to delay a German attack. However, at the same time, "the British wanted the Yugoslavs to attack northern Albania, to help out the Greeks, and above all to promise that if the Germans attacked in the direction of Salonika, they [the Yugoslavs] would treat this as an attack on Yugoslavia itself and act accordingly." (Barker, 89)

**

By this time, Churchill had abandoned the militarily sound criterion to "meet the German armies in regions where only comparatively small forces can be brought into action", as he wrote to President Roosevelt on 8 December 1940. He must have known that the German forces in Rumania were not "comparatively small".

During 1941 Churchill's Mediterranean strategy moved from the dimension of risk-taking to that of suffering the consequences. Even allowing for his conviction that Turkey could be brought into the war – which the Turks, playing a skilful hand were not unwilling to endorse – he unquestionably went too far in using small forces for large strategic ends. ... The volatility of Yugoslav politics, to say nothing of the fragility of its armed forces, made a factor of quite marginal importance in the game Churchill was playing; ... the Turks, ... , would do nothing not to their advantage; the Greeks, by contrast, were a headstrong people who gambled for high stakes. (John Keegan in Blake & Louis (eds), 335-6)

On 22 May 1940, the British had broken the German Air Force code and thus were able to follow the movement of its units. On 7 October 1940, German troops moved into Rumania. Their primary goal could not have been an attack on Greece, because Mussolini attacked Greece three weeks later, on 28 October, without Hitler's approval. Therefore, the accumulation of German troops in Rumania had to be planned for another purpose – as shortly thereafter became understood – the attack on the Soviet Union. On 23 November 1940, Rumania joined, unconditionally, the Tripartite Pact. The British Legation personnel and the SOE agents – who had to leave Rumania in February 1941 – knew the strength of the German presence in Rumania, and dutifully communicated that to London. Knowing that the German army in Rumania was not "comparatively small" – and still planning to engage it and to secure a British foothold on the Continent for further actions against Germany - the British needed the armies of Greece, Yugoslavia and Turkey. Churchill's vision of 70 Balkan divisions being able to achieve Britain's goal did not take into account that those 70 divisions were mostly ox-cart-equipped, unable to stop a lesser number – but technically and armament-wise superior German divisions. ... not to mention to withstand Germany's superiority in air-power.

The decision in favor of the Expedition in Greece was thus based also on an error in military judgment.

... the Greek government had told Wavell in January 1941 that they did not want British military assistance. Churchill determined to deliver it none the less. At a moment when Hitler ... was beginning to deploy his own forces in support of Mussolini's in Libya, a Panzer corps commanded by Rommel, Churchill stripped Wavell of his best troops, notably the Australians and the New Zealanders, and sent them to Greece. (John Keegan in Blake & Louis(eds), 336)

"A bait for the Croats and Slovenes"

The Yugoslav Ambassador in Moscow, Milan Gavrilović, suggested to Sir Stafford Cripps, the British Ambassador, that the Croats might be won over if the British would recognize the Yugoslav claim to the Istrian isthmus and Adriatic islands held by the Italians.

Cripps forwarded the idea to Eden. He "raised question of revision of Italo-Yugoslav frontier." (Dilks(ed), 359) FO considered the proposal and it was concluded (on 1 March) that "the decision of the Yugoslav government at the present juncture is of such importance that it would be worth while to disregard this rule [not to discuss any territorial changes during the war] ... if by so doing we could induce Yugoslavia to intervene forcibly on behalf of Greece". (Barker, 88; 282n59) Thus "Cabinet agreed to give A. [Eden] some latitude". (Dilks(ed), 359) On 3 March Eden was authorized to offer support for revision of Italo-Yugoslav frontier. (Barker, 88;282n60) Then, in turn, as Eden wrote:

I also authorized Campbell to tell the Prince Regent that we thought that a case could be made at the peace conference for revising the Italo-Yugoslav frontier in Istria, if Yugoslavia were our ally. This, for what it was worth, was intended as something of a bait for the Croats and Slovenes. (Eden, 216)

**

"Revising the Italo-Yugoslav frontier in Istria" was related to the frontier established after the First World War, based on the secret Treaty of London, dated 26 April 1915. According to the Treaty, Italy was to leave the Triple Alliance (Germany, Austria-Hungary and Italy) and to join the Triple Entente (the United Kingdom, France and Russia), and to declare war on Germany and Austria-Hungary. As a reward, Italy was to get certain territories from the Austro-Hungarian empire, including Istria, populated by the Croats and Slovenes.

Campbell's visit to Zagreb, early March 1941

After returning from his visit to Eden in Athens – and having the authorization to "bait" the Croats and Slovenes with the revision of the Italo-Yugoslav frontier - Campbell went to Zagreb in early March with Eden's instruction on his mind, to "encourage" Vice Premier Vladko Maček and other Croatian leaders to "resist" Germany. Pavle D. Ostović - interpreter and secretary of the British Consul-General in Zagreb, Terence Rapp - described the exchange of thoughts related to "resistance":

> Both the British and the Americans were anxious that Yugoslavia should resist Hitler's dictates. In the first half of March, 1941, Sir Ronald [Ian] Campbell, British Ambassador to Yugoslavia, came to Zagreb and, accompanied by T. C. Rapp, British Consul-General in Zagreb, in the home of Ivan Meštrović, met Dr. Maček and Krnjević and Ing. Košutić, all of the Croatian Peasant Party. In the course of the conversation and in view of Sir Ronald's interest in the attitude of Yugoslavia, Dr, Maček explained that the Croats had had no say in the planning of Yugoslav foreign or military policies. They had been given access to the necessary information, but only to a limited extent and only since the signing of the Serbo-Croat agreement [26 August 1939]. Dr. Maček then said that he thought he was betraying no state secret in telling Sir Ronald that *Yugoslavia was not prepared for war and could not resist the German steamroller for more than a week.* To Sir Ronald's remark that all Yugoslavs are a fine military race, Dr. Maček replied that brave hearts and bare hands are not sufficient to stop steel tanks. Although all Yugoslavs were anti-Nazi and anti-Fascist, sentiment cannot replace armaments. He thought that Yugoslavia should keep out of the war in her own interest and in the interest of her Western friends. Russia was bound to be involved in the war before it was over, as Hitler would want to extend his "Lebensraum" by conquering the Ukraine. Probably also the United States would be involved sooner or later. When Sir Ronald raised the question of the passage of German troops and armament through Yugoslavia, Dr. Maček replied that the Germans had assured the Yugoslavs that they would respect their territory. He declared, however, that *the Yugoslavs would never agree to the passage of German troops and material through Yugoslavia. Should the Germans try to force the passage, the Yugoslavs would resist and fight, if only with sporting rifles.*
>
> In the course of further conversation Dr. Maček explained that the Yugoslavs could wage a guerilla war in the mountains, perhaps for years, *if the British were willing to keep open and protect the Yugoslav Adriatic ports and supply war material.* Sir Ronald replied that *the British Admiralty would probably never allow its fleet to enter the lake which is called the Adriatic Sea, as it represents a veritable trap in view of the superior speed of some Italian naval units. Nor could he promise that the guerillas could be supplied by air, since Britain at that time was short both of planes and armaments.* Dr. Maček then replied that in that case the situation seemed hopeless from every point of view and that Yugoslavia should not be pressed to enter the war. *For Yugoslavia that would mean a catastrophe which would not benefit anybody.* And so the conversation ended.
>
> (P. D. Ostović, *The Truth About Yugoslavia*, Roy Publishers New York, 1952, pp.159-160. Italics added.)

In March 1941 Maček echoed what Eden had said in a broadcast on 2 June 1940, after the Dunkirk evacuation: "Brave hearts alone cannot stand up against steel. We need more planes, more tanks, more guns." (Rhodes James, 232) Nevertheless, the British disregarded Maček's rephrasing of Eden's call for weapons.

Chapter 8

Urging Prince Paul *"in the sense desired"*

Watching the development of the German-Yugoslav negotiation, Eden noticed that "On March 7th, the Yugoslav Government asked Hitler and Mussolini for assurances that their country's sovereignty and territorial integrity would be respected if it joined the Tripartite Pact." (Eden, 220) At the same time he was doing what he could – through Minister Campbell - *to persuade the Yugoslav Government to play their part.*

According to the Taylor-Masterson report to Dalton of 24 June 1941 – when they safely came to London after Yugoslavia's defeat - SOE and Campbell were working closely together when, on 7 March, Campbell reported that *Narodna Odbrana [The Defense League]* and other leading patriotic societies had addressed petitions to Price Paul urging action "in the sense desired" – (Barker, 91; 282n83) that is, desired by SOE. (British "subsidies" to these organizations are examined in **Part Two**.)

Campbell had asked the SOE to urge the Serb opposition parties to put their statement, issued a day or two later, in the form of a promise to support Prince Paul in resistance to German demands. However, the distributed statement was not written in that sense; in fact it was "pure defeatism in that (for reasons of internal politics) it threw doubt on Croat loyalty". (Barker, 91)

The patriotic associations of veterans from Serbia's resistance during the First World War "were particularly influential with the Serbian public and they submitted many petitions to Prince Paul, setting out Serb objections to giving way to German threats, while SOE published a large volume of pamphlets on the same theme, designed to arouse public opinion. In short, all possible means of bringing pressure on Prince Paul not to sign the Tripartite Pact were utilized by SOE." (Williams, 29)

And not only by the SOE; British service attachés purposefully cultivated close relationships with some high-ranking officers and Serbian veterans' associations. Most of the opposition political parties in Yugoslavia were not "loyal" in the Western sense; although patriotic, they also fought to assert their own interests and influence.

Major Milisav Perišić's talks with the British in Athens, 9-12 March 1941

Early on 8 March, Cadogan found in the FO "messages from Prince P[aul] showing he was sending an officer to Athens to find out what help he could expect." Cadogan informed Churchill, and told him that he would send a telegram to Athens "urging that the utmost encouragement should be given". … "Wonder whether Yugoslavia will do anything! What a chance to give the bloody ice-creamers [the Italians] the final kick in the pants", the FO's Permanent Undersecretary longed for. (Dilks(ed), 362)

While Prince Paul was looking for help, the Permanent Under-Secretary wanted to "encourage" him to attack the Italians in Albania – as Churchill and Eden were doing – expecting him to help the British instead.

As E. Barker put it, playing for time, Prince Paul agreed to Eden's suggestion made in the letter of 3 March, and sent an emissary of the Yugoslav General Staff to Athens to talk with the British and Greek representatives, but side-stepped a series of proposals that the Prince or his Ministers should meet Eden, openly or secretly. "This obviously offended Eden," (Barker, 88; Jukić, 56) The emissary was Major Milisav Perišić – "who traveled on a British passport under the name L.R. (Last Ray) Hope". (Barker, 88) The accounts of these talks reveal details of the then existing situation. According to Eden, the Major came on March 8th,

> only to seek answers to seven questions. … They concerned the help we could give to Yugoslav forces retreating south to the Aegean and west to the Adriatic. He had nothing to say about Yugoslav plans. In reply Pericić [Perišić] was told that *we would do all we could* to remedy his country's deficiencies in equipment. He was also reminded that if the Yugoslavs would attack the Fascist forces in Albania, they could gain large stocks of equipment, make communications up and down the Adriatic much easier and release Greek troops and British air forces to fight the Germans. (Eden, 220. Italics added.)

According to Ilija Jukić, during these talks Perišić

inquired about the strength of the Anglo-Greek forces allocated for the front against the German onslaught, the defense of Salonika, the flow of arms, and what aid the Yugoslav army could expect from Britain. Lieutenant-General Henry Maitland Wilson, commander of the British forces in Greece, noticed at once that the Yugoslav military did not understand modern methods of warfare. "It was evident that the effect of bombing on an inadequately protected port had not been appreciated and conditions similar to 1916-18 were visualized." (Jukić, 56)

> General Wavell's chief of staff, Major-General Arthur Smith, represented the British government. Almost immediatly Smith decided that as the Yugoslav attitude appeared so uncertain he and General Papagos should only give general replies. This was of little use to Major Perišić who was under strict orders to find out, in the most specific terms, what help could be given to the Yugoslav army should it be forced to withdraw either south to the Aegean or west to the Adriatic. However, even had the British been prepared to be frank, their reply would not have given the Yugoslavs much encouragement, for as long as British forces were being moved to Greece, they had no ships to spare for other manoeuvres. (Balfour & Mackay, 232-3)

Elisabeth Barker pointed out that the Major's visit brought little satisfaction to either side. As the Yugoslav attitude was so uncertain, the British and Greeks only generally replied to his questions. They did not tell him that the proposed British defense line lay south of Salonika, or that there were plans for demolitions in the Salonika area. (Barker, 88-9)

> The Major was mainly interested in finding out what help the Yugoslav armed forces could get in withdrawing either through Greece to the Aegean (that is, Salonika or Kavalla) or westward to the Adriatic so that they could if necessary be evacuated from Adriatic ports. (Barker, 89)

On the questions of withdrawals the British answered that "the naval problem was difficult"; running naval convoys up and down the Adriatic would be "onerous", although they would of course do their best if "our Allies were cut off in that sea". (Barker, 89)

> Behind this extremely vague statement lay the fact that, as Admiral Cunningham, the Naval Commander in the Mediterranean, wrote to Eden [on 8 March] so long as British forces were being moved to Greece, he had absolutely no ships to spare "except possibly an occasional submarine", though in two or three months' time, it would be possible to reconsider the situation. (Barker, 89; 282n69)

> Major Perišić's journey was a dismal failure. ... It failed because both the British and the Yugoslavs expected to have their questions answered, but to answer none themselves. (Balfour & Mackay, 233)

Jacob Hoptner – who would become Field Director and Special Representative of the American Red Cross in Yugoslavia after the war – provided more details about Perišić's talks:

> The Yugoslavs needed assurance, he said, that the Anglo-Greek forces would create a southern front if it became necessary for the Yugoslav army to withdraw toward the Aegean, would designate Salonika as a base for the Yugoslav southern army to cover it from attack as long as needed, and would provide both the northern and southern forces with naval assistance and war materials if they became cut off from their own depots. The Yugoslav particularly wanted to know how soon the Anglo-Greek forces could establish a front running from the Gulf of Orphanos to Lake Dojran. ... (Hoptner, 224)

"The British and Greeks could reply only in general terms." (Hoptner, 224) They knew that they could not provide either naval assistance or war materials, so Eden said that *they would do all they could* – without being specific. This was not enough to help the Yugoslav army; instead, the British expected the Yugoslav army to get needed war materiel from the Italians in Albania – regardless of a potentially adverse reaction by the German to such a move. Once Hitler decided to help his ally in Greece, why would he then not help him in Albania as well? It seems Churchill was not taking that probability into account.

Eden's gross misunderstanding

After Perišić left, Major-General Arthur Smith telegraphed the results of the discussion to Eden, who was by then in Cairo. Not surprisingly, the British were put out. ... Campbell sent to Eden, who was still in Cairo, constant bulletins of the latest developments. One of these Eden misunderstood. It was a message about the circumstances under which Yugoslavia might consider signing the Pact: she would resist attack, refuse passage of troops and use of the railways, and 'would not sign Tripartite Pact *with military clauses'*. Eden noted 'with satisfaction' that Yugoslavia *'will not sign the Tripartite Pact'*. This was only a slip, but it helps to explain Eden's reaction when he heard that Paul's government had signed the Pact, albeit without its military clauses. He showed little mercy. (Balfour & Mackay, 233. Italics added.)

*** German-Yugoslav negotiations: positive reply to the Yugoslav demands

While Major Perišić was getting ready to meet and confer with the Greeks and British in Athens, on 8 March, Hitler informed Mussolini that he was ready to agree to Yugoslav demands.

> No [Mussolini's] answer has been found, but on 9 March Heeren was instructed to give a positive reply to most of the Yugoslav requests. Germany was ready to guarantee Yugoslavia's sovereignty and territorial integrity; no passage for troops would be required; no military assistance against Greece would be asked for, and Salonika was to be awarded to Yugoslavia. On the other hand, Yugoslavia could not be released from article III of the pact as regards the rendering of military support by the signatories of the treaty in such cases as it applied. The Yugoslavs, however, were not satisfied; they insisted that although prepared to support the reorganization of Europe 'politically and economically', they did not want to sign an obligation that might involve them in a war with the USSR and the US. Persuasion, Heeren reported, was unavailing. (van Creveld 128)

Meanwhile, in London,

Churchill expected a change in Yugoslavia

On 9 March, Churchill telegraphed Eden in Cairo: "There seems still a chance of Yugoslavia coming in, and more than a chance of her keeping the door shut." (Churchill(GA), 107) One wonders whether he saw that chance in a potential pressure by President Roosevelt. On Monday, 10 March 1941, while informing Roosevelt of Britain's decision to aid Greece, Churchill pressed him to support one of his visions of the role of Yugoslavia:

> *At this juncture the action of Yugoslavia is cardinal. No country ever had such a military chance. If they will fall on the Italian rear in Albania there is no measuring what might happen in a few weeks.* The whole situation might be transformed, and the action of Turkey also decided in our favour. One has a feeling that Russia, though actuated mainly by fear, might at least give some reassurance to Turkey about not pressing her in the Caucasus or turning against her in the Black Sea. I need scarcely say that the concerted influence of your Ambassadors in Turkey, Russia, and above all in Yugoslavia, would be of enormous value at the moment, and indeed might possibly turn the scales. (Churchill(GA), 110. Italics in the original.)

Yugoslavia's *falling on the Italian rear in Albania,* and the concerted influence of American Ambassadors in line with the British desires ... *might possibly turn the scales of the war*? Historian A.J.P. Taylor wrote that Churchill "was believing what he wanted to believe, and not on the basis of much knowledge". (*Churchill: Four Faces and the Man,* p. 29) Basil Liddell Hart noted Churchill's tendency "to miss the wood for the trees" when absorbed in exciting details of the "war game". (*Ibid.*, 184) "He [Churchill] was always prone to count his chickens before they were hatched, and as a rule his estimates erred on the generous side." (Ismay, 197)

*** German-Yugoslav negotiations: all Yugoslavia's demands accepted, 12 March

On 9 March, the German Minister in Belgrade, Victor von Heeren, could not persuade the Yugoslav Government to drop the demand related to military support of the Axis.

On 11 March Heeren reported that there was 'strong agitation' in the population and the army caused by rumors that Germany had presented Yugoslavia with an ultimatum. Confirming Prince Paul's fears of a revolution, this report must have had its effect on Hitler, for on 12 March he conceded even this Yugoslav demand:

> *Taking into account the military situation, Germany and Italy assure the Yugoslav government that they will not, of their own account, make any demands for military assistance.* (van Creveld, 128-9. Italics added.)

On 12 March, von Heeren gave Cincar Marković a written note on the new German position:

> Germany and Italy assure the Yugoslav Government that they will not, of their own accord, make any demand for military assistance. If he Yugoslav Government should at any time consider it to be in its own interest to participate in military operations in accordance with the Tripartite Pact, it will be left to the Yugoslav Government to make the necessary arrangements for this with the Powers of the Tripartite Pact. (Ristić, 61)

> Prince Paul and the leading members of his government must have made their decision during the afternoon of the 14th. ... Cincar Marković gave Heeren a formal answer on March 17: "The Crown Council has decided in principle in favor of Yugoslavia's accession to the Tripartite Pact". (Ristić, 63)

In Professor van Creveld's opinion,

> This represented a great victory for the Serbs; with unparalleled nerve, they proceeded to demand even more. 'For compelling domestic reasons' they wanted to have the German declaration published. This went too far; Berlin had already consented to publish her submission to Yugoslavia's other demands, but to publicly confirm the fact that *Yugoslavia's accession was really a lot of humbug* was a request which Hitler could not grant. There were, Ribbentrop concluded, limits to everything. (van Creveld, 129. Italics added.)

> After months of sidestepping, the moment of truth had dawned for Yugoslavia. German troops were streaming into neighbouring Bulgaria; Hungary and Rumania were already occupied. Caught in a ring of steel the Belgrade government capitulated on 17 March. ... By dragging their feet for so long, the Yugoslavs had shown quite unequalled courage in the face of a state so much stronger than themselves. They achieved all their demands, *effectively undoing the act of accession* before it ever became known to the world. They even obtained Hitler's consent to the publication of those concessions – all except one. In the end, this was to prove Yugoslavia's undoing. (van Creveld, 129. Italics added.)

In the end, the British wanted to *"draw Yugoslavia into the war anyhow"* – and succeeded - notwithstanding the *effectively undone act of accession ...*

Churchill instructed Eden to stay in Cairo, 14 March

Eden wanted to leave Cairo and return home, but Churchill instructed him to stay:

> ... The attitude of Yugoslavia is still by no means hopeless, and *a situation may at any moment arise which would enable you to go there.* Turkey requires stimulus and guidance as events develop. No one but you can combine and concert the momentous policy which you have pressed upon us and which we have adopted. The War Cabinet needs a representative on the spot and I need you there very much indeed. (Churchill(GA), 108. Italics added.)

Churchill's hope that the situation in Yugoslavia might change *at any moment* may have been, at least partly, also founded on his knowledge of secret SOE activities in Yugoslavia. Just 12 days earlier, he thoroughly approved SOE's secret plan to deal with Prince Paul, including plan for a coup.

Another noteworthy point: Churchill wrote that it was *Eden* who pressed *the momentous policy* for the British expedition to Greece which the Cabinet adopted.

In the same telegram, Churchill continued to promote his wishful thinking:

6. Of course, if Yugoslavia came in this would justify Greek strength in Albania. But this is not yet known. Presume you and Dill have studied carefully possibilities of a Yugoslav attack on Italians in Albania. Here they might win victory of the first order, and at the same time gain the vast mass of the equipment they need to preserve their independence and can never find elsewhere in time. (Churchill(GA), 109)

How could Churchill presume that Germany would not help Italy in Albania by attacking Yugoslavia, and that Yugoslavia's attack would preserve her independence? "When Churchill wanted something, he assumed that he could have it." (A.J.P. Taylor, "The Statesman", ... , p. 32) As Lord Esher said of Churchill in 1917: "He handles great subjects in rhythmical language, and becomes quickly enslaved by his own phrases. He deceives himself into the belief that he takes broad views, when his mind is fixed upon one comparatively small aspect of the question." (Robert Rhodes James, "The Politician", *Churchill: Four Faces and the Man,* p. 70)

At this time ...

London was convinced, "*Hitler had decided to attack Russia*"

On 13 March, a report of Donovan's views reached the British Foreign Office. Of Prince Paul he had said that his training "had left him with a strong sense of doing the "right thing". He would not like his English friends to think that he had played a mean role." (Balfour & Mackay, 230; 324n24)

On 14 March, Cadogan recorded: "No decisive news. Jugs. [the Yugoslavs] still hesitant. Turks tightly enclosed in their shell. I really have more hope of the former than of the latter. Look at the latter's form: they have so far carefully evaded every obligation they ever took. But I haven't *much* hope of the former. (Dilks(ed), 363. Cadogan's Italics.)

Following Churchill's appeal to Roosevelt of 10 March, a concerted attempt to influence Prince Paul by the American State Department had intensified; Minister Bliss Lane's activities, greatly inspired during Col. Donovan's visit to Belgrade, increased. He "usefully backed" Campbell who

> ... continued his evocation of the Prince Regent and the leading Yugoslavs [including Maček]. On my instructions, he asked the Government to agree to a visit from either Dill or myself. But once again, on March 15th, the answer came that a visit was not feasible. Nor did we hear a word of Yugoslav comment on Major Peričić's visit to Athens. (Eden, 220).

When Prince Paul, "a contemporary from Oxford days", would not receive Eden, "For this he was to be much reviled, but the fact was that Yugoslavia had no armour and no air force". (Rhodes James, 249)

Without the desired backing from Yugoslavia, on 15 March, Eden telegraphed Churchill:

> You will have seen ... that I am doing all in my power to encourage Yugoslavia and to stiffen Turkey, so that she in turn may stimulate Yugoslavia. ... Commanders-in-Chiefs, while anxious that Yugoslavia should fight with us, are of the opinion that Turkey's entry into the war at this stage would constitute a military liability which they do not wish to incur. (Eden, 221)

However, "if a Turkish declaration of war proved essential to bring in the Yugoslavs", Eden and Wavell decided to try "to get the Turkish Government to make a firm statement publicly against any further acts of aggression in the Balkans. We could then use this with the Yugoslavs." (Eden, 221)

** "*... there was no sound answer*" to the questions by the Joint Planning Staff

> About the third week in March we asked for a discussion with one of Dill's advisers in order to hear of any further political or other factors which might justify this strategy. I'm afraid it was a most unsatisfactory meeting, for there did not appear to be any answers to some of the questions that were asked:
> "How could we deal with the weight of air and armour that we must expect against us?"
> "Were we going to get over sufficient forces in time to hold the Aliakmon Line?"
> "In view of the hardships and losses sustained by the Greek Army, and their acute munition problems, could we rely upon them for a sustained effort against a German attack?"
> "How could the Greek and British forces be maintained after Salonika was given up?"

> These were some of the questions asked, and to which there was no sound answer. The political factors seemed to have been given too much weight in framing our policy.
>
> Yugo-Slavia appeared to be the one potential bright spot. If they really fought the Germans, then the whole thing might be worth while. (de Guingand, 62)

Acutely aware of Britain's inability to satisfy Greece's needs for modern weapons and munitions, was not the General aware of the same needs of Yugoslavia?

18-20 January 1941, Hitler informed Mussolini about his intended attack on Greece

The chances of Churchill's vision succeeding should also be viewed in the context of the events pertaining to Albania at the time.

As early as 28 December 1940, Mussolini asked Hitler for support in Greece. Had he later needed support in Albania, it is hard to imagine that he would not have asked for that too.

On 1 January 1941, Germany began negotiations with Bulgaria to allow German troops to use Bulgaria as a springboard for their attack on Greece.

On 11 January 1941, two months before Perišić's talks in Athens, Hitler issued *Directive No. 22*, ("Assistance of German forces in operations in the Mediterranean area"), confirming his intention to send military support to the Italians in Albania. The operation was to be named "Alpine Violets". (http://www.oppapers.com/essays/World-War-2/76789 12/12/09) Here are relevant excerpts:

> The situation in the Mediterranean area, where England is employing superior forces against our allies, requires that Germany should assist for reasons of strategy, politics and psychology.
>
> Tripolitania must be held and the danger of collapse on the Albanian front must be eliminated. Furthermore, the Cavalliero army group [i.e. the Italian army in Albania] must be enabled, in cooperation with the later operations of 12th army, to go over to the offensive in Albania.
>
>> 3. German formations in the approximate strength of one corps, including 1 mountain division and armoured units, will be detailed and made ready to move to Albania. ...
>
> It will be the task of the German forces:
> (a) To act as immediate stiffening in Albania in case further critical situation should arise. (van Creveld, 105)

Between 18-20 January, Hitler met with Mussolini and informed him about an intended German attack on Greece.

On 17 February, Bulgaria and Turkey signed a non-aggression pact at Ankara. Without a potential threat to German operations in Bulgaria, it would have been easier for the Germans to support the Italians in Albania. Had Yugoslavia attacked the Italians in the first half on March, it would have been improbable for Yugoslavia to get all those armaments Churchill had been talking about.

The intent of the *Directive No. 22* made it likely that Hitler would have acted against Yugoslavia had she attacked the Italians in Albania. (Later on he supported the Italians in Greece.) Had this been the case, how effective might Yugoslavia's attack on Albania have been against the Axis? One outcome might have been visualized by analyzing the subsequent brief war of April 1941, which clearly exposed Yugoslavia's inability to "resist" Germany and thus help the Greeks and the British the way the British wanted.

While Churchill was expecting President Roosevelt to put pressure on the Yugoslav Government, Prince Paul told Campbell that he faced a terrible decision. After hearing Major Periišić's report, his military commanders told him that Yugoslavia could not hold out for more than a week; nor, in their opinion, could the Greeks, even with British assistance. "He made it clear that joining the Tripartite Pact was a possibility." (Barker, 90)

In March 1941 London knew of Hitler's plan to attack the Soviet Union

The British broke the German Air Force code on 22 May 1940. (Williams, 5) "Eden was one of the very few who knew that the British had broken the secrets of the German Enigma cypher, and although the vital and brilliant unit at Bletchley was in its early days, the British were already receiving information of unique importance." This *coup* was "one of the most jealously guarded of all secrets throughout the war and long after..." (Rhodes James, 241)

Informed of the movement of German Air Force units, the British were thus able to estimate Hitler's military intentions. In March 1941 London was

> convinced through the work of the Bletchley cryptographers that Hitler had decided to attack Russia, but would divert sufficient forces to deal with Yugoslavia and Greece. The Russians, although thoroughly alarmed by German ambitions in the Balkans, would not believe the first part of the British information. (Rhodes James, 251)

Albeit aware of Hitler's intention to invade the Soviet Union, British war leaders decided to time the *coup d'état* in Belgrade *prior to* Germany's invasion, rather than *following it* - when it probably could have been more damaging to Germany's war efforts. Hitler himself stated at the conference preceding the formulation of *Directive No. 25* that *if the overthrow of the government would have happened during the Barbarossa-action* [invasion of the Soviet Union], *the consequences for us probably would have been considerably more serious.* (The Avalon Project: Nazi Conspiracy and Aggression Volume IV – Document No 1746 www.yale.edu/lawweb/avalon.imt/document/nca_vol/1746-ps.htm 10/6/04. Italics added.)

Until mid-March, Germany *"made no preparations to attack Yugoslavia"*

Working closely with SOE's George Taylor since his arrival in Belgrade on 27 February, Campbell warned Cincar-Marković on 16 March that "popular opinion was highly excited" and was looking to the dynasty to prevent a pro-German situation as it had occurred then in Rumania. If this was not done, there might be a "strong reaction". "Up to this point the British were still hoping to prevent signature of the pact", in the opinion of E. Barker. (Barker, 91)

> The British Minister in Belgrade had kept Whitehall well informed about Germany's mounting pressure on Yugoslavia to sign the Tripartite Pact and grant transit facilities, but until the middle of March Whitehall had assumed, correctly, that Germany had made no preparations to attack Yugoslavia despite Germany's failure to secure her co-operation and despite the fact that the route through Belgrade was Germany's easiest approach to Greece. Guided by the absence of evidence for such preparations, MI [Military Intelligence] had regularly reported to this effect since the middle of January. (Hinsley *et al*, 368)

By the middle of March, the Yugoslav Premier, Dragiša Cvetković, "seemed honestly to hope that by dragging out negotiations or making unacceptable demands the Germans could be provoked into making a break. He said that in any case three things were certain: Yugoslavia would resist attack, refuse passage of troops or use of its railways, and would *not* 'sign Tripartite Pact *with its military clauses*'." (Barker 90; 282n76. Italics added.)

> Eden apparently did not notice the qualification attached to this last undertaking by Cvetković, and [on 16 March] noted 'with satisfaction' his statement that Yugoslavia 'will not sign the Tripartite pact'. (Barker, 90; 282n77)

E. Barker thought that "This misunderstanding may have added to Eden's anger when the Yugoslavs eventually *did* sign, *without* the military clauses, and his refusal to take any account of the other important conditions which the Yugoslavs have got Hitler to accept. These were strongly hinted at by Cvetković on 17 March when he told Campbell that the Germans were 'daily' pressing Yugoslavia to sign, adding that it would never agree to sign clauses requiring participation in hostilities, passage of troops or use of Yugoslav territory: 'without these, the pact would merely be an empty shell'. (Barker, 90; 282n78. Italics in the source.)

This misunderstanding may not have been the only reason for Eden's anger. After the failure to enlist Turkey, all his efforts were now concentrated on Yugoslavia. Failing in those earlier efforts was quite a sufficient additional reason for his anger.

Outflanking the British and Greek defense line

In March, with the arrival of the British forces, Whitehall and the commands in the Middle East became acutely aware that the British front in northern Greece could be turned if Germany attacked Yugoslavia and advanced through Monastir [Bitolj]. MI [Military Intelligence] drew attention to this danger on 11 March; from 14 March it was calculating the likely scale of Yugoslav resistance to an attack. On 19 March the British Military Mission in Athens feared that in their assault on Greece the Germans would cross Yugoslav territory and outflank the British and Greek defence line. (Hinsley *et al*, 369)

Without the Belgrade coup of 27 March 1941 and the resulting German attack on Yugoslavia, the Germans would not have crossed Yugoslav territory nor outflanked the Metaxas Line.

"... as early as March 16, [German] General Halder had asked himself, "When can one count on the [Marita] forces for Barbarosa?" The next day Hitler ordered the complete occupation of Greece (not merely Thrace as in the original Marita plan) and Halder noted in his diary that the forces for Marita could "no longer be counted on" for Barbarosa. Two days later he discussed "the changed Barbarosa and Marita situation" with another general staff officer. (Ristić, 139)

Eden's pressure on Prince Paul: letter of 17 March 1941

"In yet another effort to influence the Prince Regent", on 17 March Eden decided to send him a letter to be delivered by Terence Shone, former Secretary of the British Legation in Belgrade, who enjoyed friendly relations with the Regent. First, Shone gave the Regent an account of the decisions taken to strengthen British forces in the Middle East. As an example he mentioned that "The passage of Lend-Lease bill would hasten the supply of material aid, including aircraft, direct from the United States to the Middle East". After describing British successes in Africa, Eden continued:

> The attitude that you and your Government have taken up means that the German military authorities must take into account that a further aggression in the Balkans may bring them into conflict with Yugoslavia, Greece and Turkey, *backed by all the resources that we can bring to bear*. It seems to me of the first importance to hold this position, for as long as you, Sir, and your Government can do this there is always a chance of checking the German threat to the independence of Yugoslavia, Greece and Turkey before ever that threat develops into military action. (Eden, 222. Italics added.)

Then Eden turned to Albania:

> ... If Yugoslavia were to attack Albania from the north, Italian resistance would soon collapse and Italy's participation in the Balkan conflict would be at the end, except in so far as she could continue to play a secondary role with her Metropolitan air force. The elimination of Italian armies in Albania would give your army most valuable munitions of war and supplies matériel of all kinds, while it would free the Greek army and our air force for operations elsewhere. (Balfour & Mackay, 235-6)

Eden concluded with a plea for a visit to Belgrade by Sir John Dill and another British staff officer. "Dill, Wavell and I are convinced that such a talk would be of the greatest value to both our countries." (Eden, 223)

How plausible was Eden's – and Churchill's – idea of attacking the Italians in Albania?

> Eden's argument, though plausible, was one–sided. He did not spare a thought for what the Germans might do in the northwestern provinces of Yugoslavia if the Yugoslavs followed the British plan and fell upon the Italians in Albania. It would have been more honest, though equally unproductive, to have asked Paul, outright, to sacrifice half his country for the Allied cause. As it

was, Paul was unimpressed. Beside a vague promise of arms at some future date the letter contained nothing for him, and the appeal to 'old times' left him cold. (Balfour & Mackay, 236)

**

When "Mr. Hope" [Perišić] reported on his talks, Prince Paul and his Ministers singled out the question of British naval support in the Adriatic. On 17 March, Campbell suggested that "some fairly strong reassurance on the prospect of support and supply by the Navy in the Adriatic is of great importance ... to satisfy military authorities and Croats. (Barker, 89; 282n73)

Campbell's suggestion was at least partly based on his experience from the early March meeting with leaders of the Croatian Peasant Party in Zagreb, who were ready to fight if the Axis attacked Yugoslavia, but were unwilling to do so without an outside attack.

**

Well aware of Britain's *empty shops*, Eden tried to present the situation in a much more favorable light than it actually was. In doing so, he made some misleading statements. One was about the expected American supplies.

President Roosevelt signed the Lend-Lease Bill on 11 March 1941. Although his intention was to supply Britain with needed armaments, that could not be achieved immediately. A lengthy period of time was needed between placing an order, setting up the production line, and getting a final product. Eden knew that from the British experience. By 17 March he knew very well how close German troops were to the Bulgaria-Greek frontier, and how imminent their attack was likely to be. Therefore, he had to know that *hastening the supplies from the USA directly to the Middle East* could not bring the required arms to Yugoslavia in time for that assault.

And Prince Paul knew this just as well – and would not be misled by Eden's letter. He also knew of Major Perišić's discovery of the shortages in British support for Greece, and Britain's inability to support Yugoslavia.

**

All the resources that Britain could bring to bear in March 1941 did not amount to much. Both Eden and the Prince knew it. But their words were meant to be reassuring. "The British were masters in negotiations – particularly were they adept in the use of phrases or words which were capable of more than one meaning or interpretation. ... But when matters of state were involved, our British opposite numbers had elastic scruples. To skirt the facts for King and Country was justified in the consciences of these British gentlemen", wrote General Albert C. Wedemeyer, a senior officer on the US Operations and Planning Staff. Speaking from personal experience with the British, he noted:

> What I witnessed was the British power of diplomatic finesse in its finest hour, a power that had been developed over centuries of successful international intrigue, cajolery, and tacit compulsions. I recall speculating at the time on its ultimate efficacy. It is true, I thought, that the sun never sets on the British Empire. But neither does the dove of peace. Moreover, the wings of justice had constantly been clipped as British influences and possessions were increased all over the world. (Wedemeyer, 105-6)

**

Eden likewise misrepresented the role of Turkey. '*You appear to have got nothing out of the Turks.*', Churchill told him on 1 March. Yet Eden wrote as if Turkey was still going along with the British plan for a united Balkan front. Germany was threatening the independence of Greece, but not of Turkey, and therefore Turkey did not want to "resist" Germany militarily.

Prince Paul also knew that Turkey was not concerting her activities with Yugoslavia as Britain wanted it. So, Eden's letter could not persuade him to change his mind and policy.

Although Shone's talk with the Prince Regent were very friendly, he did not succeed in swaying the prince to accept Eden's views and proposal. (Eden, 223)

17 March: Hitler's decision to occupy the whole of Greece; Crown Council decided in principle to join the Tripartite Pact

While Shone was visiting Belgrade, Hitler made another important decision.

> ...if he had ever seriously pursued the path of negotiating with the Greeks, abandoned it when it became clear that British forces were arriving in strength. On 17 March he decided to occupy the whole of Greece in order to eject them. Since preparations had hitherto been made only for the seizure of the northern littoral – an operation which had been expected to take only one week - this decision necessitated the commitment of a larger force and involved the risk of further delay. In order to reduce delay, with all its implications for operation *Barbarossa,* OKH [German Army's High Command] brought forward to 1 April the date for the Greek assault, which as late as 22 March had been 7 April. (Hinsley *et al*, 364)

On 17 March, Hitler told General Halder that *Operation Marita* " [invasion of Greece] must be carried out" and a base won for air control of the Eastern Mediterranean. (Ristić, 42)

Also on 17 March, Yugoslav Foreign Minister, Aleksandar Cincar-Marković, "told the German Minister [in Belgrade] that the Crown Council had decided in principle to join the Tripartite Pact". (Eden, 225)

Chapter 9

Eden's second round of unsuccessful talks with the Turks, 18 March

Hoping that he might still change the attitude of the Turkish and Yugoslav governments, Eden invited the Turks to another conference. Meeting in Cyprus, on 18 March, the Turks did not change their stand, but the Turkish Foreign Minister, Sükrü Saracoglu, "undertook to ask Belgrade to enter upon discussions with a view of concerting measures of collective defence – though in the event he did not do so." (Carlton, 180-1) In Eden's words:

> ... Saracoglu could hardly refuse my suggestion that his Government should send an encouraging message to Belgrade. The form of the message, however, melted in discussion from a declaration that Turkey would regard an attack on Salonika as a *casus belli* if Yugoslavia would do the same, to a message suggesting an exchange of views about the threat to Salonika. I made sure that the news was conveyed at once to the Yugoslavs, but in the end the Turks never delivered it, pretexting the political uncertainties in Belgrade. (Eden, 224).

So, on 18 March, Germany's expected attack on Salonika was not a *casus belli* for Turkey, and Turkey did not cooperate with Yugoslavia about a coordinated approach against the expected invasion of Greece. Even on 28 March - one day after the *coup d'état* in Belgrade - Eden again noted: "The Turkish Government had so far failed to take any initiative with the Yugoslavs." (Eden, 231)

Thus, for the second time in 19 days, Turkey refused to join the Balkan Front and go to war. That made the British even more resolute to concentrate on Yugoslavia's "resistance" to Germany, to do it through diplomatic channels, through the Minister of Economic Warfare, Hugh Dalton, and through the Special Operations Executive. Other British services were doing it through propaganda and various specific activities. All coordinated their actions toward the same goal: either make the Yugoslav Government "resist" Germany, or replace it through a *coup d'état* - assuming that the new government would be prepared to do what Prince Paul's would not.

**

Also on 18 March: The mission successfully accomplished, Donovan returned to Washington. He reported his findings at an early breakfast with President Roosevelt, who had just received a message of thanks from Churchill for "the magnificent work done by Donovan in his prolonged tour of the Balkans and the Middle East. He has carried with him throughout an animating, heart-warming flame". (Ford, 104)

In Yugoslavia -

"... urging the necessity of action for a coup d'état ...", 18 March

Ever since the meeting of Dalton with Churchill at Chequers, on 2 March 1941, SOE was under orders to proceed with the coup if and when the Regent signed the Pact. Although the Pact was not actually signed on the 18th or 19th March, the decision was made to sign it – and that was sufficient. By the 18th,

> They [the British] knew that the Yugoslavs had won concessions from Hitler, but signature in any form was unacceptable, as they repeatedly told the Yugoslavs. Thus, when it became increasingly clear that the signature was imminent, the British mobilized their full effort to prevent it. This effort encompassed both diplomatic pressure and subversive political action, and culminated in the coup of March 27. (Stafford(cp), 401)

According to George Taylor's and Tom Masterson's report to Dalton, dated 24 June 1941, "by 18 March S.O.E. had come to the conclusion that it would almost certainly be necessary to bring down the Cvetković government." (Barker, 91-2; 282n86)

Eden's memorandum to the Yugoslav Government, 18 March

Major Perišić returned to Belgrade on 13 March. Five days later Campbell delivered Eden's memorandum to Cvetković and through him to Prince Paul. The memorandum contained arguments against signing the Tripartite Pact previously advanced by Campbell, but now supported by the British Foreign Minister. Some topics treated in the memorandum were:

Of prime importance - memorandum stated - was not to allow the Germans believe that they could attack Greece once the Pact had been signed.

Refusal to sign the Pact does not mean that Yugoslavia must now declare war on Germany.

Because limited authority was given to the Yugoslav representative in talks with the Greek and British military [9-12 March, Major Perišić], they could inform him of their plans only in general terms. That resulted in conclusion by the Yugoslav military authorities that prospects for a common action with the Greeks and British would be minimal. The British were ready to provide all needed explanations and to continue talks with the representatives of the Yugoslav General Staff in case Yugoslavia would be forced to defend her interests by force.

If the Chief of the Imperial General Staff [General Sir John Dill] could meet with the Yugoslav military leaders, he could encourage them. (Petranović & Žutić, 169-70)

Delivery of Eden's letter to Prince Paul, 18 March

On 18 March, when SOE decided to bring down the Yugoslav Government, and after Campbell delivered the memorandum to Cvetković, Shone delivered Eden's letter to Prince Paul and

> "urged repeatedly that signature by Yugoslavia of *any* pact with Germany would not only be full of peril for her but also a grave disservice to the Allied cause in as much as Germany, feeling sure Yugoslavia was 'in the bag', would no longer hesitate to attack Greece." (Stafford(cp), 402. Italics in the source.)

He " did his best but made no headway and, after hearing of the German agreement to the Yugoslav terms, felt that the situation was hopeless." (Williams, 30) "By 18th March it had become clear to Masterson and Taylor that if they did not embark on a more active policy, the Tripartite Pact would be signed. Consequently they determined to encourage as many members as possible of the existing government to resign in protest. Such a crisis, they hoped, would bring down the government." (Balfour & Mackay, 254), Therefore, "SOE's objective changed from that of endeavoring to influence Prince Paul's government to that of endeavoring to bring it down – preferably before the Pact was signed. This was the subject of discussion at a meeting of SOE, intelligence and diplomatic representatives at the British Legation on 19 March." (Williams, 30)

Shone, like Eden, used any argument he could think of in order to convince Prince Paul. In reality, Hitler had issued *Directive No. 20* for the campaign against Greece on 13 December 1940, three months before Yugoslavia was "in the bag".

Former Greek Foreign Minister Hargyropoulos arrived in Belgrade on 18 March with a special message for the Yugoslav Government. American Minister Arthur Bliss Lane believed that it also had urged resistance to German demands. (FRUS1, 958)

The Crown Council meeting on March 19

> precipitated the final crisis by agreeing in principle that Yugoslavia should sign the Pact, on condition that Yugoslavia would not be obliged to accept the transit of German troops or the use of its railways, nor sign so-called "military clauses" of the full Pact. (Stafford(cp), 402)

> ... on 19 March a Crown Council was held to discuss whether to sign the pact, on conditions which Cvetković – probably also the Prince – had hoped the Germans would reject – no passage of troops or use of Yugoslav railways, no military clauses, a guarantee of Yugoslavia's integrity. It was agreed to go back to the Germans and demand that the 'secret clauses' should be published. The Germans agreed that the Yugoslavs should publish two of them and that they themselves would not repudiate them. (Barker, 90)

The same day, Premier Cvetković informed British Minister Campbell that Germany had accepted all Yugoslav proposals related to the Tripartite Pact. (Petranović & Žutić, 174)

All-British conference, 19 March 1941

By 18 March, the British had concluded that their goals could be achieved only through a forcible overthrow of the Yugoslav Government, in favor of a new, pro-British one.

> Deciding to foment a coup was one thing; actually bringing it off was quite another. *SOE's contacts, excellent though they might be for influencing public opinion,* were not necessarily the stuff from which coups are made. SOE assessed that although the army was against the Pact its leaders were wary of provoking war with Germany, while the air force, *a small but united body,* who might be less reluctant, did not possess the political capacity to carry through after the initial overthrow. (Williams, 30-31. Italics added.)

> SOE was faced with the problem of co-ordinating all the necessary elements [to bring the coup off] while time was fast running out. " **The work of SOE during these days therefore was essentially that of urging the necessity of action for a coup d'état upon all our friends and everyone with whom we had contact** ", as Taylor put it, while hoping that once the first step had been taken everything else would fall into line. (Williams, 31. Emphasis added.)

The British Legation felt that the Serbian Peasant Party (SPP) were "the most likely long-term supporters of resistance, should German occupation occur, and it was they, under Milan Gavrilovic, and later Tupanjanin, whom we British supported with arms and finance, although we also maintained relations with the Democrats." (Glen(B), 40-41)

> With a coup d'état recognized as the only viable means of producing an alternative government, *the focus of the British side inevitably shifted away from the SOE and its political contacts and toward agencies or individuals who had contacts in the Yugoslav armed forces.* Tupanjanin and the [Serbian] Peasant Party [subsidized by the British], while valuable in publicizing the issues involved and arousing Serb public opinion, were poorly represented in state and army administrative posts, were regarded with suspicion by economically powerful interests in the country, and were thus ill suited to launch a cup d'état. The national associations [subsidized by the British], although influential throughout the country, were not sufficiently organized for such action. And *the opposition parties,* even though they included many SOE contacts, *were not prepared to take the initiative.* (Stafford(cp), 411-12. Italics added.)

To achieve their desired goal, an all-British round-table conference was held with the SOE, SIS and Legation staff on 19 March.

> The British agencies in Belgrade included not only the diplomatic mission and the attachés, but also SOE, which had originally been deployed in Yugoslavia to undertake sabotage projects for blocking the Danube and to organise resistance movements in Balkan countries that were threatened with German occupation, and the SIS, which lent its communications to SOE and provided it with essential contacts. (Hinsley *et al*, 369)

Historians pointed to this meeting as "the crucial point whereat diplomats and British personnel on the spot looked to the formation of an alternative government." (Onslow 51) At this meeting an overall plan of action was decided and tasks assigned. On 26 March 1941, Taylor informed SOE London about the decisions reached:

> As result of exhaustive round table conference here presided over by the Minister at which SO2 [SOE] possibilities were given fullest consideration, following policy decided upon.
> 1. SO2 to continue to push on with preparation for coup d'état to overthrow present Government which they began with Minister's authority approximately a week ago [i.e. 19 March] working primarily through TUPANJANIN and Serbian Peasant Party, but also endeavour to coordinate with action [*Vojvoda*] TRIFUNOVICH, RADOVICH, Slovene organisation and other small groups.
> 2. These preparations will take some time to complete, principally because of time needed by our political friends to sound Generals in order to acquire a degree of military support which is necessary

for successful coup d'état and may not be sufficiently advanced to enable action to be taken within first few days of pact when public feelings may be expected to be most violent.

3. Therefore in the meantime *direct contact is being sought through Air Attaché with military elements* to see whether purely military coup d'état could not be more quickly arranged on assumption our political friends would then throw their support behind new Government which would come into power as result such action. We are satisfied that this direct approach will not in any way compromise TUPANJANIN's attempt to organise politico-military movements.
4. As second line of action we are endeavouring to prepare through TUPANJANIN and TRIFUNOVICH demolition of vital communications, concentrating on blocking Danube, railway bridge Maribor, bridge over Sava Belgrade, railway line between Nish and Tsaribrod, and bridge near Veles indicated by C-in-C.

(Great Britain, Special Operation Executive, 91087 – 10.V, Hoover Institution Archives. Italics added.)

Sixty years later Sir Alexander Glen wrote,:

> For us [the British], it was quite simple: there was work to be done. Air Attaché Hugh Macdonald and his assistant Tom Mapplebeck virtually disappeared; Charlie Clark [Military Attaché] scarcely left the Yugoslav General Staff; while the rest of what were now 24-hour working days were spent with Tupanjanin and his friends. (Glen(B), 59)

Where did Macdonald and Mapplebeck disappear ? To maintain *direct contact with military elements,* as required by Item 3 of Taylor's report. *"The coup preparations will take some time to complete"*, reported Taylor. (Item 2) Meaning: **no preparations for the coup had been done as of 19 March,** and therefore arrangements for the coup had to be immediately expedited.

> The 'lobbying' efforts of Macdonald and Mapplebeck with the Yugoslav air force had been consistent and effective; so too was the sowing of seeds among younger officers of the General Staff, although the Yugoslav High Command was cautious and noncommittal. (Glen(B), 59)

To implement Item 3 of Taylor's report, Macdonald visited Mirković a few times after the all-British meeting, as described in **Part Two.** The honorary Air Attaché, Tom Mapplebeck, on 25 March strongly urged Gen. Mirković to launch the coup as soon as possible. (Stafford(cp), 415)

On the morning of 26 March, Macdonald had his first, secret meeting with General D. Simović, and another one in the late afternoon – as described in Chapter 10.

And the SOE operatives? They were to *continue to push on with preparation for the coup d'état* through the Serbian Peasant party and *Narodna Odbrana.* (Item 1)"Nurturing SPP" had been one of Glen's major assignment anyway. "My own work nurturing the Serbian Peasant party went ahead, again mutually reassuring, with this down-to-earth solid lot who had often seen defeat turned into victory." (Glen(B), 49) As seen in Taylor's report (Item 2), as of 19 March no decision had been made and no timing set to execute the coup. Therefore Tupanjanin, Trifunović, and other British *political friends* needed time to influence Mirković-Simović and/or other military *to enable action to be taken within first few days of pact when public feelings may be expected to be most violent.*

The coup-wishers now had to be urged to become the coup-plotters.

**

The general public knew nothing about the decision of the all-British meeting on 19 March, but rumors were spread about the government's crisis. Various protests, prepared in advance, were sent to the leadership of the state. According to SOE, the most deserving was ["Daddy"] Trifunović, who worked night and day. Thus, for example, the Association of reserve military chiefs adopted a statement in which they expressed a concern about the Pact which – for them – was against national honor and independence. On 22 March, Campbell informed the Foreign Office and the command in Cairo that the Association declared total readiness to defend the independence, sovereignty and borders of the state, faithful to the King and the homeland, in the spirit of the national tradition and ideals. (Vodušek Starić, 233; n54)

The SOE reported that ["Uncle"] Tupanjanin – encouraged by midnight talks with Masterson – applied utmost energy to force the Serbian Peasant Party to act against the pro-German Ministers. Masterson did everything to connect together the opposition political parties, the national associations, groups of University professors, and the organizations (such as the Red Cross), to persistently demand from the Regent not to surrender Yugoslavia to the German supremacy. Pamphlets, illegally printed and distributed, agitated the public. (Vodušek Starič, 232; n52)

**

Activities of *all SOE friends and everyone with whom SOE had contact* are examined in **Part Two ......** SOE had wide contacts in Belgrade, less so with the military than civilians. Because there was a ***necessity* to urge** all these contacts to carry-out the coup, that simply implies that - until the 19th March - all those contacts had no specific time-schedule for the coup, and were not prepared nor ready to execute it. The chief executor, General Borivoje - Bora Mirković, claimed that he was planning the overthrow of the regime since 1937. Some politicians actually proposed the coup to the British early in the summer of 1940 – as shown in **Appendix D.** But they sprang into action only after the British urged them to, after 19 March, actually on or after 24 March, when the British promised them full support.

The timing of the coup was linked to developments in Greece and Germany's approaching attack on Greece. General Mirković acknowledged that he was in contact with the British Air Attaché and his assistant, days before he decided on the timing which, he claimed, he did during the afternoon of March 26th. From 24 through 26 March he was in daily contact with Ilija Trifunović Birčanin ("Daddy") – the main SOE's liaison man to the conspirators – whose *Narodna Odbrana* was also "subsidized" by the British. **(See Part Two)**

**

Cyrus Leo Sulzberger, an expert on the Balkans, wrote about those days:

> The English had long been preparing for this possibility to [Yugoslavia's signing the Tripartite Pact] and acted with admirable promptness and efficiency. Leopold Amery, a cabinet member, urged the Serbs on the BBC, "Will you let your people become once more a subject race?" London's intelligence agents, including the two air attachés, Hugh MacDonald and Tom Mapplebeck, conspired feverishly with General Mirković of the Jugoslav air force and officers of the Royal Guard. ... Meantime Hugh Dalton, head of London's Special Operations Executive (SOE), a cloak and dagger outfit, told his Belgrade representative, an oil man named Tom Masterson: *"Use all means to raise a revolution."* On March 27 the plotters struck, spreading violent slogans: "No war without the Serbs," "Better grave than slave," and "Better war than a pact." (Sulzberger, 126. Italics added.)

20 March: Crown Council meeting, *"no way to avoid keeping a humiliating rendezvous in Vienna"*

By March 19th, Cincar Marković was an uneasy man, ... The Germans had agreed to all Yugoslavia's demands; notes embodying the Yugoslav proposals had been approved by Ribbentrop. There would have to be another crown council meeting, and then the cabinet meeting, and now Cincar Marković and the other could no longer raise new issues nor contrive new delays.

The council convened late the morning of the 20th. The point of decision came when Cincar Marković reported he had found a way of publishing the protocols. Yugoslavia would release them to the press, not as part of the pact but separately, and the Germans would neither confirm nor deny their authenticity. Now members of the council had to make decision. There was no way of avoiding it or delaying. Far from happy over the news that the Germans had agreed to their demands, they now saw no way out, no way to avoid keeping a humiliating rendezvous in Vienna. ... (Hoptner, 233)

20 March: Resignation of three Ministers, *"the work of SOE ..."*

The first stage of the British plan "concentrated *on the "legitimate", or peaceful, overthrow of the government, by encouraging the resignation of as many of its members as possible to force a government crisis.* (Stafford(cp), 411. Italics added.) As decided the preceding day at the round-table conference,

> Here the SOE utilized its contacts with Tupanjanin to the maximum. He was in contact several times each day with SOE representatives, and it was largely because of his efforts that three cabinet members resigned on March 20 when Cvetković announced the proposed terms of the Pact. [Branko] Čubrilović, of the Serb Peasant Party *(which was being subsidized by the SOE);* [Srđan] Budisavljević, of the Independent Democrats *(also being subsidized by the SOE);* and [Mihailo] Konstantinović, an Independent, submitted their resignation immediately, and when Konstantinović temporarily withdrew his resignation under direct pressure from the prince regent, Tupanjanin "bullied" him into line. (Stafford(cp), 411. Italics added.)

As E. Barker described it:

> Three members of the government resigned rather than agree to signing the pact – Branko Čubrilović, of the Serb Peasant Party, Srdjan Budisavljević, of the Independent Democratic Party (both parties were subsidised by S.O.E., who were in close touch with both men) and Mihajlo Konstantinović, an independent nominee of Prince Paul's, over whom Budisavljević and Tupanjanin (of the Serb Peasant Party, also in constant touch with S.O.E.) had acquired considerable influence. The rest voted for signature or abstained. (Barker, 90-91)

The resignation "was the work of SOE in close co-ordination with Tupanjanin." (Onslow, 45)

> When Tupanjanin persuaded three Serb ministers to resign in protest at the draft pact this prompted the Yugoslav government to continue its deliberations behind closed doors to counter opposition. It was apparent that they were going ahead with the Pact, leaving a *coup d'état* as SOE's only option. (Williams, 30)

> ... It is clear that Tupanjanin had believed that the resignation of three political allies, and the ensuing Cabinet crisis, would either precipitate the fall of the government, or a radical change of foreign policy. This did not happen, and the Turkish Government, much to Eden's frustration, used the political crisis in Belgrade as the excuse not to make a new approach to Yugoslavia: the Turkish Ambassador in Belgrade was instructed to act only "if he finds the occasion suitable". (Onslow, 51)

Eden confirmed the British subsidy to and the role of the (Serbian) Peasant Party: " We had for some time been supporting one of the Serb parties, which had a Minister in the Government. He had taken the lead in resigning over the Pact." (Eden, 226)

**

> Their [SOE] links with the air force conspirators, led by Bora Mirković, were only indirect – through Trifunović and Radoje Knežević on the Yugoslav side (**), and through the air attaché's contact with Mirković on the British side. Nevertheless, they were kept relatively well informed of developments. (Stafford(cp), 412)

(**) In the SOE's view, it was [Radoje] Knežević who took the initiative in fomenting the coup, and his were "the brains behind the conspiracy". The SOE considered Mirković "while enthusiastic and energetic to be unfortunately entirely without political capacity." (Stafford(cp), 412n48)

Shone's attempt to influence Maček, 20 March

After the unsuccessful attempt on 18 March to change Prince Paul's mind, Shone tried to influence the Croatian leaders. On the morning of 20 March, in the British Legation, Shone informed Ilija Jukić that he had given Prince Paul an important message from Mr. Eden. Shone asked Jukić to inform Dr Maček and other Croatian representatives that Great Britain wanted only one thing of Yugoslavia: not to sign anything with Germany. In the British opinion – explained Shone – Yugoslavia was in a good position and should not fear Germany, because the German troops in the Balkans are squeezed between Russia, Turkey and the Anglo-Greek troops. Therefore, Germany has no interest in also provoking Yugoslavia. Jukić promised to inform Maček and other Croatian representatives, and did so. (Jukić's brief survey of Yugoslavia's foreign policy, pp. 99-100. Žarko Popović Collection, Box2, Folder 2.23, Hoover Institution Archives)

Shone's arguments were evidently not convincing. At that time German troops were not squeezed in the Balkans. The Soviet Union was still allied to Germany, and continued to supply

Germany's war machine with oil and other material. Turkey did not want to get involved in a war against Germany. Jukić also knew that by then, Great Britain had sent only some 45,000 troops to support the already weakened Greek army, and by the time of Germany's invasion of Greece, on 6 April, there were reportedly some 60,000 British troops in Greece.

Urging American support for British policies

As the British attempt to sway Price Paul was failing, American support was urged and it went beyond the sphere of propaganda and diplomatic pressure, to include economic coercion.

> As Yugoslavia's acceptance of the Tripartite Pact seemed imminent, [the British Ambassador in Washington, [Lord] Halifax was instructed to get the American Government "if possible to send further instructions to their Minister in Belgrade with a view, *inter alia,* to ensuring that if Yugoslavia signs anything that instrument shall include an assurance by Germany that she will not attack Salonika." The US State Department responded by instructing the American Minister in Belgrade to inform the Yugoslav Government that "the US Government would freeze all Yugoslav assets should Yugoslavia make any agreement with Germany which would affect Yugoslavia's independence", gave military facilities to Germany, or affected the security of British military forces. (Onslow, 47-8)

On this request Professor S. Onslow commented:

> However, there was not complete unity of approach between London and Washington. Disappointingly for Britain, this American support did not extend to suggesting Yugoslavia take offensive action. Similarly, American offer of support remained deliberately vague – promises of material and moral support to maintain her independence, rather than the specific offer of armament from American production. America looked to Britain to promise to lend "material military aid with air force and ground force". ... However, American diplomats on the spot did what they could to lend Britain all possible moral support. During the final frenetic days in the lead up to the *coup*, to London's immense satisfaction, Halifax reported that America was putting "all the pressure they could in the same direction as ourselves, but that [they] would certainly consider if they could do more". Campbell saw Lane at least once a day and two exchanged information and co-ordinated their diplomatic approaches and pressure on the President of the Council and Government. (Onslow, 48-9)
>
> This marked (if not total) British success in co-ordinating policy and diplomatic pressure in the Balkans, and on Yugoslavia in particular, with the Americans was in direct contrast to UK's effort to recruit the Soviet Union. ... The Soviets refused to be drawn into a commitment to support the neutrality and independence of the Balkan states. (Onslow, 49-50)

Events were developing quickly.

20 March: "... use all means to raise a revolution"

Cognizant of these developments, on 20 March Colville recorded in his diary: "The diplomatic battle for the soul of Yugoslavia is reaching its height and sways either way with vertiginous speed." (Colville. 366)

Hugh Dalton, the head of SOE, became directly involved and issued an order for the coup *by all means.* He wrote in his *Memoirs* that on March 20th

> **We sent a wire to our friends to use all means to raise a revolution.** On March 27th there was a coup in Belgrade. The Air Force, junior officers in the Army, and the Opposition Parties took the lead. (Dalton, 373. Emphasis added.)

**

In Belgrade, on 20 March, Campbell communicated with Cvetković at least three times, attempting very hard to influence the Premier to accept British proposals related to Salonika and Turkey. The central theme was Eden's suggestion for a conference of the Yugoslav, Turkish, and Greek representatives on British territory, the Island of Cyprus. Eden was convinced that the agreement reached at the conference would keep in check Germany's plan for the Balkans. (Petranović & Žutić, 174-6)

The reason for Eden's proposal was his failure with the Turks, on 18 March, to convince them to consider an attack on Salonika as a *casus belli*. At that meeting in Cyprus Turkey agreed to exchange views with Yugoslavia about the threat to Salonika. Eden used this agreement to wishfully salvage the situation.

> To the immense frustration of the Foreign Secretary, the Turkish Government subsequently refused to send new instructions to their Belgrade minister because of the Cabinet crisis in Yugoslavia – precipitated by the resignation of three Serb politicians on 20 March. (Onslow, 44-5)

The real reason was that the Turkish Government had decided much earlier not to get involved in the war.

20 March, Prince Paul – Slobodan Jovanović meeting

Belgrade University Professor Slobodan Jovanović – described as "one of Serbia's most prolific jurists, historians, sociologists, journalists and literary critics" and "greatest authority on constitutional law" – was politically active in March 1941, meeting a great number of people. He and Prince Paul met twice – at the Prince's request, and again on Thursday, 20 March, at the Professor's. The conversation was held just prior to the Government's deliberation about the Pact. On 23 March the Professor had a walk and a long talk with his University colleague, Dragoljub Jovanović who, immediately after the walk, recorded their conversation. Following are some topics covered in the Prince - Professor meeting on 20 March.

The Prince informed the Professor that:

Yugoslavia was exempted from military clauses. Only material would be transported through the country, but no German troops.

Yugoslavia was exempted from all declarations of war.

The Prince thought that the Russians would not go to war for Yugoslavia.

He considered the attitude of Turkey uncertain.

He thought that he had secured the borders of Yugoslavia, and thus had discouraged all revisionists, Bulgarian, Hungarian, and Italian. (Petranović & Žutić, 237-8)

So: S. Jovanović was informed of the essential features of the Government's approach to the Pact.

S. Jovanović also thought that, in a recent speech, President Roosevelt had almost declared the war on Germany, and that the British were pushing the entire world into the war, while they themselves were not ready for it, and were getting ready in the course of the war itself. (Petranović & Žutić, 237, 239)

21 March, Campbell: *"Would it be preferable to delay the coup ..."*

On 21 March, hectic communications streamed between Eden in Cairo and Campbell in Belgrade. In telegram No. 171 to Eden, Campbell suggested

> the possibility of encouraging a coup d'état ...Should further arguments fail to deter the Yugoslavs, and should the alternative of breaking off relations with the Yugoslav government be rejected, then a coup might accomplish the desired objective – either by preventing signature, or, if signature occurred, by "defeating" it. (Stafford(cp) 403; 403n17)

Campbell also offered four factors for consideration:

1- If the German attack on Greece was not imminent, *would it be preferable to delay a coup* so as not to precipitate such an attack.

2- A coup or revolt could only take place 'at the moment of greatest effervescence' , that is, at or immediately after signature.

3- The people ready to revolt should be assured that the British Government would brand the present Yugoslav government responsible for signature - by breaking off relations with it, and then *would support the new government.*

4- The attitude of the Croats should be taken into account. (Stafford(cp), 403. Italics added.)

As Professor D. Stafford noted, Campbell "asked his government's authority in principle to follow this line of action". "Churchill was willing to accept the risk of precipitating a German attack if a pro-Allied Yugoslav government could be produced by a coup", (Stafford(cp), 403-4.)

**

These two points are noteworthy: 1. If on the 21st of March there existed the possibility of *encouraging a coup* - that implies that the conspirators on that day were not thinking of the coup – and needed encouragement. 2. The conspirators needed British assurance of support. No support – no coup. That was the requirement which Jovan Đonović stated to Julian Amery in July 1940, when the idea of the coup was first brought up. (See **Appendix D**.)

Campbell's warning to take into consideration the attitude of the Croats was based on his recent personal experience gained at the conference with the Croatian Peasant Party's representatives in Zagreb, who were in favor of the Pact which was without military clauses.

**

Furthermore, Campbell informed Eden that he was investigating the possibilities of a revolt against the government, and he was

> "inclined to the belief that any encouragement and support from us should be dependent on there being almost certain prospects of immediate success. There might, however, be something to be said for encouraging a movement even if we were not certain of it achieving immediate and complete success," subject to the views of Eden and the military authorities on the question of the imminence of German action against Greece. The question of encouraging a coup d'état seemed to Campbell to depend largely on the considerations of British military requirements. Pending further investigations in Belgrade, however, he asked for his government's authority in principle to follow this line of action.
> (Stafford(cp), 403)

In his *Memoirs,* Eden commented:

> On March 21st, Campbell telegraphed to ask me whether he should threaten to break off relations with Yugoslavia if the Government signed the Tripartite Pact, and so encourage the opposition to *overthrow the Government* and annul their signature. If I agreed the Ambassador wanted to know *when would it suit me,* from a military point of view, *for this to be done.* (Eden, 226. Italics added.)

So: Campbell asked *when would it suit EDEN to encourage the opposition to overthrow Prince Paul's Government!* That simply means that Campbell – whether directly or by proxy - was in a position to decide on the timing of the coup. A British Minister in a foreign country would not dare to mislead his Foreign Minister with such a question on matters as important as a *coup d'état*, if he was not sure that he could make such an important decision. He could not ask for a consideration **to time the coup** unless he was certain that the coup could really be timed by the British. This shows that the British – not the Serb conspirators – were in control of the **timing** of the coup. (More evidence on this subject is presented in **Part Two**.)

21 March: Eden's instruction to Campbell on the timing of the coup

At once, on 21 March, Eden replied to Campbell that he did not favor the threat of breaking off relations. "On the day the Yugoslav government decided to sign [21 March] Eden, from Cairo, asked Campbell about the 'practical possibility' of a coup." (Barker, 92) As for the timing of the coup, he instructed Campbell:

> "I agree that upon present information suggested *coup* would have to be staged at the moment of reaction caused by signature and this may be very soon." (Eden, 226)

Eden did not question Campbell's ability to decide on the timing at all, and directed him accordingly. Neither Campbell nor Eden mentioned the Serb conspirators as having played a decisive role in the timing, nor that they had to be asked; the timing of the coup was just that: their own decision.

Eden then continued giving Campbell his views on military matters:

> From the military point of view *it is more important that Yugoslavia should deny passage*, if necessary by force, to German troops *than that she should declare war* if Greece is invaded through Bulgaria. ... Advance thorough Monastir [Bitolj] Gap is the danger which we most fear. So long as Yugoslavia is resolute to refuse passage, it should now be difficult for the Germans to direct the attack on Greece with good prospect of success. .. (Eden, 226-7. Italics added.)

Eden *"would stop at nothing to ensure that the Yugoslavs fight to deny passage to Monastir Gap, ..."*

Having stated his priority, Eden added a further instruction in that sense, which could eventually split the Yugoslav army:

> Much will depend upon the Commander of Southern Yugoslav army. Have you any contacts with him or information as to his attitude? So long as he refuses passage to Germans he is our friend. What would be the effect on him of a *coup d'état*? While I would stop at nothing to ensure that Yugoslavs fight to deny passage to Monastir Gap, I do not yet know enough to estimate the effect of a *coup* or chance of ensuring this. (Eden, 227)

The Foreign Office preferred a policy that would "work for the secession of the Yugoslav army in South Serbia and the creation of a separatist government under its aegis: this 'would give us control of the vital passes to prevent a German attack on the flank of the Greek army.' " The British minister in Greece was already pursuing this possibility with General Papagos." (Stafford(cp), 406)

That the British contemplated on creating a separatist regime in southern Serbia is shown in **Appendix C**.

21 March: "... ensuring vehement reaction in Serbia ..."

On 21 March, 'Dalton noted gloomily in his diary the fact of "bad news from Juggery".' (Stafford[cp], 403) Cadogan entrusted to his diary: "Yugoslavs seem to have sold their souls to the Devil. *All* these Balkan peoples are trash. Poor dears – I know their difficulties. They have got no arms, and no money and no industry. But then they shouldn't have behaved as Great Powers at Geneva." (Dilks(ed), 365. Cadogan's Italics.)

As George Taylor had assessed that pro-British Serb public opinion was SOE's best hope for influencing government policy, yet another move was made in that direction to influence the Serbs.

On 20 March, Campbell sent the following suggestion to Eden, then still in Cairo:

> I suggest that B.B.C. Serb-Croat broadcasts should now adopt stronger line, *working on the feelings of Serbs in particular* with a view to (a) increasing mass opposition in Serbia to signature of any agreement with Germany and (b) *ensuring vehement reaction in Serbia* (and so far as possible in the rest of Yugoslavia) if agreement is signed. Croats and their history should not, however, be left out of the appeal.
> 2. I suggest the following line: time of decision approaches, Yugoslavia must decide now or very soon whether she is to be just another Romania or true to her glorious past, choose way of greatness and indicate her belief in freedom and democracy. Yugoslavia is a great nation – her future demands that she shall take the right decision. No pact with the devil, no encirclement, no betrayal of your belief. Serbs, Yugoslavs, we know you will be true to the spirit of Kosovo and Kaimakcalan.
> 3. It would be well, too, if American broadcast in Serb-Croat should voice the feelings of Yugoslavs in the United States in strong terms. (PRO, Premier 3 / 570/11. Italics added.)

Appealing to Kosovo and Kajmakčalan was contrived to provoke strong emotions among the Serbs, knowing that human emotions are potent impulses for motivating actions. George Taylor was recommending this kind of approach to the Serbs from the time of his arrival in Belgrade. It was expressed in thousands of leaflets financed by the British, in handsomely paid pro-British, anti-German articles in newspapers (particularly connected with the news agency *Britanova)*, in propaganda by people / institutions "subsidized" by the British, in black propaganda by the likes of the Greek journalist Pappas. Other British-inspired activities were tied to the Serb pro-Allied, anti-German pre-disposition flowing from the First World War - and to the news of young King Peter's ascendance to the throne – all this converged into emotional outbursts on the streets of Belgrade on March 27th, unrestricted by rational thought and without regard to consequences.

The broadcasts greatly contributed to the "vehement reaction" which manifested itself on the streets of Belgrade in the aftermath of the coup.

**

Whether Campbell's suggestion for the BBC broadcast was his own or not did not really matter. Baron Julian Amery wrote on this subject:

> There was little enough we could do in London; but I suggested that, as the only member of the Government who spoke Serbian, my father might usefully broadcast to Yugoslavia. The B.B.C. agreed and on the evening of 25 March he made a stirring appeal to the Yugoslavs to be worthy of the traditions of Kossovo and to choose the path of honour rather than capitulation. (Amery, 227)

22 March: *"a crushing telegram to Tsvetkovitch"*

"The diplomatic battle for the soul of Yugoslavia is reaching its height and sways either way with vertiginous speed", wrote Colville in his diary. (Colville, 366)

According to Cadogan, on 22 March "there were letters from Belgrade suggesting message from King to Prince Paul. And the P.M. with a crashing telegram to Tsvetkovitch." (Diks(ed), 365)
In the telegram Churchill "did what [he] could to rally the Yugoslavs against Germany". He envisioned "the eventual total defeat of Hitler and Mussolini", invoked the combined strength and wealth of the British Empire and the United States - as if the US already had been engaged in the war – and concluded by saying:

> If Yugoslavia and Turkey stand together with Greece, and with all the aid which the British Empire can give, the German curse will be stayed and final victory will be won as surely and as decisively as it was last time. I trust Your Excellency may rise to the height of world events. (Churchill(GA), 160)

Like Eden five days earlier, Churchill knew that Turkey would not participate in the British plan for the Balkan Front, and that Britain could not offer needed aid. Like Eden, Churchill was misinforming and misleading; the name of the game was to get Yugoslavia into the war *"anyhow"*.

22 March, Campbell: Feeling in Serbia ready, *"if led"*

Elisabeth Barker provided additional information on the British considerations of the coup, and specifically, on its would-be leaders. Responding to Eden's inquiry of 21 March on the "practical possibility" of the coup, on 22 March "Campbell replied that feeling in Serbia 'may be ready, if led' to burst out, and asked for H.M.G.'s view. " (Barker, 92)

The statement that the feeling for a coup was ready "IF LED" – implied that, on 22 March, there was nobody who would take the lead to execute the coup. Therefore, that leadership ought yet to be provided. What the British did to provide it is examined in **Part Two**……

Mirković - Mapplebeck - Legation connection

Based on an interview with Tom Mapplebeck in London, in September 1988, Professor Heather Williams wrote:

> The Briton who claimed to be closest to the makers of the coup, and the most in the know, was not a member of SOE, but Tom Mapplebeck, an honorary air attaché. Mapplebeck had lived in Belgrade since shortly after the First World War, in which he had served as an aviator, and had many contacts

in the Yugoslav air force. He was a great friend of Mirković who supplied him with copies of the Yugoslav General Staff's weekly intelligence summaries: these Mapplebeck translated and passed on to Campbell and the service attachés. (Williams, 32; 254n28)

With George Taylor's arrival in Belgrade on 27 February 1941, both the SOE and Legation personnel worked together on the objective to "resist" Germany, and to organize "post-occupational resistance". The Mirković-Mapplebeck-Legation link was a two-way communication channel – but not the only British channel with the coup-wishers. However, this channel, also, could be used to provide needed "leadership" in preparation for the coup.

Other personnel of the British Legation, of the institutions involved in propaganda, agents of SOE, etc, all did what they could - through their contacts – to effect the coup once that decision had been made.

Churchill's directive: " ...get Yugoslavia in to the war anyhow... "
22 March 1941

In the instructions to Campbell on 21 March, Eden stated that, from a military point of view, it was *more important that Yugoslavia should deny passage* to the Germans [towards Salonika]*than that she should declare war,* if Greece were invaded through Bulgaria. The Prime Minister disagreed. To him the war was more important, and the following day he directed Eden accordingly:

PRIME MINISTER TO MR. EDEN.

> Belgrade Telegram 171 of March 21, para 9.
> You must settle this in Cairo. (Stop) To me it seems more important to get Yugoslavia in to the war anyhow than to gain a few days on the Salonika front. (Stop) Play the hand as you think best. (Ends)
> (Initialed) WSC
> 22.3.41

(PREM 3/510/11, no. 369)

Get Yugoslavia in to the war anyhow --- i.e., "in any way or by any means whatever" (Webster). Tracing and examining the footsteps of Churchill, British military historian Professor Richard Holmes observed: *"He had no objection to throwing other peoples to the wolves if it genuinely helped the British sledge to reach safety."* (p. 188. Italics added.) This time "The Man of the Century" not only did not object, but actually instructed his Foreign Minister to draw another country into the war.

Subsequent instructions from Eden to Campbell reflected this directive of Churchill.

Recalling President Roosevelt's letter to Hitler

Churchill's directive brings to mind a passage from President Roosevelt's letter to Hitler of 14 April 1939:

> "Nothing can persuade the peoples of the earth that any governing power has any right or need to inflict the consequences of war on its own or any other people save in the cause of self-evident home defense. ... "

On 22 March 1941 there was no *cause of self-evident home defense of Great Britain.* Hitler's plan for the invasion of Britain had been cancelled. Still, the people of Yugoslavia were to be exposed to the consequences of war ...

Which brings to mind another sentence from the same letter:

> "Heads of great Governments in this hour are literally responsible for the fate of humanity in coming years .... "

**

On 22 March 1941 – the day of Churchill's directive - Eden gave Campbell "authority to act on his own if he had no time" to consult Eden.

> ... In considering [the chances of a successful *coup d'état]* you should bear in mind that rather than allow Yugoslavia to slip by stages into German orbit, we are prepared to risk precipitating German attack. ... (Eden, 227)

Eden's statement, that *the British* were prepared to risk precipitating a German attack on Yugoslavia, is consistent with his statement of 27 April 1941 that *"A war in Balkans was not what Hitler wanted."* (Eden, 242*)*

*** While Churchill was directing Eden's actions, on 22 March a **German ultimatum** gave Yugoslavia until the 25th **to sign the Tripartite Pact**. (Eden, 225) "Desperately searching for ways and means to encourage the national spirit" which Eden was sure was strong in Yugoslavia, the same day he instructed the British Ambassador in Moscow, Sir Stafford Cripps, to find out whether the Soviets "would be willing to encourage the Yugoslavs to resist".

> While explaining to the Yugoslav Minister in Moscow that the Soviet Government could do nothing in the matter, as the issue seemed to be settled already, he [Andrei Vyshinsky, of the Soviet Foreign Ministry] added that if this turned out not to be true, the Soviets would be ready for further discussion. (Eden, 226)

Prince Paul – Terence Shone meeting, 22 March

At Shone's request, Prince Paul met with him again in the evening of 22 March. The following day Shone reported to Eden on the arguments he unsuccessfully advanced to persuade "F" [code-name for the Prince] "for not signing the agreement in the present form or at least for delaying signature". In conclusion Shone reported:

"I regret having been unable to accomplish more. Events, he considers, worked strongly against us before my arrival (Turco-Bulgarian agreement, German occupation of Bulgaria, persistent doubts about Turkey's solidarity with us, weakening of Croat and Slovene leaders' will to resist). Acceptance by Germans of Yugoslav conditions (which happened I believe [the] day after my arrival) still further reduced any chance of success." (Balfour & Mackay, 238) Shone was not able to neutralize or invalidate the significance the mentioned events held in the decision to accept the terms of the Pact.

For Cadogan, on 23 March there were no signs of life from Churchill. "Balkans still a large question mark. Yugo[slavia] dithering and Turks drawing back into their shell." (Dilks(ed), 365)

23 March: SOE made contribution to prevent signature of the Pact; Macdonald – Mirković meeting

On 23 March, George Taylor telegraphed to London:

> I have seen Foreign Office telegram drawing attention to possibility of using organisation [SOE] for raising resistance to Government if Pact signed. ...
> A. SO2 has undoubtedly made important contribution to the struggle to prevent signature both as source of information and contacts, above all by work through TUPANJANIN, who has been heart and soul of the resistance.
> B. SO2 has undoubtedly made important contribution to the struggle t prevent signature both as source of information and contacts, above all by work through TUPANJANIN, who has been heart and soul of resistance.
> (George Taylor's report to SOE London, Great Britain, Special Operation Executive, 91087 – 10.V, Hoover Institution Archives)

On the afternoon of 23rd March, Military Attaché Macdonald informed General B. Mirković that Cvetković and Cincar-Marković would go the next day to Germany to sign the Pact – wrote the General. (Bosnić(ed), 34)

Mirković used a total of twenty five words to describe their meeting. Did they talk about anything else? Macdonald was bound to talk about the overthrow of the Government, as decided at the British round-table conference on 19 March, and acknowledged in Item 3 of Taylor's report to London, dated 26 March.

**

As a Yugoslav-Turkish-Greek conference, suggested by Eden to Campbell on 20 March, was not held, on 23 March Eden telegraphed to Campbell (No. 150) that the best he could do at the Cyprus meeting had been to extract from the Turks a statement that an attack on Salonika would constitute a "mortal danger" for Turkey (but not the desired "*casus belli*"). (Onslow, 44)

Chapter 10

Having received the Prime Minister's instructions of 22 March, [in telegram No. 137]

on 24 march Eden authorized Campbell to inform the Putschists of British support secretly

> You are authorized now to proceed at your discretion by any means at your disposal to move leaders and public opinion to understanding of realities and to action to meet the situation.
> You have my full authority for any measures that you may think it right to take to further change of Government or regime, even by *coup d'état*.
> Any new Government formed as a result of these events and prepared to resist German demands would have our full support. **You may secretly so inform any prospective leaders in whom you have confidence.**(Eden, 227. Emphasis added.)

On 20 March **SOE** was given the order to *raise a revolution by any means.* Four days later **the Legation** was instructed to do the same. *Minister Campbell was duty-bound to secretly inform the coup-wishers of Eden's instructions and promised support – through whatever "contact" was the most effective and appropriate.* This kind of support was a pre-requirement for the coup which the Trifunović – Đonović group asked of Julian Amery in the first place, in the summer of 1940. Now they got what they had wanted.

In professor S. Onslow's view,

> Eden's ultimate decision to authorise UK involvement in a *coup d'état* against Prince Paul's regime was to save Britain's Greek venture, to bolster Turkey's resolve against the German advance into the Balkans, and because of the associated perceived benefits in the United States, Vichy France, Spain and the Soviet Union. (Onslow, 40) – So, it was the UK INVOLVEMENT.

As Professor D. Stafford observed, "By March 24, ... , Campbell had full authority to encourage a change of government or regime (that is, the removal of Prince Paul), by any means, including, if necessary, a coup d'état." (Stafford(cp), 405) Having full authority and it was Campbell's duty to exercise it.

Complying with Eden's instruction to *proceed with actions to meet the situation,* the British Air Attaché, Group Captain A.H.H. Macdonald, visited General B. Mirković, the coup chief executor, on the 25th March, and General D. Simović, the nominal leader of the coup, twice on the 26th March. As requested by Dalton of British *friends to use all means to raise a revolution,* "Daddy" *Vojvoda* Birčanin was visiting and advising Mirković every day from the 24th March through the night of the coup itself, on the 27th.

Prospective leaders quietly apprised of British full support

The substance of Eden's statement of 24 March, that *any new government... would have British full support* , and that Campbell *may secretly so inform any prospective leaders ...* had specific meaning. To understand it, one must recall some of the events that occurred early in the summer of 1940.
According to Section D/SOE operatives in Belgrade, who participated in the events, there were at least two groups opposed to Government policy who proposed the *coup d'état* as a solution, and who could now be secretly informed of full support by the British.
Most prominent in the first group were Jovan Đonović – a politician and "a man of many devices" – and *Vojvoda* Ilija Trifunović Birčanin – "the greatest of Serb guerrilla leaders in the Balkan and First World Wars", the President of *Narodna Odbrana* (*National Defense League*). The other group consisted of members of (Serbian) *Zemljoradnička Stranka* (Agrarian Party), usually referred to as the Serbian Peasant Party (SPP), i.e., Dr. Milan Gavrilović and Dr. Miloš Tupanjanin, the Party's President and his Deputy, respectively.

By his own account, Brigadier General Borivoje-Bora Mirković had a change of regime and Government in mind since 1937. There were others who felt similarly. However, within the scope of this story, **Appendix D** deals with the activities of these two groups mentioned above.

As was concluded at the all-British meeting on 19 March, the Legation-SOE team had more than one channel through which to relay Eden's message. Specifically, there were at least these functioning channels:

Mapplebeck – Air Force Attaché Macdonald - Mirković ;
Macdonald – Simović;
SOE – *Vojvoda* Birčanin – Mirković - military;
Military Attaché Clarke – Mirković – military;
Masterson - military - veteran's organizations – *Narodna Odbrana* (Birčanin);
SOE – subsidized opposition political parties.

"From 24th March onwards S.O.E. worked hard, mostly through Trifunović Birčanin and Radoje Knežević, to encourage the conspirators and to prepare public opinion." (Balfour & Mackay, 255)

For the sake of historic accuracy, one should hope that one day it will be established, precisely and without any doubt, how and through whom Eden's message was communicated to the leaders of the coup.

24 March: *"Nothing is to be hoped for from the present military chiefs, with one possible exception"* ... General Dušan Simović

In answer to Eden's questions of 22 March on the chances of a *coup d'état*, and probably after he had received Eden's authorization to secretly inform prospective coup leaders of Britain's support, late on 24 March Campbell replied in a MOST IMMEDIATE "telegram of particular secrecy". Excerpts follow:

> No government can remain in power in Yugoslavia without the backing of the army. Therefore no coup d'état could have prospect of success unless new Government were either a military one or, if civilian, enjoyed from the outset or could without delay secure the support of the army. Consequently we consider that by far the best chance lies in a military movement. It is by no means certain that this can be secured specially since Yugoslavia's accession to the Tripartite pact is susceptible of presentation in a very harmless form. But if feasible a coup d'etat by the army offers by far the best prospect of success and has [grp undec] advantage of being a comprehensive solution. The defection of a few units would be of far less value, if not harmful to our purpose by removing those who might be expected to be active on our behalf (in this connection please see Athens telegram No. 165 to Cairo and your telegram No. 134 to me).
>
> 2. Nothing is to be hoped for from the present military chiefs, *with one possible exception;* probably the most senior general officers would have to be removed from their commands. We think it possible that one or two senior generals on the retired list, *if not the active Military chief mentioned above,* might be found to lead the movement. We are however convinced that in order to secure adhesion of such leaders to the idea, the possibility of offering military supplies is necessary so they could feel that if a firm attitude to Germany produced war they would be prepared with more adequate equipment in their hands. The mere promise of a share in the common pool is far too vague and would get us nowhere. The offer would also give us something with which to approach potential leaders directly.   (PRO, PREMIER 3, 570/11. Italics added.)

"The one possible exception " among the military chiefs, *"the active military chief mentioned above"* – was General Dušan Simović. Evidence: when on 26 March British Air Attaché Macdonald secretly visited Simović, he described the General as the "head of an organization intending to carry out a coup d'etat".

Based on a George Taylor's and Thomas Masterson's report to Hugh Dalton on SOE activities in Yugoslavia, dated in London on 24 June 1941, Elisabeth Barker came to this conclusion:

> What Campbell's reference to a 'military movement' meant was that while S.O.E.'s contacts with Serb political parties and patriotic organisations were very useful for purposes of agitation and

> propaganda, they were not enough in themselves to produce a coup against Prince Paul. ... The best hope lay with the Air Force, and with the younger army officers: the General Staff, *whatever bribes S.O.E. may have lavished,* were too cautious and fearful to take action. ... (Barker, 92. Italics added)

Setting the supply of arms as a prerequisite for military leadership of the coup was puzzling. Did not Campbell know there were no British arms to be supplied? That is hard to accept, for the following reason: under his watch, in May 1940, "the provision of 750,000 pound sterling credit to Yugoslavia for armament purchases could not be taken up by British production." (Onslow, 11) The issue of British military armaments is described in **Appendix F.**

The question of the timing of the coup

Communicating with Eden, Campbell dealt with another important point:

> On the question of the timing of a coup, Campbell asked Eden simply for discretion "to make offer at once with a view to exploiting feeling aroused by signature of the pact ... or at a later stage when feeling had again been aroused by German behaviour or fresh German demands. Failing immediate *coup d'état* efforts would have to be concentrated on the same objective at a later stage or in the last resort on maintaining spirit in the Army divisions in Serbia to resist any attempts by the Germans to pass through South Serbia." (Stafford(cp) 405-6)

Professor D. Stafford observed:

> It is clear from this telegram that Campbell's views on the likelihood of a coup were less than optimistic, and that he considered the offer of British arms supplies as a *sine qua non*. Because the British ability to supply arms was already stretched to the limit, however, the reaction of the prime minister and the Foreign Office was one of gloom. Churchill noted "I am very doubtful about all this.", and a Foreign Office minuted that "if a coup d'état is really dependent upon immediate material supplies the outlook is very gloomy." Eden's reaction [in telegram no. 152] was gloomy and irritable. From Cairo he told Campbell, somewhat testily, that he regretted the government could give him "no more cards to play this difficult hand", reminding Campbell that he had full authority to *handle and time matters* as he thought best, and announced that he and his party were leaving Cairo en route to London that day. Eden's decision to leave Cairo clearly implied that he did not regard a coup as imminent. (Stafford(cp), 406. Italics added.)

Thus: it was up to Campbell "*to time matters*", i.e., to time the execution of the coup.

"Put full steam on ... after consulting the Minister"

Also on 24 March, "a telegram was sent to the SOE in Belgrade telling them 'to put full steam on to assist after consulting the Minister'." So, covert SOE activities had to be reported to and approved by Minister Campbell. "Later that day, the certainty of Yugoslav signature was confirmed by Campbell, and the War Cabinet was informed accordingly." (Stafford(cp), 405)

By 24 March, all British political and military personnel and secret agents in Belgrade worked together – under the Minister's authority - on the overthrow of Prince Paul's government. As Professor D. Stafford noted: " ... when it became increasingly clear that the signature [of the Tripartite Pact] was imminent, the British mobilized their full effort to prevent it. This effort encompassed both diplomatic pressure and subversive political action, and culminated in the coup of 27 March." (Stafford(cp), 401) The SOE agents and Legation personnel worked as a team:

> Both Taylor and Masterson met daily with Campbell and Armand Dew, counselor at the legation, to exchange information. Furthermore, Taylor and Dew would usually draft a report reviewing the situation in the light of all the intelligence, which the minister could use in reporting to London. Thus, the SOE had ample opportunity to inform the minister of their activities and information, and Taylor appears to have operated on the assumption that Campbell passed all intelligence information on to London, although he never actually saw any of Campbell's dispatches. (Stafford(cp), 412-13)

Taylor had no need to see the dispatches. He was sent on the mission " with the local rank of full Colonel and Counsellor in the Foreign Office; his visit was announced to His Majesty's Representatives in various capitals on 11th January [1941], ..." (Mackenzie, 106-7) That obligated them to cooperate fully with Taylor.

So, there was full cooperation and coordination of British activities at the top, in the Legation. Tasks and roles were assigned through channels best suited to accomplish them: military attachés - with the Yugoslav military personnel and/or organizations, SOE and other agents - with political parties and/or propaganda outfits. It will be shown that Dalton, although the head of SOE, was fully informed of the air attaché's work with the military conspirators. Whether military or political personnel, overt or covert agents – they all were British. "Our Allies" to the Putschists.

The idea of blowing up the train with the Yugoslav representatives

On the evening of 24 March, Cvetković and his Foreign Minister, Aleksandar Cincar-Marković, left Belgrade for Austria, to sign the Protocol of adhesion of Yugoslavia to the Tripartite pact

On 24 March Cadogan noted in his diary:

> All the news from the Balkans is bad: the Yugoslavs are collapsing and the Turks are running out. The former are hard to blame, but the latter are the villains. So far, they've done *nothing* but evade *every* obligation. They now *refuse* to inform Yugoslavia of their declaration (*) to A. [Eden] in Cyprus ... Cabinet at 5. After we met, I got Transocean message that Jugs are off tonight to sign Pact. Told Cabinet. A. is doing all that is possible, and that is unavailing. Can only ask G.J. [Gladwyn Jebb, the CEO of SOE] to blow up the Jug train! But he probably can't do that.
> (*) Turkey had agreed to propose to Yugoslavia an exchange of views in the event of a German attack on Greece. (Dilks(ed), 365. Italics in the source.)

Professor H. Williams commented on this idea:

> The suggestion that SOE should blow up the train on which Cvetković and Cincar-Marković were returning from Vienna was in fact conveyed to Taylor in Belgrade, but according to Taylor himself, Ilija Trifunović Birčanin had informed SOE on Monday 24 March that the coup was 99 per cent certain and preparations were making good progress. To take such drastic action at this juncture would mean the introduction of martial law which would upset the plans. (Williams, 31)

Birčanin was one of the British co-operatives who, at the time, was maintaining a link with the chief executor of the coup, General Mirković. However, he was not the only "contact".

While historian Williams wrote about blowing up the train when the two Ministers were *returning from Vienna, i.e. on the 26th March,* Cadogan mentioned it when they were *traveling to Vienna, on the 24th*. It is reasonable to assume that he made the entry into his diary *at the end of the 24th*, i.e., when they were going to Vienna. In that case they would have been unable to sign the Pact.

However, General Simović also provided information about the bombing, probably even before Cadogan entered it into his diary. This is his account:

On the 24th March, about12:30 p.m., Simović went to his brother's home. While he was talking with attorney Bora Marković – his man with the ties to the Royal Palace – he noticed ((that General Borivoje Mirković leaned toward my brother and whispered to him that he *'can blow up the train with the Ministers'* , which he [the brother] enthusiastically received.))
 "da se đeneral Borivoje Mirković nagnuo prema mom bratu i rekao mu šapatom da *'može baciti u vazduh voz s Ministrima'* , što je ovaj oduševljeno prihvatio."
 Not knowing that all preparations for the coup had been completed, Simović told Mirković: ((No, by no means not now! Let them compromise themselves to the end, and when they return, then we shall.))

"Ne nikako sad! Pusti ih neka se kompromituju do kraja, pa kada se budu vratili onda ćemo!" (Simović(44), 28-9. Italics added.)

**

It is clear that the idea of bombing the train existed, but it is not clear who stopped its execution - Trifunović Birčanin and SOE (as stated by Williams), or Simović (who wrote about it in 1944). However, the evidence that both Gen. Mirković and Trifunović knew and talked about it confirms their cooperation on the coup from 24 through 27 March 1941.

Eden to Campbell: There are no weapons to supply the Yugoslav army. 25 March

To Campbell's assertion that supplying arms was a condition for a successful coup, Eden replied on 25 March - before leaving Cairo, "with more restriction to suggestions from Campbell about promising military supplies":

> As those with whom you are in touch will be aware, British forces are now in Greece. These forces include anti-tank, anti-aircraft and armoured units. Yugoslav army, if they fight with us, will thus be fighting side by side with British forces armed with equipment mentioned in your telegram.
> It would be impossible to transfer this equipment from our troops to Yugoslav troops, nor would the latter without a period of training, as suggested, make effective use of those highly specialized weapons. Furthermore *there is no other source from which we can at present supply equipment of this nature,* ... (Eden, 227-8. Italics added.)

This arms-supply picture given to Campbell is quite different from the one Eden presented to Prince Paul on 17 March. He dangled the prospect of Lend-Lease hastened armaments to the Prince, while informing Campbell that *there was no other source.*

*** Protocol of adhesion of Yugoslavia to Tripartite Pact, Vienna, March 25, 1941

On the morning of 25 March, the Undersecretary of State for Dominion Affairs informed the United Kingdom High Commissioners in Canada, the Commonwealth of Australia, New Zealand, and Union of South Africa that the Pact would be signed, and added: **"Possibility of a military coup d'etat or resistance by at least part of army is under examination."** (TNA FO 371/30206. Emphasis added.)

"Examination" was just a euphemism for an all-out effort under Churchill, Eden and Dalton's instructions to Campbell and the SOE in support for a military coup.

> To Eden, this act [of signing] obviously came as a personal blow, perhaps even an affront, in no way softened by the "secret clauses". The Yugoslavs had gone their own way, in spite of all his pressure and promises. Prince Paul and Cvetković had dropped very heavy hints about what they were doing, they had not officially informed or consulted the British. They had in fact no formal obligation to do so, but that did not make their failure less wounding. (Barker, 91)

Cadogan, on 25 March: "Jugs are signing – silly, feeble mugs." (Dilks(ed), 366)

The protocol was signed by Cvetković and Cincar-Marković, in Hitler's presence. Germany's and Italy's Foreign Ministers, Joachim von Ribbentrop and Count Galeazzo Ciano, signed for Germany and Italy. (Jukić, 59) What did they sign?

> The Governments of Germany, Italy and Japan on the one hand and the Government of Yugoslavia on the other hand, through their plenipotentiaries, acknowledge the following:
> Article 1. Yugoslavia adheres to the Tripartite Pact, which was signed September 27, 1940, at Berlin, between Germany, Italy and Japan.
> Article 2. Representatives of Yugoslavia will be present at conferences of commissions for common technical questions created under Article 4 of the Tripartite Pact so far as the commission deals with matters touching Yugoslavia's interests.
> Article 3. The text of the Tripartite Pact is added as an annex to this protocol. This protocol is drawn up in the German, Italian, Japanese and Yugoslav languages, each of which is authentic. The present protocol comes into effect on the day of signing. (Balfour & Mackay, 313)

Immediately after the signing, "the Yugoslav delegates received all the agreed notes, addressed to the Premier and signed separately by Ribbentrop and Ciano." (Jukić, 59)

The first note dealt with Yugoslavia's sovereignty and territorial integrity:

> Mr. Prime Minister:
> In the name of the German Government and at its behest I have the honour to inform your Excellency of the following:
> On the occasion of the Yugoslav adherence today to the Tripartite Pact, the German Government confirms its decision to respect the sovereignty and territorial integrity of Yugoslavia at all times. (Balfour & Mackay, 313)

The second note promised not to seek transit rights:

> Mr. Prime Minister:
> With reference to the conversations that occurred in connection with Yugoslav adherence to the Tripartite Pact I have the honour to confirm to your Excellency herewith in the name of the Reich Government that in the agreement between the Governments of the Axis powers and the Royal Yugoslav Government, the Axis power governments during this war will not demand of Yugoslavia to permit the march or transportation of troops through the Yugoslav state or territory. (Balfour & Mackay, 313-14)

The third note dealt with the Axis powers not seeking military assistance from Yugoslavia:

> Mr. Prime Minister:
> With reference to the conversations that occurred in connection with Yugoslav adherence to the Tripartite Pact I have the honour to confirm to your Excellency herewith in the name of the Reich Government that in the agreement between the Governments of the Axis powers and the Royal Yugoslav Government :
> Italy and Germany assure the Government of Yugoslavia that out of consideration of the military situation, they do not wish to advance, on their part, any request whatsoever regarding military assistance.
> If, however, the Government of Yugoslavia, would consider, at any moment, that it is in its own interest to take part in the military operations of the powers of the Tripartite Pact, the Yugoslav Government will be free to conclude such military agreements as necessary, and with these powers themselves.
> Meanwhile, I beg you to keep the preceding communication strictly secret, and to make it public only with agreement of the Governments of the Axis powers. (Balfour & Mackay, 314)

The fourth note "promised Yugoslavia Salonika, and a Yugoslav corridor, in the reorganization of the Balkans. Cvetković gave a written guarantee that Yugoslavia would not reveal the third and fourth notes without the agreement of the Axis powers." (Jukić, 59)

> In the new settlement of the frontiers in the Balkans the interests of Yugoslavia in a territorial connection with the Aegean Sea, through the extension of her sovereignty to the city and harbor of Salonika, are to be taken onto account. (Ristić, 82)

These notes show that Yugoslavia was the only signatory of the Tripartite Pact which did not include military clauses. The required secrecy of the third and fourth notes was meant to keep Hungary, Rumania and Bulgaria uninformed of Yugoslavia's military exclusion .

It seems appropriate to note comments on these Notes by Dragiša Ristić – Simović's trusted aide-de-camp and a Putschist himself, whom Simović urged to assemble all available facts on the matter and have them published:

> As Ribbentrop had unconsciously admitted, the whole treaty complex was "nothing but a lot of humbug and actually did not amount to anything." Had he been aware of all details of the negotiations, even General Simović could scarcely have objected to the actual terms although he would have still opposed signing the pact. (Ristić, 82-3)

**

On 15 March 1946, at the Nuremberg Trial, Marshal Herman Göring, the commander-in-chief of the German Air Force, stated the following about Yugoslavia's joining the Tripartite Pact:

> The entering into the Three Power Pact had the purpose of maintaining Yugoslavia's neutrality under all circumstances and of not drawing her into the war. Even at the time when the pact was signed one recognized the necessity for sending troops to Romania as a precautionary measure, and also to Greece because of the English landing there or the impending landing. In spite of that agreement it was expressly provided that no troop transports should go through Yugoslavia, so that the neutrality of that country after its entry into the Three Power Pact would be confirmed in every way. (The Avalon Project: Nuremberg Trial Proceedings Vol. 9 http://www.yale.edu/lawweb/avalon/imt/proc/03-15-46.htm 12.23/03)

**

According to General Dragiša Pandurović's story, **(see Part Two)** Simović was informed of the Government's negotiations with the Germans. On 24 March, after the conference of the highest ranking commandants of the Belgrade garrison, in the office of General Milorad Petrović, the Commandant of Belgrade, the attendees went to see the War Minister, General Petar Pešić, to present their views and to hear his.

They entered the Minister's office **about 11 a.m.** The Minister explained all exemptions from the military clauses of the Pact, and Yugoslavia's right to "activate" her military units. In that Pact there was nothing humiliating for Yugoslavia as an independent state. She stands and remains an armed state ((and if Germany would ask anything besides the pact - there we stand in defense of our rights, there we are to perish honorably and gloriously like Tzar Lazar at Kosovo)) , "pa ako bi Nemačka tražila nešto pored pakta - eto nas na braniku naših prava, eto nas poput Cara Lazara na Kosovu da izginemo časno i slavno." Until then this ought to be accepted as an inevitability, with heavy heart, but in the interest of the people and the state; there was no other way out. (Pandurovć, 6)

All listened carefully, especially Simović, wrote Pandurović … but Simović still opposed the signing of the Pact – as Ristić suggested.

German radio report on the signing of the Pact, 25 March, 5 p.m.

At 5 p.m. on 25 March, the American Chargé in Germany (Leland B. Morris) informed the Secretary of State:
> At 3:30 this afternoon at the Belvedere Palace in Vienna, Yugoslavia signed a protocol of adherence to the Three-Power Pact identical in terms with that signed by the previous adherents. …
>
> The German radio announced at 5 p.m. that simultaneously with the signing of the protocol the German and Italian Governments addressed notes to Yugoslavia stating that it is their intention always to respect the sovereignty and territorial integrity of Yugoslavia and that in accordance with the understanding reached with the Yugoslav Government, the Axis Powers will not demand the right of passage of troops or war materials during the present war. (FRUS1, 967/8)

Apparently assuming that the Pact with Yugoslavia – which *"actually did not amount to anything"* in Ribbentrop's view – protected his flank for the forthcoming invasion of the Soviet Union, Hitler ordered some units to leave the Balkans. "Decrypts had revealed as early as 26 and 27 March that the movement of two German Army HQs and three armoured divisions from the Balkans to Cracow had been ordered soon after Yugoslavia had signed the Tripartite pact, …" (F.H. Hinsley in Blake & Louis (eds), 420-21)

Macdonald – Mirković meeting, afternoon of 25 March

After getting Eden's authorization for the coup on 24 March, "Campbell, while indicating clearly in his telegrams of March 25 that the *legation was in touch with army and political figures,* still considered an offer of arms essential, and held out little hope of early action." (Stafford[cp], 408. Italics added.) One such contact was the Macdonald – Mirković meeting in the afternoon of the 25th.

Reportedly offended and angered that the Tripartite Pact had been signed, Mirković vowed that he would fell the Pact down. (Bosnić(ed), 34)

This meeting took place one day after Eden's instruction to Campbell to inform the conspirators of His Majesty Government's support. Was Mirković informed of Eden's message? What did Macdonald relay to Campbell about this meeting?

It is shown in **Part Two** that from the 24th March, *Vojvoda* Trifunović Birčanin – SOE's favorite contact-man, "Daddy" - consulted Mirković daily. The *Vojvoda's* long-desired *coup d'état* was now an order-of-the-day by the British. Thus his advice to Mirković could only be one thing: for the coup - Putsch (PUČ). But Mirković claimed that he met *Vojvoda* for the first time in the evening of the 26th - and then gave two different explanations for the *Vojvoda's* role, not mentioning his political advice at all.

Macdonald – Simović first meetings, morning of 26 March, 1941

As decided at the all-British conference on 19 March (Item 3), Macdonald was to establish *a direct contact with military elements to see whether a purely military coup could not be arranged more quickly*. Consequently, at Macdonald's request, he met with Simović secretly on the morning of 26 March. In the evening Macdonald reported Simović's statement that *"We [the British] should not have to wait more than a few days before the coup d'etat."* (Macdonald's report is quoted in **Part Two**.)

In addition to the timing of the coup, they also talked about Yugoslavia's attack on the Italian troops in Albania. From Macdonald's report it is clear that Simović was not convinced that Yugoslavia's intervention in Albania would provide needed war matériel for Yugoslavia.

> The British agencies in Belgrade included not only the diplomatic mission and the attachés, but also SOE, which had originally been deployed in Yugoslavia to undertake sabotage projects for blocking the Danube and to organize resistance movements in Balkan countries that were threatened with German occupation, and the SIS, which lent its communications to SOE and provided it with essential contacts. (Hinsley *et al*, 369)

Dalton: Macdonald went to Simović *"and finally persuaded him to act"*, 26 March 1941

Referring to the Macdonald -Simović meeting, Hugh Dalton – in charge of SOE - wrote in his diary for 27 March:

> It was the Air Attaché who went to Simović *and finally persuaded him to act.* (Pimlott(ed), 176. Italics added.)

IF, indeed, Macdonald *did persuade Simović to act* – it is clear from Macdonald's telegram that he *had not persuaded him to act* **during the morning meeting of the 26th**, because Simović stated that *"We should not have to wait more than a few days before the coup d'état"*, i.e., that the British should wait a few more days for the coup. Dalton's statement would imply that Macdonald persuaded Simović to act **during their late afternoon meeting.**

What was the subject of the conversation during their afternoon meeting? Simović provided two different explanations. One, as stated above, that Macdonald inquired about the "new situation of Yugoslavia." (Simović(44), 39) Then another one: that Macdonald informed him of a "delivery" of supplies for the air force armaments. (Simović(51), 14)

Would not a lower-rank officer handle such a delivery? Such difference in explanations of the scope of the visit raises the question of the credibility of its author.

**

In his speech on 28 March 1941 (discussed in **Part Two**) and in some documents he left behind, Simović did not mention his secret meeting with Macdonald **in early morning on 26 March**. However, in the documents referred to as "Simović(44)" and "Simović(51)" - the General left the evidence of his contact with Macdonald **in the afternoon of 26 March.**

26 March: Publication of first two Notes of the Protocol

On the morning of 26 March – when Simović was secretly conferring with Macdonald – on the front page of Belgrade's daily *Politika,* Belgraders could read the first two Notes attached to the Protocol of adhesion. So could Simović, Mirković and all other Puschists - if they had wanted to be informed.

The text of the Pact and of first two Notes – on respecting the sovereignty and territorial integrity of Yugoslavia, and not demanding transportation of troops through Yugoslavia – was also published in "The Official Gazette". (Maček, 215; Ristić, 85). Therefore, it is puzzling to read: "Prince Paul, the elegant, art-loving Regent, was forced, to his distaste, to grant Berlin permission for its armies to cross Jugoslavia." (Sulzberger, 126) Even more puzzling, why would Sandy Glen – a former influential SOE operative in Belgrade in March 1941 – write some sixty years later, "It was certainly Germany's intention that war should be avoided through concession by *Yugoslavia*, permitting full transit rights for the Wehrmacht, *formalised by the adhesion of Yugoslavia to the Tripartite Pact."* (Glen(B), 58. Italics added.)

Churchill to Campbell, 26 March: *"... do not neglect any alternative ... "*

Another related event occurred in the afternoon of 26 March. Churchill sent Campbell an additional green-light-for-the-coup directive after a consultation with Cadogan, the Foreign Office Permanent Under-Secretary:

At about 3 PM, Churchill sent for Cadogan to show him a telegram he wanted to send to Campbell. His main idea was not to break relations with the Yugoslav Government. Cadogan thought that to be the right approach, *"provided he [Campbell] at the same time does not relax efforts to put another Government in their place! P.M. agreed and added a sentence I drafted."* (Dilks(ed), 366. Italics added.)

Professor Dilks then quoted the telegram sent to Campbell:

> Do not let any gap grow up between you and Prince Paul or Ministers. Continue to pester, nag and bite. Demand audiences. Don't take NO for an answer. Cling on to them pointing out Germans are already taking the subjugation of the country for granted. This is no time for reproaches or dignified farewells. Meanwhile, at the same time, *do not neglect any alternative to which we may have to resort if we find present Government have gone beyond recall.* Greatly admire all you have done so far. *Keep it up by every means that occur to you.* (Dilks(ed), 366. Italics added.)

Dilks added that Eden had already authorized Campbell to secure the change of government by any means, including coup d'état. (Dilks(ed), 366) Churchill's instruction now strengthened Eden's. Did Macdonald inform Simović of Churchill's order?

Macdonald – Simović second meetings, late afternoon of 26 March 1941

Simović wrote that, after meeting with Mirković the afternoon of 26 March, he remained in his office awhile longer:

> ((During that time the British Air Force Attaché Colonel Macdonald visited me inquiring about *the new situation* of Yugoslavia. Not telling him anything about our decision, after a shorter conversation I took leave of him.))."
> "Za to vreme posetio me je britanski vazduhoplovni izaslanik pukovnik Macdonald interesujući se *za novu situaciju* Jugoslavije. Ne govoreći mu ništa o našoj odluci, ja sam se posle kraćeg razgovora oprostio s njime." (Simović(44), 30. Italics added.)

The "new situation", arisen since their early-morning meeting? What was *"new"* was the publication of two Notes to the Protocol by *Politika*. Even **IF** Simović did not tell Macdonald about their decision, what did Macdonald tell the General? What **did they** talk about? Could it be that the decision-making British were not satisfied with the General's morning statement that ***"We [the British] should not have to wait more than a few days before the coup d'etat.",*** and they wanted to be sure that the coup was executed "If and when the Regent signed a deal with Hitler", as decided at Chequers on 2 March, ... 'at the moment of greatest effervescence' – as Campbell suggested to Eden? On the 24th March, Eden authorized Campbell to inform the Putschists that His Majesty's Government would recognize and support the new government. Did they discuss this at their meetings on the 26th ?

The *"new"* in the afternoon of the 26th was also Churchill's order to Campbell, *"do not neglect any alternative to which we may have to resort if we find present Government have gone beyond recall".* Was this discussed at their second meeting?

While on the 26th March Macdonald was meeting with Simović, Tom Mapplebeck, was on the 25 March 1941 strongly urging Mirković to launch the coup as soon as possible. (Stafford(cp), 415) The same was done by the SOE's "contact" "Daddy" Trifunović Birčanin since the 24th.

26 March: Leo Amery exhorting ... without supporting

Whether Julian Amery's or Campbell's suggestion of 20 March, to *work on the feelings of Serbs*, and to *ensure vehement reaction in Serbia* if the Pact was signed, was readily implemented. Leopold "Leo" Amery, a close friend of Churchill, delivered "the speech, on 26th March, in which he exhorted the Yugoslavs, and particularly the Serbs, to acts of heroism in keeping with their ancient traditions" (Balfour & Mackay, 257-8)

Jacob Hoptner wrote about this speech:

> ... On March 26th Leopold Amery, British secretary of state for India, appealed to Yugoslavia in a radio message over the BBC. Actually he addressed his remarks not so much to all Yugoslavs as to the Serbs alone. Recalling their valor in the First World War, he asked why the Serbs should now leave all the glory to the Greeks and class themselves with the Bulgars and the Rumanians. The Allies would win the war, he assured the Serbs; Hitler could not prevail against England and America together. Then he appealed more specifically to clergymen and students. ... He reminded them of the tradition of Kosovo and the heroic King Lazar, who preferred a heavenly kingdom to the one on earth. Reaching the climax of his inflammatory broadcast, Amery asserted that the Yugoslav government could not
>> "claim the right to sign away the honor and independence of sixteen million people. If the people clearly show that accession to the Axis pact is regarded by them as a betrayal of honor and independence, then surely it is the duty of government to consult the people before the pact is ratified. No, it is not too late for that. The whole future of Yugoslavia is on razor's edge." (Hoptner, 241-2)

Leopold Amery's son Julian stated the following about the speech:

> The speech was widely herd in Belgrade and may have contributed to the general spirit of resistance. More important, perhaps, it was heard by some of the officers who were preparing the coup d'état. They afterwards told me that they took it as a public sign of British support for themselves and were strengthened by it in their determination to act. (Amery, 227)

This was another appeal to somebody else's honor and a preference for a heavenly kingdom – to the benefit of the British short-term war objectives for their earthly empire. The speech indeed contributed to the *vehement reaction in Serbia* on 27 and 28 March 1941, just as Campbell had wanted.

27 March 1941: The *coup d'état* in Belgrade

The *coup d'état* (known domestically as *PUČ, the Putsch*) was executed in Belgrade the night of 26/27 March 1941. Prince Paul's Government was overthrown, and a new Government formed under the premiership of General Dušan Simović. (See **Part Two**)

As Professor David Stafford noted, "a great deal [about the Putsch] undoubtedly will remain unclear for a long time, and much on the British side probably will never be revealed." (Stafford(cp), 401) However, some reactions by the British shapers of events - showing their complicity - were recorded and are shown herein.

One of SOE's reports stated: When at 2:30 a.m. on 27 March tanks rolled on Belgrade's streets, it showed that their midnight meetings contributed to the unification of all anti-German-oriented Yugoslavs and in a few hours the regime was overthrown. (Vodušek Starič, 234, n57)

**

"Within twelve hours of the coup in Belgrade", the order to move some German units from the Balkans to Cracow has been canceled. (F.H. Hinsley in Blake & Louis(eds), 421) That was an indication that Germany would attack Yugoslavia.

Chapter 11

Churchill: " ... the Yugoslav nation found its soul".
***The coup d'état – "one tangible result"* of British desperate efforts ...**

"For propaganda purposes the British government made out that it [the coup] was a strictly Yugoslav rebellion, but in private there was no restraint." (Balfour & Mackay, 257)

The British shapers of events were jubilant.

> On the morning after the coup, the *New York Times* correspondent phoned the British legation [in Belgrade]. "Who's there?," he asked; back came the answer "Bloody well everybody. We're having champagne. Come on." Despite this unrestrained and understandable enthusiasm, the British were quick to emphasize *for public relation purposes that a coup was a Yugoslav affair,* however much it was to be welcomed. *But this restraint clearly was not exercised internally.* (Stafford(cp), 419. Italics added.)

The Putsch, as Cadogan experienced it on 27 March:

> Good news on arriving at F.O., of coup d'état in Belgrade. Went to see P.M. at 11.40. He due to make speech at 12. Gave him his phrase 'Yugoslav nation has found its soul', which was featured by evening papers. We sent off telegrams to the President (U.S.), Belgrade and Angora. And he advised A. (hung up by weather at Malta) to return to Cairo. ... Somewhat puzzling and rather discouraging news from Belgrade. Government seem to have put out a statement that their foreign policy isn't changed! Cabinet at 5. P.M. very elated. I threw a little cold douche, but pointed out that independent, and previous, reports on Simovich (from Athens and Angora) were good. ... P.M. said King ought to send a message 'before we went to bed' ... Back to F.O. 7.45 and dictated message from King and arranged for it to be submitted to P.M. ... (It looks as if Yugs *may* attack Italians at midnight! Prince P[aul] asking to come here! We can't allow that, but we'll get him out somewhere.) (Dilks(ed), 366-7. Italics by Cadogan.)

Years later, Churchill wrote about the coup:

> The news of the revolution in Belgrade gave us great satisfaction. Here at last was one tangible result of our desperate efforts to form an Allied front in the Balkans and prevent all falling piecemeal into Hitler's power. I received the earliest telegrams only an hour before I had to address the Conservative Central Council for the first time as leader of the party. I ended as follows:
>
> Here at this moment I have great news for you and for the whole country. Early this morning *the Yugoslav nation found its soul.* A revolution has taken place in Belgrade, and the Ministers who but yesterday signed away the honour and freedom of the country are reported to be under arrest. This patriotic movement arises from the wrath of a valiant and warlike race at the betrayal of their country by the weakness of their rulers and the foul intrigues of the Axis Powers.
> We may, therefore, cherish the hope – I speak of course, only on information which has reached me – that a Yugoslav Government will be formed worthy to defend the freedom and integrity of their country. Such a Government in its brave endeavor will receive from the British Empire, and, I doubt not, in its own way, from the United States, all possible aid and succour. The British Empire and its Allies will make common cause with the Yugoslav nation, and we shall continue to match and strive together until complete victory is won. (Churchill(GA), 168. Italics added.)

Churchill's speech merits a bit of commentary.
By his own admission, this so-called *revolution was one tangible result of BRITISH desperate efforts to form the Balkan Front.* A strange *revolution* it was: kept in utmost secrecy, without the people's participation, explained to the nation as something that had been done in the name of the darling young King, the son of the assassinated King Alexander – who knew

nothing about it. However, one result of these British efforts was tangible indeed: Hitler's decision to attack and dismember Yugoslavia.

Among other British efforts was Taylor's assessment of "pro-British Serb public opinion as SOE's best hope of influencing the Yugoslav government's policy", as Professor Williams observed, and the resulting tremendous agitation and propaganda activities. The outcome was a systematic "black propaganda", financed by the British, to provoke *the wrath of a valiant warlike race* – specifically the Serbs, who could not forget the terrible acts committed against them by the Central Powers in the First World War.

The Prime Minister talked about the Yugoslav Ministers who had "signed away the honour and freedom" of Yugoslavia - but did not mention another British effort - **his own** directive to Eden "*to get Yugoslavia in to the war anyhow*".. He did not mention what his Foreign Minister stated: "A war in Balkans was not what Hitler wanted." He was talking of giving the new, *putschist* Government , "*all possible aid and succour*", while Britain was not able to do much at the time ... so he advised them to get arms by taking them from the Italians in Albania.

Churchill to Dalton:
"*...patient work of your people had reaped such a rich reward*"

Probably after the speech to the Council,

> Churchill instructed [General Sir Hastings] Ismay [then Churchill's Chief Staff Officer] to write to Dalton that
> "it was a source of great satisfaction that the careful patient work of your people had reaped such a rich reward" and to convey cordial congratulations to all concerned. (Barker, 151)
>
> When the Cabinet met on 27 March they were told that 'the repudiation of the government which had signed the three-power pact was a clear rebuff to our enemies'. Churchill said he had authorised Campbell to tell the new government that, 'on the basis that they were determined to denounce the pact with Germany, *and to help in defence of Greece*', Britain recognized them as the government of Yugoslavia. He had also sent a telegram to Roosevelt urging him to encourage resistance in the Balkans. (Barker, 93. Italics added.)

"Dalton's people" were secret agents of the Special Operations Executive. According to Churchill: it was *their* careful patient work that led to the coup. Colonel W.S. "Bill" Bailey, former head of SOE in Belgrade - [and later the chief of the British military mission with General Dragoljub-Draža Mihailović] – wrote in a letter to George Taylor, dated 28 March 1941:

> I feel very strongly that although *the action immediately preceding the coup d'état* may have been directed by others, *the necessary preliminary conditions* were established largely through the work of the S.O.2 [S.O.E.] staff in Belgrade during the past six months. (Barker, 151; 289n14)

According to Bailey, credit for the coup should be shared by SOE operatives in Belgrade and others. SOE had been *establishing the necessary conditions since October 1940* – i.e., since Italy's attack on Greece, which much increased SOE's work in the Balkans (Sweet-Escott, 52), and "the others" – who may have been *directing the action immediately preceding the coup* – probably since the all-British meeting on 19 March. Although Bailey did not identify "the others" – it is clear that in this context "the others" were the British, Legation personnel and others, but not Serbs.

On the theme of *establishing conditions* for the coup, Trevor J. Glanville, the British Consul in Zagreb [and SOE agent D/H4, "Nero"], wrote in a report, dated 27 September 1941, "that one can honestly attribute some measure of the popular feeling which endorsed it and made possible the formation of the new Government to our activities and that one can regard it as the fruit of 18 months [i.e. since September 1939] of hard work by all concerned." (Great Britain, Special Operations Executive, 91087-10V, Hoover Institution Archives)

Indeed, SOE activities were feeding popular sentiment to endorse the coup.

Hugh Dalton was more explicit. Among the successful operations of SOE he included the coup in Belgrade:

As I have stated, S.O.E. agents were in Belgrade on March 27th 1941, when the coup took place which chased out Prince Paul and the pro-Axis Government, and placed General Simovic in command and the young King Peter on the Throne. ***This had been well prepared beforehand***. (Dalton, 375. Emphasis added.)

Sir Alexander-Sandy Glen, one of more important SOE operatives in Belgrade during 1940-1941, shed even more light on this point. He wrote, in 1975:

There has been considerable speculation in Yugoslavia recently as to how much the events of 27 March were influenced and encouraged by the British. The answer as regards the latter must be a considerable amount, as Hugh Macdonald and Charlie Clark [Air and Military Attaché, respectively] were too close to the organizers for this to have been otherwise. (Glen, 63)

Preparing Serb political and popular opinion; Dalton was delighted

In E. Barker''s opinion, "It is clear in fact that Mirković was the director of the operation, keeping in touch with the British, but in no way their agent. ... But the British equally clearly gave every encouragement. ... Yet S.O.E. could fairly claim that they had done a great deal to *prepare Serb political and popular opinion,* so that the coup was accepted in Serbia with enormous enthusiasm. (Barker, 93. Italics added.)

Bickham Sweet-Escott, a close associate of George Taylor, formerly of the SOE's Balkan section, wrote of SOE's "three successful operations, though for two of them Baker Street [SOE headquarters] could not take *all* the credit. " (Sweet-Escott, 59. Italics added.) Some *partial* credit, then.

... At four o'clock on the morning of 27th March I was telephoned by the duty officer to come to the office to decipher a most immediate telegram from George [Taylor] in Belgrade. It contained the news of the successful pro-allied *coup d'état* organized by General Simović with the backing of the Serbian Peasant Party, the first reverse of this kind which Hitler had so far received.
    It would be a gross exaggeration to say that the *coup d'état* was organized by George Taylor and Tom Masterson. For it was the result of a spontaneous revulsion of Serbian public opinion against the axis. All the same subversion by third parties can never succeed unless public opinion was ready to back it, and it was I think fair to say that as our organization existed for the purpose of creating subversion, we were entitled to some credit. At all events our part in it certainly improved our standing in Whitehall and was good for morale in Baker Street. (Sweet-Escott, 62-3)

**

While Sweet-Escott thought that *It would be a gross exaggeration to say that the coup d'état was organized by George Taylor and Tom Masterson,* in Dalton's opinion: *his chief organizer of the coup was George Taylor* (Pimlott(ed), 178) – *who really got down to work* when he came to Belgrade [on 27 February], and who worked through the Serbian Peasant Party and *Narodna Odbrana* – who were "*in our pay*" !

**

Indeed, the British SOE in Belgrade has claimed some small credit for persuading the initiators of the uprising *to act fast*. (Roberts, 14. Italics added.)

"Some small credit" for *acting fast* – once the coup was authorized and the conspirators informed... It was a rather large credit ...

(How the British – among them the SOE operatives - and their subsidized and non-subsidized local co-operatives influenced and promoted that "spontaneous revulsion" - and thereby earned "some credit" - is examined in **Part Two.**)

Professor Ben Pimlott, the editor of Dalton's diaries, commented:

On 27th March, a coup, led by an Air Force General, Bora Mirković, and backed by junior army officers and Opposition politicians, overturned the regime and forced Prince Paul into exile –

placing General Simović in command, and putting the young King Peter on the throne. S.O.E. agents had given every encouragement and *had done much to prepare Serb opinion for the event.* Hence Dalton was delighted by what seemed like a tangible triumph for his organisation. (Pimlott(ed), 175. Italics added.)

About Prince Paul's efforts and the *coup d'état* in Belgrade, Professor Robert Rhodes James wrote that the Prince was "desperately trying to prevent the invasion of his country", and that he was ousted "with the full approval and involvement of the British". (Rhodes James, 251)

In Professor Hinsley's opinion:

> The coup was brought off on 27 March, ... by Air Force and Army officers. That they had joined forces with the dissident political parties owed something to encouragement from the British attachés and SOE, and Whitehall was alerted to the fact that a coup was imminent before it occurred.
>
> While British participation in the plans no doubt contributed to their success, it is clear that even without *direct British encouragement* there would still have been a coup; its origins were deeply rooted in the Yugoslav political situation (Hinsley *et al*, 370. Italics added.)

The British attachés and SOE "encouraged" the officers-conspirators to join with dissident political parties, while direct British participation contributed to the coup's success. However, even without the British involvement – according to Hinsley - there would still have been a coup.

The question then becomes - **When?**

General Mirković – the principal executor – claimed that he had thought about a change of government since 1937 – but had done nothing. The Serbian Peasant Party had considered a coup since 1938 – but nothing was done. Đonović and Birčanin suggested the coup in July 1940: HMG said it was premature **then** - and there was no coup. On 21 March Minister Campbell asked Eden "*when it would suit **him***, from the military point of view, for this to be done," and Eden replied "*at the moment of reaction caused by signature*". On 24 March Eden instructed Campbell: Any new Government formed as a result of these events and prepared to resist German demands would have our full support. **You may secretly so inform any prospective leaders** in whom you have confidence. (Eden, 227) And the coup was executed exactly at that time – i.e., **after** the coup-wishers / plotters were informed of support from His Majesty's Government. **When, how** and **to whom** was that promise of support communicated ?

On the morning of 26 March, Simović told the Air Attaché **to wait for a few more days**. Mirković claimed that **he** had decided for the coup **after 2 p.m. on the 26thMarch**. Simović afterward claimed that **he** had ordered the execution **at 1 p.m. on the 26th**. They contradicted each other and had different description of details related to the coup, each stressing the significance of his own role.

Professor D. Stafford correctly noted that "a great deal [about the Putsch] undoubtedly will remain unclear for a long time, **and much on the British side probably will never be revealed.**" (Stafford(cp), 401. Emphasis added.) One of the reasons might be that there was "stuff in the British archives that would make your hair stand on end ", as Baron Julian Amery commented (Onslow, 17) – so it would not be desirable to reveal it. As presented in **Part Two**, the evidence shows that, from the 24th of March through the coup itself, "Daddy" Trifunović Birčanin was in contact with Mirković and SOE operatives, keeping them informed of the preparations and the progress of the operations – thus serving as a channel of communication between Mirković and SOE ... whether Mirković knew it or not.

"Fullest possible measure of aid" ... which Britain did not have

Churchill also made it clear that recognition of the new Yugoslav Government would depend not only on denouncing the Tripartite Pact, but also on Yugoslavia's "*help in defence of Greece*". Indeed, *the defense of Greece* - not the protection of Yugoslavia from dreadful Nazism and

German domination - was *the reason* for the coup and drawing Yugoslavia into the war. The defense of Greece, in turn, served strategic British needs and goals.

On 27 March 1941 Churchill wrote to President Roosevelt:

> I hope you will agree that in the present situation we are bound to do all we can to help and encourage the elements prepared to resist German penetration. *If the new government shows readiness to share in Greek heroic resistance, we propose to recognise it at once as Government of Yugoslavia, and extend to it in the fullest possible measure the aid which we are already giving to Greece.* We should encourage the Yugoslavians to roll up the Italians in Albania which would produce result of prime importance and give them a good packet of arms. I trust that you will take similar line and will sustain the new government *with promise* of America's powerful support and backing. (Loewenheim *et al* (ed), 135-6 Italics added.)

The fullest possible measure of aid was a well-sounding but misleading phrase, because Churchill knew that Britain did not have badly-needed armaments to send to Yugoslavia; so he instigated Yugoslavia to attack the Italians in Albania. Also, he did not ask Roosevelt **to send arms** to *the elements prepared to resist German penetration,* but only to **promise** them support and backing – because he knew very well that the US supplies would be available only "in the near future". (Loewenheim *et al* (ed), 136)

**

While the Prime Minister, in London, was *cordially congratulating* all British involved in the coup, his Foreign Minister was on the way back to London.

> On 27 March Eden arrived in Malta *en route* for London. Here to his delight news reached him of an anti-German *coup d'état* in Belgrade. Eden at once decided to return to the Balkans and arrived on the following day at Athens. *The fall of Prince Paul was the first and only real success of Eden's personal policy during the whole of his protracted Mediterranean odyssey.* (Carlton, 181. Italics added.)

Coup d'état ... magnificent news for Eden, warmest congratulations for Campbell

Eden recorded his reaction in his diary:

> Just before luncheon local press telephoned to say that there had been *coup d'état* in Belgrade, Government out, Paul fled and a pro-ally administration established. Magnificent news which so delighted me that I almost hugged Lady Dobbie! Collected Dill and Service Chiefs and we agreed that right course was to leave for Athens by Sunderland tonight. (Eden, 228-9)

In Eden's and Dill's conference, first with Gen. Wilson and then with the Greek authorities, it was decided that the Yugoslavs should be told, "if they moved into Bulgaria and Albania when the Germans entered Greece, the Allies would reinforce the defences along the Nestos River and the boundaries of Bulgaria. At all costs they would protect the route up the Axios [Vardar] valley from Salonika into Yugoslavia." (McClymont, 131-2)

Eden also acknowledged: "Campbell meanwhile did everything in his power to encourage the more robust among the politicians and the military through his many useful contacts." (Eden, 229)

Some of those *"more robust among the politicians"* were "subsidized" by the British. Before he flew off from Malta to Athens, Eden telegraphed Campbell:

> *Warmest congratulations on your share of this most happy turn of events.*
> Please telegraph, to reach me on arrival at Athens, your appreciation of the situation and your views on how we can best help. What we most desire is to establish contact with members of the new Government and with army and air force leaders. From every point of view, by far the most valuable means of doing this would be by meeting in Belgrade and I earnestly hope that it may now be possible to arrange this. Failing this, meeting might be held at some place in southern Serbia. If visit by us to Yugoslavia is not practicable, I shall be glad to see Yugoslav representatives with sufficient powers in Athens and I have no doubt that Greek Government would likewise welcome them.

> While change of Government in Yugoslavia must have disjoined the Germans' plans, it is of first importance that we should make the utmost use of the time thereby gained to concert our own plans against all eventualities. (Eden, 230. Italics added.)

Dalton: *"Our chaps have done their part well"*

In December 1940, when Eden became the Foreign Minister, his relationship with Dalton – who was in charge of SOE – became tense. "There was obvious personal rivalry over the Belgrade coup of March 1941: both men had sent messages to Belgrade urging action; Eden, then in the Middle East, had less chance of claiming credit for the coup, when it happened, than Dalton did in London." (Barker, 151)

In London, on Thursday, 27th March, Dalton recorded in his diary:

> What a day! Gladwyn [Jebb, SOE's Chief Executive Officer] comes into my room this morning with a smiling face and says, 'There was a *coup d'état* early this morning at Belgrade.' As the day goes on, we hear more detail, and *it is clear that our chaps have done their part well*. It was the Air Attaché who went to Simović and finally persuaded him to act. When Simović asked what arms we could supply, the Air Attaché *was authorized to say that we would do what we could, but his best chance of getting arms was to attack the Italians in Albania*. There was a lot to collect there. The money we spent on the *Serb Peasant Party and other Opposition Parties has given wonderful value*. We knew before that the Air Force would be all right, and, *if necessary, would fly away to Greece*, but many of those near the top of the General Staff were rotten, and this *coup* was mainly carried out, apart from the Air Force, by Colonels, Majors and junior officers. Prince Paul, 'Our Friend' (Eton and Oxford), has been a complete skunk. He has deceived our diplomats as such gentlemanly skunks always do.
>
> [Bickham] Sweet-Escott who has been in our job for a long while, says he remembers the black looks he first met at the Foreign Office when it was proposed that we should subsidise the Opposition Parties. 'Prince Paul would be so vexed if he ever found out,' they said.
>
> I had a yap at Gladwyn later in the day because, through some stupid oversight, he had not shown me the telegram he had last night, though he had sent a copy to Cadogan and shown a copy to [Major Desmond] Morton [Personal Assistant to Churchill] at lunch.
>
> Cabinet this afternoon. P.M. [Prime Minister] says now is the time to go ahead with The Danube. **(1)** I say that a telegram went this morning. (It did, because the Chiefs of Staff wanted it, but it was only a repeat of earlier orders.) (Pimlott(ed), 176-7. Italics added.)

> **(1)** The S.O.E. plan to block the Danube. This was carried out, with only limited success, early in April. (Pimlott(ed), 177 n1)

An important question to consider is: Whether the Air Attaché was authorized to say only *that the British would do what they could*, or was he also authorized to relay Eden's authorization to Campbell of 24 March **to secretly inform any prospective leaders that the new Government would have full British support?** (Eden, 227) As Macdonald reported, the conversation with Simović *ranged over various subjects*, and his report was summarized for the sake of simplicity. Was Macdonald authorized to relay Eden's message also to Mirković when they met in the afternoon of the 25th March?

When necessary, editor Pimlott supplemented Dalton's war diary entries with relevant explanation. For the entry of 17 June 1941, he noted that the "S,O.E. agents had helped to inspire "the coup in Belgrade on 27th March, but that the coup had been swiftly nullified by the Axis invasion of Yugoslavia a few days later. (Pimlott(ed), 230)

Julian Amery: *"… climate of opinion in which the coup became inevitable"*

Baron Julian Amery of Lustleigh, former Section D/SOE agent and one of the coup-conspirators, wrote in 1973:

> It would be idle to claim that S.O.E. organised the coup d'état of 27 March. … But S.O.E.'s co-operation with the Djonovich-Birchanin group and with Gavrilovitch's Peasant Party undoubtedly strengthened both these and *helped them to create climate of opinion in which the coup became inevitable*. (Amery, 227-8. Italics added.)

Indeed: First - the *climate of opinion was **created***; and then, after the coup, it was said to have been a ***spontaneous*** *revolt of the people.*

John Colville: *"The Prime Minister is overjoyed"*

John Colville, Assistant Private Secretary to Churchill, recorded in his diary on 27 March:

> A great day. Revolution in Belgrade, which puts an entirely different complexion on events in the Balkans and turns darkness into dawn. The P.M. is overjoyed .... He announced the glad tidings in two speeches, at a Conservative Association meeting and at T.U.C. [Trades Union Congress] meeting. The whole country is in ecstasies." (Colville, 367-8)

**

In historian Sue Onslow's opinion:

> ... The events in Belgrade were seen as, and presented as, a remarkable propaganda victory for the British cause. The *coup* proved a tremendous, if ephemeral, boost to British morale, coming rapidly upon the victories against Italian forces in North Africa and the Sudan. Even provincial British papers printed the news from Belgrade as their banner headline. Prime Minister Churchill, above all, understood the value of gesture, and the *coup* was perceived as giving Nazism a bloody nose. (Onslow, 2)
> ... the *coup* was indeed a crucial propaganda victory for the Allied cause - and Britain thereby succeeded in Churchill's aim of 'drawing Yugoslavia into the war anyhow'. (Onslow, 3)
> In one sense only was British policy successful: the *coup* was seen as defiance to the Axis and it did indeed precipitate a German invasion of the country, as Britain had foreseen. (Onslow, 5)

... as Britain had foreseen it, and had worked to achieve it.

SOE and Legation worked together

As for the timing of the coup, one has to recall the Churchill-Dalton meeting at Chequers on 2 March 1941, during which a secret plan to deal with Prince Paul was thoroughly approved by Churchill: "If and when the Regent signed a deal with Hitler, SOE undercover agents in Belgrade would support a *coup d'état*." ... (Stafford (C), 211-12) Although Macdonald was not an SOE agent, it is important to note that Dalton, in charge of the SOE, stated, "When Simović asked what arms we could supply, the Air Attaché *was authorized* to say that we would do what we could, but his best chance of getting arms was to attack the Italians in Albania." That was Churchill's line, reiterated by Eden, and even told to President Roosevelt, when Churchill requested his support on 10 March 1941. Dalton's knowledge of the authorization is additional evidence of the concerted and cooperative efforts by the SOE agents and the Legation personnel to arrive at their political goals. Dalton's evaluation of the usefulness of subsidies to the Serbian opposition parties was correct. They were particularly effective in influencing public opinion and creating a fertile atmosphere for British propaganda. Both the Legation and SOE personnel participated in these undertakings. Under the circumstances, all British institutions and services were obliged to co-operate in an effort to achieve the goals of His Majesty's Government.

> ... S.O.E. was not the only British Intelligence Agency operating in Yugoslavia. S.I.S. (Secret Intelligence Service or MI6) had been in the Balkans far longer than S.O.E. and was generally considered better informed and more trustworthy. S.I.S. reports went only to the highest levels in government, and in utmost secrecy, and to this day [1980] their contents are shrouded in mystery. The role of S.I.S. in Yugoslavia in 1941 has still to be explained but there is evidence to suggest that, at the very least, some members of the British cabinet had prior knowledge of the coup d'état. How otherwise could Leo Amery have timed his speech on B.B.C. radio so perfectly – the speech, on 26th March, in which he exhorted the Yugoslavs, and particularly the Serbs, to acts of heroism in keeping with their ancient traditions? (Balfour & Mackay, 257-8)

> SIS .. had established excellent networks of information and intelligence gathering throughout the country, using vice-consular and pro-consular cover in Zagreb, Split, Dubrovnik, Susak [Sušak], Ljubljana and Skopje. ... the Stephen Clissold papers at the Bodleian Library show that in

Yugoslavia at least there was remarkable co-operation and concord between SOE and SIS before April 1941. (Onslow, 15-16)

There is every reason to believe that the SIS was as active in Yugoslavia as the SOE during this period. It is also worth noting that while SOE contacts with Yugoslavia were broken by the German invasion, this was not the case with the SIS. (Stafford(cp), 108n37)

From April 1934 to the spring of 1939 Sir Cecil Parrott was the tutor to young King Peter II. He wrote this about the coup:

There would certainly have been no *coup d'état* if the British had not planned it. When the British government found out that they could get nowhere with Prince Paul's government, they decided to overthrow it. Eden stated this in his memoirs. 'You have my full authority for any measure you may think it right to take to further a change of government or régime, even by *coup d'état,*' he telegraphed to Campbell. 'We sent a wire to our friends to use all means to raise a revolution.' wrote Hugh Dalton, the Minister in charge of S.O.E. This was a unique case of the Foreign Office and the British Legation together with 'the Ministry of Ungentlemanly Warfare', as Dalton called it, engineering a *coup* against a government with which they enjoyed more than friendly relations and which was presided over by a British Knight of the Garter! (Parrott, 105)

"The triumph of hope over reality"; "wild rejoicing in the streets of Belgrade"

While all of Britain was *"in ecstasies"*, there was also *"wild rejoicing in the streets of Belgrade"* ... for a brief time.

... News of the coup, and King Peter's assumption of the royal prerogative six months before his official coming of age, sparked off scenes of wild rejoicing in the streets of Belgrade – although these were not echoed in Zagreb. It produced a frisson of optimism in Britain where, for a short time, it gave a fleeting glimpse of early victory, coming as it did at the time of British successes in North Africa and signs of Italy weakening. This, in the event, turned out to be the triumph of hope over reality. (Williams, 32)

The attitude of the new Yugoslav government, especially with regard to military preparedness and tactical deployments, was thought highly unsatisfactory by British ministers, and caused great anxiety as to whether Britain would be able to gain full benefit from the coup. It put SOE back into virtually the same situation as in the pre-coup days, attempting to put pressure on the government through its various friends and contacts. SOE had not been too pleased with Simović heading the new government, but he was the only figurehead on whom all parties could agree. SOE's closest associates, especially Tupanjanin and Trifunović Birčanin, were equally disappointed and within a few days, *according to Taylor, were discussing the possibility of another coup.* (Williams, 33. Italics added.)

This is very important information because it came from G. Taylor. For Tupanjanin and Trifunović Birčanin - whose organizations were "subsidized" by the British – it was more important to promote the British agenda than to get rid of the "White Russian Prince" Paul – as Đonović criticized him. (Amery, 174-5)

**

On the day following the installation of the Simović government, the Defence Committee noted that "an expression of appreciation should be conveyed to Doctor Dalton for the part played by his organization in bringing about the coup d'état in Yugoslavia." (Stafford(cp), 417)

George Taylor's letter to Dalton, 27 March 1941: "Trifunovich had kept us informed of conspiracy ..."

After the coup, Taylor sent reports to Dalton, who forwarded them to the Prime Minister on the 28th. The third of Dalton's attachments sent to Churchill was Taylor's telegram, written after the formation of the new Government, (Belgrade) to London, 27 March 1941, which is partially quoted herein:

A. Coup d'état carried out under undisputed leadership of SIMOVICH and his assistant MERKOVICH [MIRKOVIĆ] with help of TRIFUNOVICH and certain officers. No Generals were included in plot which was executed by Captains, Majors and Lt. Colonels.
B. TRIFUNOVICH had kept us informed of conspiracy under strictest promise of silence. He had promised to give us 12 hours' notice so that we could advise you but coup was precipitated by departure of Prince for Ljubljana last night.
C. Provisional Government consists of two Generals, SIMOVICH, Minister President of Council, and ILICH, War Minister, together with leaders of Peasant, Radical, Democratic and Nationalist Party, with whom we are in closest touch. Croatian and Slovene Ministers have been invited to remain in office for the present.
D. TUPANJANIN remains outside Cabinet but has nominated Milan GAVRILOVICH, CUVRILOVICH [ČUBRILOVIĆ] and DAKOVICH to represent the Party.
E. MASTERSON has done marvelous work and deserves greatest praise. Credit also due [John] BENNETT who discovered TRIFUNOVICH and would like to emphasise that thanks are due to HANAU for originally picking winner in TUPANJANIN.
(Great Britain, Special Operations Executive, 91087-10V, Hoover Institution Archives)

Thomas Masterson's report, 27 March 1941: misled about the role of the Knežević brothers

On 27 March 1941, Thomas Masterson also reported on the Putsch, and the role of the brothers Knežević, Radoje and Živan-Žika in it. Excerpts follow:

> The following information was given to me today in connection with the Coup d'Etat.
>
> Radne KNJEVICH, Professor of Belgrade, who is also a member of the Democratic Party Executive and with whom, *some 6 weeks ago, we discussed the possibility of developing propaganda, appears to have spoken to General MERKOVICH and suggested the idea of a coup d'état.* After discussing questions of detail, they agreed to ask General SIMOVICH if he would take the lead. He agreed. General MERKOVICH and Professor KNJEVICH thereupon spoke to General ILICH. He agreed. Radne KNJEVICH has a younger brother, one Jika KNJEVICH, to whom he spoke after his agreement with General MERKOVICH. Young Jika, who is a major, then spoke to a number of captains, majors and lieutenant-colonels. With the exception of 2 or 3, they all agreed to play. Jika was then asked to take command of the coup d'état, made the plan and divided the roles. 300 planes were made available at Zemun. ... SIMOVICH gave the order at 2 am when all left their barracks with Jika at the head of his battalion on horseback.
> They at once occupied the War Office, the Presidency and Council. Radne KNJEVICH, together with General MERKOVICH with others, were in Zemun whence operations were conducted. At 2:30 am it was announced that all vital points had been occupied. ...
> At 4 am, Jika went to SIMOVICH's house, announced that everything had been completed and took him to the War Office where KNJEVICH and General MERKOVICH had already arrived. CVETKOVICH, Cinzar MERKOVICH [Cincar-Marković] and 3 Croat ministers were brought to the War Office when General SIMOVICH told the Croats that the revolt was not against them and there would be no alterations in their positions.
>
> General SIMOVICH produced list of people he was going to invite to form a Cabinet. ... KNJEVICH was asked for advice. He replied that the matter could be solved in two ways. Either a cabinet of soldiers or of civilians. He advised that he should constitute his cabinet largely from the existing political parties. General SIMOVICH eventually agreed, tore up his list and asked KNJEVICH to form a new one on the basis of party collaboration.
> (Great Britain, Special Operations Executive, 91087-10V, Hoover Institution Archives. Italics added.)

**

On the basis of Simović's, Mirković's and other coup-participants' accounts - presented in **Part Two** - this information, given to Masterson, seems inaccurate and biased in favor of the Knežević brothers. When this information is compared to accounts provided by the brothers Knežević, it is evident that one of them had influenced Masterson. Because *some 6 weeks ago* [i.e., in middle-February]*, we* [i.e. Masterson/SOE and Radoje] *discussed the possibility of developing propaganda,* it was probable that Radoje – who already had a connection to Masterson

- rushed this information to Masterson soon after the formation of the new Government on the 27th March - to score points in the brothers' favor.

Both Mirković and Živan Knežević asserted that Mirković met Radoje for the first time the afternoon of 26 March. (Karapandžić(AB), 135) (Knežević, 172) Mirković claimed that Simović had agreed *in principle* to take formal leadership of affairs after a coup, upon Mirković's urging him to do so. (Bosnić(ed), 17) Simović acknowledged their long-time association and discussion of a coup. (Simović(44), 1-2) Therefore, it follows that it was not true that Radoje had *spoken to General MERKOVICH,* and *suggested the idea of a coup d'état*, that Radoje and Mirković *discussed questions in detail*, and then *they agreed to ask General SIMOVICH if he would take the lead*.

It is likewise not true that *Jika was then asked to take command of the coup d'état, made the plan and divided the roles*. Both Mirković and Simović claimed that role for themselves. Mirković and Dragiša Ristić described in detail how and when Mirković had assigned specific tasks to individual participants. Žika's role in the physical execution of the coup was equivalent to the roles of other junior officers; his deployment was at the intersection of *Miloševa* and *Nemanjina* streets. (Knežević, 239)

Early in 1940, Mirković talked with General Bogoljub Ilić about a *coup d'état* - as he had with other Generals – but Mirković did so by himself, without any collaboration with Professor Radoje. Ilić refused to participate. (Bosnić(ed), 16)

At 4 am, Jika did not go *to SIMOVICH's house* - as Masterson's informant claimed -did not *announce that everything had been completed*, and did not take *him to the War Office where KNJEVICH and General MERKOVICH had already arrived*. Captain Dragiša N. Ristić did that. Radoje was sent along in order to give to Simović a draft of a Proclamation which Radoje had sketched and which was to be published after the coup. (Bosnić(ed), 23-4) (Knežević, 242) Ristić also claimed that this had been the first encounter Simović had with Radoje.

Of major importance is the claim in the information, given to Masterson, that Simović wanted a Government of soldiers and Knežević of civilians; that, eventually, Simović tore up his list and then asked Knežević to make a new one on the basis of party collaboration. This line was later expounded by Radoje's brother Živan in his book, *27 mart 1941.* Mirko Kosić claimed that Simović intended to include political parties' representatives in the new Government. More details are provided in the account related to the formation of the new government.

**

It appears that Masterson's report had some unintended consequences.

Once the information from reliable Masterson was available in the Prime Minister's archives, it seems that Sir Winston used it in his history of the Second World War when writing about the coup of 27 March 1941: " ... The leader of the projected rising was General Bora Mirkovic, commander of Yugoslav Air Force, aided by Major Knezevic, an army officer, and his brother, a professor, who established political contacts through his position in the Serb Democrat Party. ..." (Churchill(GA), 161)

This version of the role the brothers Knežević played was not appreciated by the supporters of Gen. Simović. Dragiša Ristić – Simović's former aide and a participant in the execution of the coup - wrote to Gen. Mirković on 27 August 1955, wondering whether one should allow Churchill's statement to stand. Because Churchill had earlier reacted positively to the need of correcting some inaccuracies in his memoirs, Ristić pleaded for an action in this sense. If corrections are not made, "brothers Knežević will have a great moral support against us." (Karapandžić(AB), 142)

More than a year later, Ristić acted. With a letter dated 30 November 1956, he sent his account of the events of 27 March 1941 to Sir Winston, so that he "might know the facts" as Ristić remembered them, and they were not favorable to the brothers. (Dragiša Ristić Collection, Box 2, Hoover Institution Archives)

Masterson's report is also important because it confirms that the SOE had discussed British-desired-and-directed propaganda with the Democratic Party – which was subsidized by the British. Namely, around 20 January 1941, Dr. Milan Grol, president of the Democratic Party, had a long conversation with Masterson. After the talk, Masterson proposed SOE's financial support for the Democratic Party: The Party's help would increase the propaganda reach, and in the public mind it would fortify consciousness of the danger of German penetration into Bulgaria. Campbell consented with the proposal of 1,000 pound sterling per month. (Vodušek Starič, 214-15)

Although Masterson spelled Radoje's name incorrectly, as "Radne KNJEVICH", he correctly identified him as "Professor of Belgrade, who is also a member of the Democratic Party Executive" - "who has a younger brother, one Jika KNJEVICH" - "and with whom, *some 6 weeks ago, we discussed the possibility of developing propaganda*". "Some 6 weeks ago" puts their discussion at the middle of February, about one month after the Masterson-Grol conversation.

Report by *"Daddy"*, Ilija Trifunović Birčanin,
The coup d'état in Yugoslavia, Belgrade, 27 March 41:

During the afternoon and evening of the 26th and the night of the 26th / 27th March, *Vojvoda* Trifunović Birčanin was in Zemun with General Mirković. Following the Putsch they went to Belgrade together. After 6 a.m. on the 27th, *Vojvoda* was interviewed about the sequence of events. A report on the coup was then prepared and sent to London. Here are excerpts:

> It was decided **between the hours of 7 and 9 last night** to carry out the Coup that had been planned if the King [Peter] had not left Belgrade. The conspirators learnt that the Prince had gone away and they were not sure if he took the King with him. They passed the word to hold up the train, giving as a pretext that the line was mined. They then ascertained that the King was at home and asleep. As soon as this was learnt, **they decided to execute the plan that night**. Orders were given that the troops begin their movements **at 2 am** after the telephone lines were cut. (Before cutting the lines, however, they ordered the Divisional Commander at Ljubljana to get the Prince back to Belgrade and not molest him.)

**

This is the third version of the time when it was decided to execute the coup. As stated above, Mirković claimed to have made that decision **after 2 p.m. on the 26th March,** and Simović **at 1 p.m. on the 26th**. *Vojvoda* - who was with Mirković on the 26th – put the time **between 7 and 9 p.m.** In any case, the decision was made **after** the coup-plotters were assured of British support.

**

Vojvoda's report continues. After the designated buildings were taken,

> General SIMOVICH was brought from his house to the War Office. General MARKOVICH [Mirković] and TRIFUNOVICH and a number of officers waiting at the Zemun Aerodrome left to inspect the troops and see that they were all in place. They ascertained that they were and that no resistance was intended. They took charge of CVETKOVICH and Cinzar MARKOVICH, who were both found in their houses, and they were taken to the War office, where they are imprisoned at this moment. All was over **at 3:30 am** and there was no resistance.
>
> The execution of the Coup d'Etat was carried out by colonels and lieutenant-colonels, majors and captains, ...
>
> **Between 4 and 4:30 am,** General SIMOVICH called all chiefs of the political parties and the representatives of the Croat party who were in Belgrade and in their presence prepared the King's Proclamation declaring that the King has taken charge and appointed General SIMOVICH to form a Cabinet. The Proclamation was taken to the King's Palace **at 5 o'clock** and **was signed by him**. Immediately afterwards, General SIMOVICH formed his Cabinet. **At 6 o'clock,** the Cabinet informed all the commanders of the Army in the Provinces and all approved. There are manifestations of joy all over the country and peace reigns. The Cabinet is provisional. No blood was shed anywhere.
> (Great Britain, Special Operations Executive, 91087-10V, Hoover Institution Archives. Emphasis added.)

**

The Proclamation was not signed. (See **Part Two**) Major Knežević took it to the Royal Palace for the King's signature, but he was not successful. He wrote about this episode that, suspecting a trap had been set for him, he returned from the Palace without having seen the King, arriving *circa* **6:30 a.m.** in front of the General Staff Headquarters. Hundreds of officers, looking through the windows of the Ministry of the Army, were eager to know what was happening. Questioned about what had happened with the Proclamation, the Major raised the paper, and waving it said:

"**Potpisana ! Živeo Kralj !**" ("**Signed! Long live the King!**") (Knežević, 257. Emphasis added.)

He did not tell the truth. At that moment *Vojvoda* Trifunović, and all others present, were not aware of Knežević's deception.

Dalton's letter to Churchill, 28 March 1941:
"... the coup d'état itself was largely the work of Trifunovich ..."

In a letter with three attachments sent to Churchill on 28 March, Dalton informed the Prime Minister, *inter alia:*

> Last January I decided to send TAYLOR out to the Balkans, of which he has special knowledge. He was then acting as number two to Sir Frank Nelson here at Headquarters but, in view of the obvious German threat, I felt that we must temporarily part with one of our best men for work in the field.
> ... he arrived in Istanbul on 20 Feb **(#)** and promptly visited Sofia, Belgrade and Athens, returning to Belgrade. *Then he really got down to work.*
>
> In order of importance TAYLOR's instructions were:
> 1. To move heaven and earth to get a Danube blocking scheme finally laid on by our friends on the Yugoslav General Staff;
> 2. To complete the preparations for a revolt in Romania;
> 3. To organise bands of saboteurs in Bulgaria, Yugoslavia, Greece and Albania for use in the event of those countries being over-run;
> 4. To continue the work, *already well in hand,* of encouraging the Yugoslav opposition parties to bring pressure to bear on the Government in a sense favourable to this country.
>
> Of these No. 4 concerns us most today. Since I took over the SOE, we have spent in Yugoslavia no less than £100,000. This has mainly gone to financing the Serb Peasant Party and *to bribery of various sorts,* including payment for recurrent acts of minor sabotage. We also succeeded in creating an emergency reserve of 16 million Dinars to be used if remittances from London should become impossible. I think we have had good value for this expenditure!
> By these means our agents were able to maintain the friendship of the principal anti-Axis Yugoslavs (such as TUPANJANIN of the Serb Peasant Party, and TRIFUNOVICH of the Narodna Odbrana) *and our secret propaganda agencies constantly stimulated the national will to resist.* You will, in fact, see from the third of my enclosures that the <u>coup d'état</u> itself was largely the work of TRIFUNOVICH, while the real political backing without which it could hardly have been made, lay outside the old Cabinet and in the Serb Peasant Party – the principal instrument of our policy and (like Narodna Odbrana) in our pay. I am proud of the result, for which I feel that great credit attaches to TAYLOR and his chief lieutenants in Yugoslavia – [TOM] MASTERSON and [JOHN] BENNET.
>
> As for no. 3, ... In Yugoslavia and Greece the bands are now formed and have been supplied with the necessary explosives and devices. ...
>
> No. 1 is the most important objective of all. ... You will remember that even your own eloquent appeal to Prince Paul to complete the preparations for blowing in the rock at Kazan [defile] failed, owing to the infirmity of purpose of that miserable figure. Thanks to Prince Paul, Kazan, at any rate, can not now be completed in time.
> Yet there is hope. ... As soon as I heard the news of the coup d'état I sent yet another telegram to TAYLOR. Nothing, I can assure you, that it is humanly possible to achieve our end will be left undone. Still, *the coup d'état was a success* and we must pray that the final stroke will also be successful.
> (Great Britain, Special Operations Executive, 91087-10V, Hoover Institution Archives. Italics added.)

(#) Taylor reported to Nelson that he had arrived in Istanbul on 8 February 1941. Perhaps he came to Athens on the 20th, just before the Tatoi Conference between the British and Greek representatives.

Churchill's reply to Dalton: Destroy the railroad lines

On 28 March Churchill replied to Dalton instructing him to pay the utmost attention to Yugoslavia:

> with the execution of the *coup d'état,* there mightily grew possibilities for successful subversive activities such as destroying the railroad lines in the southern part of the state and the Vardar River valley, in order to inhibit German advances; the demolitions to be entrusted to the Yugoslav troops, with the help of *Vojvoda* Trifunović's organization, which should influence the officer corps; all reserves ought to be concentrated on the southern region of the state, not on the northern, because these sabotages would require great quantities of explosives. (Vodušek Starič, 239; n68)

In Dalton's opinion, the chief organizer of the coup was George Taylor

On 28 March Dalton recorded in his diary:

> More congratulations on my Jug achievement. Letter from Ismay on behalf of P.M. and Defence Committee. We are well on top! I make an order of the day and write thanks and appreciation. A wonderful reply comes two days later from my Chief Organiser. (3) It is quite touching.
>
> (3) Marginal note: Taylor.   (Pimlott(ed), 178)

In Dalton's opinion: the chief organizer of the coup was George Taylor – who really got down to work when he came to Belgrade [on 27 February], and who worked through the Serbian Peasant Party and *Narodna Odbrana* – who were "*in our pay*" !

> In London, ... , the Chiefs of Staff sent their congratulations to Dalton on the SOE's achievement in sowing the seeds of the *coup.* Dalton found this gracious on the part of the Chiefs of Staff and acknowledged that SOE had done well and that their considerable investment in the Serbian peasant party had been "thoroughly justified". (Glen(B), 59)

In Baron Julian Amery's opinion:

> ... The coup d'état of 27 March may well have been a turning point in the war. ... And yet I believe that Britain missed an even greater opportunity by not supporting the Djonovitch proposal to overthrow Price Paul when this was first made to us in the summer of 1940.
> Had we given our blessing then to a coup d'état in Yugoslavia it would probably have been attempted in the autumn [of 1940]. (Amery, 229)

Three decades after the coup, this influential former participant in the events clearly implied that the coup was accomplished only when the British gave their blessing for it.

John Bennett: Trifunović and Đonović *pushed and planned ...*

John H. Bennett wrote about the same subject to the head of SOE; here are some excerpts:

> First, I should like to record my own views and, I think, the views of TAYLOR and MASTERSON, that the grounds for eventual Coup d'etat were laid by TUPANJANIN who, ... , delayed the signing of the pact allying Yugoslavia with the Axis for 3 days. The resignation of 3 members of the Government, was due to TUPANJANIN's effort. Further, after CONSTANTINOVICH had withdrawn his resignation, it was TUPANJANIN who made him re-resign. When he heard that CONSTANTINOVICH had withdrawn his resignation, he immediately went into CONSTANTINOVICH's room and said: "You are like all other members of the Government, weak and gutless and your fate would be decided at the end of this war". This shook CONSTANTINOVICH so much that he immediately re-resigned. ...

Secondly, I think that TRIFUNOVICH and DJONOVICH played an important part in the actual Coup. It was they who pushed and planned how the Coup should take place. ...

... I am also certain that *the propaganda emanating from SO2 in Belgrade was largely responsible for the spirit maintained until their final entry into the war on the side of the Allies.*

(Great Britain, Special Operations Executive, 91087-10V, Hoover Institution Archives. Italics added.)

Chapter 12

The coup raised Churchill's hope

Persisting in his plans, and now more hopeful of forming the Balkan Front, on 27 March 1941 Churchill telegraphed Ismet Inönü – the President of Turkey:

> Your Excellency: The dramatic events which are occurring in Belgrade and throughout Yugoslavia may offer the best chance of preventing the German invasion of the Balkan Peninsula. Surely now is the time to make a common front which Germany will hardly dare assail. I have cabled to President Roosevelt to ask him for American supplies to be extended to all Powers resisting German aggression in the East. I am asking Mr. Eden and General Dill to concert all possible measures on common safety. (Churchill(GA), 169)

American supplies could not arrive on time, even if Roosevelt complied. This appeal to Turkey remained unsuccessful as well.

The news of the coup prompted Eden to return from Malta to Athens immediately. An Anglo-Greek meeting was held on 28 March in the renewed hope of forming the Balkan Front. General Papagos wanted to form "a solid continuous defensive front from the Adriatic to the Black Sea", to clean up Albania with Yugoslavia's help, and to move all available Anglo-Greek forces northwards because "we were practically obliged to defend Salonika if the Yugoslavs came in". Eden proposed a four-power conference between Britain, Greece, Yugoslavia and Turkey, "to form a common front to aggression". (Barker, 104; 284n50) Eden, Dill and Wilson were against moving the troops because they still did not know what Yugoslavia would do. (Eden, 231)

Still counting on Yugoslavia's participation, on 28 March, Churchill drafted a lengthy message to Eden, who was still in Athens. Churchill compared seventy divisions (from Yugoslavia, Greece, Turkey and Britain) against not more than thirty German. "Therefore, the seventy could say no to the thirty, 'If you attack any of us you will be at war with all'." "This is Turkey's best chance of avoiding war", he wrote, aware that Turkey did not want to be drawn into it. He continued to speculate:

> If Germany, notwithstanding the objections, attacks in the Balkans, we must play our part with our full available strength. If, on the other hand, she pretends that she never wished to bring war into the Balkans, and leaves Greece, Yugoslavia, and Turkey alone, then we might turn our forces to a strong summer and autumn campaign in the Central Mediterranean … (Churchill(GA), 169-71)

Once Churchill had decided on a course of action, he persisted in carrying it out, sometimes inspired more by his wishes than reality. He accounted for the number of divisions, but discounted the armament superiority of the German army and air force. As for developments in Greece, the *coup* upset all previous calculations.

> Since the Yugoslavs disregarded Papagos' pleas to abandon the northern part of their country in order to concentrate on the defence of its southern regions against the coming German onslaught, the Allied forces on both lines were exposed to outflanking movements over Yugoslav territory, which was in fact just what the Germans were planning. When the Wehrmacht attacked at dawn of 6 April there was 55,000 British troops in Greece; within less than a month there were only 10,000 left, and they were prisoners. (van Creveld(G), 92)

Had Yugoslavia not been drawn into war, there would have been no outflanking the Metaxas line.

First shocks of cruel awakening

In the meantime, in Belgrade, " In the first flush of enthusiasm after the *coup*, the new Yugoslav Prime Minister, General Simović, had sent a message to the British Air Attaché in Belgrade [Macdonald] to say that the army was now being fully mobilized and would be concentrated in the south, and that an attack on the Italians in Albania was imminent. A statement was being issued that Yugoslavia remained faithful to her policy of neutrality but this was only to gain time." (Eden, 231-2) This message was a sequel to the secret Simović-Macdonald conversation of 26 March, when Simović "foresaw that Yugoslavia would go to war in Albania immediately after the coup d'etat. He asked if Turks would then join in, to which I [Macdonald] replied that it was very possible but that I had no positive assurance regarding exact circumstances he described." However,

> Two days later Yugoslav policy was already being toned down. The General now told Campbell that the Government were not going to denounce the Tripartite Pact, although they would not ratify it, if it needed ratification. Salonika, the General stated, was a vital Yugoslav interest and if it were attacked the Yugoslavs would attack the Germans in Bulgaria and the Italians in Albania; but they would not make a public declaration of their intentions. Campbell thought that the new Government would resent any assumption on our part that they had definitely ranged themselves on the side of the democracies. (Eden, 232)

The Tripartite Pact did not need ratification, and the new Vice Premier, Professor Slobodan Jovanović, informed the new government accordingly. Simović's "tough" statement to Macdonald, that he was going to fight the Italians ... was negated by reality.

**

Hugh Dalton, who on 20 March issued the order for a revolution *by all means,* and stated that *the coup had been prepared well beforehand,* was quickly disappointed by the less-than expected benefits from the coup for the British war efforts:

> But the sequel [of the coup] was deplorable. The Yugoslav Government formed after the coup contained a number of very elderly politicians who, though their coup was a flagrant defiance of Hitler, believed that, if they sat as quiet as mice, he would not notice them. Therefore they stated publicly that their foreign policy was unchanged, and privately that they were still neutral and could enter into no staff talks with us. They never issued a general mobilisation order ... (Dalton, 373)

> After the events of 27 March, the Southern Department [of the Foreign Office] complained that the *coup* had been hijacked, and Campbell lamented the reappearance of yesterday's men, but there was no appreciation of the extent to which British policy had contributed to the outcome. (Onslow, 56)

It was not the age of the politicians that affected their attitude: for most of them it was the cruel reality of the situation.

Conference of Hitler and the German High Command on the situation in Yugoslavia, Berlin, 27 March 1941, at 1300 hours

After summarizing the coup-related developments of March 27, Eden recorded: *"Hitler's reaction was fury.* By mid-afternoon he had announced to Göring, Ribbentrop, the High Command and Army staffs his decision to 'smash Yugoslavia militarily and as a state'." ... (Eden, 229. Italics added.)

A fury it was, indeed, "one of the wildest rages of his entire life". (William L. Shirer) Churchill later wrote:

> Hitler was stung to the quick. He had a burst of that convulsive anger which momentarily blotted out thought and sometimes impelled him on his most dire adventure. In a cooler mood, a month later, conversing with Schulenburg, he said:
>> "The Yugoslav *coup* came suddenly out of the blue. When the news was brought to me on the morning of the twenty-seventh I thought it was a joke."
>
> But now in a passion he summoned the German High Command. Goering, Keitel and Jodl were present, and Ribbentrop arrived later. ... *He [Hitler] deemed it fortunate that the Yugoslavs had revealed their temper before "Barbarosa" [invasion of the Soviet Union] was launched.* (Churchill(GA), 163. Italics added.)

In that "convulsive anger", at a conference on 27 March, Hitler formulated his overall plan for the military operation against Yugoslavia.

Present: Fuehrer, the Reich Marshal [Goering], Chief OKW [Keitel], the Chief of the Wehrmacht Fuehrungstab [Generaloberst Alfred Jodl], Major General Bodenschatz, Colonel Schmundt, Commander von Puttkamer, Lieutenant-Colonel Scherff, Major von Below, Major Christian.

Later on the following persons were added: Supreme Commander of the army (Ob.d.H.), Chief of General staff of the army (Chef Gen St d. H.), Colonel Hensinger, Lieutenant-Colonel Sieverth, Reich Foreign Minister, Ambassador Hewel, Brigadier General (Gen.Maj.) von Waldan, Colonel Schmidt, Brigadier General (Gen.Maj.) von Rintelen.

The Fuehrer describes Yugoslavia's situation after the coup d'etat. Statement that Yugoslavia was an uncertain factor in regard to the coming Marita-action [attack on Greece] and even more in regard to the Barbarosa-undertaking [invasion of the Soviet Union] later on. Serbs and Slovenes were never pro-German. These governments never sit securely in the saddle, because of a nationality problem and the officers caste (Kamarilla), which is always inclined to start a coup d'etat. In the present time, the country had only one strong man, namely Stojodinowitsch [Stojadinović], and Regent Price Paul had him thrown over, to his own disadvantage.

The present moment is for political and military reasons favorable for us to ascertain the actual situation in the country and the country's attitude toward us, for *if the overthrow of the government would have happened during the Barbarosa-action, the consequences for us probably would have been considerably more serious.*

The Fuehrer is determined, without waiting for possible loyalty declarations of the new government, to make all preparations to destroy Yugoslavia militarily and as a national **unit.** No diplomatic inquiries will be made nor ultimatum presented. Assurances of the Yugoslav government which cannot be trusted any how in the future will be taken note of. The attack will start as soon as the means and troops suitable for it are ready.

It is important that actions will be taken as fast as possible. An attempt will be made to let the bordering state to participate in a suitable way. An actual military support against Yugoslavia is to be requested of Italy, Hungary, and in certain respects of Bulgaria too. Rumania's main task is the protection against Russia. The Hungarian and the Bulgarian ambassador have already been notified. During the day, a message will still be addressed to the Duce.

Politically, it is especially important that the blow against Yugoslavia is carried out with unmerciful harshness and that the military destruction is done in a lightning like undertaking. In this way, Turkey will become sufficiently frightened and the campaign against Greece later on would be influenced in a favorable way. It can be assumed that the Croats will come to our side when we attack. A corresponding political treatment (autonomy later on) will be assured to them. The war against Yugoslavia should be very popular in Italy, Hungary, and Bulgaria, as territorial acquisitions are to be promised to these states; the Adria coast for Italy, the Banat for Hungary, and Macedonia for Bulgaria.

This plan assumes that we speed up the schedule of all preparations and use such strong forces that the Yugoslav collapse will take place within the shortest time.

In this connection, the beginning of the Barbarossa-operation will have to be postponed up to 4 weeks.

The military operations are to be carried out in the following way:

1. Begin the operation Marita as early as possible with the limited aim to capture Greek-Thracia and the basin of Saloniki and to win the high terrain of Odessa; for that purpose march (Ausholen) across Yugoslav territory.

2. Push from neighborhood of Sofia in direction of Skoplje in order to relieve the flank of the Italian front in Albania.

3. Push with stronger forces from the area around Sofia in direction towards Nis, then towards Belgrad, in cooperation with

4. Stronger German forces penetrating from the area around Graz and Klagenfurt in direction South-East with the aim to destroy the Yugoslav army.

5. The main task of the air force is to start as early as possible with the destruction of the Yugoslavian airforce ground installations and to destroy the capital Belgrad in attacks by waves; besides the air force has to support the advance of the army.

For this purpose, it is possible to make use of the Hungarian ground installations.

(The Avalon Project: Nazi Conspiracy and Aggression Volume IV – Document No 1746
www.yale.edu/lawweb/avalon.imt/document/nca_vol/1746-ps.htm   10/6/04. Italics added.)

**

Churchill also described the conference according to minutes found in the Nuremberg records:

> The Fuehrer is determined, without waiting for possible loyalty declarations of the new Government, to make all preparations in order *to destroy Yugoslavia militarily and as a national unit.* No diplomatic inquiries will be made nor ultimatums presented. Assurances of the Yugoslav Government, which cannot be trusted anyhow in the future, will be "taken note of". The attack will start as soon as the means and troops suitable for it are ready.
>
> Actual military support against Yugoslavia is to be requested of Italy, Hungary, and in certain respects of Bulgaria too. Rumania's main task is the protection against Russia. The Hungarian and Bulgarian Ambassadors have already been notified. During the day a message will be addressed to the Duce.
>
> Politically it is especially important that the blow against Yugoslavia is *carried out with unmerciful harshness* and that the military destruction is done in a lightning-like undertaking. In this way Turkey would become sufficiently frightened and the campaign against Greece later on would be influenced in a favourable way. It can be assumed that the Croats will come to our side when we attack. A corresponding political treatment (autonomy later on) will be assured to them. The war against Yugoslavia should be very popular in Italy, Hungary, and Bulgaria, as territorial acquisitions are to be promised to these States: the Adriatic coast for Italy, the Banat for Hungary, and Macedonia for Bulgaria. This plan assumes that we speed up the schedule of all preparations and use such strong forces that the Yugoslav collapse will take place within the shortest time. ... The main task of the air force is to start as early as possible with the destruction of the Yugoslav Air Force ground installations and to destroy the capital, Belgrade, in attacks by waves. (Churchill(GA), 163-4. Italics in the source.)

**

According to Colonel General F. Halder, Chief of Staff of the German Army, Hitler had decided to invade Yugoslavia for the following reasons:

> 1, To protect the flank of the offensive to be launched from Bulgaria against Greece. 2. To gain possession of the railway line from Belgrade via Nisch to the south. 3. To make sure of his right flank before starting 'Barbarossa'. (van Creveld, 147)

The plan outlined by Hitler at the afternoon conference was drawn up that evening as the *Directive No. 25*.

"Directive No. 25" – excerpts

> 1. The military revolt in Yugoslavia has changed the political position in the Balkans. Yugoslavia, even if it makes initial professions of loyalty, must be regarded as an enemy and beaten down as quickly as possible.
> 2. It is my intention to break into Yugoslavia in the general direction of Belgrade and to the south by a concentric operation from the Fiume-Graz area on one side, and the Sofia area on the other, and to deal an annihilating blow to the Yugoslav forces. Further, the extreme southern region of Yugoslavia will be cut off from the rest of the country and will be occupied as a base from which the German-Italian offensive against Greece can be continued. The opening of the traffic on the Danube as soon as possible and the seizure of the Bov [Bor] copper-mines are important for economic reasons. Efforts will be made to induce Hungary and Bulgaria to take part in operations by offering them the prospect of regaining the Banat and Macedonia. Internal tensions in Yugoslavia will be encouraged by giving assurances to the Croats.
> 3. I issue the following detailed orders ... (Balfour & Mackay, 263-4)

Churchill also wrote about Hitler and *Directive No. 25* :

> My intention is to invade Yugoslavia by powerful thrusts from the area of Fiume and Sofia in the general direction of Belgrade and further to the south, with the objective of inflicting on the Yugoslav army a decisive defeat, as well as to cut off the southern part of Yugoslavia from the rest of the country and to turn it into a base for further operations of German-Italian forces against Greece.
> In detail I order the following:
> (a) As soon as the concentration of sufficient forces is concluded and meteorological conditions permit, all Yugoslav surface installations and Belgrade must be destroyed by continuous day and night air attacks.
> (b) If possible simultaneously, but under no circumstances sooner, Operation "Marita" must be started, with the primary limited objective of seizing the harbour of Salonika and the Dios Mountains. (Churchill(GA)], 164)

Vauhnik informed American colleagues of Hitler's plan

One hour after Hitler decided to break up Yugoslavia before attacking the Soviet Union, Vauhnik was informed of Hitler's decision. Within a few hours he also had the plan of the attack against Yugoslavia.

At that moment he considered it necessary to reveal details of the plan to attack the Soviet Union to the American Attaché, Colonel Peyton, and his assistant, Major Lovelt. How did they handle this information – Vauhnik did not know. He provided the same information to his friend, the Brazilian Attaché, Colonel Holt. (Vauhnik, 133)

Hitler's letter to Mussolini

After the conference at the *Reichskanzlei,* Hitler dictated a letter to Mussolini. (van Creveld, 147) As Churchill recorded it:

> Duce, events force me to give you, by this, the quickest means, my estimate of the situation and the consequences which may result from it.
> From the beginning I have regarded Yugoslavia as a dangerous factor in the controversy with Greece. Considered from the purely military point of view, German intervention in the war in Thrace would not be at all justified as long as the attitude of Yugoslavia remained ambiguous and she could threaten the left flank of the advancing columns on our enormous front.
> 2. For this reason I have done everything and have honestly endeavored to bring Yugoslavia into our community bound together by mutual interests. Unfortunately these attempts did not meet with success, or they were begun too late to produce any definite result. Today's reports leave no doubt of the imminent turn in the foreign policy of Yugoslavia.
> 3. I do not consider this situation as being catastrophic, but nevertheless it is a difficult one, and we on our part must avoid any mistake if we do not want, in the end, to endanger our whole position.
> 4. Now I would cordially ask you, Duce, not to undertake any further operations in Albania in the course of the next few days.
> I consider it necessary that you should cover and screen the most important passes from Yugoslavia into Albania with all available forces. These measures should not be considered as designed for a long period of time, but as auxiliary measures to prevent for at least fourteen days to three weeks a crisis arising.
> I also consider it necessary, Duce, that you should reinforce your forces on the Italian-Yugoslav front with all available means and with utmost speed.
> ... If silence is maintained, Duce, on these measures I have no doubt we shall both witness a success that will not be less than that of Norway. This is my granite conviction. (Churchill(GA), 164-5)

During the following night Hitler drafted more detailed military instructions for the Italians: they were to redeploy their forces in Albania, stage an offensive from across the Julian Alps, and take care of the Yugoslav naval forces. (van Creveld, 147)

> The Germans submitted a memorandum containing suggestions to promote the coordination of the German and Italian operations against Yugoslavia. The memorandum outlined the German plans and assigned the following missions to the Italian forces:
> a. To protect the flank of the German attack forces, which were to be assembled around Graz, by moving all immediately available ground forces in the direction of Split and Jajce;
> b. To switch to the defensive along the Greek-Albanian front and assemble an attack force, which was to link up with the Germans driving toward Skoplje and points farther south;
> c. To neutralize the Yugoslav naval forces in the Adriatic;
> d. To resume the offensive on the Greek front in Albania at a later date.
> Mussolini approved the German plans and instructed General Guzzoni to comply with them. As a result, the Italian army group in Albania diverted four division to the protection of the eastern and northern borders of that country where they faced Yugoslavia.
> (Hyper War: The German Campaign in the Balkans (Spring 1941) – Part 1
> www.ibiblio.org/hyperwar/ETO/East/Balkans/Campaigns-1.html 10/6/04)

Hitler asked Hungary and Bulgaria to cooperate

In addition to Mussolini, on 27 March Hitler also contacted the Hungarian and Bulgarian representatives. "The Yugoslavs, he raged, had gone stark mad. Him who the gods would destroy they first struck blind. Budapest and Sofia were asked to cooperate in the liquidation of Yugoslavia and would receive slices of her territory for their pains. Here, however, Hitler faced a disappointment; King Boris politely refused to help, while the Hungarians limited their participation to some ten military and armoured brigades which were to attack on 14 April." (van Creveld, 147-8)

The coup in Belgrade, a part of a *"large design"* – Churchill claimed

On 29 March, Churchill instructed Eden that the Yugoslavs, Greeks and Turks send a 'triple note' to Germany, saying that if it attacked any one of them, it would be at war with all three. (Barker, 106; 284n51)

On 30 March, Eden telegraphed Campbell: If the new government would not have him, then get approval for Dill's visit. (Eden, 232)

Also on 30 March, Churchill informed Eden about the movements of the German troops, concluding, "This can only mean in my opinion intention to attack Yugo at earliest or alternatively act against the Turk." (Eden, 234)

**

Attempting to dispel serious doubts about the Greek campaign, and hoping for benefits from the coup in Belgrade, on 30 March, Churchill sent a personal, most secret message to the Acting Prime Minister of Australia, Arthur W. Fadden, explaining:

> When a month ago we decided upon sending an army to Greece it looked rather a bleak military adventure dictated by *noblesse oblige* . Thursday's events in Belgrade show the far-reaching effects of this and other measures we have taken on the whole Balkan situation. German plans have been upset, and we may cherish renewed hopes of forming a Balkan front with Turkey, comprising about seventy Allied divisions from the four powers concerned. This is, of course, by no means certain yet. But even now it puts "Lustre" [the expedition to Greece] in its true setting, not as an isolated military act, but as a prime mover in a large design. Whatever the outcome may be, everything that has happened since our decision was taken justifies it. Delay will also enable full concentration to be made on the Greek front instead of piecemeal engagement of our forces. Result unknowable but prize has increased and risks have somewhat lessened. … (Churchill(GA), 171)

In order to implement his *large design* at that moment, Churchill was still hoping to draw Turkey into the war, although after two meetings with Eden, the Turks resolutely rejected that idea. "They [the British] were unfailingly tolerant towards the Turks, who had stubbornly resisted all of Eden's pressures – even more stubbornly than Prince Paul." (Barker, 107) By 30 March, there was no statement from the new Putschist Government in Belgrade of its readiness to "join in" and to defend Salonika. Actually, *the Simović Government did not renounce the Tripartite Pact*, and was moving in the direction traced by the maligned and ostracized Prince Paul. However, when it had been decided that General Dill should go to Belgrade, Churchill still wishfully hoped that Yugoslavia might strike

> a deadly blow at the naked rear of the disorganised Italian armies in Albania. If they acted promptly they might bring about a major military event, and while their own country was being ravaged from the north might possess themselves of the masses of munitions and equipment which would give them the power of conducting the guerrilla in their mountains which was now their own hope. It would have been a grand stroke, and would have reacted upon the whole Balkan scene. In our circle in London we all saw this together. The diagram below shows the movements which was deemed feasible. (Churchill(GA), 172)

Regarding *the masses of munitions and equipment* supposedly available in Albania, the Air Attaché Macdonald reported that, during the secret meeting on the morning on 26 March, Simović "feared, however, that the *types of weapons were not the same and that Italian ammunition could not therefore reinforce Yugoslav units.* Reserves of 76.5 and 75 mm. ammunition for field artillery would be required." Churchill did not care about the *ravages of Yugoslavia from the north,* as long as there could be the guerrilla in the mountains. That appears to have been his goal since he first tried to push Yugoslavia into the war against the Axis in Albania. But he did not elaborate as to how the guerrillas could impede the German advance toward Salonika along the Vardar valley, which was not protected by the mountains in Albania. He just wanted to get Yugoslavia into the war by any means, to keep the Germans engaged - which would benefit Britain - regardless of the consequences for Yugoslavia and her people.

**

From J. Colville's diary, on 31 March:

> The P.M. has been elated by the naval victory [off Cape Matapan] following so close on the Yugoslav revolution, ...
> The P.M. told me he was now sure Germany would attack Yugoslavia before Greece or Turkey *and he is very hopeful on that front.*" (Colville, 369. Italics added.)

General Dill's secret visit to Belgrade, 31 March – 1 April:
Simović *"quite unwilling to sign anything that would commit the Yugoslav Government."*

Dill's visit to Belgrade was approved also on 31 March. Eden and Dill then decided what the Yugoslavs' tasks should be in concert with the Greeks. Dill would also suggest staff talks between the Yugoslavs, Greeks and British, pointing out that, because of necessary political decisions, Eden should be invited to Belgrade (Eden, 232-3)

On 31 March and 1 April, General Sir John Dill [with Pierson Dixon of the FO and Brigadier A.W.S. Mallaby of the War Office (Williams, 33)] secretly visited Belgrade and had highly clandestine talks with the Yugoslav military. Dill urged the Yugoslavs to attack Albania before Germany was ready, "where they would have an easy victory and secure quantities of much needed equipment". But Simović — who, according to Macdonald's report of 26 March, "foresaw that Yugoslavia would go to war in Albania immediately after the coup d'etat" -- said that the attack would provoke an immediate German attack from south-west Bulgaria and Yugoslavia was not yet ready. (Barker, 105)

> As Prince Paul had done earlier, Simović "regretted his inability to receive Mr. Eden", since this would provoke the Germans. And as Prince Paul had done he stressed the Croat problem: if the government took any "provocative action" the Croats would defect. But if the government could show that they had not provoked a German attack, then the Croats and Slovenes would fight. Agreement to hold British-Yugoslav-Greek talks at Florina was the only outcome of the Dill visit. (Barker, 105; 284n57)

On the evening of 31 March, Dill met with Simović, the Minister of War, General Bogoljub Ilić, and the acting Chief of the General Staff. In a report to Eden that evening, Dill emphasized that the Yugoslav Government resolutely opposed any act which the Germans may interpret as a provocation. (Petranović & Žutić, 528) Eden described the meeting in more details : Because of the tenuous internal situation, the Yugoslavs were

> "determined to avoid provoking a Nazi assault. ... [They] agreed to sign a brief statement saying that if Yugoslavia were attacked by Germany, the British government would give her *all the aid in their power* and that, if the Germans attacked Greece and not Yugoslavia, the Yugoslav Government would join with us in giving Greece all the aid in their power. ... Dill inquired what was happening about the Tripartite Pact and was told that the Yugoslavs regarded it as having lapsed, but were leaving it in suspense. (Eden, 233-4)
> Next morning [April 1st], however, the General Staff refused to agree to the statement Dill had prepared, without putting in an amendment limiting Yugoslav help to Greece to the case of a German attack west of the Struma. Dill in turn refused to accept this and asked to see Simović again. He now found the Prime Minister quite unwilling to sign anything that would commit the Yugoslav Government. He said that if he asked his Government to accept such obligations, or if I came to Belgrade, there would be a split and the home front would disintegrate. (Eden, 234)

No other Ministers knew of Dill's visit. The C.I.G.S. had already discovered that the General Staff did not know his identity and thought that he was one of Wilson's divisional commanders. The staff talks, now fixed for April 3rd, the Prime Minister said, could only be to exchange views and must not lead to a military convention. Simović added that he could do no more *unless the Government changed their mind* or the Germans attacked Yugoslavia or Salonika. Even an attack on Salonika would only bring in the Yugoslavs if it passed the Struma. (Eden, 234. Italics added.)

**

As Eden stated, Simović would not accept the British plan *"unless the Government changed their mind"* or if the Germans attacked Yugoslavia or Salonika. To understand Simović's stand, one ought to keep in mind the ongoing internal developments within Yugoslavia and the new Government's activities from its inception on the morning of 27 March until the moment of Simović's talk with General Dill on 1 April. (Related information is presented in **Part Two**.) The following is relevant to the observation of *the Government changing their mind.*

During its formation, most of the new government's ministers declared themselves "for peace". Simović reportedly said, "For peace, if possible". (Kosić(50), 16-17) "If possible" showed Simović's personal leaning to side with the Allies – as he had professed to Col. Donovan. Campbell knew of Simović's leaning when he informed Eden, late on 24 March, about *"The one possible exception* "among the military chiefs, *"the active military chief mentioned above"*.

Siding with the Allies was Simović's essential reason for overthrowing Prince Paul's Government in the first place. According to Simović: When William Donovan asked him, on 24 January 1941, would Yugoslavia go with Hitler or not, Simović promptly replied:

((What are the intentions of our responsible factors I do not know and I can not tell you. But I can assure you that the Yugoslav people will never abandon their true friends and Allies and go with Hitler, even if that should be against the will of the leading factors.)) . (Simović(44), 10) (See **Appendix A.**)

But, once in power, he had to be cautious. Although he wanted to side with the Allies, most of the Ministers wanted Yugoslavia to remain neutral. The non-Serbian ministers, holdovers from the previous government, were all for adhesion to the Tripartite Pact as a means of avoiding war. On 1 April, the representative of the Croatian Peasant Party, Vladko Maček – the First Vice-Premier-designate ... still negotiating his conditions for joining the new Government ... was not in Belgrade. Without the non-Serbian representatives, the new Government could not claim to be the representative one, "with the roots in the people". Any commitment now to the plan proposed by Gen. Dill would have meant the breakup of the new Government. Simović could not afford that. Therefore, *"unless the Government changed their mind"*, the talks with the British , "could only be to exchange views and must not lead to a military convention".

In his speech to the Holy Assembly of Bishops on 28 March 1941, Simović stated that the Government was doing everything possible to convince the Axis Powers that the intent of the Government was only to preserve peace. The Government desired to secure the peace, security and borders of the state; they did not desire to give reason for provocations. The Foreign Minister was taking steps in that direction.

After a talk with Simović the evening of 28 March, American Minister Lane reported to Washington that "... Yugoslavia does not wish to provoke Germany or Italy but will resist by force any attempt to take Salonika, which is vital to national interest, nor will it tolerate move against sovereignty of country."

On 30 March – a day before the first meeting with Gen. Dill - the Yugoslav Foreign Minister, Momčilo Ninčić, summoned von Heeren and made a formal statement on behalf of the Government:

The Present Royal Yugoslav Government remains true to the principle of respect for international treaties which have been concluded, among which the Protocol signed on the 25th of this month at Vienna belongs. It will insist in the most determined fashion on not being drawn into the present conflict. Its chief attention will be devoted to the maintenance of good and friendly relations with the neighbors, the German Reich and the kingdom of Italy. (Ristić, 114)

Consequently, the same day the Government declined Eden's request for a visit, and only approved the visit to Belgrade by Gen. Dill. (Jukić(65), 143)

**

Here is Gen. Simović's description of this first round of talks with the British (translated):

>((The Minister of Great Britain, ... Campbell, visited me on 27 March, and insisited on the coming of Mr. Anthony Eden, the Minister of Foreign Affairs, and General ... Dill, the Chief of the Imperial Staff. Because Hitler could understand the coming of Mr. Eden to Belgrade as an intentional provocation – and the goal of the Government was to gain at least the most needed time for the mobilization and concentration of the military and the preparation of the country for war – after the consultation with the Minister of Foreign Affairs, I declined the visit of Mr. Eden, but allowed the coming of his Chief of Cabinet Dixon in the company of General Dill.
>
>((The Chief of the Imperial Staff, General Dill, was in Belgrade on 31 March and 1 April. His coming, stay and return were kept in the strictest secrecy. The goal of his coming was to get information about our preparations, potential and needs; and our goal was to get assistance in material and support from the British troops.The meetings were held in the office of the MInister of the Army; present were – in addition to the Minister, General of the Army B[ogoljub] Ilić – the representatives of the Main General Staff, as follows: ... General Milutin Nikolić, ... General Radivoje Janković, ... Colonels Branko Popović, Bor. Josimović and Vasa Petković. I also attended, partially. In the course of talks, General Dill was setting for us prospects of certain material help and cooperation of the British troops sent to Greece.
>
>((As General Dill was returning, General Radivoje Janković was sent with him to Greece in order to get information about the strength and condition of the British troops who, under the command of General Wilson, were landing in Greece. ... .)) (Simović(51), 16)

**

While Dill was still conferring in Belgrade, on 1 April 1941 Churchill sent him this message: "A variety of details shows rapid regrouping against Yugoslavia. To gain time against Germans is to lose it against Italians. Nothing should stop Yugo developing full strength against latter at earliest. By this alone can they gain far-reaching initial success and masses of equipment in good time." (Churchill(GA), 172-3)

Prime Minister Churchill was talking about *masses of equipment* that Yugoslavia could get in Albania because he knew very well that *all the aid in British power,* which Eden had spoken of, amounted to very little .

But the best Dill could do was to arrange another conference near the border of Yugoslavia between Gen. Miloje Janković, Yugoslavia's Director of Operations, and Generals Wilson and Papagos. (McClymont, 132) As Eden stated, even this second round of talks "could only be to exchange views and must not lead to a military convention."

**

In order to create good will of the Croats for the British policies, on 2 April – a day before the next scheduled British-Yugoslav meeting at Farina - the Foreign Office asked Eden: would it be useful if a Crown Minister, in the near future, in a radio emission mentions the Croats in a special way. (Petranović & Žutić, 531)   The question was related to the authorization given to Campbell on 3 March for eventual revision of the Italo-Yugoslav frontier related to Istria, about which Eden commented at that time: "This, for what it was worth, was intended as something of a bait for the Croats and Slovenes." (Eden, 216) In another telegram the same day the Foreign Office suggested to Eden the content of that proposed message for the Croats. (Petranović & Žutić, 532)

The conference in Greece, 3-4 April 1941
"... in Belgrade Dill had said that Britain would ultimately have 150,000 men on the Aliakmon line ..."

In the railcar near Farina, Greece, the night of 3 April, Gen. Miloje Janković stated that – if the Axis group attempted to take Salonika with the goal of encircling Yugoslavia from the south – Yugoslavia would resist and be prepared to cooperate with the Allied armies. However, Yugoslavia herself would decide just when she would make that move, and she was quite willing to have plans prepared for any eventuality. "Jankovitch has brought with him the draft plans by which she was willing to commit her divisions. Five British divisions were to go forward to the Lake Doiran area as a link between the army of Yugoslavia and the Greek forces along the Metaxas line. At the appropriate moment, which would be decided in Belgrade, the Allied forces were to open an offensive against the Italians in Albania and to the rear and right flank of the Germans advancing toward Salonika." (McClymont, 133-4)

"Gen. Janković proposed that the Greek troops deployed on the fortification line would remain there, and the British troops would assume defence positions between the Greeks and the Yugoslavs near Lake Dojran and in the valley of river Struma. He was surprised when Gen. Wilson presented the real strength of the British forces in Greece (in Belgrade Gen. Dill overstated the numbers) and declined a commitment to swiftly deploy British units in the vicinity of Dojran." - As to the Albanian front, Janković stated that the Yugoslavs would start offensive activities with four divisions by 12 April, in directions Podgorica – Shkodra, Prizren – Kukesi, and from Debar and Struga westward, where they would co-operate with the Greeks. "However, neither the date of the beginning of the operation nor the forms of activities' co-ordination were agreed upon." "Practically it meant that it did not come to establishment of a common strategic plan among Yugoslavia, Greece and Great Britain,"

(Paul Newman, "Enemies on all the sides", http://2ndww.tripod.com/Balkans/r41.html 2/4/04)

"... Wilson did not wish his troops be caught on the move at this stage of the campaign; he preferred to remain where he was until the political situation was less obscure. So the final decision was that there should be no move beyond the Aliakmon line for at least eight days." (McClymont, 134)

As E. Baker described it: the Yugoslav representative read a note declaring that if the "freedom of Salonika" should be threatened by the Axis, the Yugoslav army would intervene to ensure its security, but that "the necessary decision will be taken by the Yugoslav government at the appropriate moment". (Barker, 105)

There was only a vague general discussion of Yugoslav military plans. One point which caused trouble was that while in Belgrade Dill had said that Britain would ultimately have 150,000 men on the Aliakmon line and was already "somewhere near the half way mark", General Maitland Wilson now said that Britain would have one armoured brigade and three infantry divisions "in about six week's time". Janković declared that Yugoslav plans had been based on Dill's considerably higher figure of the forces already in place, and that "news of the lesser British force would be an acute disappointment". The meeting ended without any clear agreement and – to judge by the British record – left a feeling of mutual distrust. (Barker, 105; 284n58)

Eden – who was in the area but did not attend the meeting – described it differently. Some excerpts:

General Janković, the chief Yugoslav representative, was only authorized to discuss certain points about common action in the event of an attack on Salonika, and the plan he put forward was based on *such faulty information about the size* and disposition of the British and Greek forces that it could not be used. When General Wilson insisted on being allowed to reconnoitre the Dorian-Strumica area where the plan suggested our forces should concentrate, Janković could only promise to refer back to Belgrade. He gave the same reply when General Papagos suggested that army and air force representatives should be sent to Athens to continue the conversations. He refused to give any information about the disposition of the Yugoslav forces, except in the south-east, where there were four divisions, and on the Albanian front, where there were also four. Although we knew that these were forty thousand strong and therefore twice the size of an ordinary division, General Janković emphasized that the Yugoslav divisions were not designed to repel an armoured attack. (Eden, 236. Italics added.)

Understandably, Eden did not record that *such faulty information about the size* of 150,000 men *and disposition of the British and Greek forces* came from Sir John Dill himself.

In the discussion of 3-4 April, the Allied representatives explained that such an ambitious plan – as proposed by Gen. Janković - was impossible. Gen. Wilson also noted the Greeks' desire to strengthen the Yugoslav army in southern Serbia:

> General Papagos urged General J. to persuade his Government to send two more divisions into southern Serbia so as to ensure no break in the hinge joining the Allies; whilst I again stressed the importance of stopping a tank break through and of fighting on ground where the Yugoslav soldier would find himself superior to the German. At two o'clock on the morning General J. departed; opportunity for meeting him again never recurred. This closed the most unusual and at the same time the most unsatisfactory conference I have ever attended, (McClymont, 133)

No soldier without anti-aircraft or anti-tank weapons would be superior to a soldier in an aircraft or in a tank.

> ((... Upon returning, General Janković submitted an unfavorable report: that the British forces, who arrived in northern Greece, were weak (up to two infantry brigades), that they are located around Olympus, and that we cannot count on their help, at least not now.)) (Simović(51), 16)

The coup and Turkey

Eden also thought that the coup in Belgrade could be used to induce Turkey to actively support British plans. "During the week since the *coup* I, and the Foreign Office at home, had made several attempts to induce the Turkish Government to give the Yugoslav Government political support". Noticing that Turkish policy was becoming increasingly equivocal, he asked the British Ambassador at Ankara for an explanation of the reasons. "It is common ground that strategically Turkey's role is to remain on the defensive. But we have never agreed that politically she should play a negative part." (Eden, 236-7)

He recorded that: "The new Yugoslav Government now asked the Turks to receive a staff officer and inquired whether they [the Turks] would regard an attack on Salonika as a *casus belli*." Knowing that Turkey would not automatically go to war over Salonika, the Turkish Foreign Minister asked the British Ambassador for advice. The ambassador consulted Eden, who replied:

> ... Best contribution Turks could make would be (a) to create a diversion by troop movements on Turco-Bulgarian frontier and (b) to assure Yugoslav Government that in the event of a German attack on Yugoslavia directed toward Salonika, Turkey would at least declare war. (Eden, 236-7)

However, "The Turkish Government refused to accept these suggestions and were unconvinced by any arguments in favour of political action." (Eden, 237)

As it had been before the coup in Belgrade, so it was after it. The Turkish Government was putting the interests of Turkey above those of Great Britain; the coup did not advance the argument in favor of the Balkan Front.

Instead of the promised attack on the Italians in Albania ... negotiations

> ... the Simović government did not denounce the pact or offer to help Greece, and pursued Prince Paul's foreign policy with little change. In any case, the German invasion of Yugoslavia soon negated most of the supposed beneficial effects. (Pimlott(ed), 175)

On 3 April – the day of negotiations at Farina - Air Attaché MacDonald informed the British Air Ministry that negotiations between the Italians and the Yugoslavs were proceeding, and while they were still going on, Yugoslavia would not attack Albania. These negotiations made General Papagos' idea of "a solid continuous defensive front from the Adriatic to the Black Sea" unrealistic. (Barker, 104-5; 284n56)

When the talks at Florina did not produce the desired results, and possibly not yet aware of Macdonald's report from the preceding day, on 4 April Churchill - still stubbornly persisting in directing Yugoslavia against the Italians in Albania – appealed to Gen. Simović:

> From every quarter my information shows rapid heavy concentration and advance towards your country by German ground and air forces. ... I cannot understand argument that you are gaining time. The one supreme stroke for victory and safety is to win a decisive forestalling victory in Albania, and collect the masses of equipment that would fall into your hands. When the four German

mountain divisions reported by your General Staff as entraining in the Tyrol reach Albania, a very different resistance will confront you than could be offered by rear of the demoralized Italians. ... (Churchill(GA), 174)

**

That same day British troops began sailing to Greece, Campbell talked with Simović and reported to Eden, who was still in Athens: The best the British could do to ensure a resolute stand and resistance of Yugoslavia was to use propaganda, with which they would maintain the mood to force the Government to behave accordingly. (Petranović & Žutić, 536)

Use propaganda to create a fighting mood, and when the mood fades, use propaganda again to revitalize and maintain it.

Chapter 13

Sunday, 6 April 1941: Germany attacked Yugoslavia

On 27 March 1941, in the conference with the German High Command Hitler requested: Politically, it is especially important that the blow against Yugoslavia is carried out with unmerciful harshness and that the military destruction is done in a lightning like undertaking."
(http://avalon.law.yale.edu/imt/1746-ps.asp   12/17/09)

In Moscow - Utterly opposed to the idea of a military alliance, advanced by Yugoslavia, the Soviet Union agreed only to a nonaggression and friendship pact with Yugoslavia. "The signing of the agreement had originally been scheduled for 10 p.m. on 5 April. By midnight [Vladimir] Dekanozov [Soviet special ambassador to Berlin] informed Stalin from Berlin that a German invasion of Yugoslavia was imminent." Subsequently, the agreement "was signed around 3 a.m. on 6 April. ... Stalin insisted, however, that the date of the signing should be 5 April, so as not to suggest that it had been signed with preknowledge of or concurrently with the German invasion of Yugoslavia." (Gorodetsky, 149-50)

No promised help from the Soviet Union.

In Belgrade: The Coup on 27 March - the war on 6 April. What did the British, involved in promoting the coup, do to help Yugoslavia *with all resources at their disposal?* The British sent no *resources to bear* on the outcome of "resistance" to Germany about which Eden wrote to Prince Paul on 17 March. No military supplies were sent by the USA, which Simović had reportedly told Donovan were urgently needed. The following is how some British war leaders described what had happened in Yugoslavia on 6 April.

* **The air bombardment of Belgrade**

    The Luftwaffe opened the assault on Yugoslavia by conducting a saturation-type bombing raid on the capital in the early morning hours of 6 April. Flying in relays from airfields in Austria and Romania, 150 bombers and dive-bombers protected by heavy fighter escort participated in the attack. The initial raid was carried out at fifteen minutes. Thus, the city was subjected to a rain of bombs for almost one and a half hours. The German bombardiers directed their main effort against the center of the city, where the principal government buildings were located.
    The weak Yugoslav Air Force and the inadequate flak defenses were quickly wiped out by the first wave, permitting the dive-bombers to come down to roof-top levels. Against the loss of but two German fighters, twenty Yugoslav planes were shot down and forty-four were destroyed on the ground. When the attack was over, more than 17,000 inhabitants lay dead under the debris. This devastating blow virtually destroyed all means of communication between the Yugoslav high command and the forces in the field. Although some elements of the general staff managed to escape to one of the suburbs, coordination and control of the military operations in the field were rendered impossible from the outset.
    Having thus delivered the knockout blow to the enemy nerve center, the [German] VIII Air Corps was able to devote its maximum effort to such targets of opportunity as Yugoslav airfields, routes of communication, and troop concentrations, and to the close support of German ground operations. (Blau, 48)

Churchill's note on the bombardment of Belgrade:
    On the morning of April 6 German bombers appeared over Belgrade. Flying in relays from occupied airfields in Rumania, they delivered a methodical attack lasting three days upon the Yugoslav capital. From rooftop height, without fear of resistance, they blasted the city without mercy This was called Operation "Punishment". When silence came at last on April 8 over seventeen thousand citizens of Belgrade lay dead in streets or under the débris. Out of the nightmare of smoke and fire came the maddened animals released from their shattered cages in the zoological gardens. A stricken stork hobbled past the main hotel, which was a mass of flames. A bear, dazed and uncomprehending, shuffled through the inferno with slow and awkward gait down towards the Danube. He was not the only bear who did not understand.
    Operation "Punishment" had been performed.   (Churchill(GA), 175)

Eden: "After a slightly better night, up early and went to Gezira for a swim. News reached us while there of German invasion of Greece and attack on Jugs, as foretold." (Eden, 239)

Cadogan:

> Rung up at 7.45 with news (fully expected) that Germany has declared war on Yugoslavia and Greece. This should put an end to all the dither in Belgrade. (*) No news at all. Soubbotitch [the Yugoslav Ambassador] called at 12.45 but *he* had no news. Asked for a 'message' and I gave him what I could, though I can't make pronouncements on behalf of the British Government.
>
> (*) Simović had refused to allow a visit by Eden. Dill, who did go to Belgrade, failed to make an agreement. Fruitless staff talks were held on 3 April. (Dilks(ed), 369)

Dalton: "And up she went according to forecast! I hear this at breakfast." (Pimlott(ed), 183)

Colville: "We heard on a wireless that Germany had invaded both Greece and Yugoslavia." (p, 371)

General F. de Guingand:

> Sunday April 6th in Cairo was indeed a black day. That morning news arrived that the German attack against Greece had begun. ... Not only was Salonika immediately threatened, but in view of the threat through Yugo-Slavia towards the Monastir [Bitolj] gap. An immediate danger existed to the Greek forces in Albania. In addition the news from the Desert was very bad. ... That afternoon a meeting took place at which the Commander-in-Chief [Gen. Wavell], Eden and Dill were present.. The atmosphere was certainly tense. The subject was Tobruk. ... (de Guingand, 62-3)

Not a word or worry about Yugoslavia.

William J. M. Mackenzie, an official SOE historian:

> The German attack began early on 6th April and was instantly successful in dislocating organised resistance. *SO2 [SOE] had expected early Yugoslav defeat, and was making plans for post-occupational sabotage and guerilla warfare. In particular it had been ceaselessly pressing the Yugoslav General Staff to make effective preparations to block the Danube at once in the event of war.* (Mackenzie, 112. Italics added.)

Yes, *up she went according to forecast*, as *fully expected*, a few hours before Eden *went to Gezira for a swim .... Operation "Punishment" was being executed, with unmerciful harshness.* Writing some nine years later, Sir Winston used 72 words to describe the three days of bombing of Belgrade, mentioning over seventeen thousand dead citizens of Belgrade, and 63 words to describe maddened animals released from their cages.

His three top officials involved in the events which led to Operation "Punishment" did not waste even that many words on the bombings. They were not surprised by the bombings ... which are a part of the war ... into which they were expected to draw Yugoslavia. *"And up she went according to forecast"* – wrote Dalton who made sure that – before she went up – his SOE planned to successfully organize a "post-occupational resistance" in Yugoslavia. That was one of the major tasks of his principal man, George Taylor. "Perhaps the most delicate part of his allotted task was to organize post-occupational planning and make preparations for guerrilla resistance if – or when - the Balkan peninsula was overrun." (Williams, 28) As the bombs were falling, he also was fleeing the city and the country.

The Simović Government were fleeing, too

When the German bombs began to fall, Simović's cabinet ministers fled from Belgrade to Užice, a town in western Serbia, while Simović and High Command went to Koviljača; the British retreated hurriedly, as did most of their domestic co-operatives and Putschists.

7 April 1941 – "There is no news from the Balkan front but that from Libya is bad. The German attack has taken us by surprise and an armoured brigade has been cut up." (Colville, 372)

London updated President Roosevelt daily on the preceding day's military situation. Thus, for April 7th, 1941, a report was sent to the President relating to Greece and Yugoslavia:

> 6. MILITARY. At 6.00 P.M. April 6th enemy positions reliably reported as follows: XL Army Corps advancing on Skoplje; second armoured division from PETRIC advancing westward in the direction of STIP. Opposition in this sector reported slim. Sixth mountain division east of Lake Doran and believed moving southward. This division being met by determined counter attacks. Fifth mountain division with one infantry effectively blocked in Rupel Pass in spite of heavy German dive bombing attacks. Enemy thought to have suffered considerable casualties here. No reference to any enemy movements in N. Yugoslavia. (www.fdrlibrary.marist.edu/psf/box35/a319i02.html   10/31/08)

Human losses from the bombings of Belgrade

And what were the human losses from the bombings? Accounts vary on the losses of that day. Churchill stated over seventeen thousand. Others give a number closer to twenty. Quoted here is the estimate by an American journalist who lived through the first day of bombings in Belgrade:

> Twenty thousand out of a population of three hundred thousand! One of every fifteen killed! And God only knows how many of the other fourteen had been injured. Had lost legs or arms or other pieces of their bodies. One out of fifteen dead. Just as if half a million people were to be killed in New York City in a two-day raid. Or two hundred and twenty thousand in Chicago. Or a hundred thousand in Los Angeles, or nearly six hundred thousand in London in two days. (St. John, 120-1)

During The Blitz – the German bombing campaign on British cities on 7 September 1940 through 10 May 1941 – over 43,000 civilians have been killed by bombing across Britain, half of them in London.   (http://historylearningsite.co.uk/blitz_and_world_war_two.htm   5/3/10) (http://en.wikipedia.org/wiki/The_Blitz   5/2/10)

Over a period of eight months – over 43,000 civilians in Britain.
In Belgrade, in three days - between 17,00 and 20,000 , according to some sources, "more than 5,000 civilians" (Roberts, 16), and up to 10,000, according to others. Whatever the number of victims of the merciless German bombings of Belgrade, that was just the first carnage, a most dreadful omen of an unfolding national tragedy.

In March 1941, London was "convinced through the work of the Bletchley cryptographers that Hitler had decided to attack Russia." (Rhodes James, 251) Had London and the coup-wishers-and-plotters in Belgrade waited until King Peter II came of age, on 6 September 1941 – when the Regency was to expire, and Germany was deeply involved in the war in the Soviet Union - Germany would have been hard pressed to fight on another front, in the south. In the meantime, armament production would have increased in both Great Britain and the USA, and even without the Putsch, a more advantageous blow to Hitler's plan might have been dealt him instead.

After the Germans blasted Belgrade *"without mercy"*,

on 9 April Churchill spoke in the House of Commons

about the war situation. He did not minimize the hazards the British faced in Greece and North Africa, but still stood by the idea he had expounded on 28 March: "If Yugoslavia, Greece and Turkey had stood firm together, they could have presented to Germany a strong front defended by seventy divisions." (Colville, 372) He still stuck to his idea that seventy ill-equipped divisions, with an inferior and inadequate air force, could have deterred Germany from the invasion of Greece.

> … He did not seem to understand that infantry on the Second War battlefield had very little power unless properly organised in trained formations with good communications and a real command structure, and backed by artillery and anti-tank weapons as well as armour. (Sir Ian Jacob, Military Assistant Secretary to the War Cabinet 1939-45, in Wheeler-Bennett(ed), 201)

Dalton referred to Churchill's speech, in his diary entry for 9 April:

> Bad news this morning. German mechanised column is threatening Salonika, ... P.M. will have a job today when he moves a motion, now a bit time-soiled, of congratulations to our Forces for recent victories in North Africa, Mediterranean and Greece. ...
>
> Gladwyn [Jebb] asked yesterday ... whether I thought, if we were chased out of the Balkans, this would react against Eden. I said I thought not much, for the reason just given and because principle of collective responsibility pretty well accepted at this moment.
>
> P.M. has a difficult job in making his statement this afternoon. It was to have been a triumphal vote of thanks to the Forces and the workers at home for recent victories in Africa, Greece and the Mediterranean. The speech was a strong and somber performance. Less rhetorical ornament than usual. He announced the fall of Salonika and warned various possible victims, including Turkey and the U.S.S.R. (Pimlott(ed), 183)

Following are some passages from Churchill's *strong and somber performance* related to Yugoslavia:

> Once again we see the odious German poison technique employed. In this case, however, it was to the government rather than to the nation that the dose of inoculations were administered. ... Presently the weak and unfortunate Prince and afterward his Ministers were summoned, like others before them, to Hitler's footstool and a pact was signed which would had given Germany complete control *not over body but over the soul* of the Yugoslav nation.
>
> Then at last *the people of Yugoslavia* saw their peril, and with a universal spasm of revolt swept from power those who were leading them into a shameful tutelage, and resolved at *the eleventh hour* to guard their freedom and their honor with their lives.
>
> A frightful vengeance was vowed against the Southern Slavs. Rapid, perhaps hurried, redispositions were made of German forces and German diplomacy. Hungary was offered large territorial gains to become the accomplice in the assault upon a friendly neighbor with whom she had just signed a solemn pact of friendship and non-aggression. Count Teleki, Hungarian Premier, preferred to take his own life rather than join in such a deed of shame.
>
> A heavy forward movement of the German armies, already gathered in Austria, was set in motion through Hungary to the northern frontier of Yugoslavia. A ferocious howl of hatred from the supreme miscreant was the signal for the actual invasion. The open city of Belgrade was laid in ashes and a tremendous drive by the German armored forces in Bulgaria was launched westward into Southern Serbia. (http://www.ibiblio.org/pha/timeline/410409awp.html   4/26/11. Italics added.)

No German control *over [the] body* of the Yugoslav nation: as stated in the first three Notes to the Protocol of adhesion to the Tripartite Pact. The *soul* would have been kept in the body – if the country had not been exposed to war which resulted in more than a million graves, known and unknown, marked and unmarked.

The eleventh hour: the *coup d'état* of 27 March 1941.

The people of Yugoslavia: the coup-wishers-and-plotters, in co-operation with those British who were acknowledged and praised by the British war-leaders immediately after the coup - as shown above. On 9 April, when German troops were already in Salonika and the disastrous ending of the British military intervention in Greece was in sight, it was not easy to acknowledge one's own failures and mistakes. As Dr. Dalton observed: *"P.M. has a difficult job in making his statement this afternoon."*

The disastrous end of the Eden – Dill mission

Eden and DIll returned to London on 10 April. "The situation in Greece on that day was that the German armies had advanced through the southern end of Jugoslavia, and they had also occupied Salonika. ... The Greeks in Macedonia and Thrace had been cut off and had surrendered, except for some who had escaped into Turkey." (Kennedy, 89)

Eden first went to see Churchill, then talked with Cadogan. "P.M. had been rather tiresome to him [Eden] – saying he had never wished to help Greece! I [Cadogan] said that must be his mood: no one could have supported A. [Eden] more stoutly and consistently in his absence than P.M. had done." (Dilks(ed), 370)

Referring to days in early April, Eden wrote:

> ... In the Balkans the Germans had invaded Greece and Yugoslavia before General Wilson's troops were all in position. One division of the three which Wavell had advised should be sent to Greece, and the Polish brigade, had to remain to face the threat in Cyrenaica. The rapid collapse of Yugoslav resistance left the flank of the Aliakhmon line open and the Greek army was battle weary after its long winter campaign.
> To those external factors must be added the crippling shortages which had hampered our operations since the beginning of the war. The Royal Air Force performed prodigies of valour in Greece but was outnumbered by the Germans and Italians, so that a long and complicated line of supply lay open to enemy attack. Our troops also suffered from faulty equipment, some of the tank tracks failed, while the Germans had specially trained mountain troops and more up to date weapons. (Eden, 241)

One division instead of the 150,000 men Dill spoke of in Belgrade on 31 March – 1 April; *crippling shortages; German and Italian air force superiority; faulty equipment, etc* , ... this was quite a different picture than the one presented by Eden to Prince Paul, telling him of *all the resources that the British can bring to bear.*Especially damning was the fact that the British knew of the German-Italian air force superiority for the Balkan operations. This justified the skepticism of Prince Paul, who was quite aware of Britain's *empty shops* at the time.

The Independent State of Croatia on the 10th, the fall of Belgrade on the 12th of April

Also on 10 April 1941, the Independent State of Croatia was proclaimed, in Zagreb – in the presence of high German officials - as an outright consequence of the war, in fulfillment of "*Operation Punishment's*" objective *to destroy Yugoslavia militarily and as a national unit.* This opened the doors to the most tragic sequence of events which finally resulted in the loss of more than one million human lives ... a true national tragedy. Unfortunately, not much was written about it by the British war leaders.

On 13 April, German troops entered Belgrade. (Churchill(GA), 222) The vanguard had entered on the 12th. That same day, Churchill sent a message to Campbell, then at Vrnjačka Banja:

> we do not see why the King or government should leave the country, which is vast, mountainous and full of armed men. German tanks can no doubt move along the roads and tracks but to conquer the Serbian armies they must bring up infantry. Then will be the chance to kill them. Surely the young King and the Ministers should play their part in this. (Barker, 106; 284n61)

Churchill had reason to expect resistance to the Germans in the mountains of Yugoslavia. One of the tasks for George Taylor's SOE mission to Belgrade was to organize post-occupation resistance. At considerable overall cost to Britain, SOE agents had been engaged in that respect for some time, smuggling "toys and chocolates" – i.e. explosives and arms needed for a guerrilla warfare – into Yugoslavia, first from Britain and then from Greece, and distributing them to groups who were supplied with wireless communication sets, ample funds and propaganda-generating equipment. The details were described in a 26 February 1941 report in Athens, from SOE's Taylor to his chief, Sir Frank Nelson. But the would-be organizers of the post-occupational resistance fled the country in a rush, just like the Simović government and the organizers of the coup of 27 March 1941.

From *"The triumph of hope over reality"* to the death-bringing reality ...

John Colville, on 13 April: "... The Chiefs of Staff, Eden, [Leopold] Amery, Horace Seymour and [Gen. Ismay] Pug met all morning to discuss Iraq, ... , and Yugoslavia, where resistance to the Germans by semi-mobolised army seems to be stiffening a little. ..." (p. 374)

On 14 April, convinced that he himself could hardly secure the best armistice terms, Simović empowered General Danilo Kalafatović to sue for armistice from the enemy. (Ristić, 129-30)

From Colville's diary, 16 April: "Organised resistance in Yugoslavia has ceased. In Greece the Germans are entering Volo and there is much talk of a stand in the pass of Thermopylae. ... " (p. 374)

On 17 April, in Belgrade, Yugoslavia's representatives signed the unconditional surrender. (Hoptner, 292;) The armistice became effective at 1200 on the 18th. (Blau, 153)

On 20 April - Churchill asked Eden to go to London and "take command" of situation in respect to Greece and help to Wavell. (Eden, 242)

On 21 April - Gen. Wavell ordered the immediate evacuation of British troops from a collapsing Greece. (Kennedy, 100) "It seemed to me providential that we were being forced to go so quickly. If we had had to maintain a front in Greece, our depleted reserves in Egypt would have been used up, and the Nile Delta left unprotected from the German threat through the desert," commented General Kennedy. (p. 101) "Today is a critical day in the history of the war as far as Greece is concerned. Final decision to evacuate was taken." (Colville, 376) The British withdrew air force from Greece, and redeployment of German troops from the Balkans began. (Blau, 153)

On the afternoon of 21 April, Eden saw the Greek Minister, who complained to him "that his people felt wounded by British argument whether or not they had been worth helping". (Eden, 242)

On 23 April - "The surrender of the Western Greek armies and departure of the Government were made public." (Colville, 377)

On 27 April - The Germans entered Athens. That day the Prime Minister broadcast "Report on the war" – which became known as "But westward, look, the land is bright!" Carefully prepared, as all his reports and speeches always were, the report could not possibly contain details of the planning of the Greek expedition which have been, in a small way only, mentioned above. And besides, they would not fit well into a public relation picture of the British engagement he wanted to project to the British people. Here are excerpts related to Greece and Yugoslavia:

> You will remember how, in November, the Italian dictator fell upon the unoffending Greeks and without reason and without warning invaded their country, ... Hitler, ... , suddenly made it clear that he would come to the rescue of his fellow-criminal. The lack of unity of the Balkan States had enabled him to build up a mighty army in their midst. ...
>
> In their mortal peril the Greeks turned to us for succour. Strained as were our resources we could not say them nay. By solemn guarantee, given before the war, Great Britain had promised them her help. They declared they would fight for their native soil even if neither of their neighbours made common cause with them and even if we left them to their fate.
>
> But we could not do that. There are rules against that kind of thing and to break those rules would be fatal to the honour of the British Empire, without which we could neither hope nor deserve to win this hard war. Military defeat or miscalculation can be remedied. The fortunes of war are fickle and changing. But an act of shame would deprive us of the respect which we now enjoy throughout the world and thus would sap the vitals of our strength. ...
>
> We, for our part, were, of course, bound to harken to the Greek appeal to the utmost limit of our strength. ...
>
> We knew, of course, that the forces we could send to Greece would not by themselves alone be sufficient to stem the German tide of invasion. But there was a very real hope that the neighbours of Greece would, by our intervention, be drawn to stand in line together with her while time remained. How nearly that came off will be known some day.
>
> The tragedy of Yugoslavia has been that these brave people had a government who hoped to purchase an ignoble immunity by submission to the Nazi rule. But, when at last the people of Yugoslavia found out where they were being taken and rose in one spontaneous surge of revolt, they saved the soul and future of their country, but it was already too late to save its territory. ...
>
> Great disasters have occurred in the Balkans. Yugoslavia has been beaten down. Only in the mountains can she continue her resistance. The Greeks have been overwhelmed. ... (Prime

Minister Winston Churchill's broadcasts, http://www.ibiblio.org/pha/timeline/410427awp.html 8/22/09)

In his diary Eden wrote this about the broadcast:

> Winston broadcast after dinner. Another good effort in admirable perspective. I am sorry, though, that he based help to Greece solely on *noblesse oblige*. **A war in Balkans was not what Hitler wanted.** (Eden, 242. Emphasis added.)

"A war in Balkans was not what Hitler wanted." Ergo, a war in the Balkans was what the British war leaders wanted.

Noblesse oblige was neither the essential nor the sole reason for the support of Greece, but Churchill liked to recall it to show how high-principled British policies were. He mentioned *noblesse ...* also to the Acting Prime Minister of Australia on 30 March 1941, along with other reasons for his "high design" – as he wanted them to be recognized by others.

And if *"noblesse oblige" was not the sole reason to help Greece,* then what could have been the others? Elisabeth Barker provided some explanation:

> The reasons why the British insisted so strongly that Prince Paul should abandon his benevolent neutrality and that Yugoslavia should go to war, *whatever the cost, why they in fact forced Hitler to undertake an operation against Yugoslavia which he had not intended, at any rate at that time,* can be understood only in the light of their doubts and fears about the outcome of the Balkan campaign of 1941. This campaign – so strongly criticized after the event – was seen from the start as a military gamble, justifiable only in so far as it enabled Britain to keep or win allies on the continent of Europe. (Barker, 96. Italics added.)

Whether or not the gamble was justified, the cost to the people of Greece and Yugoslavia was not factored into the planning of this campaign and it should have been. Regrettably, for some British war-participants, that cost was of no consequence - even more than three decades later – as will be shown below.

> " ... there was a very real hope that the neighbours of Greece would, *by our intervention*, be drawn to stand in line together with her while time remained. *How nearly that came off will be known some day"* – said the Prime Minister on 27 April, when the Germans entered Athens. By 22 March 1941, when he ordered Eden to draw Yugoslavia into the war, they both knew very well that there was no hope that Turkey *would stand in line together* with Greece, in spite of all *British interventions.*

**

Colville's diary, 29 April:

> An afternoon of busy operational discussions: we must save Egypt and Suez at all costs. The evacuation of Greece seems to have been fairly successful and we have got over 40,000 away out of 55,000 all told. (p. 378)

Slightly different numbers:

> On 2nd May our troops were out of Greece and, according to our information, 45,000 or more men had been taken off, out of 60,000. But all the heavy equipment was lost. (Kennedy, 114)

On 9 May, in Moscow, the Executive Committee of the Communist International (Comintern) issued its "Directive for Future Work" which "contained the Comintern's main directives for the Yugoslav Communist Party..." (Clissold, 238) It can be shown that the directives were followed by the Communist Party of Yugoslavia in the course of a subsequent "resistance" and a civil war.

On the night of 12 May, in Yugoslavia, Colonel Dragoljub-Draža Mihailović "reached the plateau of Ravna Gora south of Valjevo [Serbia] with seven officers and twenty-four non-commissioned officers and men." (Roberts, 21) His subsequent participation in the "resistance" and civil war was examined in detail in many sources.

On 19th May the Germans launched their attack on Crete, ... (Kennedy, 119) On the 29th orders were sent from London to evacuate Crete, but Wavell had already decided to do this, and his telegram crossed ours. (Kennedy, 127)

On 22 May: "The Navy are having a heavy task off Crete and have lost a lot of ships, including *Gloucester* and *Fiji*." (Colville, 389)

On 24 May: "Crete is now serious, as became clear during the afternoon and evening. The Germans are fighting with blind courage and have complete control of the air. The crux of the matter is how long the navy can carry out its dangerous task of preventing seaborne landings." (Colville, 390)

On 25 May: "... in the Mediterranean the navy shows, he [Churchill] thinks, a tendency to shirk its task of preventing a seaborne landing in Crete since [Admiral Andrew] Cunningham fears severe losses from bombing. The P.M.'s line is that Cunningham must be made to take every risk: the loss of half the Mediterranean fleet would be worthwhile in order to save Crete." (Colville, 391)

26 May: "... The Cretan situation seems slightly better and at the P.M.'s instigation the Chiefs of Staff have sent a signal to the C.-in-C. that no risk can be considered too heavy to win the battle." (Colville, 391) "...We face defeat in Crete. ... " (Eden, 243)

On 27 May: "The Crete situation is deplorable. It seems that we are finished here owing to lack of air support." (Colville, 392) Just as General Ismay expected, "*concentrated air-attack, with little opposition, will break Greece as it broke Poland and France.*" (Colville, 286. Italics added.)

On 28 May: " ... Decision to withdraw from Crete was taken." (Colville, 392)

On 30 April, hostilities ceased in Greece. (Blau, 153)

On 1 June: "[The Prime Minister] rang me up on the morning to discuss Iraq situation and told me Cretan evacuation was at an end.... Winston said he wanted to overrule C.-in-C. Mediterranean and carry on another night, but he had found that Wavell had already issued orders to capitulate. The naval losses are heavy. *Calcutta* to add to a long list." (Eden, 244) German forces completed the seizure of Crete. (Blau, 153)

In the battle for Crete, "The naval losses had been crippling. Three cruisers and six destroyers had been sunk, and three battleships, one aircraft carrier, six cruisers and seven destroyers had been damaged. The army casualties had been close to twelve thousands." (Ismay, 207)

Chapter 14

"Misplaced optimism" for the British enterprise in Greece

Writing about the initial opposition to giving support to Greece, General Kennedy observed that something unexpected happened: both Dill and Wavell changed their mind and began reporting to London that they both considered that there was a fair chance of success. (Kennedy, 85) Ralph Bennett – writing about the British Mediterranean strategy - pointed to one possible reason for their change of mind:

> ... Eden's uncritical conviction that the Greek expedition was politically sound may have combined with a soldier's habit of obedience and his own sense of honorable obligations to make Wavell overlook his primary duty of calculating the balance of military advantage or disadvantage in cold blood. ... (Bennett, 34)
> The major share of the blame must nevertheless rest on Eden's shoulders. The soldier is the servant of the politician in a democracy, and Churchill had taken the unusual course of investing Eden with plenipotentiary powers to decide about Greece. (Bennett, 34)

Professor Sue Onslow remarked:

> Eden has been heavily criticized, both in the House of Commons on his return in April 1941, and by subsequent writers, for his role in the disastrous Greek campaign. Certainly, the Foreign Secretary was a politician who relied heavily upon his civil servants and, in his peripatetic tour of the Near East between February and early April, he was accompanied only by Pierson Dixon of the Southern Department, and Sir John Dill, ... This naturally enhanced the importance of Eden's own perceptions and decisions. While this policy of pursuing a Balkan front, and then endorsing a *coup* in Belgrade, was clearly a highly personal one for Eden, the Foreign Secretary was acting on Churchill's instructions and was in close contact with the War Cabinet in London. Eden was in essence holding the ring between the Prime Minister – who desired to wear the Germans down in every theatre – and the Mediterranean Commander-in-Chief who only reluctantly accepted the political arguments for the Greek campaign. (Onslow, 39-40)

On Eden's role in the Greek expedition, historian Robert Rhodes James observed:

> Churchill did not hold Eden accountable for the Greek disaster.
> ... Eden never considered that his ill-fated Greek expedition had been a mistake, and he was always fiercely defensive about the decision to aid Greece.
> ... The debate in the House of Commons was in itself a near disaster, and Eden was acutely sensitive to the bleak atmosphere – 'cold' he described it in his diary – that greeted him. His was not a good speech, and he set down in complete silence, Duff Cooper later commenting waspishly that it was the best speech made against the Government. (Rhodes James, 252-3)

In Elisabeth Barker's opinion:

> Eden's own political stock slumped in the summer of 1941 because of his personal sponsorship of the Greek campaign, even though his enthusiasm for it had almost certainly been fired by Churchill's own eagerness for a Balkan front against Hitler, and even though Churchill 'covered' Eden in the House of Commons. (Barker(CE), 23)

Eden's biographer, Carlton, commented on the subject:

> In Cairo, ... , there was wholly misplaced optimism that the enterprise might turn out to be militarily sound. They disliked a justification solely based on what Eden later called *noblesse oblige*. Judging from the formal record, this mood was created by Dill and Wavell, Eden being recipient of their expert advice. But if the personalities of those involved are taken into account, it may reasonably be contended that Eden was actually the moving force behind the policy. The fact is that Dill and Wavell owed their survival in their posts to Eden and were on extremely friendly terms with him. (Carlton, 180)

Assessment of the Balkan Front idea and of the British Expedition in Greece

According to the military historian Basil Liddell Hart:

> The Balkan theatre had long fascinated Mr. Churchill, since his boldly conceived but ill-fated Dardanelles venture in World War I. Now [in late 1940], his imagination was fired by the way the Greeks had withstood Mussolini, and he became filled with the idea of giving Hitler a slap in the face if he pushed his nose into Greece. Mr. Churchill's eagerness outran the practical possibilities, however, and showed little regard to the limited extent of his resources compared with Hitler's. (Liddell Hart, 17)

The idea of the Balkan Front has been characterized many ways: as "wishfully-minded" (Kennedy), "a political decision" (Lord Strang), not based on a realistic military assessment, "errors of judgment" (Ralph Bennett), and the British Expedition in Greece ended in "a second Dunkirk" (Liddell Hart), "Norway, Dunkirk and Dakar rolled into one" (Charmley), "a humiliating disaster" (A.J.P.Taylor). Mostly, it was a prelude to a great tragedy for Yugoslavia. Following are several opinions about the idea and the expedition.

Field Marshal Harold Alexander wrote that sending British troops to Greece happened "at a time when we could ill afford to weaken our forces in the Middle East." (Alexander, 145)

Elisabeth Barker stated:

> Politically, the outcome of the Balkan campaign was more difficult to assess [than military losses]. Against the British, it could with reason be said that they had egged on small countries to oppose *overwhelming force*, knowing that this was *a gamble* without giving anything like adequate support. It could also be said that they had – perhaps *carelessly* rather than deliberately – led these small countries to believe that British aid would be large-scale and quicker than was possible. The British themselves ran risks and made sacrifices, but on no scale remotely comparable to the Greeks and Yugoslavs, now facing years of enemy occupation. Of the '300,000' Yugoslav troops who - it was once hoped in Belgrade - were to have been evacuated by the British, about 1,000 reached the Middle East. (Barker, 108. Italics added.)

With all due respect for the late Elisabeth Barker's opinion, a few well-intentioned comments to her conclusion seem to be appropriate. To egg small countries against a power with a known *overwhelming force* is more than *a gamble* – i.e., more than taking a risk, because the outcome is foreseeable. It was more like recklessness – no regard for consequences. As it was originally conceived, the Balkan Front was to be formed by three countries. At the beginning of March it was known that Turkey "stubbornly resisted all Eden's pressures" and was out of consideration. There remained only two: Yugoslavia – with her ox-cart army – and Greece, with her military strength already being sapped in Albania. This altered the original concept of the Balkan front. Under changed circumstances, Churchill's instruction to Eden on 22 March, "*to get Yugoslavia in to the war anyhow*", was surely worse than a gamble.

"The total number of army personnel in Greece had been between 55,000 and 56,000". (Barker, 107) Sir John Dill had to know that number because he participated in determining it. It is hard to accept that he – the Chief of Imperial General Staff – forgot it and *carelessly* almost tripled it during the talks in Belgrade on 31 March – 1 April.

In the letter to Prince Paul on 17 March, Eden mentioned that the American armaments supplies should be hastened to the Middle East – while telling Campbell a few days later that "there is no other source from which we can at present supply equipment of this nature". Unfortunately, Eden's statement to Prince Paul should be characterized as deliberately misleading.

The coup of 27 March 1941 - so appreciated and praised by the British war leaders, who wanted it and worked for it – started a sequence of events in Yugoslavia that ultimately took more than one million lives out of almost 16 million. Indeed, Britain's human losses were *on no scale remotely comparable.* And on top of that, at the end, the war made possible the installation of a Communist regime in Yugoslavia – with very sizeable material and political support by Great Britain's war leaders ... the same leaders who, by armed force, prevented a similar Communist regime from being installed in Greece.

George E. Blau of the US Foreign Studies Branch, Special Studies Division, Office of the Chief of Military History:

> The British did not have the necessary military resources in the Middle East to permit them to carry out simultaneous large-scale operations in North Africa and the Balkans. Moreover, even if they had been able to block the German advance into Greece, they would have been unable to exploit the situation by a counter thrust across the Balkans. It is worth noting that the British planners in Cairo secretly started to work on evacuation plans from Greece at the time when the expeditionary force was being transferred from Egypt to Greece. The ill-fated expedition was considered a hopeless undertaking by those who knew how little help Britain would actually be able to offer to Greece. General Papagos also had strong misgivings about the effectiveness of assistance the British were able to furnish and the soundness of their planning. (Blau, 113)

General Sir Alan Brooke, who succeeded General Dill as CIGS, called the Greek expedition "a definite strategic blunder ... a dangerous dispersal of forces." (Bennett, 36) In September 1941 Churchill said that LUSTRE [code name for the Greek expedition] was the only error the government had yet made. (Bennett, 36) "Errors of judgment, not lack of information about the enemy, were the primary cause of all this," concluded **Ralph Bennett** (Bennett, 36) - well qualified to form an opinion, because "he served as a senior member of the Bletchley team dispensing Ultra information".

> ... although the transfer of 30,000 men, 240 guns, and 140 tanks fatally weakened the defense of Cyrenaica, not even all the men and matériel in the whole Middle East could match the German armies now shown by secret intelligence to be assembling along the eastern frontier of the Reich for the invasion of Russia and the Balkans. (Bennett, 28)

Whether errors in judgment or other motivations to blame, ultimately the consequences for Yugoslavia were that more than a million human lives were lost.

Eden's biographer **David Carlton** concluded that Eden's hopes to draw both Yugoslavia and Turkey into collective resistance to Hitler "proved vain, being based on unrealistic assessment of Turkish and Yugoslav intentions and capabilities. Thus a broadly unfavourable verdict on his general Balkan policy during this period would appear to be justified. Moreover, *Greece was required to pay an unnecessarily high price for this flawed diplomacy.* (Carlton, 170. Italics added.)

Field Marshal Lord **Michael Carver,** Chief of the Defence Staff, 1973-1976, called the short campaign in Greece and Crete "disastrous" (Blake & Louis(eds), 360, 362)

John Colville, the Assistant Private Secretary to Churchill in 1940-1941, entered into his diary on Sunday, 28 September 1941:

> The P.M. [Churchill] talked to me while he was dressing for dinner. He said that so far the Government had only made one error of judgment: Greece. He had instinctively had doubts. We could and should have defended Crete and advised the Greek Government to make the best term it could. But the campaign, and the Yugoslav volte-face which it entailed, had delayed Germany and might after all prove to have been an advantage. (Colvlle, 443)

The great man admitted that the British expedition in Greece was an error of judgment and that the Greek campaign had entailed the coup in Belgrade. Colville added his comment:

> I was surprised at the P.M.'s assertion that he had doubted the wisdom of going to Greece. I seem to remember *his influencing the decision in favor of an expedition and Dill being against it.* Incidentally he has now got his knife right into Dill and frequently disparages him ... (Colville, 443. Italics added.)

However, after initially opposing the expedition, Sir John Dill later changed his mind.

Had the British *advised the Greek Government to make the best term it could* , there would have been no need to *draw Yugoslavia into the war anyhow,* and there would have been no *Greek fiasco* – as Colville magnanimously called it.

Professor Martin L. van Creveld concluded:

> ... Limited aid to Greece served to draw Italian forces away from Africa, but when the Germans appeared on the scene any attempt to keep her in the war, in so far as this was possible at all, would require so many British forces as to reverse the order of priorities and put Greece, instead of Africa, at the top of the list. On 22 February [at the Tatoi Conference] Eden himself put the German forces in the Balkans at 23 divisions, and since no British force could be brought up that might match this number, hopes for success were ultimately based on Turkish and Yugoslav intervention. Even so, however, it is hard to see how such an allied force, whose 70 divisions would have to be supplied by the Cape route, could hope to hold up for long against the unlimited resources of the Wehrmacht whose communications were incomparably shorter and by land.
>
> This, in fact, was the initial opinion of Wavell and Dill, both of whom started from the assumption that driving the Italians out of Africa was more important than fighting the Germans in Greece, that only such aid should be given to Greece as to keep her in the war, that no force the British could send to the Balkans could hope to match the Germans there, and that 'the locomotive and petrol engine will always beat the ship, especially when the ship has to go round the Cape'. Both subsequently modified their opinions, the reason for this being not so much military as political, i.e. hope for Turko-Yugoslav intervention. (van Creveld(G), 91)

General Francis "Freddie" de Guingand, a participant in the Anglo-Greek negotiations in February and March, 1941, wrote about them in 1946:

> We must ask ourselves whether intervention in Greece was *necessary* at that time from either the political or the military angle. Then there is a question of whether our forces were committed to Greece with any hope of success – in other words, was the task a feasible one, and did it suit our best interests?
>
> We can dispose of the military necessity business quite shortly. We were not in a position to start large scale operations in the Balkans at that time. We did not have the military resources. We would, therefore, not have been in a position to exploit a lodgment gained in Greece. We would be killing Germans, which in itself was a desirable object, but not a good one if in the process we were likely to lose far more than the enemy. This was in fact the case. Germany was now virtually master of Europe and we needed time to build up our strength, and for America to come to our aid. This demanded a defensive strategy unless some cheap success were possible.
>
> The political necessity obviously hinged around our Treaty of Alliance with Greece. Initially I don't doubt that the Greeks wished for our help, but presumably the acceptance was conditioned by whether the assistance that could be given would be of any real value. Early in March, however, there was undoubtedly a period when the Greeks were convinced that our assistance would either be insufficient or would not arrive on time. They were also extremely worried because it looked as if neither Turkey nor Yugo-Slavia would fight the Germans. I feel sure that if we had agreed that our intervention would be ineffective, Greece would have let us off any obligations. (de Guingand, 67-8. Italics in the source.)

Then the General continued:

> There seemed to be few grounds at that time to support the expectations of Turkish and Yugo-Slav active co-operation. As regards Turkey, surely nothing would have acted more as a damper upon her help than a demonstration of our impotence in Greece. It is also very doubtful whether the eventual partisan fight in Yugo-Slavia against the German oppressor was due to our action in Greece. (de Guingand, 68)

Finally his conclusion on the "Greek adventure":

> I contend that from the military point of view an intervention in Greece never had any chance of success. ...
>
> If Greece had asked for assistance then we were in honour bound to do the best, but I contend we misled her as to our ability to help. We led her to believe that this help would be effective. The

grounds for arriving at this view appeared extremely scanty. And the result was that we lost many lives, all our valuable equipment, and jeopardised our whole position in the Middle East. We brought about disaster in the Western Desert and threw away a chance of clearing up as far as Tripoli. Whether the politician forced the soldier's hand I do not know.

This brings me to the end of a sorry tale. But the real sufferings of brave little Greece had only just begun. Her valiant efforts against Italy, her readiness for sacrifice, and her trust in our ability to protect her country from the ravages of war, were of no avail. (de Guingand, 68-9)

In **Professor Gabriel Gorodetsky**'s opinion:

When Operation 'Marita' was contemplated the Wehrmacht had an ample pool of troops to draw on. Naturally preparations for 'Barbarossa' [invasion of the Soviet Union] were disrupted, but only fifteen divisions out of the enormous force of 152 earmarked for Russia were actually diverted for the operations in Yugoslavia and Greece. Because of the leisurely pace of the build-up for 'Barbarossa' most of the divisions assigned for Russia had not yet departed. In practice only four divisions were detached and sent to the south ahead of their scheduled deployment in the East. Only the 14th division out of the five divisions earmarked for the south, whose movement had alerted Churchill, had started rolling east before being ordered to change course. As the military historian M. van Creveld has most convincingly proved in his debunking of the established myth, the Greek diversion, far from overstretching the Wehrmacht, only produced a negligible delay of the build-up for 'Barbarossa'. (Gorodetsky, 177)

Historian Francis Harry Hinsley *et al*:

At the same time [in February 1941, when the German Afrika Corps was reaching North Africa], and not least because it remained ignorant of Greek military planning, the Defence Committee decided to send Mr Eden, the Foreign Secretary, and Field Marshall Dill, the CIGS, to Cairo and Athens. Throughout this period British intelligence of Greek, Turkish and Yugoslav plans was conspicuously less good than that about Germany's preparations, and it is also clear that Whitehall's hopes of co-operation from these countries were based on wishful thinking. As has been said by the official historian, 'it is indeed surprising that in view of Germany's military record, her vastly superior armament and her proximity we should have expected the Balkan countries to join the war against her or, if they did, to withstand her. It would appear that in such matters the Norwegian campaign had taught us little'. (Hinsley *et al*, 359-60)

Dr. Jacob Hoptner:

Britain's policy was clear. The decision to aid Greece sprang from purely political motives. It contradicted all military advice given to Churchill, for it meant he had to take men and material from Britain's thin defenses in the Near East. Yugoslavia's function was to underpin his *beau geste*, to supply men and arms as a barrier, no matter how temporary, against the Germans as they came to the aid of the faltering Italians. (Hoptner, 233-4)

If Churchill pondered the political consequences for the Yugoslavs should they go down to defeat, he gave no evidence. *They, the last of the Balkan neutrals, were expendable.* He saw a magical shift in the balance of power – if only the Yugoslavs would fall on the Italian rear in Albania. (Hoptner, 234. Italics added.)

General Sir Hastings Ismay, Chief of Staff in Churchill's Defence Department:

It may be claimed that to have fought and suffered the defeat in Greece was less damaging to us than to have left the Greeks to their fate. A military failure may be excused, but failure to keep a promise to help a friend in trouble is not easily forgiven, or forgotten. It may also be claimed that, on a long-term view, our action was vindicated in that it delayed the German attack on Russia for four or five weeks. Nevertheless, there can be no doubt that the immediate military results of the decision to intervene on the mainland of Greece were disastrous, and that the ultimate responsibility for that decision rested with the Prime Minister and the Cabinet. (Ismay, 201-2)

About the expected resistance to the German invasion at the Aliakhmon Line, **military historian John Keegan** observed:

Neither Greek valor nor British arms would avail to postpone an armistice. The Greek plan was flawed, and neither advice nor deployments from Britain could avoid defeat. ... He [General Papagos, the Greek Commander] counted on the Yugoslavs to protect the left flank of both positions and had even arranged a scheme with the Yugoslavs to react to an Axis attack by opening an offensive into Albania against the Italians, ... , with the bulk of the Greek army, fourteen divisions. Professor Martin van Creveld describes the dispositions – without exaggeration - as "suicidal". ... In two days of fighting , 6-7 April, the Germans broke the resistance of the Yugoslavs in Macedonia and forced the Greek defenders of the Metaxas line, who had stoutly resisted frontal assault, to surrender on 9 April. They were thus freed to turn the left flank of the Aliakhmon Line, defended by the New Zealanders, and press on down the ancient invasion route which leads from the Vardar Valley in Macedonia into central Greece. ... (Keegan, 156-7)

Elsewhere the Graeco-British front was collapsing concertina-like as one position after another was outflanked by the invaders. ... In fact the British had been in full retreat from the Aliakhmon Line since 16 April. ... the Greek army, like the Yugoslav, belonged to an earlier age of warfare and 20,000 of its soldiers fell into German hands in the wake of the British retreat. (Keegan, 157)

... The Greeks, with British help, had fought to defend their homeland from conquest. The Germans had battled to overcome them and had triumphed, but in token of respect to the courage of the enemy had insisted that the Greek officers should keep their swords. This was to be almost the last gesture of chivalry between warriors in a war imminently fated to descend into barbarism. (Keegan, 158)

**

"*Directive No. 25*" precluded any such chivalry in Yugoslavia. Some 250,000 prisoners, almost all Serbs – because the Croats, German, Hungarian and Bulgarian nationals were soon released – were taken to POW camps in Germany; unlike Greece - Yugoslavia as a state was dismembered. Drawn into the war to protect Greece, Yugoslavia fared much worse.

The losses sustained by the German attack forces were unexpectedly light. During the twelve days of combat casualty figures came to 558 men: 151 were listed as killed, 392 wounded, and 15 as missing in action. During the XLI Panzer Corps drive on Belgrade, for example, the only officer killed in action fell victim to a civilian sniper's bullet. (Blau, 62)

**

After the fateful Greek Campaign, **General Sir John Kennedy** made an analysis of the "strategic errors" which, in his view, had been committed. One was "the commitment in Greece". Here are some excerpts:

> There is no doubt now that this was a major error. From a purely military point of view, which was never given its proper weight, we could not afford to send a strong force to Greece. ... it was clear to all, except the wishfully-minded, that we could never have held the Germans for long in Greece. ... And we should have been prepared to lose anything we sent. The political pressure put upon the Commanders–in-Chief, Middle East, was tremendous. ... Wavell accepted, without a murmur, a proposition that he should send to Greece four infantry divisions and an armoured division. ... It seems inconceivable that the Commander-in-Chief have accepted and attempted to carry out such an unsound project. (Kennedy, 138-40)

In General Sir John Kennedy's view:

> The military opinion [on the expedition to Greece] tendered to the Cabinet by the Chiefs of Staff and by Wavell was proved wrong in every aspect. Nor is there any truth in the belief, at one time widely held, that our intervention delayed the German attack on Russia, and helped to save the Red Army by shortening what remained of the campaigning season, before winter set in. It is clear from German documents that *Hitler confirmed the 22 June as the date for the offensive as early as 30 April,* and that our operation in Greece caused no postponement. The most that can be claimed is that some forces were diverted. (Kennedy, 87. Italics added.)

**

During World War II, **historian William Leonard Langer** was volunteer head of the Research and Analysis branch of the Office of Strategic Services, which was headed by Colonel W.

Donovan. He and his co-author, **historian S. Everett Gleason**, reached the following conclusion about the American position related to the Balkan countries in the spring of 1941:

> It is certainly problematic whether any action the United States Government could have taken, short of direct intervention in the war, would in fact have influenced the course of Balkan politics. America was far away and not even Donovan could promise immediate, substantial aid. On the other hand, the Nazi divisions were already massed on the frontiers. Considering their military weakness, the Balkan states could not hope successfully to resist a Blitzkrieg. It was therefore almost inevitable that they should knuckle down when the pressure became great. Promises of favorable treatment at the peace settlement, such as Donovan had in mind, could hardly compensate for the material destruction certain to befall them in the event of resistance. To believe in the ultimate victory of the democracies was difficult enough; to face in the meantime military subjugation and years of occupation was too much to ask. (Langer & Gleason, 400)

Yet the British war leaders did ask.

**

In the opinion of **Dr. Sheila Lawlor**:

> ... militarily Greece fitted into the scheme of imperial defence whereby not only Crete but the Aegean islands and Athens could all be seen as vital to the Mediterranean position and the defence of Egypt. Furthermore, the military case for helping Greece could be made in terms of its affecting the Turks, thought to hold the key to Britain's imperial position. (Lawlor, 132-3)

> In pressing the case for Greece against military advice and that of Eden, Churchill began the process which led to the commitment just over four months later, to aid Greece against Germany, and the bargain with Stalin just four years later to secure influence over Greece, even if it meant abandoning to the Soviets most of Eastern Europe. In each of these cases Churchill had, through his military arguments for Greek intervention – based as they were on the need to influence Turkey – come to be convinced that Greece in itself was strategically important; almost as much as Turkey had been; and that given Turkish refusal to co-operate, Greece could and must now play the role in the Mediterranean traditionally accorded by Britain to the Turks: that of guaranteeing the key to Britain's imperial position.. (Lawlor, 121-2)

**

During the 'Munich crisis' and in the following years, Churchill sometimes asked **Basil Liddell Hart** for military advice at private meetings of his 'Focus', "a small group of people who shared his views about the German danger". Liddell Hart knew Churchill's views, attitude and *modus operandi* well. In a contribution to a book published in London in 1969, he also provided his assessment of Churchill's involvement in Greece, in the spring of 1941.

> ... while the defeat of the Italian forces in Africa was incomplete, Churchill tried to open up another fresh avenue in the Balkans. The landing of a British force in Greece naturally precipitated a German invasion of that country. Yet the force was dispatched at a time when it was clearly recognized that Hitler did not intend to move against Greece. The outcome was a second 'Dunkirk', together with a reverse in Africa. ("The Military Strategist", *Churchill: Four Faces and the Man*, p. 189)

Liddell Hart then continued:

> As a direct result of this rash move, British incurred a serious loss of prestige, and sacrificed a large part of the scanty equipment she then possessed. As an indirect result, she sacrificed the chance of completing her conquest of Libya – owing to the diversion of troops to Greece. By spurring the Germans on to establish themselves on the Greek coast, and the Aegean Islands, she also blocked the way for any subsequent Balkan move on her part when better prepared to undertake it. (*Ibid.,* 189-90)

As for the question of the wider strategic importance of the British expedition in Greece, Liddell Hart argued:

> Churchill's Greek venture cannot be justified by the retrospective argument that it delayed the invasion of Russia. For the Cabinet, as he himself admits, was not aware at the time [of the start of Eden-Dill mission, 12 February 1941] that Hitler was planning such a step. Moreover, the postponement was not due to the British effort in Greece, with which Hitler had reckoned, but to his sudden fit of anger over the Yugoslav *coup d'état*. In any case, the weather in Russia ruled out an earlier start there. (*Ibid.,* 190)

In another book, Liddell Hart wrote that Churchill and Eden "wanted to send an army to Greece and forestall any German move there, even though it meant halting the advance on Tripoli. That army was quickly thrown out of Greece, but by then the opportunity in Africa had passed." (Liddell Hart, 15)

> "… the only armoured division Britain had at home … was … split up between Greece and Cyrenaica, and overtaken by defeat in both places, losing all its tanks." (Liddell Hart, 15)

> The account presented to the public after the failure was that the British Government had embarked on the venture at the pressing appeal of the Greeks, and that Britain could not in loyalty abstain, whatever the cost to herself. This was a long way wide of the truth. In reality, the British Cabinet had pressed the Greeks to accept support about which they were dubious. (Liddell Hart, 17)

Sir Cecil Parrott, the former tutor to King Peter II:

> The *coup d'état* which took place on 27th March 1941 was a disaster for the country. Even Hugh Dalton admitted that the sequel was deplorable. It precipitated German attack on Yugoslavia, when her main nationality problem had not yet been entirely solved and she was desperately unprepared for it. It sparked off a convulsion of maniacal rage in Hitler, who determined to punish Yugoslav 'faithlessness' by most brutal means. The result was 'Operation Punishment' – the bombardment of Belgrade in which reportedly seventeen thousand people lost their lives in a single night. There followed in twelve days time the deepest humiliation a nation can suffer in its history, the utter defeat of its army and a degrading capitulation, while leaders of the *coup* fled the country and left the people to suffer the consequences. (Parrott. 103-4)

> … The *coup d'état* was presented by its instigators as a protest against the Yugoslav government's capitulation to Germany. But in reality their motives had been entirely different. The signing of the Pact was only the pretext for it. The army had been misled into supporting it and the people into acclaiming it, because they genuinely believed that it would not only extricate the country from its predicament but bring them honour, victory and liberty. (Parrott, 104)

> … Undoubtedly the British government were ruthless in their treatment of the Yugoslav government, and Prince Paul in particular. Churchill believed that there were no neutrals in the war – only non-belligerents – and that they must not be allowed to stand in the way of great powers fighting for their existence. For this reason he ordered the British Minister in Belgrade to 'pester, nag and bite' Prince Paul. But in judging his attitude we must also consider that *small powers conduct a struggle for their existence too and have the right to seek their own ways of securing it*. Churchill was not only very unsqueamish about the welfare of other countries during the war: *he did not bother his head much about their future,* as can be seen from his notorious remark to Fitzroy Maclean: 'Do you intend to make Yugoslavia your home after the war?' 'No? Neither do I.' (Parrott, 112-13. Italics added.)

**

During Germany's attack on Yugoslavia on 6 April 1941, **the AP correspondent Robert St. John** fled from burning Belgrade in great haste. Along with some of his Anglo-American colleagues, he reached the Peloponnesus and joined soldiers of the British Expeditionary Force in their perilous retreat to Crete. In his book, published in 1942 – while the Second World War was still raging – he also wrote about the casualties as they were estimated at that time:

> Out of approximately forty thousand British troops in Greece, about twenty thousand had come out to fight another day. The other twenty thousand had either been killed in that devastating rear-guard action the Anzacs fought so bravely down through Greece or had been so badly wounded they had to be left behind, or had been taken prisoner, or had been lost at sea when dozens of ships went to the bottom. Twenty thousand! Fifty per cent of the original force! At Dunkirk the loss had

been about ten per cent, and yet that evacuation was considered terrible. This was so much worse than Dunkirk that there just wasn't any comparison. Five times worse by actual account. (St. John, 319)

In the view of Robert St. John, whose description of Greco-British black propaganda spread in Serbia is presented in **Appendix B** :

Forty thousand [British troops in Greece]. ... Even three hundred thousand men with a real air force would have had a tough job holding back that sea of men and machines that I had seen sweeping down like a wild cascade from Germany, Rumania, and Bulgaria into Yugoslavia and Greece. Forty or fifty thousand against millions of German soldiers who had no other job on their hands at the moment than to take the Balkans at all costs. (St. John, 269)

In **Professor Bradley F. Smith**'s words:

A Balkan league tied to Britain was a political impossibility because everyone in the Balkans knew Germany was too strong and Britain too weak. But Churchill pressed ahead anyway, out of fear of a continued German advance on the Middle East, determined to use whatever influence and leverage Britain had in the region to move the Balkan states into a position of opposition to Germany. No longer would a position of cautious aloofness, such as that advocated by the regent of Yugoslavia, Prince Paul, satisfy London. The British government demanded not neutrality but alliance and dangled hints of the arrival of shipments of arms and invasion forces to encourage the Yugoslavs and Turks. Such efforts were not merely pointless. As some British official and semiofficial historians have recently suggested, to have "egged on" these small countries by promises of assistance that could not be fulfilled while encouraging them to oppose Nazi Germany with her "military record" and her "vastly superior armament" was simply irresponsible. In light of the horror that an extended occupation and civil and guerrilla war would bring to the region in the following four years, *London's pressure on the Balkan governments to become overt enemies of Nazi Germany in the spring of 1941 is one of the heavier ethical burdens that has weighed on Britain's official postwar conscience.* (Smith 46. Italics added.)

In the opinion of the British diplomat **Lord William Strang**:

The British decision to send forces to Greece to meet the German attack in March 1941 was a political decision taken with the support of a firm local military judgment that it had 'a reasonable fighting chance'. (Lord Strang, "War and Foreign Policy: 1939-45", *Retreat from Power, Studies in Britain's Foreign Policy of the Twentieth Century, Volume Two, After 1939,* The Macmillan Press Limited, London, 1981, p. 98)

Historian A.J.P. Taylor's view:

He [Churchill] 'prodded' the British commanders into premature offensives. He encouraged, though he did not alone promote, the rash expedition to Greece, which was supposed to enhance the British name and instead brought humiliating disaster. He counted unthinkingly on the ability of British sea power to hold Crete and shared responsibility for that disaster also. ("The statesman", *Churchill: Four Faces and the Man,* p. 43)

Chapter 15

"A revolutionary stroke" ... with Britain's complicity

Even if *London's pressure on the Balkan governments was one of the heavier ethical burdens that has weighed on Britain's official postwar conscience* - as Professor Smith stated - it did not weigh on Britain's wartime conscience. London applied the pressure, "egged on" Yugoslavia, and British leaders admitted that internally, in the afterglow of success.

The response by Churchill, Eden, Dalton, and the Defence Committee, to the news of the coup, was immediate and spontaneous, mirroring their insight into the participation of the SOE / Legation / other personnel in the coup, and their delight in its success.

Nine years later, after seeing the fateful consequences, **Sir Winston Churchill, the Historian,** wrote for posterity, as if the British had nothing to do with the *coup d'état,* claiming that it was just a domestic Yugoslav "revolution", and thus implying that Britain did not deserve "credit" for the ensuing consequences:

> Direct action, ... , had been discussed for some months in the small circle of officers around Simovic. A revolutionary stroke had been carefully planned. ... Knowledge of the plan was confined to a small number of trustworthy officers, ... The network extended from Belgrade to the main garrisons in the country, Zagreb, Skoplje, and Sarajevo. ...
>
> When during March 26 ... rumors of the pact began to circulate in Belgrade, the conspirators decided to act. ... Few revolutions had gone more smoothly. ...
>
> The plan had been made and executed by a close band of Serb nationalist officers without waiting upon public opinion. It let loose an outburst of popular enthusiasm which may well have surprised its authors. ... On March 28 the young King, who by climbing down the rain-pipe had made his own escape from Regency tutelage, took the oath in Belgrade amid fervent acclamation. (Churchill(GA), 161-2)

(Regarding participation of garrisons in Zagreb, Skoplje, Sarajevo, ... the King climbing down the rain-pipe ... Churchill, the Historian, did not carefully verify the facts ... to say the least.)

While the plan was physically *executed* by the military, it was not prepared and timed without participation by the British who, as Taylor put it, were **"urging the necessity of action for a coup d'état upon all our [British] friends and everyone with whom we [the British] had contact "** (Williams, 31. Emphasis added.) Actually, Taylor was dutifully implementing the decision to support the coup if and when the Pact was signed – the decision which "Churchill thoroughly approved" at Chequers, on 2 March. (Stafford (C), 211-12)

Churchill, the Prime Minister, was informed by Dalton on 28 March that one of Taylor's assignment was *"To continue the work, already well in hand, of encouraging the Yugoslav opposition parties to bring pressure to bear on the Government in a sense favourable to this country."* Furthermore, that "TRIFUNOVICH had kept us [SOE] informed of conspiracy under strictest promise of silence", and ""that the coup d'état itself was largely the work of TRIFUNOVICH, while the real political backing without which it could hardly have been made, lay outside the old Cabinet and in the Serb Peasant Party – the principal instrument of our policy and (like Narodna Odbrana) in our pay." Also that "MASTERSON has done marvelous work and deserves greatest praise. Credit also due [John] BENNETT who discovered TRIFUNOVICH and would like to emphasize that thanks are due to HANAU for originally picking winner in TUPANJANIN. (Great Britain, Special Operations Executive, 91087-10V, Hoover Institution Archives.)

To the point: The Prime Minister was informed that the coup was not only a domestic Yugoslav "revolution", but that there was British complicity in the coup. His own statements confirmed it:

Churchill ordered Campbell: " .. do not neglect any alternative to which we may have to resort if we find present Government have gone beyond recall. Greatly admire all you have done so far. Keep it up by every means that occur to you." What could have been *any alternative* he ordered, but the overthrow of the Government ?

Churchill to Dalton: "it was a source of great satisfaction that the careful patient work of your people had reaped such a rich reward and convey cordial congratulations to all concerned". Churchill knew about the SOE participation. So did other war leaders:

The Defence Committee: " ... an expression of appreciation should be conveyed to Doctor Dalton for the part played by his organization in bringing about the coup d'état in Yugoslavia."

> In London, ... , the Chiefs of Staff sent their congratulations to Dalton on the SOE's achievement in sowing the seeds of the *coup*. Dalton found this gracious on the part of the Chiefs of Staff and acknowledged that SOE had done well and that their considerable investment in the Serbian peasant party had been "thoroughly justified". (Glen[B], 59)

British complicity was confirmed also by the British participants in the events, as already presented above :

Julian Amery: "... S.O.E.'s co-operation with the Djonovich-Birchanin group and with Gavrilovitch's Peasant Party undoubtedly strengthened both these and helped them to create climate of opinion in which the coup became inevitable."

Bill Bailey: ""I feel very strongly that although the action immediately preceding the coup d'état may have been directed by others, the necessary preliminary conditions were established largely through the work of the S.O.2 [S.O.E.] staff in Belgrade during the past six months."

John Bennett: "... I am also certain that the propaganda emanating from SO2 in Belgrade was largely responsible for the spirit maintained until their final entry into the war on the side of the Allies."

Dalton: "We sent a wire to our friends to use all means to raise a revolution."

Dalton: "It was the Air Attaché who went to Simović and finally persuaded him to act. When Simović asked what arms we could supply, the Air Attaché was authorized to say that we would do what we could ..."

Dalton : "S.O.E. agents were in Belgrade on March 27th 1941, when the coup took place ... This had been well prepared beforehand."

Dalton : "I make an order of the day and write thanks and appreciation. A wonderful reply comes two days later from my Chief Organiser. (3) It is quite touching."   (3) Marginal note: Taylor.

**

It is important to note: In Dalton's opinion: *the chief organizer of the coup was* **George Taylor**, *who really got down to work* when he came to Belgrade [on 27 February], and who worked through **the Serbian Peasant Party and *Narodna Odbrana*** who, in turn, were "subsidized" by the British.

**

Eden to Campbell: "You have my full authority for any measures that you may think it right to take to further change of Government or regime, even by *coup d'état.*
  Any new Government formed as a result of these events and prepared to resist German demands would have our full support. You may secretly so inform any prospective leaders in whom you have confidence." When the SOE-instigated resignation of three Ministers was unsuccessful to cause the Government's crisis, the only other measure available at that time was a military coup.

Eden: "Campbell did everything in his power to encourage the more robust among the politicians and the military through his many useful contacts." A clear admission of complicity.

Eden to Campbell:"Warmest congratulations on your share of this most happy turn of events."

Eden: "... *coup d'état* in Belgrade, ... Magnificent news which so delighted me that I almost hugged Lady Dobbie! "

Sandy Glen: "For us, it was quite simple: there was work to be done. Air Attaché **Hugh Macdonald** and his assistant **Tom Mapplebeck** virtually disappeared; **Charlie Clark** scarcely left the Yugoslav General Staff; while the rest of what were now 24-hour working days were spent with **Tupanjanin** and his friends." Another admission of complicity.

Sandy Glen: "There has been considerable speculation in Yugoslavia ... as to how much the events of 27 March were influenced and encouraged by the British. The answer as regards the latter must be a considerable amount, as **Hugh Macdonald and Charlie Clark** were too close to the organizers for this to have been otherwise."

Thomas Masterson and **Radoje Knežević** "some 6 weeks ago [mid-February 1941], discussed the possibility of developing propaganda ..."

George Taylor: "Coup d'état [was] carried out ... with help of **Trifunovitch** and certain officers. ...
Trifunovitch kept us informed of conspiracy under strictest promise of silence. ...
Masterson has done marvelous work and deserves greatest praise. ...
Bennett ... discovered **Trifunovitch** ...
Hanau originally [picked] winner in **Tupanjanin**."

British policies towards Greece and Yugoslavia

Following are some opinions on the subject of British policies towards Greece and Yugoslavia, expressed over time –

In September 1943: *Churchill was prepared to send troops to Greece to fight against the Greek Communists.*

> As far back as September 1943, he [Churchill] addressed a minute to the Chiefs of Staff drawing attention to the possibility of a Communist *coup d'état* in Greece in the event of a German withdrawal, and asking that preparations should be made to meet that eventuality by sending 'five thousand troops with armoured cars and Bren gun carriers into Athens. ... Their duty would be to give support at the centre to the restored lawful Greek Government.' (Ismay, 367)

On 23 September 1943, Brigadier Fitzroy Maclean was parachuted to the Headquarters of Josip Broz Tito - the Secretary General of the Communist Party of Yugoslavia, the leader of the Communist-controlled Partisans – to lead the British Military Mission as Churchill's personal representative, providing political and military support to the Partisans. This was one year before Churchill proposed to Stalin the division of the spheres of influence in Europe.

In January 1944: *Churchill and Maclean would not live in Greece, but ...*

> We have observed the equanimity with which, in autumn 1943, Mr. Churchill had contemplated Russian dominance in the Balkans. In December Brigadier Maclean - [Commander of the Allied Military Mission to Tito, 1943-45] - fresh from his mission to the Yugoslav partisans, had reported to him that Tito would certainly swing Yugoslavia strongly towards the Soviet Union. (Howard, 63)

In Maclean's words:

> ... I went [from Alexandria] up to Cairo to report, taking Bill Deakin with me. ...
> The first thing was to see the Prime Minister. We found him installed in a villa out by the Pyramids. He was in bed when we arrived, smoking a cigar and wearing an embroidered dressing-gown. He started by telling us some anecdotes about the Teheran Conference and his meeting with Stalin. This, it appeared, had been a success. ...
> ... we slid into a general discussion of the situation in Jugoslavia. He had read my report, and in its light and in the light of all other available information, had talked over the Jugoslav problem with Stalin and Roosevelt at Teheran. As a result of these talks, it had been decided to give all-out support to the Partisans. ...
> I now emphasized to Mr. Churchill the other points which I had already made in my report, namely, that in my view the Partisans, whether we helped them or not, would be the decisive factor in Jugoslavia after the war and, secondly, that Tito and other leaders of the Movement were openly

and avowedly Communists and that the system which they would establish would inevitably be on Soviet lines and, in all probability, strongly orientated towards the Soviet Union.

The Prime Minister's reply resolved my doubts.

'Do you intend,' he asked, 'to make Jugoslavia your home after the war?'

'No, Sir,' I replied.

'Neither do I,' he said. 'And, that being so, the less you and I worry about the form of Government they set up, the better. This is for them to decide. What interests us is, which of them is doing most harm to the Germans.' (Brigadier Fitzroy Maclean, 411-13)

This was in early January 1944. By the end of the war, Maclean and Tito became good friends. His doubt resolved by the Prime Minister, Maclean did not live in Yugoslavia after the war, but he did possess a house there, in which he used to occasionally spend time. When he died on 15 June 1996, there were conflicting reports on the way he got the ownership of the house. According to these reports,

"Tito had given them a house on the island of Korčula, "(Frank McLynn, "Sir Fitzroy Maclean Bt: Obituary", *The Independent,* 19 June 1996.), and "he [Tito] bought a house on the island of Korcula", (Anne de Courcy, "This James Bond stirred but not shaken". *The Daily Telegraph,* June 19, 1996) In either case, it seems that "One of only three foreigners allowed to own property in the country during the Tito period, Maclean spent part of each year at the seaside villa on the Adriatic island of Korcula." (Frank McLynn, "Sir Fitzroy Maclean Bt: Obituary", *The Independent,* 19 June 1996.)

However Maclean came into the possession of an old palazzo on the seaside, he only visited, but did not live in Yugoslavia. The Prime Minister never did, either.

Nor did they live in Greece, either. Yet, the Prime Minister worried – so very much – what form of Government the Greeks would set up. He did not let the Greeks decide. HE decided that it should not be a Communist one, as it was imposed in Yugoslavia.

In August 1944 -   *"We don't want to interfere in Yugoslavia."*

On the morning of 12 August 1944, in Naples, Italy, Churchill met with Tito, the secretary general of the Communist party of Yugoslavia and the supreme commander of the Partisans. In a lengthy conversation, *inter alia,* Churchill talked with Tito about his son's presence among the Partisans: "Randolph has sent me many photographs of your country. He is a great Partisan – I find this rather worrying sometimes", the Prime Minister added with a smile. *"But I too am wholeheartedly for you. We don't want to interfere in Yugoslavia.* We only want to see the greatest possible unity against the Germans, and after that a quiet and peaceful Yugoslavia." (Clissold, 196-7. Italics added.)

While Churchill was assuring Tito that *Britain would not interfere in Yugoslavia* – i.e., that it would give him a free hand ... and arms, Churchill had been already planning how to interfere with the Communists in Greece ... to make it impossible for them to organize a system in Greece similar to the one Britain was helping Tito to set up in Yugoslavia.

By August 1944 the Germans were being hammered in Russia, France and Italy, and it looked as though they would soon have to evacuate Greece and other Balkan countries. The Prime Minister therefore decided that the time had come for the force earmarked for Greece to be held at instant readiness to embark. He emphasized that the operation was to be "regarded as one of reinforced diplomacy and policy rather than an actual campaign." (Ismay, 368)

On 9 October 1944, in Moscow, before he "produced what he called a 'naughty document' showing a list of the south-east European countries with the proportion of interest in them" by the Soviet Union and Great Britain, Churchill said he was "not worrying much about Romania"; that was very much a Russian affair, but Greece was different: *"Britain must be the leading Mediterranean power",* and he hoped Stalin would let him have the first say about Greece in the same way as Stalin about Romania. (Barker(CE), 283. Italics added.)

Regarding Germany's evacuation of Athens, in the Prime Minister's words:

On October 12 [1944] General Wilson learnt that the Germans were evacuating Athens, and the next day British paratroopers landed on the Megara airfield, about eight miles west of the capital. On the 15th the rest of the paratroopers arrived, and occupied the city on the heels of the German withdrawal. Our naval forces entered Piraeus, bringing with them General Scobie and the main part of his force, and two days later the Greek Government arrived, together with our Ambassador. (Churchill(TT), 285. Emphasis added.)

At the end of October 1944, Eden visited Athens on his way from Moscow to London. **On 7 November** Churchill sent him a message:

> In my opinion, *having paid the price we have to Russia for freedom of action in Greece,* we should not hesitate to use British troops to support the Royal Hellenic Government ...
> 2. This implies that British troops should certainly intervene to check acts of lawlessness. ...
> 3. I hope the Greek brigade will soon arrive, and will not hesitate to shoot when necessary. ... We need another eight or ten thousand foot-soldiers to hold the capital and Salonika for the present Government. ...I fully expect a clash with E.A.M., and we must not shrink from it, provided the ground is well chosen. (Churchill(TT), 286-7. Italics added.)

[E.A.M. - The Greek "National Liberation Front" - Communist-led resistance ; E.L.A.S. - The Greek "People's National Army of Liberation" - Communist armed forces]

On 8 November, Churchill instructed General Wilson (in Italy) and the British Ambassador R.W. Allen Leeper (in Athens):

> In view of increasing threat of Communist elements in Greece and indications that they plan to seize power by force, I hope that you will consider reinforcing our troops in Athens area by immediate dispatch of the 3rd Brigade of the 4th Indian Division or some other formation. ...(Churchill[TT], 287)

As the Communists took measures designed to seize power by force, and the British troops resisted, the situation greatly deteriorated and, as Churchill wrote:

> At this moment [Sunday, December 3], I took a more direct control of the affair. On learning that the Communists had already captured all the police stations in Athens, murdering the bulk of their occupants not already pledged to their attack, and were within half a mile of the Government offices, I ordered General Scobie and his 5,000 British troops, ... , to intervene and fire upon the treacherous aggressors. It is no use doing things like this by halves. ... (Churchill(TT), 288)

In December 1944 - *"We have to hold and dominate Athens."*

> Crisis in Greece where E.L.A.S., the left wing organisation, is getting out of hand. The P.M. stayed up till 4.00 a.m. dictating telegrams, and reading tomorrow's newspapers. Bob [Pierson] Dixon [Principal Private Secretary to Anthony Eden] came over from the F.O. and he and I remained with the P.M. while he dictated, ... ("Treat Athens as a conquered city", he wrote in his telegram to [Lt. Gen. Ronald] Scobie [Commander of the British troops in Greece from 1944 to 1946.].) (Colville, 532-3)

On 5 December, at 4:50 A.M., that telegram was sent to General Scobie (Athens) and General Wilson (Italy). Churchill told them, in part:

> You are responsible for maintaining order in Athens and for neutralising or destroying all E.A.M.-E.L.A.S. bands approaching the city. You may make any regulations you like for the strict control of the streets or for rounding up of any number of truculent persons. ... *Do not however hesitate to act as if you were in a conquered city where a local rebellion is in progress. ... We have to hold and dominate Athens. It would be a great thing for you to succeed in this without bloodshed if possible, but also with bloodshed if necessary.* (Churchill(TT), 289. Italics in the source.)

> Scobie threw his troops into the battle. ...

> All through December the fighting raged. Athens, ... , was battered by British tank cannon, rocket-firing Spitfires, 75mm artillery in the hands of ELAS ... The British fought against their former allies, and Greeks mercilessly battled Greeks ...
> ... on the 25th of December, Churchill arrived by plane and joined the battle for Athens. ...
> ... Churchill's tactics in Greece did resemble an old-fashioned imperialistic power play. He was fighting there to make the country [Greece] politically safe for Britain's postwar aim to resume its dominant role in the Mediterranean. ... (Bailey et al., 182-4)

A lot of blood was shed. Churchill and Eden landed at the Athens airfield about noon on Christmas Day. A decision was made to form a Government without any Communist member. On 11 January 1945 the Communists accepted the truce. (Ismay, 370)

In 1951, British historian **Professor Hugh Seton-Watson** – a former influential Section D/SOE operator - elucidated Britain's action in Greece:

> Events in the rest of Eastern Europe since 1944 have shown what kind of regime Greece would have had if E.L.A.S. and the Communist Party had had a free hand. For two reasons at least there should be satisfaction in Britain that they did not. One is that a totalitarian regime would have been imposed on the Greek people, ... Some indication of how communist rule would have begun was given by the massacres of hostages which E.L.A.S. committed during its days of power in Athens. The corpses, in many cases mutilated, of murdered men and women, including besides some 'collaborators' a large number of innocent and harmless persons, were found after the E.L.A.S. withdrawal. The second reason is that the triumph of E.L.A.S. would have extended the Soviet block far into the Eastern Mediterranean, including Crete and the Dodecanese, and threatened the Middle East. It is indeed probable that this was the main consideration affecting Mr. Churchill's policy. A Soviet threat to British interests did not at that time seriously alarm most British people, who thought of the U.S.S.R. as a gallant ally. But the events of last five years had shown it in a different light.
> British troops prevented the Greek communists from seizing power. ... Looking back in 1950 one must be thankful that the British intervention took place. ... (Seton-Watson(ER), 320-1)

So, while the Communists in Yugoslavia were helped – politically and militarily – to establish a totalitarian Communist system in Yugoslavia, the Communists in Greece were denied the same goal by the British military force. Yugoslavia was not a Mediterranean country. ... The massacres in Athens, thankfully, could not compare with the ones committed by the Communist regime in Yugoslavia after the war had ended. These massacres were a part of the terrible national tragedy in Yugoslavia that deserves a separate examination.

In December 1944: *"Greece had higher priority"*

> In both Yugoslavia and Greece considerations of short-term strategic necessity had come into conflict with considerations of postwar politics. ... In the delicate balance to be struck between long-term and short-term considerations, the former was deemed to be more important in Greece than the latter. In both countries the British desired non-communist postwar governments, but Greece had higher priority, as a hostile Greece would threaten British postwar interests in the Eastern Mediterranean. (Stafford(so) 126)

In March 1945: *Yugoslavia was needed to protect British position in Greece*

After the infamous Churchill-Stalin sharing of influence zones in Europe, on 18 March 1945, Eden wrote to Churchill who was inclined to withdraw from further interest in Yugoslav affairs:

> Our present policy towards Yugoslavia is, I think, realistic and not overambitious. It recognises that *Yugoslavia has not the same long-term strategic and political importance for us as Greece or for that matter as Italy,* and that *Yugoslavia lies outside or rather on the edge of our major interests.* It is based on the 'fifty-fifty' agreement, the principle of which is in effect that Yugoslavia should be a sort of neutral area between British and Russian zones of influence.
> Since a half share of influence in Yugoslav affairs does not fall to us naturally, the agreement has meant in practice that we have to exert ourselves to produce some influence on Yugoslav affairs to counterbalance the otherwise overwhelming Russian influence.... My idea has been that by aiming in this way to make Yugoslavia as far as possible a 'neutral' area, *we shall be providing an*

important protection of our position in Greece and to a lesser degree in Italy as well. ... From the political point of view it seems to me that we should not draw out and leave the whole business to Tito and Moscow. (Eden, 523-4. Italics added.)

Chapter 16

The July 1973 Conference

Clogg, Barker, Sweet-Escott, Seton-Watson, ... , all were participants at the July 1973 Conference organized by the School of Slavonic and East European Studies of the University of London. Here are some excerpts from the proceedings related to Greece and Yugoslavia:

Richard Clogg (Lecturer in Modern Greek History, University of London) :

> Was there ever any explicit mention in the documents that Greece was, as Sargent cabled to Eden during the August 1943 crisis, a vital British interest? Is there any indication that Yugoslavia was not regarded as a vital British interest in the sense that Greece was? (Auty & Clogg(ed), 274-5)

Elisabeth Barker(former Head of Balkan Region, Political Warfare Executive) :

> Obviously it was regarded in a different category but there was some talk at some stage as to whether we could maintain our influence in Serbia as a sort of a buffer state protecting Greece. But this never got beyond loose talk in minutes. (Auty & Clogg(ed), 275)

Bickham Sweet-Escott, (on the SOE Staff Headquarters, London; missions to Cairo and elsewhere) :

> But surely there was this difference in 1943-4, that Greece was supposed to be essential because it guarded the route to India. Our pre-war policy, or policy in 1941, in Yugoslavia – was expendable, more expendable than in Greece. (Auty & Clogg(ed), 275)

Barker:
> Quite obviously they would have liked to keep their hold on Yugoslavia but I do not think they said it was vital. (Auty & Clogg(ed), 275)

Professor Hugh Seton-Watson – a former Section D / SOE agent in Rumania, Yugoslavia, Cairo and Istanbul, who evolved from an internationalist in the early 1940s to a British nationalist in the 1970s:

> The question raised by Woodhouse which is the crucial issue emerging from our discussions, namely why the British government took opposite decisions in Yugoslavia and Greece, cannot be answered with complete certainty, but there are some relevant points that can be enumerated.
> Greece was always seen to be geographically more important, and physically more controllable, than Yugoslavia. Greece in hostile hands would undermine British security in the eastern Mediterranean; and conversely, British naval power would make it possible for Britain to hope to impose its will on Greece, at least on the assumption that Britain was going to remain a Great Power. Neither of these things were true of Yugoslavia, even though it was undoubtedly desirable that Yugoslavia should be in friendly hands. (Auty & Clogg(ed), 293)

> Yugoslav or Greek readers may be shocked at the crude calculus of British politicians, generals or officials of 'who is killing most Germans'; at the thought that Yugoslav and Greek lives were treated as mere commodities, *expendable according to British military interests*. Yet this should not really cause shock or surprise. Men's lives are the currency of war, and in this war the survival of Britain was at stake. Britain's leaders had to be ruthless... (Auty & Clogg(ed), 294. Italics added.)

So: Greece was more important and more controllable than Yugoslavia, and Britain could easier impose her will on Greece. *Britain's leaders had to be ruthless ...* with other peoples' lives – while doing whatever they could to save the British.

On Churchill's Greek expedition:

> British military experts are almost unanimous in their condemnation of Churchill's decision to land troops in Greece and to push Yugoslavia into the war. "The sequel was," wrote B.H. Liddell Hart, "that within three weeks Greece and Yugoslavia were overrun, and the British forces driven to

a second 'Dunkirk.' ... It brought appalling misery on the people of Greece and Yugoslavia, and the bitter fruits are still being harvested in the troubles that followed the war." *The Economist* called it "a cardinal strategic error." Lord Harding called it "a major strategic mistake," and Lord Alanbrooke (General Alan Brooke) termed it "a definite strategic blunder." Eden had told Dill that he felt largely responsible for the catastrophe in Greece and Cyrenaica and said that he was going to resign. However, Dill persuaded him not to do so. George Thompson called the Greek expedition "the most disastrous British blunder of the war." (Jukić, 87-8)

**

As has been already shown, *"the end of Sea Lion"* came in September 1940, Britain was not politically alone after Harry Hopkins' visit to Churchill in January 1941. Britain was also in position to control all of North Africa before 27 March 1941.

In March 1941, the British expedition to Greece was not the only option, a military necessity in service of the survival of Britain. To send troops to Greece was a political decision, a strategic error, etc., as quoted above. The expedition did not help the survival of Britain; it brought her defeat and, ultimately, a catastrophe for the peoples of Greece and Yugoslavia. Most unfortunately, *"Yugoslav and Greek lives were treated as mere commodities"*, expendable because of an ill-conceived, unrealistic, "wishful-minded" idea.

In July 1943, when Churchill asked Brigadier Fitzroy Maclean to find out *'who is killing most Germans'*, so he could support them, the *"survival of Britain"* was not at stake. The German armies had been stopped on the Eastern Front, the Allies controlled North Africa, Mussolini's government was to capitulate within weeks, and Italy was going to change sides in the war.

A comparison of ultimately-suffered losses of human lives shows the magnitude of the catastrophe for Greece and Yugoslavia:

Out of   47,760,000 inhabitants, the United Kingdom lost   449,800 dead, or 0.94%.
Out of   7,222,000   Greece lost   311,300   4.31%.
Out of   15,400,000   Yugoslavia lost   1,027,000   6.67%
(http://en.wikipedia.org/wiki/World_War_II_casualties   2/15/09)

"... human lives... mere commodities ...., expendable ... "

Historian, Professor Richard Holmes, observed this about Churchill: *"He had no objection to throwing other peoples to the wolves if it genuinely helped the British sledge to reach safety."*

Yet one third of a century after the British sledge reached safety, not a word of sorrow, commiseration, sympathy, of regret ... Not a sign of *"one of the heavier ethical burdens that has weighed on Britain's official postwar conscience"*, as Professor Bradley F. Smith thought – at least not among the former shapers of events in Greece and Yugoslavia. For at least one of them – a very influential one – it seems that

"All peoples were equal, but some were more equal."

Appendix A - William Donovan's missions

Drawing Yugoslavia into World War II was supported by William Joseph Donovan, who earned the nickname "Wild Bill" in World War I. He was the only American who had received America's four highest awards: The Medal of Honor, the Distinguished Service Cross, the Distinguished Service Medal, and the National Security Medal. (http://www.arlingtoncemetery.net/wjodonov.htm 12/23/11)

"By the end of the war he received a promotion to colonel." A graduate of Columbia Law School, Donovan became an influential – and well to do - Wall Street lawyer. "Donovan ran unsuccessfully as a Republican for Lieutenant Governor of New York in 1922, and for Governor in 1932."

> During the interwar years, Donovan traveled extensively in Europe and met with foreign leaders including Mussolini of Italy. Donovan openly believed during this time that a second major European war was inevitable. ... Following Germany's invasion of Poland in September 1939 and the start of World War II in Europe, President Roosevelt began to put the United States on a war footing. ... On the recommendation of Donovan's friend, United States Secretary of the Navy Frank Knox, Roosevelt gave him a number of increasingly important assignments. In 1940 and 1941, Donovan traveled as an informal emissary to Britain ... (http://en.wikipedia.org/wiki/William_J._Donovan 12/23/11)

Actually Donovan went on a confidential mission to the Balkans and the Middle East for both President Roosevelt and Prime Minister Churchill. His mission had been planned for some time and was well organized, lasting from late December 1940 to early March 1941. Because his findings and recommendations were influential in subsequent Anglo-American relations and involved Yugoslavia, due attention should be paid to them.

Donovan's first trip to Britain (14 July to 4 August 1940)

The December 1940 mission followed his earlier visit to Britain, undertaken with intent of aiding Great Britain. Here is some background information related to Donovan's first trip to Britain.

President Franklin Roosevelt and Winston S. Churchill had been corresponding since 11 September 1939, when Churchill was First Lord of the Admiralty. On 15 May 1940 – five days after becoming Prime Minister – Churchill wrote to the President: "Although I have changed my office, I am sure you would not wish me to discontinue our intimate, private correspondence. As you are no doubt aware, the scene has darkened swiftly." (Loewenheim *et al* (ed), 94)

The swift darkening referred to Germany's attack on France, the Low Countries and Luxemburg on 10 May.

On 16 May, the President replied, *inter alia* : "... I am sure it is unnecessary for me to say that I am most happy to continue our private correspondence as we have in the past." (Loewenheim *et al* (ed), 95)

In their letters "the basis for Anglo-American cooperation was established and the means for implementing it devised long before the United States actually entered the war." (Loewenheim *et al* (ed), 4)

One of these means was Donovan's first trip to Britain.

**

> ... with fewer than four months remaining prior to the election that would determine whether Franklin Roosevelt would serve an unprecedented third term, it behooved the president to move with extreme caution on the issue of aid to Britain. Privately, he seems to have been inclined to the belief that Britain had a chance to withstand a German assault and that it was in America's interest to play that chance and to send aid, but the issue was far from simple. ...
>
> ... What he needed most was accurate information on Hitler's power and intentions, as well as a solid estimate of Britain's ability to withstand German air attack and a cross-channel invasion. ... (Smith, 25-6)

After Donovan accepted the President's assignment at a meeting in the White house, held on June 1940, the secretary of State, Cordell Hull, wrote a letter "for the personal attention only" of Prime Minister Churchill, to be hand-carried by Donovan, pledging America's assistance to

Britain "in all ways possible", providing Donovan was satisfied after his visit to London. (Thomas, 86, 88)

According to the historian Bradley F. Smith,

> Important though Donovan's mission to Britain was in July 1940, some words of caution need to be added. Despite much subsequent exaggerated and loose comments, Donovan's trip was not analogous to a holy mission arranged by American internationalists to save Western civilization. ... The trip was primarily a hard-headed, ad hoc survey-and-coordination operation organized by [Frank] Knox [the Secretary of the Navy] and approved by the president." (Smith, 33)

Donovan arrived in London on 17 July, and within a few hours of his arrival went to Buckingham Palace to see the King. George VI cordially welcomed him and showed him a deciphered message from Hitler to his field commanders – without disclosing that Britain had broken Germany's [Air Force] code [on 22 May 1941]. (Dunlop, 209) (Smith has 15 July as Donovan's arrival day in London. Donovan's biographer, Anthony Cave Brown, a Briton, sets 16 July as the arrival date, while Professor Thomas F. Troy has it as 19 July.)

> "On his first day in London (15 July) he met with Director of Naval Intelligence (D.N.I.), Adm. John Godfrey, ... Donovan was free to talk with important British officials, ... After three weeks of observation and a final set of conferences with the American military attachés in London, Donovan concluded that the R.A.F. [Royal Air Force] and British resoluteness gave the United kingdom a better than even chance of beating off a German attack." (Smith, 34-5)
> However welcome, "he was not privy to the "Ultra secret" – the increasingly successful deciphering achievement attained by the staff of the Code and Cypher School at Bletchley Park in unraveling the mysteries of Germany's Enigma coding machine. (Smith, 36)

> Donovan was also introduced to all the top personalities in the British intelligence community. [Major-General Stewart] Menzies [the head of the Secret Intelligence Service (SIS), or MI6] personally briefed him on SIS's overseas organization; ... the Director of Military Intelligence, Paddy Beaumont-Nesbitt, gave him a tour of the War Office and explained the German order of battle; Sir Frank Nelson [of SOE] received him at the Baker Street headquarters of SOE and introduced him to his senior staff [which included Nelson's Chief of Staff, George Taylor]; Desmond Morton described the Industrial Intelligence Centre's strategy of an economic blockade [in which SOE was heavily involved]; ... Finally, he was escorted into the maze of tunnels under Great George Street to meet the Prime Minister in the Cabinet War Room. (West(6), 204; Dunlop, 212-13)

Donovan was scheduled to meet Churchill on Thursday, 25 July, at 5:30 P.M. (Troy, 52) He dined with Churchill and King George, learned of Britain's top-secret invention of radar, saw the production of fighter planes, visited Britain's coastal defenses, was briefed on the successful propaganda war MI5 and MI6 were already conducting in Europe, and how the SOE had already begun infiltrating its saboteurs into enemy-occupied France. "The surest sign of the trust in which the soft-spoken Donovan was held by his hosts came when Churchill personally authorized he should be shown the highly secret interrogation center that had been prepared for captured Nazi generals – 'and captured they will be', the prime minister had repeated, waving one of the Cuban cigars Donovan had brought as a personal gift." (Thomas, 88-9) "The prime minister assured Donovan of his government's complete cooperation on his mission." (Dunlop, 213)

> Donovan spent his last evening in England at Braddocks, the home of Rear Admiral John Godfrey, ...In the morning Godfrey reported to Vice Adm. Tom Phillips on his evening with Donovan, who forwarded this account to First Sea Lord Sir Dudley Pound, who handed it to Churchill with the notation, "This is very satisfactory". (Dunlop, 216-17)

**

Donovan left England on 3 August, at 2:00 P.M. (Troy, 55) Once back home, "Donovan had done yeoman service in helping to convince American opinion makers that generous assistance to Britain was in America's interest." (Smith, 38) He expressed the opinion that British morale was excellent, that Britain would withstand a German invasion, and that Britain's military needs were both great and urgent. (Troy, 57) Donovan pressed at the highest level "for the supplying to the British of the supplies they so badly needed from the United States. Destroyers topped the list; behind them came the

Sperry bomb sights, flying boats, flying fortresses, ... " (Troy, 58) Donovan was "instrumental in giving impetus" to the Destroyers-for-Bases agreement between the USA and Britain. (Troy, 58)

After a dinner with Donovan, Henry L. Stimson, the US Secretary of War, wrote about Donovan in his diary on 6 August 1940:"He [Donovan] was determined to get into the war some way or other and was the same old Bill Donovan that we have all known and been so fond of". (Troy, 61) With such an attitude, it was natural for Donovan to help further the British cause and goals as much as he could. On 17 August 1940, Sir Arthur Salter [of the Ministry of Shipping] telegraphed Churchill: "Colonel Donovan was working with great energy in our interest. We now had a firm friend in the Republican camp [with the presidential election in process] and this was proving of immense value." (Troy, 60; 220n46)

Unceasingly advancing Britain's cause in the eyes of the American public and Government, Donovan's trip was of great benefit to Britain; British officials could feel satisfied with it. However, Donovan "had not grasped how appallingly weak the British ground forces were (something on the order of 3 or 4 modern divisions against 150 German ones), and thus tended to be too optimistic about what could be accomplished once Germany was checked at the Channel." (Smith, 35)

Donovan's second trip to Britain (6 December 1940 to 18 March 1941)

Between Donovan's first and second trip to Britain, two major events occurred: "the end of Sea Lion" in September, and Italy's attack on Greece in October 1940. Well aware of Donovan's support for their cause, the British still did not inform him of the first event. Both events, however, were going to affect Yugoslavia, with Donovan contributing his share.

**

On 27 November 1940, the US Secretary of the Navy, Frank Knox, asked the British Ambassador to the United States, Lord Lothian, if Donovan could pay a short visit to the Middle East front. (Troy, 78) On 1 December, Donovan was called to Washington, and the President asked him if he would go and make a strategic appreciation of the Mediterranean area from an economic, political and military standpoint. (Troy, 78) This area was selected " for it was here that Britain's position was most critical; the Italians had opened hostilities in Libya and had invaded Greece; the Germans seemed posed for thrusts either through Spain into North Africa or into the Balkans and the Middle East; from Gibraltar to Suez, the land, the passageways, and the waters were problems for the British." (Troy, 78)

As Donovan told historians William L. Langer and S. Everett Gleason,

> His mission was to journey to the Middle East, to collect information on conditions and prospects and, more importantly, *to impress on everyone the resolution of the American Government and people to see the British through* and provide all possible assistance to countries which undertook to resist Nazi aggression. (Langer & Gleason, 397. Italics added.)

Described by Lothian as "one of our best and most influential friends here with a great deal of influence both with the Service Departments and the Administration", Donovan was approved for the visit. On 5 December, the Foreign Office sent assurances that Donovan was welcome both in London and the Middle East. (Troy, 79)

As historian Bradley F. Smith wrote,

> The Foreign Office was told in December 1940 to start putting the squeeze on the Balkan leaders, and the carrot of promised arms shipments together with the stick of British political and economic pressure were soon applied. Just as this was occurring, William Donavan arrived on the London scene. ... (Smith, 46)

**

The London scene at this time encompassed Britain's insistence that Yugoslavia should stand four-square against any Axis demand, and that the Balkan situation would the acid test for the Special Operations Executive – which resulted in George Taylor's mission to the Balkans and the Middle East. Discussions between Cairo-Athens-London whether or not to help Greece were still going on – and this offered Donovan a chance to express the President's and his own opinion. The Foreign Secretary Lord Halifax was going to be replaced by Anthony Eden within a week of Donovan's arrival to London. Thus Donovan's mission fit well with the Prime Minister's policies of squeezing the Balkan leaders, especially as President Roosevelt had resolved to help Britain.

* **More on Donovan's lunch with Churchill, 18 December 1940**

(As stated in Chapter 4, Donovan informed Churchill "that the United States and Britain must help each other in this crisis in history in a "relationship of mutual selfishness". (Dunlop, 239))

To facilitate a study on the economic, political and military cooperation between the two countries, Churchill assigned to Donovan as traveling companion

> "the best man in the Cabinet Secretariat," Lt. Col. Vivian Dykes of the Royal Engineers, "who has been present at meetings of the Joint Board and combined arms." Churchill also gave Donovan all the studies that had been done on the Mediterranean and Middle East situation, studies which, Donovan noted, covered all the parts but did not include "a comprehensive view combining all points as part of one strategic front." (Troy, 81)

Anthony Cave Brown wrote the following about this meeting:

> Although Donovan left no account of his long conversation with Churchill, he did tell a law partner, Otto C. Doering, that the prime minister discussed at length his strategy for the defeat of Germany. Churchill believed that Britain would surely founder as a world power if it suffered again casualties on the scale of those of World War I, and that to avoid such casualties, he had started to look at the map in other ways. Churchill showed on a globe in his study how Germany was more vulnerable to an attack from the Baltic or the Mediterranean than from the West across the Channel. Donovan ... found much wisdom in Churchill's concept ... He liked especially Churchill's ideas to make all Europe rebel against the Germans, "to set Europe alight", as the prime minister put it, as a precursor to a general attack by the armies. (Cave Brown, 152-3)

After a long private lunch with Churchill on 18 December Donovan met with numerous high-ranking British military and civilian officials. The mood in Britain had changed since his first visit. Ultra intercepts of German signals and aerial reconnaissance showed the withdrawal of German air and support forces, indicating that the threat of invasion – *Operation Sea Lion* – had passed. However, *this was not revealed to Donovan* (Smith, 41-2. Italics added.)

Donovan's tour of the Mediterranean

On 24 December 1940, two days after Anthony Eden became the Foreign Minister, the Foreign Office alerted British Ambassadors throughout the Mediterranean area to expect an important visitor:

> Colonel Donovan, who is visiting this country as an observer for President Roosevelt, with whom he has great influence, is leaving on a six weeks' tour of the Mediterranean in the course of which he proposes to visit Gibraltar, Malta, Egypt, Palestine and Greece. His object is to study and report to the President on our strategical situation in the Mediterranean but his terms of reference are very wide. The Prime Minister has directed that every facility should be afforded to Colonel Donovan, who has been taken fully into our confidence. (Danchev(ed), 19; 229n1)

Bulgaria, Yugoslavia and Turkey were not mentioned in this alert. "At the Prime Minister's personal request, Colonel Donovan extended his tour to Bulgaria and Yugoslavia." (Ford, 100)

The Director of Naval Intelligence sent a signal to Admiral Andrew Cunningham, Commander-in-Chief of the Mediterranean Fleet: "Donovan exercises controlling influence over Knox [the Secretary of the Navy], strong influence over Stimson [the Secretary for War], friendly advisory influence over President and Hull [the Secretary of State]. ... Being a Republican, a Catholic, and of Irish descent, he has following of the strongest opposition to the Administration. ... There is no doubt that we can achieve infinitely more through Donovan than through any other individual." (Ford, 99)

Professor Troy concluded that the FO's message to the British Ambassadors made it clear that the trip was financed by the Secret Intelligence Service. "Colonel Dykes has been told to draw on His Majesty's Embassy (or Legation) for funds which should be charged to the funds of the Assistant to the Oriental Secretary (or the Passport Control Officer)." (Troy 81)

* Churchill's confidential agent

> On his Mediterranean journey Donovan was to fly in British bombers and use British base facilities. For all effects and purposes he was now Churchill's as well as Roosevelt's confidential agent. (Dunlop, 243)

The editor of Dykes' diaries wrote in the Introduction: "Donovan was bear-lead round the Mediterranean by Lieutenant Colonel Vivian Dukes, 'the best man in the Cabinet Secretariat'." (Danchev(ed),19)

> ... Dykes recorded – and actively helped to influence – the development of Donovan's own thinking, fully reported to Secretary Knox in Washington, and shared with a select circle around the president, including his 'best friend' and closest adviser, Harry Hopkins. For his part, Dykes reported direct to the CIGS [Chief of the Imperial General Staff], carefully including copies of Donovan's dispatches as well. ... (Danchev(ed), 21-2)

It was not hard for Dykes to do all these things because Donovan himself wanted to promote and re-enforce Britain's war policies and objectives.

> During the entire three-and-a-half-month trip, Donovan depended almost entirely on the secondhand information given to him by British officials of all ranks and positions. ... In general terms, the British sought to create a "Balkan front" against the Axis. (Petrov, 138)

* Donovan's message: the USA is solidly behind Great Britain

> The Balkan situation was the cause of the high point of Donovan's trip, namely his meetings in Cairo with British leaders as they wrestled with the question whether and how to help Greece resist a German onslaught. The British consulted him as a representative of the President, as someone who was passionately interested in their welfare, and as a clear-sighted strategist - as one who had been on the ground, talked with the leaders, understood the issues and fully appreciated the consequences of action and inaction. (Troy, 85)

> In Greece, his talks with the leaders covered Greek preparations, strategy, and tactics for the resistance they were determined to offer to any German advance. They covered also the supplies and armaments needed by the Greek army: antiaircraft guns, mountain guns with ammunition, Ford trucks, donkeys eleven hands high, uniforms, shoes, and socks. (Troy, 84)

> In Athens, and everywhere he went, he delivered his own message that Britain was fighting, that America would support the democracies, and that the President himself was being given "overwhelming support" in this regard. (Troy, 84-5)

> Everywhere he went, his message was the same: the United States was solidly behind Great Britain. ... Donovan asserted that America would withhold her favors not only from those who flirted with Nazis or Fascists, but also from those who failed to resist Axis pressure. Those countries that did not line up with Britain stood to lose American sympathy and all prospect of American assistance. (Smith, 48)

> ... Donovan was fully initiated into British plans and negotiations with the Greeks and Turks. Like the British, he was convinced that if the Balkan states and Turkey could be induced to form a united front, Nazi aggression might yet be averted. He therefore readily agreed to postpone his visit to the Albanian front and to make the rounds of the Bulgarian, Yugoslav and Turkish capitals in an effort to bring those governments in line. (Langer & Gleason, 397)

Donovan in Cairo

For a more complete understanding of how "British policy toward Yugoslavia early in 1941 became a function of the British desire to save Greece", a rather detailed account can be taken from Col. Dykes' diaries.

> On Tuesday, January 7, 1941, Donovan and Dykes reached Cairo and were given comfortable rooms at the British Embassy. .... he [Donovan] spent most of the next several days with British leaders, including the commander-in-chief in the Middle East, Gen. Archibald Percival Wavell, with whom Donovan struck up an immediate friendship. (Dunlop, 244)

On 8 January, at 9:35 a.m., Dykes recorded that he and Donovan met with General Wavell and Air Chief Marshal Arthur Longmore:

> Wavell gave a very interesting general survey of the position in his area. ... At the start of the war our position in the Middle East was weak and the policy had been not to annoy the Italians, ... As for Turkey, the Tripartite plans which had been worked out before the collapse of France were all now a dead letter. They had been based on the hypothesis of a friendly Italy, and Turkey now wanted to start fresh conversations. General Marshall-Cornwall [General Officer Commanding British Troops Egypt] was shortly going to Turkey for that purpose. ... (Danchev(ed), 26-7)

> The war in Greece has brought new commitments for us. The Greeks were crying out for more aircraft, but the aerodromes were so bad that we could not operate more than we have already sent even if we could spare them. ... If we have to send troops to the Balkans we should want to liquidate the Dodecanese [Islands] first. ... If Yugoslavia was drawn in too, there would be fresh demands from them for aircraft, anti-aircraft and anti-tank guns. To meet these contingences in this area, schemes of aerodrome construction and improvements of ports and roads in Turkey were being pressed on. It would however always be difficult to operate in the Balkans against Germany since she possessed the advantage of interior lines. (Danchev(ed), 28)

> ... Speaking of German intentions, Wavell thought that they would try to keep the Balkans quiet and consolidate in the south-east, thus avoiding operations on two fronts. They had put in strong defences in Romania to protect their oil and were using Bulgarians as a buffer zone. (Danchev(ed), 28

After leaving Wavell, Donovan called on the American Minister and then, in the afternoon, he and Dykes saw the British Deputy Quartermaster General. Next they saw General Marshall-Cornwall, about whom Dykes recorded in his diary: " Marshall-Cornwall thinks that we should strive to bring in the Yugoslavs and the Turks on our side and go in through Salonika, thus forming a wide front for attack on Germany on the south-east; this is the only way we can get at her." (Danchev(ed), 28-9)

On January 10, Wavell showed Donovan a message from Churchill:

> ... Destruction of Greece would eclipse victories you have gained in Libya and might affect decisively Turkish attitude, ... You must now therefore conform your plans to larger interests at stake.
> Nothing must hamper capture of Tobruk but thereafter all operations in Libya are subordinated to aiding Greece.
> We expect and require prompt and active compliance with our decisions for which we bear full responsibility. Your joint visit to Athens will enable you to contrive the best method of giving effect to the above decisions. It should not be delayed. (Dunlop, 245)

On the same day the Defence Committee decided that it was of the utmost political importance to provide Greece with the fullest possible support, and the Cabinet instructed General Wavell and Air Marshal Longmore to fly to Athens and offer immediate reinforcement. His forces having been in hot pursuit of the Italians in north Africa, Wavell questioned the instruction: "It fills me with dismay." (Hinsley *et al*, 353-4)

Donovan in Greece

General Wavell and Air Vice-Marshal Longmore left for Greece on the morning of 13 January, to consult with the Greeks. Dykes and Donovan came to Athens on the 15th. Donovan stayed with the British Ambassador, Sir Michael Palairet, and Dykes with the archaeologist Wace, who was working in the Passport Control Office. (Danchev(ed), 33-4)

> During his various meetings in Athens Donovan spoke forcefully and eloquently, stating the United States' firm determination to assist the British in securing the defeat of the Axis; urging the Greeks to form a united front with other Balkan states and Turkey; and taking copious notes of Greek needs for military equipment which could be filled by American aid. (Petrov, 140)

> Donovan spent considerable time with Premier John Metaxas, the veritable dictator of the country, and Gen. Alexander Papagos, the commander-in-chief who was Metaxas' chief of staff. At the British Legation the British military delegation kept Donovan abreast of negotiations with the Greeks. *Metaxas declined an offer of British troops* to help Greek soldiers who were still driving back the Italians on the Albanian front, *but he welcomed whatever arms and supplies* the British could provide to strengthen the forces preparing to defend Macedonia against a probable German assault. It was Metaxas' position that any British military assistance short of overwhelming strength would merely goad the Germans into action. Only supplies and military aid on the scale that America alone could provide would secure Greece against Germany. Donovan carefully noted exactly what supplies and equipment would most help the Greeks. (Dunlop, 247. Italics added.)

Martin van Creveld provided more information on these Anglo-Greek conferences:

> From 13 to 17 January they [the British] met with Metaxas and the Greek CIC, General Alexander Papagos, in a series of conferences of which we have several records. ... Papagos explained that he had fourteen divisions in Albania and could concentrate four more on the Bulgaro-Greek frontier. ... he wanted Wavell to supply nine British divisions ... Wavell replied that in view of his commitments in Cyrenaica and Ethiopia he had only two or three divisions available, and even these would be able to arrive only late in March, whereas the German attack might start at any time after the beginning of March. At this point Metaxas interfered to say that such small aid would be worse than useful, since it might provoke the Germans without being sufficient to aid effectively in their repulse. Hence he did not want any British aid, and with that the conference adjourned. (van Creveld(G), 75-6)

Van Creveld observed the following about these conferences:

> From a summary of the talks sent by the British Military Mission to the War Office, it appears that, during the conference of 15 January, Metaxas and Papagos at first asked for equipment to fight the Italians in Albania, *not the British units to fight the Germans in Bulgaria.* Wavell refused; possibly because he wanted to make sure of continued Greek participation in the war, he offered not material, but complete units, including some armoured and anti-aircraft forces. This the Greeks refused; and the British, speculating as to their motive, again saw the spectre of a separate Italo-Greek peace. (van Creveld(G), 76. Italics added.)

**

Copious notes of Greek needs taken by Donovan may have been suggestive of aid, but in reality, no American military equipment or armaments could have been delivered to Greece (and Yugoslavia) before the expected German invasion. The US Congress passed the Lend-Lease Act on 11 March 1941 – almost two months after this meeting in Athens - with the intention to equip Britain first and foremost, and not Greece and Yugoslavia.

**

> While Donovan was busily collecting and sending to Washington lists of Greek requirements in matériel, the Administration was still wrestling with the problem of finding for the Greeks the thirty modern combat planes which the President, in a moment of misguided generosity, had long since promised. Since the Greeks had refused the obsolete Navy planes offered them and since Secretary Knox would not hear of turning over any of the new planes so desperately needed by both the American and British services, a deadlock was reached at the end of January [1941]. (Langer & Gleason, 400)

As for Donovan's attitude and activities,

> British officials, quite naturally, were delighted with the Colonel's effort and showed their appreciation in many ways. Donovan was put up handsomely, encouraged, honored, and treated like a trusted friend. While in Athens he stayed at the British rather than the American legation, even when General Archibald P. Wavell ... was there. Dispatches praising his efforts were filed by many British officials, including the new Foreign Secretary, Anthony Eden. ... In addition, both to broaden Donovan's understanding and to give his reports to America as much pro-British coloration as possible, he was provided with a large number of interviews and briefing papers. Donovan's dispatches to Washington show the full mark of this information and reflect his admiration "for the superb job which the British have done in this area." His mission had convinced him that Germany's sole aim, the driving force that animated every action, was to defeat Great Britain. Every feint, every maneuver, whether in Western Europe or the Balkans, was, in the colonel's opinion, directed solely to effect the overthrow of the United Kingdom. It therefore followed that the United States must support and assist the British at every threatened point. (Smith, 48-9)

Purposefully not informing Donovan of *"the end of Sea Lion"*, the British made sure to keep him convinced that all German actions were directed solely to the overthrow of the United Kingdom.

On 16 January, Dykes wrote in his diary that he and Donovan were informed of the discussions with the Greeks the previous day about furnishing British troops :

> The Greeks would not have any formed units from us, nor would they allow us to send anything to Salonika. They fear the acceptance of troops might precipitate German action against them and ask only for material, quite regardless of the fact that their men are untrained in its use. Metaxas said that the Yugoslavs had hinted that they would disclaim all responsibility if the Greeks accepted help from us. ... (Danchev(ed), 35)

The same day, after lunch, "Donovan had a good long talk with the King." In the evening he saw Prime Minister Ioannis Metaxas, and General Alexandros Papagos, and told Dykes that "he had impressed on them that the US would see the Allies through." He got a list of the principal things the Greeks needed from Papagos, promising to press for them to be supplied. In the evening Donovan informed Wavell of his interviews with Metaxas and Papagos. (Danchev(ed), 35-6)

From Dykes' diary entry for 17 January:"In the morning we heard that Papagos had rather changed his attitude during the night (as a result of his talk with Donovan?) and was now more disposed to favour acceptance of our offer of troops. He had an interview with Wavell early in the morning before Wavell left." ... "At 11.00 p.m., after discussion with Palairet and Heywood, Donovan agreed to go straight to Sofia in the hope that he would be able to put some stiffening into the Bulgars." (Danchev(ed), 36)

Trip to Sofia and Belgrade

The trip to Sofia - and then on to Belgrade – was not a planned part of his mission. They were now requested by the British in the field because of the apparent need to "stiffen" the Bulgars and Yugoslavs.

> Having spent a busy week in Athens - he [Donovan] barely had time to talk with [American] Minister [Lincoln] MacVeagh – Donovan took train to Sofia where he had an important task to accomplish. The British feared that Bulgaria was on the verge of reaching an accord with the Germans on the passage of German troops through the country and hoped that Donovan's intervention would forestall this development. (Petrov, 140)

On 17 and 18 January Donovan sent six telegrams to Secretary Knox. One of them, relating to his interviews with Metaxas and Papagos on 16 January, Dykes recorded in his diary. Here is the excerpt regarding Yugoslavia:

> Metaxas fears that to anticipate Britain's strengthening her foothold here Germany may attempt to seize Salonika and that this Yugoslavia and Bulgaria may not resist, and British force is not yet

sufficient. General Wavell asked me to say that he has drawn, and is drawing, heavily on his resources to aid her but due to existing commitments and limitations of shipping cannot at this moment do more. (Danchev(ed), 35)

On 18 January, Dykes changed into civilian clothes. "After buying a felt hat (known in Greek as a 'republica') ... I changed into mufti and got packed up ready for our journey into the Balkans." (Danchev(ed), 37) On the 19th, in Salonika they boarded the train for Sofia, via Niš. "At Skopje, Lawrence, our Vice-Consul, joined the train. ... Lawrence told us that sentiment in that part of Yugoslavia is still strongly Macedonian and that the population have no very solid national feeling. Generally speaking however they dislike the Germans intensely and are all for resisting them if it comes to the point of invasion." (Danchev(ed), 38-9) (F. Lawrence was formerly an agent of Section D of the Secret Intelligence Service, and in January 1941 of the Special Operations Executive, which replaced "D" in July 1940. His code name was D/H24. (Vodušek Starič, 56, 430)

On 19 January, the American Minister in Athens, Lincoln MacVeagh, sent a letter to Roosevelt which stated, *inter alia*:

> ...General Wavell has come to Athens not only to discuss with the Greeks the problem of supplying their army, but to seek their aid in the prompt preparation of Salonika for action against Germany, either defensive or offensive, as circumstances may dictate. At the same time, a British Military Mission now in Turkey is trying to influence that country to enter the war on Britain's side without further delay. ...
> .... [Donovan] was planning to go to the Albanian Front, but the British Minister and General Heywood, Chief of the British Military Mission here, were anxious to rush him up to Sofia and Belgrade without delay, believing that the present moment is truly critical and that he might help to give the leaders in these capitals a very timely steer. (Dunlop, 248-9)

On 22 January, Donovan and Dykes had a very comfortable journey from Sofia in a *wagon lit* and arrived in Belgrade at 10:00 p.m. Donovan was immediately set upon by a crowd of reporters and photographers. Dykes made an unobtrusive get-away by the other door of the carriage. Donovan was going to stay with the US Minister, Arthur Bless Lane. (Danchev(ed), 40)

**

Although Donovan contacted American diplomatic officials, the tour was arranged by the British, and focused on British operations centers. His assigned companion, Vivian Dykes, wore civilian clothes, and usually did not stay in the same hotel as Donovan. Rather than hide, Donovan displayed his ties with the British. (Smith, 47-8)

Donovan's visit in Belgrade

Donovan was to go to the Balkans and the Middle East in support of the British plan to create a front against Hitler. (Jukić, 45) Roosevelt had approved Churchill's plan for a Balkan front and the U.S. Minister in Belgrade, Lane, worked hard to promote it. In January 1941, he had been assisted by a special envoy from Roosevelt, Colonel William Donovan. (Balfour & Mackay, 230)

Lane, "learned through the British legation that Colonel William J. Donovan, a Republican politician and successful Wall Street lawyer known to be close to President Roosevelt, was coming to the Balkans and the Middle East on an important mission." (Petrov, 136) "During the entire three-and-a-half-month trip, Donovan depended almost entirely on the second-hand information given to him by British officials of all ranks and positions. ... In general terms, the British sought to create a "Balkan front" against the Axis." (Petrov, 138)

> Lane met Donovan at the Belgrade railroad station on the evening of January 22 and took him directly to his residence. There he was closeted with the presidential envoy for several hours, listening to his outline and evaluation of the current British strategy in the Balkans. ... Lane obtained a fair idea of the role the British assigned to Yugoslavia in their plans. This role was infinitely more important than that envisaged by the State Department or anything Lane himself had imagined. Lane could no longer doubt that Roosevelt had decided to throw the full diplomatic weight of the

United States behind the British policy, thus reversing a much more cautious State Department policy. (Petrov, 142)

> On January 23, accompanied by Lane, he [Donovan] met Prime Minister Cvetković, had a press conference for Yugoslav newspapermen, had lunch with Prince Paul, visited the tomb of the Unknown Soldier at Avala, and had conference with the Croatian leader Vladko Maček and Foreign Minister Cincar-Marković. All events went smoothly except for the meeting with Cincar-Marković, and Lane recorded, not without annoyance, that the latter's attempt to snub Donovan was due to his commitment to the pro-Axis orientation for Yugoslavia. At the end of the day Colonel Donovan was entertained at an elaborate dinner at Lane's residence, followed by an enjoyable poker game. (Petrov, 143)
>
> The next day [January 24], this time accompanied by [American Military Attaché, Col. Louis L.] Fortier, Donovan visited General Pesic [Pešić], minister of war; General Kosić, chief of the general staff; General Simović, chief of aviation; and Admiral Luterotti, chief of naval operations. He inspected the military academy and the general staff school, as well as the 6th aviation regiment, chief preserve of General Mirković who, together with Simović, was the head of the conspiracy. (Petrov, 143) (*)
>
> After that he had a prolonged lunch with British Minister Ronald [Ian] Campbell and his aides, gave informal interviews to American newsmen accredited to Belgrade, and joined the Lanes at a late dinner party. (Petrov, 143)
>
> (*) Conspiracy to overtrow Prince Paul's Government.

When in Belgrade, Donovan was acutely aware that the British Government was no longer satisfied with Yugoslavia's neutrality, as maintained by Prince Paul, but wanted to «encourage» him and his Government to «resist» the Germans. Totally supportive of that British policy, Donovan skilfully promoted it in conversations with the civilian and military representatives he met.

US Foreign Service officers were present during all of his conversations, except for one with Prince Paul. (Smith, 47)   Here are some notes on the meetings with the Premier Dragiša Cvetković, the Regent Prince Paul, the Vice Premier Vladko Maček, and the Chief of Aviation, General Dušan Simović.

* Donovan – Cvetković meeting

> Cvetković assured him that attempts by the Germans to enter Yugoslav territory by force would mean war. Yugoslavia would not permit German war materials or troops to cross its frontiers. (Hoptner, 205)
>
> Although Donovan's mission failed – for the Yugoslavs did not agree to enter the war – it had a psychological side-effect. It led many in Belgrade to believe that he brought from President Roosevelt a moral commitment to supply them with arms and planes as soon as they attacked the Italians. (Hoptner, 205)
>
> Donovan's reports contradict Churchill's comments that "fear reigned" in Belgrade and that "ministers and leading politicians did not dare to speak their minds". (Hoptner, 205n12)
>
> ... Donovan's appearance in Belgrade was upsetting, but Cvetković appeared friendly and cordial. He assured Donovan that the Germans would not invade the Balkans. Hitler, he said, had no immediate designs on either Britain or Turkey but would strike next at the Soviet Union. Cvetković explained that the Serbian part of the Yugoslav population would reject any alliance with the Axis, but the Croats, for their part, would oppose siding with the Allies. Donovan contented himself with telling the prime minister what President Roosevelt had to say about nations that did not stand up to Hitler. (Dunlop, 256-7)

* Donovan – Prince Paul meeting

Because Donovan's trip was formally covered as a mission for Knox's newspaper, *Chicago Daily News,* Prince Paul was so afraid that his conversation might be published in the American press that Donovan had to reassure him repeatedly on this point before he could get the Prince to say anything at all. (Smith, 50)

> Vital to the success of the British plans was the position of Yugoslavia. ... During his stay (January 23-25) Colonel Donovan had a long talk with Prince Regent Paul. ... Prince Paul thought there was

a bare possibility that, under American influence, the Bulgarians might refuse the Germans permission to transit their territory, but, like all other Yugoslavs, he was full of distrust of his neighbor and really expected the Bulgars to yield to Nazi pressure. In the event of a German occupation of Bulgaria, Prince Paul thought the Yugoslavs might fight, but he recognized that they were not united. (Langer & Gleason, 398)

> ... Donovan told the prince of Roosevelt's view. Prince Paul commented that his country might resist the Germans but that he distrusted the intentions of the Bulgarians, and that his own countrymen were hopelessly disunited. The Serbs, Croats and Slovenes were at loggerheads.
> "I talked with Prince Paul, and it was very apparent that he was in difficulty," Donovan said in a speech [on 29 April 1941] after he returned to the United States. "He was working for the unity of his people and he said, 'If the German comes in and attacks us, then we will fight.'
> "I said, if they go into Bulgaria and are on your flank, what will you do:, and he said, 'Then we can do nothing, because Croatia will not be with us.' So there was a man attempting to get unity of his people, not being able to get it because at the crucial moment [he] would find that disintegration he feared, and upon that Germany played." (Dunlop, 257)

Richard Dunlop, who later worked for Donovan, commented on this topic:

> There was no real possibility of Yugoslavia's joining a Balkan entente. At least the regent maintained that his country would remain neutral at all costs and that he would refuse German demands for war material, bases, and the passage of troops through Yugoslav territory. Donovan assured the prince that if the Yugoslavs let the Germans cross their boundaries without opposing them, the United States would not intercede on their behalf at the peace conference after the Allied victory. Donovan was impressed by Prince Paul. (Dunlop, 257-8)

**

It turned out that, two months later, in dealing with the Germans, Prince Paul succeeded indeed in maintaining his country's integrity and sovereignty, disallowing the passage of German troops and materiel through Yugoslavia.

**

Donovan's escort, Col. Vivian Dykes, summarized his conclusion of the Donovan – Prince Paul meeting: "Donovan described Prince Paul as a Serb with an Eton and Oxford veneer, which might influence him strongly to do what he felt was the correct thing by English standards." (Danchev(ed), 41)

> At the end of the mission, a report of Colonel Donovan's views [dated 13 March 1941] had reached the British Foreign Office. Of the Prince Regent he had said: 'While his early training had unfitted him for dealing with people like the Yugoslavs, it had left him with a strong sense of doing the "right thing". He would not like his English friends to think that he had played a mean role.' (Balfour & Mackay, 230; 324n24)

The Prince's English "friends" knew that, for the British policy-makers, the *right thing* was the role which ***they*** had assigned to Yugoslavia, and not that of the Prince Regent.

* **Donovan – Maček meeting**

Years after the meeting, Maček wrote :

> His [Donovan's] mission was to find out the attitude of Yugoslavia in the event of a Nazi military assault on Rumania and Bulgaria. When he asked me this question, I frankly answered that insofar as it depended on me, Yugoslavia would not intervene. I told him further that I had no doubt Great Britain would defeat Hitler in the end, but that *we had to preserve our skins until that British victory seemed assured.* (Maček, 207. Italics added.)

While Maček claimed that the conversation lasted one hour (p. 264), Dykes recorded in his diary: "He [Donovan] had a short time with Macek, Leader of the Croatian Peasant Party, who did his usual trick of removing his collar and tie before receiving him, to emphasise his peasant sympathies!" (Danchev(ed), 41)

According to Dunlop, Maček told Donovan that Germany had been amassing troops on Yugoslavia's northern border; that Yugoslavia had hoped to forestall an invasion until she was able to resist effectively; that it would help if the Soviet–German conflict would break out; and this was imminent. "If the German asks to pass through freely, we will not permit it," Maček told Donovan. (Dunlop, 258)

**

While Donovan was busy on the 23rd of January visiting Yugoslav officials, Dykes "had spent most of the day with Macdonald [British Air Attaché], Dew (First Secretary), and Garron (Second Secretary) giving them news from home and collecting information." (Danchev(ed), 41)

**

Group Capt. A.H.H. Macdonald carefully cultivated contact with General Borivoje-Bora Mirković. the chief executor of the coup d'état of 27 March 1941. Macdonald was authorized to give misleading statements to General Dušan Simović, the nominal leader of the coup, at a secret meeting on the morning of 26 March, the day before the coup. From 27 February 1941, Armand Dew closely collaborated daily with George Taylor, the No. 2 man of SOE, who directed his agents and their local co-operatives in activities leading up to the coup.

* Donovan - General Simović meeting (24 January 1941)

The meeting took place at Zemun, across the Sava River from Belgrade, at the headquarters of Gen. Simović, commander of the Yugoslav air force. Because of the importance of and controversy about the meeting, accounts by several authors are presented.

Historians William L. Langer, former head of the Research and Analysis branch of the Office of Strategic Services (OSS), and S. Everet Gleason commented (in 1953):

> Donovan had ample opportunity, in his conversations with Belgrade politicians and military men, to realize that the chances of Yugoslav intervention were slim indeed. All agreed that their country would fight rather than allow the German transit rights or other concessions that might infringe Yugoslav sovereignty, but a number of them, notably Prime Minister Cvetkovich and Foreign Minister Cincar Markovich, apparently deluded themselves into thinking that Hitler would not disturb the Balkan breadbasket, while General Simovich, later to lead a coup of March 27, was inclined to believe the Nazis would turn on the Soviet Union rather than on Britain or Turkey. (Langer & Gleason, 398)

Planning the invasion of the Soviet Union, Hitler needed "the Balkan breadbasket" and therefore did not want to disturb it, at least for the time being. The British war leaders were acutely aware of the importance of food-stuff and oil supplies from the Balkans. Blocking these supplies to Germany on the Danube River was a long-standing and one of the most important assignments to Section D of SIS and its successor, SOE.

Corey Ford, former Air Force Colonel and former OSS official, stated (in 1970) that

> President Roosevelt sent a personal message to the Colonel [Donovan] in Belgrade, suggesting that some means should be found of impressing the Yugoslavian leaders that
>
>> "the United States is looking not merely to the present but to the future, and any nation which tamely submits on the grounds of being quickly overrun would receive less sympathy from the world than a nation which resists, even if this resistance can be continued for only a few weeks". (Ford, 102-3)

**

The President's message to Donovan implied that the President had expected Yugoslavia's "resistance" to last "a few weeks". It lasted eleven days. Toward the end of the war, before he died, the President did not even actively concern himself with Yugoslavia: she was in the British sphere of interest.

**

> … Learning through private sources that Yugoslav Air Force General Simovic and a group of Serbian officers had formed an underground opposition to Nazi domination, Donovan paid a

clandestine visit to the General at the Air Force headquarters across the river from Belgrade in Zemun. Shortly after his visit, on March 25, the Yugoslav ministers signed the Axis pact in Vienna. Simovic organized a revolution two days later which led to the overthrow of Prince Paul and his government. ... (Ford, 103)

As it is not known whether or not Donovan maintained his own private contacts in Belgrade, the "private sources" mentioned by Ford were probably the SOE operatives and the Legation personnel with whom his escort, Col. Dykes, met. They were eagerly working on the "encouragement" of the opposition to "resist" the Germans. However, the visit was not clandestine. The Air Force units conducted air exercises for Donovan. Who "organized a revolution" of 27 March, and how it was executed is examined in **Part Two.**

Professor David Dilks(in 1972): "General Simović, to whom Colonel Donovan had spoken confidently of Allies' prospects on his visit, became Prime Minister ." (Dilks(ed), 366)

Richard Dunlop, who later worked for Colonel Donovan, wrote (in 1982), without the usual reference to a source:

> Simović told Donovan that he believed concessions to Germany would be deadly and would destroy Yugoslavia's chance to resist invasion. ... *Donovan and Simović talked over Simović's plans for a coup d'état* against the government of Prince Paul. The patriots would strike as soon as the government signed an agreement with the Axis and would place royal authority in the hands of 17-year-old King Peter, *who agreed that Paul had outlived his usefulness.* (Dunlop, 259. Italics added.)

> Donovan was back at Minister Lane's residence for a late dinner party. He briefed naval and military attachés so they could send his reports to Washington by diplomatic pouch, safe from Axis surveillance. He was able to furnish them with a probable timetable for Hitler's move into the Balkans. He said nothing to the minister about what he had learned from Simović... (Dunlop, 259-60)

Whatever Donovan and Simović talked about, one thing is certain: King Peter did not in reality agree that Prince Paul had outlived his usefulness. The young King was not consulted about the coup and had nothing to do with its eventual execution.

Historian Bradley F. Smith wrote (in 1983) about Donovan's role:

> ... He surveyed the Mediterranean area, made an estimate of the situation, and used his journey to assist the British in every way possible . ... Donovan played no part in preparing the coup which toppled the Yugoslav government shortly after his visit. Among his various meetings in Belgrade, he did have a discussion with Gen. Dusan Simović, who later emerged as head of the government which followed the coup, but all that happened during the Donovan-Simović talk was a series of assurances by the Yugoslav general - stronger than those made by any other official in Belgrade – that Yugoslavia would fight if Hitler made *any* offensive move against Greece. Such words were music to Donovan's ears, and he appears to have passed on Simović's remarks to the British. Recent research has made it abundantly clear that Donovan himself took no *active* part in preparing the coup. (Smith, 50-51. Italics in the source.)

> ... Though he [Prince Paul] made no military commitments and still refused passage to German troops, various Yugoslav factions, *aided initially by S.O.E. and later by the British air force attachés in Belgrade,* overthrew the government on 26 [27] March and put Simović in power. The Simović government then tried to snuggle close with the British while making various reassuring noises to the Germans. Hitler was infuriated by the coup and immediately set in motion preparations to smash Yugoslavia as well as Greece. The German invasion and rapid Allied defeat followed in late April. *The consequences were severe: the British were driven from their continental toehold and the Balkans began a four-year period of Nazi hell.* (Smith, 51. Italics added.)

> Donovan deserves only limited credit or blame for what happened in the Balkans. None of the *specific acts* that produced the disaster were caused by him. ... The real significance of Donovan's role in Balkan developments was his work as a reinforcer of British policy. To the degree that the

Balkan policy made the situation worse, some measure of responsibility falls to him. ... (Smith, 51. Italics added.)

Considerable detail concerning Donovan's role was recorded in the diaries of Colonel Vivian Dykes, his escort during their mission, "who bear-led [Donovan] round the Mediterranean." (Danchev) Dykes' diaries were published seven years *after* Smith's book. Some of the evidence, examined herein, shows that Donovan's role was more than that of reinforcer. He was also an advisor on strategy.

In his appreciation of the situation, edited by Dykes, and telegraphed to Secretary Knox on 20 February 1941 – two days before the Anglo-Greek agreement at Tatoi – Donovan wrote, *inter alia:*

> ... I consider present moment offers vital opportunity for decisive action by President in offering services for promotion of Balkan front. ... Mediterranean once cleared will provide lateral communications and put Britain on interior lines. Essential for this purpose that Great Britain should retain foothold in the Balkans. ...
>
> .... Her [Germany's] armies must somewhere be beaten when on the defensive and Balkans offer perhaps the only place for this. To enable Britain to retain her foothold all Balkan countries must be brought into one front with Britain who would supply mainly technical services and troops. ... (Danchev(ed), 58-9)

Donovan's credit or blame for what happened in the Balkans is commensurate with his role both as an reinforcer and a strategist. He urged the British to engage the Germans in the Balkans.

**

Referring to a personal message Roosevelt sent to Donovan in Belgrade, Donovan's biographer Anthony Cave Brown – who claimed to have been given "complete access to the Donovan papers and complete editorial freedom" (p. xii) - wrote:

> The telegram obviously constituted something less than an inducement to revolution; nevertheless, it was later asserted that Donovan promised military assistance to Simović if he mounted a revolution against the prince and entered into an alliance with Britain. Of that assertion there is no evidence in the Donovan papers, nor, it seems, was any inducement necessary. For as Donovan related later:
>
>> [Simović was] emphatic in his determination to resist any German infringement on Yugoslav territory. He said that the people of Yugoslavia, if they needed any further lesson, could now clearly see in Rumania [which the Germans had virtually occupied in preparation for Barbarosa] what happened when a country let itself be occupied without resistance. He stated that Yugoslavia would not permit the passage of German troops through its territory, as ... people would not stand for it. **(10)**   (Cave Brown, 156-7)
>
>> **(10)** "Highlights of Conversation Between Col. Wm. Donovan and the Chief of the Aviation, Army General Simović," January 24, 1941. Balkans Trip. vol. 1, CIA Collection (Cave Brown, 843)
>
> Moreover, General Simović also assured Donovan that the Yugoslav Army would fight the Germans if either Greece or Bulgaria was invaded by the Germans, as such an invasion would constitute "intolerable dangers". (Cave Brown, 157)

The biographer continued:

> There would also be a powerful school of thought that the upset in Hitler's timetable was caused by Donovan's assurances to Simović. Donovan always denied that he gave any assurance to Simović; nevertheless the protagonists of the idea were able to present such formidable evidence to support the case that there is no reason to doubt that Donovan set light to the fuse that led to Simović's coup d'état – the event that led Hitler to march into Yugoslavia and Greece and to postponement of the Barbarosa D-Day. (Cave Brown, 157-8)

While the coup in Belgrade precipitated Hitler's attack on Yugoslavia, his attack on Greece was totally unrelated to the coup.

Thomas F. Troy, former CIA staff officer and analyst, presented a different view of Donovan's *lighting the fuse that led to the coup:*

> Bulgaria and Yugoslavia were critical points because of their exposed position vis-à-vis German moves to the southeast. ...
> ... Yugoslavia provided him [Donovan] with another celebrated event, this time alleged responsibility for the anti-Nazi coup pulled off in Belgrade shortly after he left the country. Donovan wrote "No" to this charge, and Langer and Gleason concluded: "There is no evidence ... to show that either American or British influence played *an important part* in this dramatic overturn." Even so, the occasion was grist for the Nazi propaganda mill. **(38)** (Troy, 85. Italics added.)

> **(38)** Donovan's "No" is written opposite the statement: "There is no doubt that it was entirely due to the line he took in Yugoslavia that General Simovic was persuaded to eject the then pro-German Government," which appears in "British Relations with OSS," OSS Records, job 62-271, box 29, folder 2 (typescript, 1). (Troy, 223n38)

Contrary to Langer's and Gleason's conclusion, it will be shown that British influence played a vital part in the coup.

Donovan's British escort, Colonel Vivian Dykes:

> Donovan had interviews with the Minister of War, Chief of Staff, Minister of Marine, and Head of the Air Force and visited the aerodrome. Simović [Air Force] impressed him very favourably and the Yugoslav Air Force though small seemed very efficient indeed. Simović is all out to fight the Germans at the first possible opportunity; he is said to be going to succeed the present Minister of Air very shortly." (Danchev(ed), 41)

Although *Donovan always denied that he gave any assurance to Simović,* and although Simović was probably not *entirely and solely* persuaded by Donovan, Donovan's statements and Roosevelt's telegram were reinforcing British policy and thus adding to Simović's persuasion of the need to *eject* Prince Paul's government. "In February 1941, he [Donovan] saw the issue purely in terms of assisting Britain, and despite much talk of democracy, he was prepared to deal with nearly anyone who might improve the position of the United Kingdom." (Smith, 49) Allegations that Donovan steered Simović toward the coup are found in OSS Records. See above). Awareness of the disastrous consequences of the coup for the people and state of Yugoslavia could have been reason enough to disclaim the steering. For the sake of historical truth and fairness to this great American patriot, Donovan's influence toward the Belgrade coup should be re-examined and verified - if that is at all possible.

Donovan's visit with Simović at his headquarters in Zemun, lasted "about 45 minutes". (Dušan Simović Collection, Box 1, Folder 9, Hoover Institution Archives) During such a long period for serious discussion a lot could be said, more than a series of assurances mentioned by B. Smith. As shown above, varying accounts were given probably because the conversation was not recorded. Accounts by some authors are presented above. However, Simović left his own accounts of the meeting which are excerpted below.

* **General Simović's own account of the meeting with Donovan, written in exile**

According to a summary of Simović's account of the "conversation with the emissary of the President of the United States of America", written in exile:

Escorted by the American Military Attaché, Col. [Louis L.] Fortier, Col. Donovan visited Simović in his office in Zemun between *circa* 11 a.m. and noon, on the 23rd of January, 1941. [It was actually on the 24th.] After the usual exchange of thoughts, Donovan asked his opinion on the situation in Europe.
    Simović first informed Donovan: The Yugoslav officers, procuring air force materiel in Germany, for 1941 foresee Hitler's move south-east, through Turkey and the Middle East, in

order to conquer India. In favor of such a move and goal – they point out – is tremendous superiority of the German war machine and the German-Soviet Pact of August 1939. As for Yugoslavia – they think – Hitler is ready to protect her interests against Italy's unjust pretensions, and to satisfy Yugoslavia's just aspirations, without requesting any favors and sacrifices. (Simović(44), 7)

Then Simović gave Donovan his own views: That the Soviet Russia always presents the greatest threat and danger to Hitler's Germany; she can plunge a sword into Germany's heart at the moment when Germany least expects it and is over-stretched in the south-east direction. As long as a strong and highly-populous and vast Russia should find herself unconquered at the open flank of Germany, all Hitler's conquests are temporary. He can not secure the domination of Europe, and even less of the world, as long as he does not defeat Russia. Every excessive stretching out of German forces in the south-east direction to conquer India would damage that goal. Every delay in attacking Russia would give her time to get stronger and ready to repulse that attack. (Simović(44), 7-8)

Accordingly, Simović expressed his conviction: 1 - Hitler will attack Soviet Russia, his principal enemy, at the latest by May of 1941; the main attack will be directed through Ukraine, with the goal of seizing the harvest, mines, and industrial regions in Southern Russia and the oil sources in the Caucasus. 2 – The attack on Russia will be preceded by entry of German troops into Bulgaria, by the attack on Turkey, and the conquest of the Near and Middle East in order to secure his right flank of the front in Russia and to capture the oil sources in Mosul, Baku and Batum. Therefore, the conquest of India is not Germany's goal. 3 – To achieve those objectives, Germany must conquer Yugoslavia willy-nilly, by right or might. (Simović(44), 8-9)

Then Donovan asked Simović about Soviet Russia. Whether she would be able to withstand Hitler's attack, and what were Hitler's chances for victory? In a lengthy answer Simović replied: Initially, there would be deep German penetration, to Moscow, and even to the Urals. However, the rains, the winter, lack of roads, water-soaked ground, and deep snow would make the motorized units immobile. The logistics for a huge front from the Baltic to the Black Sea will be the greatest difficulty for the Germans. That will be the time for the Russians to engage in their traditional conduct of war. "Hitlera stoga ocekuje ista sudbina kao Napoleona 1812, samo mozda gora, ukoliko Nemci dublje prodru u Rusiju u toku leta svojim motorizovanim kolonama, … " ((The same fate is awaiting Hitler as it did Napoleon in 1812, only even worse, in as much as the Germans penetrate deeper into Russia with their motorized columns during the summer.)) (Simović(44), 9-10)

At the end of the conversation, Simović added that the attack on Russia will help England. The main goal of the policy of Great Britain will be thereby achieved: to unite the largest human reservoir – Russia, with the largest material reservoir – America and the British Empire. It was clear who will come out as the winner. "Ja mislim da će Saveznici tući Hitlera onim istim sredstvima - tenkovima i avijacijom, kojima on sada pobeđuje sve." ((I think that the Allies will defeat Hitler by those same means – the tanks and aircrafts, with which he is now defeating all.)) (Simović(44), 10)

**

Although William Stephenson, "The Intrepid", was active in New York from June 1940 to influence the American public opinion in favor of aiding Great Britain, by 24 January 1941 there was no certainty of his success. True, Harry Hopkins told Churchill, a couple of weeks earlier,

> The President is determined that we shall win the war together. Make no mistake about it.
> He has sent me here to tell you that at all costs and by all means he will carry you through, no matter what happens to him – there is nothing that he will not do so far as he has human power." … (Churchill(GA), 22-3)

However, Simović did not know this, the average American did not know this, and the American public opinion at that time was strongly opposed to the USA's engagement in the war. The Soviet Union was allied with Germany, and Britain – USA were not yet "Allies". Also true, by 24 January, Germany was strengthening her forces in Rumania, but the British expected – correctly – they would be used for the invasion of Greece.

Simović reportedly told Donovan that *Hitler would attack the Soviet Union at the latest by May 1941, and that the Allies will defeat Hitler.* Was Simović's prediction a case of prescience, prophecy – or of using the hindsight of 1944 as his foresight in 1941?

At Simović's insistence for a speedy delivery of US arms to Yugoslavia, Donovan wondered how the arms would be used, and asked the General: ((Will Yugoslavia go with Hitler or not?)) "Hoće li Jugoslavija ići s Hitlerom ili ne?" Simović replied:

((What are the intentions of our responsible factors I do not know and I can not tell you. But I can assure you that the Yugoslav people will never abandon their true friends and Allies and go with Hitler, even if that should be against the will of the leading factors.))
"Kakve su namere naših odgovornih faktora ne znam i ne mogu Vam reći. Ali mogu Vas uveriti, da jugoslovenski narod neće nikad napustiti svoje prave prijatelje i Saveznike i poći sa Hitlerom, makar to bilo i protiv volje vodećih faktora." (Simović(44), 10)

Following the conversation, Simović took Donovan and Fortier to the airport to inspect the units and to watch the fliers' exercises. Simović concluded his story:

((After the March 27th, I got a telegram from Colonel Donovan from America of the following content: "I remember our conversation of 23 January. *Congratulations.* Greeting – Donovan.))
"Posle 27 marta, dobio sam depešu od pukovnika Donovena iz Amerike sledeće sadržine: "Sećam se našeg ragovora od 23 januara. *Čestitam*. Pozdrav - Donoven." (Simović(44), 11. Italics added.)

**

If Simović expected Germany to attack the Soviet Union in May 1941 – as he reportedly told Donovan - why did he not wait with the coup until **after** the attack, when the German war machine was deeply involved, and her chances of crushing Yugoslavia were weaker?

**

Now from

* **Simović's account of the meeting with Donovan, as given in Belgrade, in July 1951,**

to the *Institut za istorijska pitanja(The Institute for Historical Inquiries),* after his return to Belgrade. *Institute's* question No. 4 was related to his meeting with Colonel W. Donovan, and here isSimović's answer (translated):

((ad 4.Colonel Donovan, special emissary of US President [Franklin Delano] Roosevelt, visited Belgrade in January 1941. He had an audience with the Prince Regent and then visited Prime Minister Dragiša Cvetković, Minister of the Army and Navy, General Petar Pešić, and the Chief of the General Staff, General Petar Kosić. It is unknown to me what the mission of Colonel Donovan was, or the [subjects of] talks he held with the Prince, Cvetković and Pešić, and in the General Staff quarters. As much as I could judge from his conversation with me, I think that he was not satisfied with those talks.
((To free themselves from him, those officials directed Colonel Donovan to me, to visit the airport and Air Force units. I received him in my office in the new building of the Air Force Command. With him was the American military attaché, Lt. Colonel Fortier. After expressing [his] first impressions in Belgrade, Colonel Donovan asked for my opinion about the situation on the borders of Yugoslavia and Hitler's eventual intentions. In a rather lengthy exposition I stated to him my anticipations of Hitler's grandiose plan for subduing the world, which basically included:
((- The intention to conquer the Balkans, the Near and Middle East, and the oil sources in Iraq and Iran;
((- The inevitability of the attack on Soviet Russia, with which he would unite against himself the largest stock of manpower with the largest material resources;
((- The inability of Hitler's war machine to win a victory, due to climate conditions and the huge size of Russia.
((Explaining to him the dangers of our situations and the insufficiency of our forces for a decisive defense, I insisted that America send us, promptly, help in armaments, especially in airplanes and arms for anti-aircraft and anti-tank defense.

((With [head] nodding and facial expression, Colonel Donovan was showing that he was agreeing with my explanation, but he made no proposals at all, he was not even trying.

((After that, I took Colonel Donovan to the airport. ... I also took this opportunity to tell him of our needs for urgent assistance in armaments and I insisted on his personal engagement. Thereupon, looking me straight in the eyes, he posed the question: **"And on which side will Yugoslavia fight in the case of war?" I did not expect this question and was surprised, but my heart replied without meditation: "I do not know what those higher in authority think, but I can tell you only one [thing]: that our people will never betray our friends and allies from the past war." ...**))

((After March 27th, 1941, I received a telegram from Washington: "I remember our conversation of January 20th. Greeting, Donovan."

((Colonel Donovan had no conversation with the Air Force Brigadier Bor[ivoje] Mirković, and did not even see him. General Mirković, as my aide, was busy with administrative matters in the Air Force Command.)) (Simović(51), 6-7. Bold type in the source.)

**

It is important to note that his answers to the Institute were not published in Yugoslavia during his life, but in America, almost six years after his death. There were no «*congratulations*» from Donovan is this document, as shown in the preceding description. Also, the «Yugoslav people» was replaced with «our people».

**

Speaking "without meditation" "*.... our people will never betray our friends and allies from the past war*" ... Simović acted in contrast to the advice President George Washington had given to the people of the United States in his Farewell Address:

... nothing is more essential, than that permanent, inveterate antipathies against particular Nations, and passionate attachments for others, should be excluded; and that, in place of them, just and amicable feelings towards all should be cultivated. The Nation, which indulges towards another an habitual hatred, or an habitual fondness, is in some degree a slave. It is a slave to its animosity or its affection, either of which is sufficient to lead it astray from its duty and its interest. ...

... a passionate attachment of one Nation for another produces a variety of evils. Sympathy for the favorite Nation, facilitating the illusion of an imaginary common interest, in cases where no real common interest exists, and infusing into one the enmities of the other, betrays the former into a participation in the quarrels and wars of the latter, without adequate inducement or justification. ...
(http://www.earlyamerica.com/earlyamerica/milestones/farewell/... 5/24/10)

Simović should have meditated: "*... an habitual fondness [of a favorite Nation], is in some degree a slave ... Sympathy for the favorite Nation, facilitating the illusion of an imaginary common interest ...*"

Because France had been defeated in June 1940, Turkey's Government considered the Anglo-Franco-Turkish Pact of 19 October, 1939, non-binding. Although Great Britain was still in the war, the Turks remained neutral. Turkey thus spared her people the terrible destructions of war. Simović behaved as if Britain were an Ally of Yugoslavia – although there was no Alliance and there were no mutual obligations.

At the end of the war "*the friends and the allies from the past war* "mightily assisted the Communists to install a system in Yugoslavia which the Western Allies did not want in their own countries.

**

Some time after Donovan's departure and the coup, it was discovered that Simović had also met an American army general staff representative in Planica, Slovenia. (Jukić, 60)

**

The above-reported conversation between Simović and Donovan makes one wonder: On January 24, 1941, the General spoke of Germany's losing the war against the Soviet Union *due to climate conditions.* Did he, in January 1941, indeed foresee the unusually harsh winter which greatly contributed to Germany's defeat ? Donovan's reported question as to which side Yugoslavia would fight on, and Simović's reported answer, appear to have been so important to Simović that he had empasized them in his typescript – so they deserve special attention.

To be loyal to friends and allies from the past is an admirable quality. Yet, in international relations, when the destiny of one's country is at stake, it is the mind, not the heart, which ought to be the guide: a cool, objective analysis of reality, and not feeling without reasoning.

Simović could not have been more loyal to Britain and the British people than was Prince Paul.

Alleged *"White Russian Prince"* was a British Knight of the Garter

> He had been educated at Oxford and before becoming Prince Regent had spent much time in England, ... , where he had many friends. His two sons were born in this country and he always spoke English at home with his wife and family. His children had English nurses and went to school in England. His wife's sister was the Duchess of Kent. Even the palace he had reconstructed for his official use was built in Adam style. Excellent French speaker and scholar tough he was, he seemed most at home in our own language which he spoke and wrote faultlessly, and with a style and polish I envied. (Parrott, 95)
>
> When he learnt of the assassination of his cousin, King Alexander, in 1934, his first action was to send a telegram to the British Minister, Sir Neville Henderson, then on leave, urging him to return at once. ... Prince Paul was on terms of personal friendship not only with Henderson and Sir Ronald [Hugh] Campbell, his successor, but also with other members of the staff nearer his age such as first secretaries 'Jock' (Sir John) Balfour and (Sir) Terence Shone. He even set up a direct telephone line with the Embassy. ... When I compare what Prince Paul told me at the time, or has told me since, with what was reported in official documents by the British Legation to the Foreign Office, I can see that he must have kept few secrets from successive British Ministers. They knew what was in his mind, and understood and appreciated his attitude. He even refused to permit our Legation to be subjected to the police supervision which was imposed on other missions in Belgrade. This was incautious of him because partly, no doubt, thanks to his tolerance *S.O.E. agents in Belgrade were able to complete their plans to overthrow him in 1941 and remove him from Yugoslavia without hindrance.* (Parrott, 95-6. Italics added.)
>
> «His [Prince Paul's] own personal preference was strongly with the British; he enjoyed our culture, our history and hid friends were British, including several politicians.» (Glen(B) 41)

Under Prince Paul's direction, on 20 May 1939, 7.34 gold ingots – worth $47,000,000 . was transferred from Yugoslavia to the Bank of England.

Accused by his opponents at home of being a "White Russian Prince", he was actually a British Knight of the Garter. Still, the Prince's loyalty to Britain could not stand in the way of reality which showed him that Yugoslavia could «resist» Germany for about two weeks at a tremendous loss of lives and property and the destruction of the state. In spite of his genuine feelings for the welfare of Britain, he was honor-and-duty-and-legally-bound to protect the interests of the country for which he was the Regent..

Simović behaved differently. Did he really expect to receive *prompt help in armaments, especially in airplanes and arms for the anti-aircraft and anti-tank defense,* upon which he reportedly insisted with Donovan? If he did, he was mistaken.

British arrangements for Donovan's mission

As Thomas Troy pointed out, throughout his travels Donovan met and talked with several military and naval intelligence people, and with all kinds of specialists on all subjects that pertained to winning the war. Did he have contacts with the Secret Intelligence Service and the Special Operation Executive agents?

> The former [SIS] was paying the bill for his travels, and Dykes regularly contacted the passport control officer [PCO]. In Athens this was the man named «Edge». In Sofia Donovan «met Smith-Ross, our P.C.O. there and brought him back for a talk in the hotel.» In Belgrade, Dykes had «a long talk with [Robert] Lethbridge the P.C.O. ... and discussed with [the Air Attaché] MacDonald the D. organization [Section D of SIS] which was apparently in a very bad state in [Lt. Col. Laurence] Grand's time but now shows some sign of improvement. This corroborates what Alec Ross told me in Belgrade.» Back in Athens, Dykes had «a long talk with Forbes ... about our C. and D. organization [SIS] in the Balkans with which he is profoundly dissatisfied like everyone else I have talked to in these parts.» (Troy, 87)

Lethbridge became chief 'Passport Control Officer' in Belgrade in 1940. ... He is suspected of some involvement in encouraging the coup d'état that unseated Yugoslavia's Prince Regent in March 1941 and precipitated the Axis invasion. ... In 1942 he was sent to North America to help recruit émigré Yugoslav left-wingers for infiltration to Tito's Partisans. (Some personalities in SIS operations in Yugoslavia www://oocities.org/sebrit/personalities2.html 9/18/12)

«C» refers to the Secret Intelligence Service, and «D» to its section [for Destruction]. The PCOs were the SIS personnel. As stated by Troy, SIS was covering the cost of Donovan's travels. In Sofia, Donovan talked directly with the local PCO. Dykes had a long talk with the PCO in Belgrade, where SIS agents were establishing contacts between local people and SOE agents. In London, before his journey, Donovan met the leaders of SOE. In Belgrade, Dykes also discussed the situation with the Air Attaché who had solid contacts with the conspirators. Because the British had full confidence in Donovan, and in turn he was so willingly promoting their goals, it is logical to expect that Dykes was sharing with Donovan at least some information obtained from his contacts with the SIS and SOE agents and/or other British personnel in Belgrade.

**

At 6:40 a.m. on 25 January 1941, Donovan and Dykes reached the Belgrade airport. «The Yugoslav civil air line produced free of charge for Donovan a very nice Lockheed 14 in which we took off at 7.00.» They went to the Albanian front. (Danchev(ed), 41) After they left Belgrade, Minister Lane sent a message, «personal for the Secretary [Hull]». Excerpts:

> On January 25, Bliss Lane reported to Secretary of State Cordell Hull on the Donovan talks. «From remarks made by Prince Paul, Cvetković and Maček,» he wrote, «... it is clear that [the] Yugoslav Government is ... determined to protect its territory against attack.» (Jukić, 46)

The Yugoslav Government repeatedly confirmed a determination to protect Yugoslavia's borders.

Assessments of Donovan's visit in Belgrade

On 28 January 1941, Churchill wrote to Roosevelt about Hopkins' and Donovan's missions:

> ... It has been a great pleasure to me to make friends with Hopkins, who has been a great comfort and encouragement to everyone he has met. One can easily see why he is so close to you. Colonel Donovan also has done fine work in the Middle East. (Churchill(GA), 26)

However, in his *History of the Second World War*, Churchill's record for posterity of Donovan's visit in Belgrade was brief and non-revealing:

> At the end of January, 1941, in these days of growing anxiety, Colonel Donovan, a friend of President Roosevelt, came to Belgrade on a mission from the American Government to sound opinion in Southeastern Europe. Fear reigned. The Ministers and leading politicians did not dare to speak their minds. Prince Paul declined a proposed visit from Mr. Eden. There was one exception. An air force general named Simovic represented the nationalist elements among the officer corps of armed forces. Since December his office in the air force headquarters across the river from Belgrade at Zemun had become a clandestine centre of opposition to German penetration into the Balkans and to the inertia of the Yugoslav Government. (Churchill(GA), 158)

Prince Paul was cautious because of Donovan's cover as a representative of Knox newspaper.

Professor B. Smith noted that Donovan "appears to have passed on Simović's remarks to the British". (Smith, 51) On the crucial event that determined the fate of Yugoslavia and her people in World War II, Smith stated:

> ... Though he [Prince Paul] made no military commitments and still refused passage to German troops, various Yugoslav factions, *aided initially by S.O.E. and later by the British air force attachés in Belgrade,* overthrew the government on 26 [27] March and put Simović in power. The Simović

government then tried to snuggle close with the British while making various reassuring noises to the Germans. Hitler was infuriated by the coup and immediately set in motion preparations to smash Yugoslavia as well as Greece. The German invasion and rapid Allied defeat followed in late April. *The consequences were severe: the British were driven from their continental toehold and the Balkans began a four-year period of Nazi hell.* (Smith, 51. Italics added.)

After Donovan's trip to Sofia and Belgrade ...

Having completed the trip to Sofia and Belgrade, Donovan continued his mission in the Middle East in close collaboration with the British.

> Once again in Greece, Donovan was taken to the Albanian front ... Upon his return to Athens (where he stayed at the British legation) Donovan found time to share with [American Ambassador Lincoln] MacVeagh his overall impressions. "He said he believed that Germany would refrain from making any attack on the Balkans," reported MacVeagh to the State Department, "if she were convinced of united opposition on the part of Bulgaria, Yugoslavia, and Turkey, and that despite the forces tending to keep their nations apart, their common desire for American moral support and material assistance might well be sufficient to bring them together should a move in this direction be made by the president. Doubtless such an idea will seem ingenuous to those who have had long experience in Balkan affairs, added MacVeagh cautiously, "but even in the Balkans circumstances alter case, and the immense interest taken hereabouts in the colonel's visit may be a sign that he is not altogether wrong." (Petrov, 143-4)

On 6 Feb. Donovan raised the issue with Eden of what action Pres. Roosevelt could take to assist British diplomacy in the Balkans. (Onslow, 45n136)

> Donovan's further travels took him to Ankara; ... he flew to Egypt, stopping on the way to Jerusalem ... After a night's rest in Cairo, Donovan made a whole-day inspection of the British front in Libya, sending a long message to Roosevelt on February 20, summarizing his impressions and conclusions.
> He wrote that the British "simply must" retain and widen their footholds in the Balkans because this might force Germany to "*abandon the attempt at invasion of England*" and instead "gamble on over-running in a short war not only the Balkans but Turkey as well." In this attack, Germany would be likely to employ a new secret weapon ... and finish the job quickly because the Reich "*wants tranquility and security in the Balkans so as to maintain uninterrupted her supplies of oil, food, and raw materials.*" His conclusion was that the British should not be discouraged by such a threat of a German attack; that, on the contrary, *Yugoslavia, Greece, Turkey, and, if possible, Bulgaria, should be induced to stand together with England.* "Such a joint venture would result in economy of time, of force, and of administration," Donovan pointed out gravely, and advised the president to cooperate with the British in their endeavor to form a "Balkan front". (Petrov, 144-5. Italics added.)

"In Belgrade and Ankara he [Donovan] talked optimistically of the prospects of a Balkan front." (Smith, 48)

**

Conferring with Turkish officials and army leaders, Donovan "brought encouragement from President Roosevelt for Turkey to stand fast against any Axis threats, assuring them that the United States was determined not to see Britain lose the war." (Ford, 103)

However, even with the President's encouragement, Turkey steadfastly rejected any efforts to be drawn into the war.

**

On 11 February,

> the Defence Committee decided to send Mr. Eden, the Foreign Secretary, and Field Marshal Dill, the CIGS, to Cairo and Athens. Throughout this period British intelligence of Greek, Turkish and Yugoslav plans was conspicuously less good than that about Germany's preparations, and it is also clear that Whitehall's hopes of co-operation from these countries were based on wishful thinking. As has been said by the official historian,
>> 'it is indeed surprising that in view of Germany's military record, her vastly superior armaments and her proximity we should have expected the Balkan countries to join the war against her or, if they did, to withstand her. It would appear that in such matters the Norwegian campaign had taught us little.' (Hinsley *et al*, 359-60)

> ... by 11 February, if not earlier, the Enigma had established Greece as the first objective of the German preparations for a large scale Balkan campaign. By its lack of any reference to the transit of stores or personnel or to other preparations for an attack on or through Yugoslavia, the Enigma traffic had left no doubt that *the attack on Greece would come only through Bulgaria*, but the timing of the attack remained unknown.' (Hinsley *et al*, 360. Italics added.)

By this time, the British knew that Germany had not intended to attack or send her troops through Yugoslavia. However, George Taylor and SOE agents were already instructed to prepare for "post-occupational resistance" in Yugoslavia – additional evidence of the British plan to draw Yugoslavia into the war, expecting her occupation.

> Accompanied by CIGS John Dill, Eden left London on 12 February. Bad weather delayed their flight, and it took two weeks to reach Cairo. The talks of mid-January had shown that, by themselves, the British could not match the German force in the Balkans; hence they now hoped to get Turkey, and especially Yugoslavia with her excellent strategic position in the rear of the Italian forces in Albania, to join them in resisting a German attack on Greece. (van Creveld(G), 79-80)

**

Delighted with Donovan's attitude and efforts, the British "showed their appreciation in many ways". The new foreign secretary, Anthony Eden — who replaced Lord Halifax in December 1940 – was particularly appreciative (Smith, 48) Donovan was on his way to Sudan when a message from Eden "asked him to wait in Cairo for the arrival of himself (Eden) and General Dill, ... (Troy, 85) The editor of Dykes' diaries pointed out: "A high point of the trip was Donovan's intersection in Cairo with Eden and Dill, also touring the Mediterranean, for a somewhat similar purpose." (Danchev(ed), 22)

"On the day they were to arrive, Donovan had dinner alone with General Wavell, who then outlined what he intended to tell Eden and Dill." (Troy, 85)

Donovan-Eden meeting in Cairo

On 19 February, about 11 p.m., in Eden's words:

> After supper I had some talk with the Ambassador, read the telegrams from home, and finally had a discussion with Colonel William Donovan. He had been touring the Balkans for the United States Government and was able to give me a first-hand account of recent developments. His blunt speech in those countries had been useful and I was grateful to him for waiting several days to see me. I asked him to send the President a message emphasizing that any action we might take in the Mediterranean would overstrain our shipping resources and inviting him to help if he could. (Eden, 195)

Eden's biographer wrote:

> ... In a brief meeting with the Foreign Secretary, Donovan urged British resistance to German encroachment upon the Mediterranean, not least on the grounds that a passive attitude would be unfavourably received by American public opinion. ... Eden had long been optimistic regarding the extent to which the United States might be drawn back into European affairs and he was only too ready to give disproportionate weight to Donovan's counsel. (Carlton, 172)

> Donovan also sat in conference with Eden, Dill and Wavell in Cairo on 20 Feb. 1941. (Onslow, 45n136) Eden met Colonel William Donovan on 20 February 1941 and asked him to convey a message to Roosevelt requesting help with British overstrained shipping resources in the Mediterranean. (Onslow, 46-7)

**

According to Dykes, there were more conferences that evening, where questions were asked and Donovan answered them. Here are some of his answers:

> The British should make up their own mind as to the course which was best for their ultimate good. If, bearing in mind all the risks run from not being fully prepared, they decide that it is best to

> go into Salonika, let them tell the Greeks so quite plainly and act accordingly. If it is in British interests, it must ultimately be in the interest also of the Greeks.
>
> It is quite certain that Germany will never tolerate Great Britain getting on to the Continent, either now or in the future. Therefore it is best to leap in now while the going is good.
>
> [British support should now be given primarily] to Greece, who is now fighting hard. Britain has kept her in the fight and discouraged her from coming to terms … This policy would be sound *psychologically* for its effect on Germany, and on opinion in U.S.A. Even Turkey would be impressed by this unselfish action. Militarily there might be some risk of a complete debacle, if Greece collapsed completely; but it must not be forgotten that Turkey would indirectly obtain a certain advantage from British support of Greece.
>
> Get her [Turkey] in as an ally now, if possible. One never knows what German pressure and penetration may achieve. Turkish opinion is basically loyal to the British alliance and they take pride in being the "defenders of the gate". Cash in now on this sentiment and it might bring in Yugoslavia and even have some effect on Bulgaria. (Danchev(ed), 59-60; 231n53. Italics in the source.)

Dykes then wrote: "The net result was the dispatch of a telegram to Athens offering to meet and discuss in great secrecy before Eden and Dill went to Turkey." (Danchev(ed), 60)

While Donovan was making various calls during the morning of 20 February, Col. Dykes made "a précis of his final draft of his appreciation. The full text was telegraphed by the American Legation to Washington [to US Secretary for Navy, Frank Knox]". Here are excerpts from that appreciation, prepared at Eden's request:

> … I consider present moment offers vital opportunity for decisive action by President in offering services for promotion of Balkan front. Speedy action is essential. Only if Balkan front is formed can American munitions aid Balkan states, and German move south-eastward be stopped. Without it British may find it impossible to pass to offensive later. I am encouraged to suggest this move by President's recent telegram to Prince Paul and confirmed by admiration of magnificent British achievements in this theatre with very limited means.
>
> … Great Britain holds a salient in Greece and must now plan advance northward against enemy line. Task will be difficult till Mediterranean can be cleared. … Essential for this purpose that Great Britain should retain foothold in the Balkans. For this shipping and naval escort are vital, also aircraft and ammunition for Balkan States. …
>
> In Balkans Germany is doing all possible to disintegrate potential resistance. She wants peace there to keep undisturbed her food and oil supplies. … Her penetration of Bulgaria is doubtless largely dictated by considerations of defence of Romanian oil-fields against British air attack. Germany will stay ready to strike and forestall Britain in Salonika which she herself may need in connection with ore extended operations. … (Danchev(ed), 58-9; 231n52)

Uninformed of *"the end of Sea Lion"*, Donovan continued:

> Assuming all German plans aim at destruction of England it is not enough for England to liquidate Italy in Africa, securing herself in Pacific by naval arrangements in U.S.A. and beat off attack on British Isles. … Blockade and air attack will not complete her [Germany's] defeat. Her armies must somewhere be beaten when on the defensive and Balkans offer perhaps the only place for this. To enable Britain to retain her foothold all Balkan countries must be brought into one front with Britain who would supply mainly technical services and troops. Britain needs American aid to achieve this end. (Danchev(ed), 59; 231n52)

Dykes' diary entry for 20 February further notes:

> Meanwhile, Eden and Dill were discussing with Wavell and Longmore what our policy should be regarding the dispatch of British forces to the Balkans. In the evening Donovan had a long talk with Dill about Balkan policy. I have no doubt he put a good deal of stiffening into Dill in the course of it. (Danchev(ed), 58-9)

Donovan's putting *a good deal of stiffening into Dill* may explain, at least partially, Dill's change of opinion from opposing to supporting military assistance for Greece. One wonders to what extent, then, Donovan and Dill affected the "stiffening" of Wavell, who initially also opposed aid to Greece.

Professor B.F. Smith noted:

> ... By February 1941, the British were convinced that Greece would be attacked but they were still uncertain that Russia would be Hitler's next target. Donovan, for his part, worried only about the threat to Britain and in his reports to Washington never raised the possibility of a German attack on Russia. Obviously, the British were not letting him in on all their secret thoughts, and he was so much under the influence of what they did tell him that he continued to believe England was the focus of all Germany's efforts. (Smith, 49)

"... the colonel never realized that he had missed the crucial point that Germany was then preparing to attack Russia." (Smith, 49-50) According to Simović, on 24 January he told Donovan of "the inevitability of the attack on Soviet Russia". As stated by Dunlop, Churchill told Donovan on 18 December 1940 that Germany would attack the Soviet Union in May.

**

This is an important point and indirectly relates to Yugoslavia as well.

> ... long before any reliable evidence had arisen, he [Churchill] had warned Stalin as early as June 1940 that Germany would turn east, and had told a meeting of senior commanders in October 1940 that she would inevitably attack Russia in 1941. (F.H. Hinsley in Blake & Louis(eds), 421)

Expecting Germany's attack in May, why did the British war leaders not postpone the coup in Belgrade until **after** Germany's attack, when her war machine would be engaged on a massive scale?

**

According to E. Barker, Donovan's report from Cairo, dated 20 February, contained this passage:

> ... it is a truism to say that the will of [the German people] must be broken and her armies must be at some point thrown on the defensive and beaten in the field. The Balkans offer perhaps the only place for such a defeat. The British must then retain a foothold there, and this can only be done by inducing Jugoslavia, Greece, Turkey and if possible Bulgaria to stand together with England. (Barker, 101. 284n34)

Quoting the same passage, Eden's biographer Carlton noted that Churchill was conscious of having received this paper from Donovan. (Carlton, 179)

**

From Dykes' diary for 21 February:

> Donovan had a good talk with Eden after lunch and seemed gratified to find that his ideas were accepted, ... The Greeks had sent an immediate reply accepting the invitation to a conference. Donovan sent a message to the President, at Eden's request, on the need for shipping from the USA. ... In the evening we went round G.H.Q. [General Headquarters] saying good-bye to all. ... Eden had sent off a very laudatory message to the Prime Minister about Donovan, which I think is very well deserved.... (Danchev(ed), 60-61)

**

Donovan's statement of 20 February, that "The British should make up their own mind as to the course which was best for their ultimate good.", supported Churchill's opinion that Greece should be discouraged from coming to terms with Italy. On this subject Dr. Lawlor wrote:

> Churchill wanted the Germans' advance stopped and Greece prevented from making a separate peace. ... The Greeks must not make a separate peace and – Churchill continued to allude to the need to keep them in the field. He maintained that 'sustaining of [the] Greek battle, thus keeping in the field their quite large army [becomes] an objective of prime importance'; and that 'the massive importance of taking Valona and keeping the Greek front in being must weigh hourly on us.' He did

not think it 'right' for the sake of Benghazi to lose the chance of the Greeks' 'taking Valona, and thus to dispirit and anger them, and perhaps make them in the mood for a separate peace with Italy.' (Lawlor, 178)

Back in London: "... an extremely interesting visitor ..."

Donovan and Dykes left Cairo on 22 February, and traveling via Alexandria-Malta-Gibraltar-Madrid-Lisbon arrived in London on 3 March 1941. Dykes reported in at the Cabinet Offices, met with some generals (including the Director of Military operations, General John Kennedy) and then went home. (Danchev(ed), 61-5)

Donovan's mission, however, did not end on the day of his arrival to London. He was satisfied with his survey, and more supportive of Britain and her prospects than ever. "His reception in London was in some respects even more cordial than it had been in July and December 1940. The colonel had established close American ties with British operations and procedures, and in a sense he was a foreign associate rather than a foreign observer. He had another meeting with Churchill [on 4 March], and, in what must be a nearly unprecedented opportunity for a foreigner, was allowed to address the operations and intelligence directors of the three service ministries on the subject of his Middle Eastern mission." (Smith, 52)

General John Kennedy, A.C.I.G.S. (Operations) – described by Sir Robert Bruce Lockhart as "a shrewd calculator who rarely indulged in speculations about the future" - wrote about this address:

> We had an extremely interesting visitor about this time in the shape of Colonel "Wild Bill" Donovan. ... On 7th March he came by invitation to attend and address a meeting of directors of operations and intelligence from each of the three ministries, and talked about his trip.
> He spoke first of the Balkans. For King Boris of Bulgaria he had the greatest contempt. ... Boris had said to him, 'We feel it a great injustice that nations like Bulgaria, who wish only to live in peace, should be condemned to death.' 'I do not call it sentence of death,' Donovan had answered. 'I call it suicide. If you let the Germans in, we shall not intercede for you at the peace.' He had spoken in the same sense in Jugoslavia, where he had seen the Regent. The small Balkan nations reminded him of children looking into a shop window full of modern toys – tanks and aeroplanes. They all complained that their military equipment was out of date. He had found a general feeling of helplessness everywhere, and a great fear of Communism if Germany did not win the war.
> In Turkey he had been told that Britain had entered the war before she was ready, and that the Turks were determined not to make the same mistake. 'The new Prime Minister of Greece.' he said, 'is not half the man Metaxas was. He is a man of great integrity, but his stomach is weak, both morally and physically.' (Kennedy, 87-8)

The more Turkey refused to enter the war – even with American "encouragement" - the greater the pressure that had to be exerted on Yugoslavia to "join in".

On 9 March, Donovan had another meeting with Churchill and talked with Colville about his Balkan and Peninsular tour. (Colville, 364) "In 1941 [March 9] Churchill paid high tribute to Donovan's 'magnificent work' in the Balkans, telling Roosevelt that he had carried everywhere an 'animating and heart-warming flame." (Barker, 119. 285n28)

Afterward, Donovan surveyed a number of SOE stations in the United Kingdom, and on 11 March Hugh Dalton informed him that, as the Minister of Economic Warfare, he was the man in charge of SOE. (Smith, 52) Sir Frank Nelson gave Donovan a "conducted tour" of selected SOE stations. (Mackenzie, 388)

> ... Under the guidance of ... Sir Frank Nelson, chief of the Special Operations Executive (SOE), Colonel Donovan had been shown the various SO stations, including the propaganda division (later PWE [Political Warfare Executive]) ... , and the sabotage and subversion branch (SO-2) ... It was imperative, he [Donovan] was convinced, to establish an agency in the United States which would prepare for similar unorthodox activities in the event of war. (Ford, 107)

Donovan was shown everything there was to see about British Secret Intelligence as well as Special Operations (SO), ... Sir Frank Nelson, made certain that Donovan was welcomed at stations throughout Britain. (Dunlop, 212)

"... increasing co-ordination of policy and diplomatic activity ..."

> Building upon Colonel Donovan's tour of the Balkans, and Harry Hopkins's extended visit to London, there was increasing co-ordination of policy and diplomatic activity with the United States. Eden attempted to use American diplomatic support and pressure upon both Turkey and Yugoslavia. He also approached the American Ambassadors in both capitals to request that the State Department in Washington try and persuade the President to offer Lend-Lease material to each, rather than channeling it through Britain. ... London continued to urge Washington to encourage Turkey and Yugoslavia 'to work together in resisting outside aggression'. This had the wholehearted support of Lane, who used all opportunities to reinforce the message; the lure of American support for post-war political and geographical readjustments was extended. (Onslow, 45-6)

It was like promising the proverbial pigeon in a tree in exchange for a sparrow in the hand.

An assessment of Donovan's role in the Balkans and Middle East

Sir Douglas Dodds-Parker, a distinguished SOE operative, who "helped to build up SOE", and closely cooperated with Colonel Donovan and his Office of Strategic Services, wrote about the Colonel: "Donovan had paid a visit to some of our establishments in the Summer of 1941. He had been second to none in the previous decade in doing all possible for the cause of freedom, *and more recently of Britain in particular.*" (Dodds-Parker, 103. Italics added.)

> Donovan deserves only *limited credit or blame* for what happened in the Balkans. None of the specific acts that produced the disaster were caused by him. As we have said, he did not create or even contribute to the Yugoslav coup, and he did not play a *direct* part in Britain's decision in early March to sharply increase her forces in Greece. It must be acknowledged that when Churchill urged his cabinet colleagues to send the British army into Greece, he noted that since Donovan had tried to sell the Americans on the Balkan front, Britain could not forsake Greece without it having a "bad effect in the United States". But this was a thin causal thread and without it, the prime minister, who was determined to act, would surely have found another supplemental supporting argument. *The real significance of Donovan's role in Balkan developments was his work as a reinforcer of British policy. To the degree that the Balkan policy made the situation worse, some measure of responsibility falls to him. Without British pressure, "peaceful" German occupation or a shaky satellite status would have* fallen to every Balkan country. As it was, *the British came first*, which led to the panzers and the Luftwaffe. The British, having quickly lost the battle, departed, and the Balkan people were left to face the victorious Germans in the highly unpleasant role of defeated enemies. To the British and to Donovan, it appeared that they had simply gambled and lost; *in retrospect it seems to have been more like irresponsible folly.* Britain never had the strength to stop Hitler in the Balkans, and it is therefore difficult to ignore the point that Prince Paul made to America's ambassador to Yugoslavia, Arthur Lane, in late March 1941. "You big nations are hard," Paul said, "you talk of our honor, but you are far away." (Smith, 51-2. Italics added.)

The Regent could have justifiably added: "You talk about *our honor,* but in doing so you concern yourselves primarily with *your own interests."* Even if Donovan did not play a *direct* part in Britain's decision to increase her forces in Greece, his influential opinion was taken into consideration, and thus he played an *indirect* part. Even *limited* credit or blame is still credit or blame. And if, in retrospect, the British expedition in Greece had been *an irresponsible folly,* then Donovan's advocating and enforcing British policy contributed to that folly.

**

In the years to come, Donovan closely collaborated with the SOE. In 1942, for instance, he assisted SOE in recruiting Communists from Yugoslavia – who were then residing in the USA and Canada – for an SOE-training program at Camp X, in Canada, before they were to be parachuted into Yugoslavia to establish contact with the Communist-led Partisans.

Appendix B - Black propaganda about the British Expeditionary Force in Greece

Eden's biographer David Carlton considered that Eden correctly attributed the influence on events in Yugoslavia to the presence of British troops in Greece. (Carlton, 181) How was that achieved? By combining regular diplomatic and multifaceted clandestine activities, including "black propaganda". One aspect of the latter is outlined below.

Robert St. John, Balkan correspondent for the Associated Press for two years, was in Belgrade during the fateful March-April 1941 events. Describing his experience, the events and atmosphere in Belgrade during that time, he wrote in some detail about the effects of the British troops' landing in Greece. Their arrival was indeed used as the basis for an excellently thought-out, very effective and misleading "black" – i.e. un-attributable-propaganda in Belgrade, skillfully spread by a Greek journalist called Pappas, and those who believed him. The news Pappas was spreading was accepted as truth not only by its targeted domestic confidants, but also by most Anglo-American nationals then in Belgrade. In the words of St. John:

> There was only one gap in the [Axis'] necklace of steel [around Yugoslavia]. That was to the south. The border with Greece. The narrow Vardar valley. They said there were three hundred thousand British troops in Greece waiting to back up the rebellious Yugoslavs. Three hundred thousand British troops with plenty of tanks, planes and munitions. Who said so? Well ... of course it wasn't exactly official. Not exactly. But for three weeks a tall, slim young Greek journalist, Pappas by name, had been shuttling back and forth from Athens to Belgrade. He carried a diplomatic passport and he whispered that he was on a "diplomatic mission." (St. John, 20-21)
>
> While the Cvetkovich government was negotiating with the Axis about signing up, the ubiquitous figure of Greek Pappas slithered here and there. He chose his confidants carefully. Foreign correspondents he felt he could trust. Serbian oppositionists, like the Simovich crowd. A few selected diplomats. It was dangerous business. He was dealing in dynamite. Not the kind of dynamite you use to blow up bridges but the kind of dynamite you use to blow up nations. He had just come from Athens. From "our friends down in Athens," he said, and winked slyly. "You know, *our* friends!" (St. John, 21)
>
> "Our friends" wanted Yugoslavia to know that a hundred thousand British troops had landed at half a dozen different ports in the south of Greece. He even gave us the names of the ports. The blue waters of the Mediterranean were black with ships. British ships. Ships carrying a mighty Balkan army that would help Greece and Yugoslavia defy the Axis, if Yugoslavia only had the nerve to do any defying. (St. John, 21)

Then St. John continued on about his own personal involvement:

> I was one of the correspondents Pappas chose to confide in. I was introduced to him by a reputable, honest British newspaperman whom I knew and trusted. What Pappas said was hot news, because up to then [the first week of March] there had been only vague rumors about British troops landing in Greece. He said I was welcome to use the figures and all the details he gave me if I swore not to disclose where they came from. "Of course," he explained, "I must warn you that the British will deny the story. They will deny if officially, but they will confirm it unofficially. They don't dare to admit it for publication. You can understand why. It would give the Germans just the excuse they may want to attack us. But you can take my word for it that it's all true. The easiest way to check up on the story is to check up on me." (St. John, 21)

> I did. It was too serious a story to put out without careful checking. All of us were bending over backward trying not to fall for anyone's propaganda. I asked some of the boys who had been in Athens all about Pappas. They gave me detailed reports. They were sure he was all right. Fine reputation. Important connections inside the Greek government. Very close to the British High Command. Often was given important diplomatic missions.

...a hundred...two hundred...three hundred thousand troops...and they believed every word ...

> And then I went to the British Legation and asked them flatly how about these landings of British troops in Greece? Officially, they said, they were obliged to deny it. Categorically, in fact. But unofficially ... well ... and they hesitated and smiled. Who gave me the information? Pappas? Well, Pappas was a very reputable man, all right, and he had just come from Athens, and he ought to know what was going on down in Greece. So I sent the story about a hundred thousand British troops in Greece, with planes and tanks and munitions. Then I sent a story about the blue Mediterranean being black with British ships. Later I boosted the number to two hundred thousand and eventually to three hundred thousand, all on the say-so of the Greek Pappas and the unofficial confirmation (but official denial) of the British Legation in Belgrade. (St. John, 22)

And St. John concluded:

> How seriously General Simovich himself took the Pappas reports and how much these reports inspired his *coup d'état* and his defiance of Hitler no one will never know definitely, but weeks later some of his little circle of advisors, ministers, and army officers told me they had believed every word of the reports and had been convinced that at least fifteen British divisions and hundreds of British planes would rush to Yugoslavia's aid when the zero hour came. (St. John, 22)

**

Pappas was not the only Greek in Belgrade spreading black propaganda. The Greek Minister in Belgrade, [Bibica-Rosetti], told Ilija Jukić, the Yugoslav Assistant Foreign Minister, that 200,000 British troops had already landed in Greece. The Yugoslav Minister in Athens, however, reported that, by that time, [the first half of March], scarcely 45,000 British troops of all service branches had arrived. (Jukić(65), 130)

**

The St. John's story continued. --- Germany attacked Yugoslavia by bombing Belgrade on Sunday, 6 April 1941. St. John fled a burning Belgrade in great haste – like most of the foreign correspondents. Eight days later, in Plevlje, he met Captain Obrad Obradović, aide-de-camp to General Dušan Simović, now the head of the new Government who was likewise hurriedly retreating southward toward the Greek border. The Captain was on an important mission for the General. "He was leaving town in a few minutes. We couldn't follow behind him because his car would be racing ahead much faster than our Chevrolet could go. But this was the best route. And he drew it for us on one of our maps." (St. John, 148)

> Then Obradovic wrote out a military pass for each of us, and finally he looked us straight in the eyes and said, "I've done a lot for you and now I'm going to ask you to do something for me." He bent forward while he talked.
> "You know who I am. You know the fix Yugoslavia is in. We haven't had a bit of help from either the British or the Greeks. We're going to go under soon if we don't get it. We need planes and tanks and gasoline. And we have to have them in a hurry. We've got to have real help if they expect us to hold out. We were told that the British had three hundred thousand men and plenty of planes down in Greece. We can't understand why they haven't done anything for us. We can't seem to get in communication with them any more. I want to start out from the Dalmatian coast tomorrow for Greece by power boat and see how quickly I can get in touch with the British. I've got to let them know how desperate our situation really is. ... (St. John, 148-9)

**

Captain Obradović was indeed one of the "Simović crowd", who on 26 March was charged with an intelligence task. "General Simović had assigned Captain Obrad Obradović to watch the offices of the Belgrade police as well as the German "travel bureau". (Ristić, 88) This chance-encounter occurred on 14 April, the same day Gen. Simović empowered Gen. Danilo Kalafatović to sue for armistice with the Germans, and King Peter and his entourage flew from Yugoslavia to Greece. Obradović's lamentation illustrates at least two points: The mighty influence of propaganda, and a great gullibility by those who uncritically believed it.

First, there were not nearly so many British troops and aircrafts in Greece. Then, those who were there simply could not help. Indeed, the British and the Greeks wanted Yugoslavia to help them – and not the other way around. That is why they did whatever was necessary to make Yugoslavia to "come in". Unfortunately, the coup-wishers-and-plotters fell for the British and Greek propaganda, like did so many people who wanted to believe in "our allies".

**

Through great hardship St. John found his way to Greece, and wanted to reach Athens via the Peloponnesus. One day, in his own words:

> As soon as it got dark we found we were in a caravan of hundreds of British lorries. Huge lorries. Lorries packed with Anzac troops. Where they suddenly came from I don't know. When we got on a hill we could look back and see the road black with the parade of British lorries. It suddenly dawned on us what was happening. The British were evacuating Greece! These were some of the three hundred thousand soldiers who had been sent up from the Middle East to help the Greeks and the Yugoslavs. This was the army Pappas had told us about when he was back in Belgrade. But now they were in flight. They were heading south to get ships and sail away. The Balkan War must be nearly over. Greece must be collapsing fast. The parade to the sea had begun. (St. John, 267-8)

"… there had been not three thousand British troops in Greece."

And then St. John realized:

> And that was the first time I found out that there had been not three hundred thousand British troops in Greece; only two divisions. One division of Australians, one division of New Zealanders, and about ten thousand miscellaneous English and Canadian soldiers attached to units like R.A.F., ambulance corps, and headquarters companies. Forty thousand in all, the men told me. Forty, not three hundred. Forty thousand all together. I didn't believe them at first. I asked men in other trucks. I asked dozens of soldiers. I checked up on the figures later in Argos, and still later in Crete, and after that in Cairo. The figure wasn't ever exactly the same. Some said forty-one thousand, some said forty-nine thousand, but they all agreed that there were just two full divisions. And when told them about our figures of one hundred, then two hundred, and then three hundred thousand, they just laughed. (St. John, 268-9)

> I was stunned. Probably just as stunned as the Yugoslavs were when they learned the grim truth. I know, because later I talked to some Yugoslav General Staff officers in Cairo. They told me how stunned they had been. They told me they had believed the officially-denied-but-unofficially-confirmed stories that were sent up to Belgrade about the British strength in planes and men. (St. John, 269)

> Forty thousand. No wonder we hadn't seen any British help for the Yugoslavs. No wonder Yugoslavia was able to hold out only ten days. And no wonder what was left of the British Expeditionary Force was fleeing now toward the sea. Even three hundred thousand men with a real air force would have had a tough job holding back that sea of men and machines that I have seen sweeping down like a wild cascade from Germany through Hungary, Rumania, and Bulgaria into Yugoslavia and Greece. Forty or fifty thousand against millions of German soldiers who had no other job on their hands at the moment than to take the Balkans at all costs. (St. John, 269)

Did the presence of British troops in Greece influence events in Yugoslavia, as Eden claimed? Through deceitful propaganda – and thanks to "the Serbian oppositionists" and "the Simović crowd" - yes, it did. And what about Yugoslav General Staff officers in Cairo? Let us end this story with St. John's words again:

> … We had had a tip that the [Yugoslav] government had left Ilidže, near Sarajevo, the same day we pulled out, on Easter Sunday [13 April1941], and that they had been heading for Nikšic [Nikšić] ….
> We knew there was an airport in Nikšic. We knew that a whole fleet of big planes had recently been flown to the Nikšic airport. Now we discovered that the planes were no longer at the airport. Yes, Simovich and his Ministers, and probably Obradovic too, had disappeared all right. … The government had fled. Yugoslavia was through. It was all over except the carving up. (St. John, 154)

Appendix C - The idea of separation of Southern Serbia

Eden *would stop at nothing to ensure that the Yugoslavs fight to deny passage to Monastir* [Bitolj] *Gap.* For a better understanding of the meaning of Eden's statement and his questions about the Southern Yugoslav army, here is some pertinent background information.

It is shown in **Chapter 9** and **Part Two** that the British Military Attaché, Colonel Charles S. Clarke, had maintained good relations with high-ranking active officers and the reserve officers' association in Belgrade – mostly Serbs - especially after the fall of France in June 1940. Part of his normal duty was to gather information on Yugoslavia's defense strategy and deployment of troops in the event of war with the Axis. The same topic was also broached by Minister Campbell with the Prince Regent. Sharing the views with some high-ranking officers, his official and non-official contacts, Clarke came to the conclusion that it would be wrong to defend Croatia. In reports to the War Office (12-14 November 1940), he stated that the Yugoslav General Staff had two main plans. First – to defend Yugoslavia's frontiers. Second – to concentrate armed forces "for active defence of Serbia". Although this meant the sacrifice of much territory, he thought that the second plan should be adopted.

> The Yugoslav Chief of Staff, [General Petar] Kosić, himself told Clarke that for strategic reasons there was no doubt that the second plan was right, but the government might veto the movement of forces away from Croatia and the army might be forced to adopt the strategically unsound first plan. (Barker, 83; 281n36)

Related to the second plan was an inquiry by a secret government committee in Belgrade.

On 22 November, British Naval Attaché, Captain Max Despard, reported that a "secret [Yugoslav] government committee" was studying the problem of defending old Serbia ... possible retreat and withdrawal ... and "continuing the fight on foreign soil", as in the 1914-1918 war. The committee contacted Miloš Tupanjanin, the acting leader of the British-subsidized (Serb) Peasant Party since July 1940 – known to have a close relationship with the British – and instructed him to approach Despard unofficially to find out whether Britain would be able to supply "at least part of shipping required and organize supply of local shipping" for the evacuation of a force of 300,000 men, probably through Salonika or Kavalla. (Barker, 84; 281n39) This was in line with the second strategy, favored by the British.

Well aware of the impossibility of such shipping and supply, the Foreign Office replied on 23 November that Campbell should urge "a spirit of resistance without too much thought of withdrawal". (Barker 84; 281n40)

As Elisabeth Barker noted: *"British demands – no British aid"*. They were pressing for the second plan but were not capable of supporting it. On the contrary, the British wanted Yugoslavia to support *British* demands.

> In response to a lengthy telegram from the Military Attaché in Belgrade reporting Yugoslavia's increasingly precarious strategic position and her war plans, Pierson Dixon of the Southern Department [of the Foreign Office] minuted that the report 'confirms our supposition that political decisions will militate against the adoption of the right strategic plan in the event of invasion, i.e. the abandonment of Croatia and withdrawal to old Serbia.' (Onslow, 8n19)

Clearly, the second alternative was preferred by the British because it suited their plans for Greece.

To defend the Vardar and Monastir gaps

> Southern Department was already devoting considerable thought of how best to manage Yugoslavia's adherence to the Tripartite Pact: either by maintaining relations with Prince Paul's Government, or by seeking to foster a separatist regime in southern Serbia with the support of the strategically key Southern Serb Army. The British Minister in Athens, Sir Michael Palairet, had already been instructed to co-operate with General Papagos in a joint effort to 'bring about the secession of the Yugoslav Southern Army.' **(#)** (Onslow, 52-3)

(#) [On 24 March] Eden telegraphed from Cairo to report that he, Dill and Wavell were 'agreed there need be no question of disintegrating Yugoslav armies *at present*. But it is of first importance to secure maximum Yugoslav forces to defend the territory of southern Serbia against German forces and in particular to protect the Vardar and Monastir gaps.' He urged Sir Michael Palairet to co-ordinate with General Papagos and General Haywood (head of BRITMILMIS in Athens) to 'get in touch with Yugoslav military commanders in southern Serbia and to co-ordinate plans'. (Onslow, 53n166. Italics added.)

In Professor Onslow's opinion, an authoritarian separatist regime in Southern Serbia – one of the options contemplated by the Foreign Office - would have better served immediate British interests than the democratic government produced by the March 27 coup. (Onslow, 55)

On the subject of involving the Yugoslav Southern Army fighting for Greece, but outside the accepted national strategy, E. Barker wrote:

> ... A few days before the coup, they [the British] had been toying with an alternative scheme. The Greek Commander, Papagos, who was anxious to win over the Commander of the Yugoslav Third Army [General Ilija Brašić] in the extreme South, had sent an emissary to Skoplje to get in touch with him and encourage him to resist the Belgrade government's policy and combine operations with the Greek Army on the Albanian front. The British commander in Greece, General Maitland Wilson, warned Papagos against the danger of disintegrating the Yugoslav army and so playing the German game, but [on 24 March] referred the matter to Cairo. (Barker, 93; 283n98)

So Eden got involved. After the discussion with the Middle East Command, on 25 March ... one day after he instructed Campbell in Belgrade to secretly inform the coup leaders of the British support ... Eden suggested that General Wilson – the Commander of the British forces in Greece - should arrange for British officers to get in touch with the Yugoslav military commanders in southern Serbia to "secure maximum Yugoslav forces ... to defend Vardar and Monastery gaps", "and if possible coordinate plans". (Barker, 93; 283n99)

> The same day, in London, Orme Sargent, at the Foreign Office, "minuted views which clearly reflected ... general tone of pessimism. Noting that 'the prospects of a successful *coup d'état* ... are not very bright,' he said that three different policies would now have to be pursued more or less simultaneously." One of the policies would have to "work for the secession of the Yugoslav army in South Serbia and the creation of a separatist government under its aegis: this 'would give us control of the vital passes to prevent a German attack on the flank of the Greek army.' He noted that the British minister in Greece was already pursuing this possibility with General Papagos." (Stafford(cp), 406)

According to D. Stafford, Campbell's views on this subject did not differ much from Sargent's and Cadogan's:

> In a long analysis sent from Belgrade late on March 25 ... , Campbell reaffirmed that he still regarded an offer of arms to the military as being essential if early success was to be achieved in the creation of an alternative government (civil or military). The army was of paramount importance even if a coup did not take place, because in the last resort it would represent "the only remaining possible form of resistance to the German threat to Greece through Southern Serbia." ... Campbell feared that divisions between the component parts of the kingdom would be exploited, with the Croats and possibly Slovenes likely to push for a separate solution. Therefore, "our efforts must be directed in the main to stiffening Serb resistance the more so as South Serbia is for us and Greece the vital point." (Stafford(cp), 407)

The next day, 26 March, Permanent Under-Secretary Cadogan agreed with Sargent's recommendation. Ultimately, he thought that this policy would be the best, as "the defence of the Greek-Yugoslav frontier is really vital to Greece." (Stafford[cp], 406-7) "The guiding consideration [of the Foreign Office] was to ensure that the Greek flank would not be turned and to secure southern Serbia." (Stafford[cp], 418)

On 25 and 26 March, Papagos, Generals Wilson and Cairo discussed what "financial assistance" or "personal inducement" should be offered to Yugoslav officers or men. (Barker, 93; 283n100)

Simply put: how to bribe them. However, the coup altered this scheme.

On 28 March the British considered that Simovic 'could maintain the unity of the country, in any case in the south'. It was hoped that the Yugoslav army, whose morale was supposed to be high, would stage an offensive against the Italian rear and liquidate them 'in two or three weeks'. The Germans, in the meantime, were supposed to be held up by the 'difficulty of the ground and communications on the Balkan frontier'. Papagos regarded the *coup* as a vindication of his demand to hold on to Salonika, and was eager to push forward the Greek and British forces that had in the meantime occupied the Kaimaktsalan-Vermion-Olympus line. This, however, was not done, possibly because the Greek government under Alexander Koryzis - .... – feared lest the presence of British troops in Salonika would present Germany with a *casus belli,* or because Simovic government continued to vacillate. Thus the allied forces remained split, ... Meanwhile, the Yugoslavs also disappointed Papagos. Not only did a conference between him and the deputy chief of the Yugoslav general staff on 3-4 April result in Belgrade rejecting out of hand proposal to attack in Albania, but the Yugoslavs refused to adhere to Papagos' strategic plan to concentrate the bulk of their army in Southern Serbia in order to prevent the outflanking of the Metaxas line and prevent a link between the Germans and Italians from being formed (a link which would cut them off from Greece). The adoption of this strategically correct plan meant the abandoning of more than 50 per cent of Yugoslavia's national territory, and this was the decision which Simovic and Co. could not bring themselves to make. All they did was to allocate one army – or, rather, one corps – of four divisions for the protection of South Serbia. The rest of the Yugoslav army with its million men and eight armies remained where it was, that is strung out all along the very long frontiers of the Kingdom. (van Creveld, 157-8)

Uncertain of the outcome of the coup, the British were ready to partition Yugoslavia, in order to defend Greece - for British own interests. Enraged by the coup of 27 March, Hitler not only defeated but also dissolved the Yugoslav state by partitioning it.

Appendix D – Ideas for a military coup

In the summer of 1940 there were at least two groups in Belgrade who were considering a *coup d'état:* the Đonović - Trifunović group, and the (Serbian) Agrarian Party, in British sources usually called the Serbian Peasant Party (SPP). Leaders of the second group were Dr. Milan Gavrilović and Dr. Miloš Tupanjanin, the President and his deputy, respectively. On 24 March 1941, Campbell was authorized by Eden to secretly inform any prospective leaders of *British full support.* The story about the Đonović - Trifunović group first.

The Đonović - Trifunović group

In early 1940, Lieutenant Alexander-Sandy Glen - an agent of Section D of the Secret Intelligence Service (SIS) - joined the British Belgrade Legation under cover of the Assistant Naval Attaché. In early April 1940, "The Chief" of his "Show" - George Taylor, Chief of the Balkan Unit of Section D – visited Belgrade in utmost secrecy, "and proceeded to hold several meetings with Sandy and other members of the British community whom, in my innocence, I had hitherto regarded as ordinary businessmen" – wrote three decades later baron Julian Amery. (Amery, 158)

Julian was the son of Leopold "Leo" Stennett Amery, the Secretary of State for India, "a close friend of Churchill" (Barker). Julian also worked for some months for Section D, but officially was the Deputy Press Attaché, and on the payroll of the Legation. (Amery, 139, 184)

Amery wrote that "The Chief" was interested in the situation in Albania. As Glen had no knowledge about it, he asked Amery for assistance, and Amery successfully complied and "concocted a short memorandum". He explained the situation:

"Now it so happened that Lawrence Grand [the head of Section D] and the "Chief" had set their hearts on organising a revolt against the Italians in Albania. They believed that it would tie down large numbers of Italian troops and weaken Italy's ability to wage war." (Amery, 159-60)

" 'D' Section was authorized to prepare plans for a revolt in Albania and to open communications with potential Albanian centres of resistance." Consequently, Julius Hanau – the head 'D' man in the Balkans – was then instructed to engage Amery for this project. (Amery, 160)

On the advice of Jacob Altmaier – about whom more will be said in this story – Amery went to consult Jovan Đonović [code-named "Monkey"]. "Djonovitch had at one time been leader of the Republican Party in Yugoslavia. Later on, however, he accepted an invitation from King Alexander to become Minister in Tirana for the specific purpose of countering the growth of Italian influence in Albania." (Amery, 162)

Đonović had ties with some Albanian refugees in Yugoslavia who were subsidized by the British. (Barker, 48) When Amery approached him for advice related to the Albanian affairs, Đonović steered the conversation to Yugoslavia. Here are excerpts from Amery's detailed description of their first meeting:

> I told Djonovitch about our Albanian problems but he brushed them aside. Albania, he said, was no longer the issue. The issue was Yugoslavia itself. Then, ... , he began to analyse his country's political situation. The Serbian people in their great majority were bitterly anti-German. The German was their traditional foe. They were pro-British because Britain has been Serbia's ally in the First World War and one of the founders of Yugoslavia. They were pro-Russian and, in their hearts, still looked on the Russians as the protectors of the Slavs. These were the true feelings of the people and of their representatives in the Political Parties, the Army, the Patriotic Societies and the Church. (Amery, 174)

It should be noted here that Đonović talked specifically about the Serbian people, the Serbian political parties and patriotic organizations, and the Serbian Orthodox Church – without giving the visitor his views on the non-Serbian political parties and institutions. Then he continued giving Amery his views:

> Even if they wanted to, the Yugoslavs could not do a deal with Germany. Whether they fought or surrendered, the Germans were bound to carve Yugoslavia up to meet the claims of Italy, Bulgaria and Hungary. But, if they surrendered without fighting, the soul of the nation would die; and even if

the war ended in an Allied victory they would never be able to put the country together again. Honour was the soul of the nation. Serbia had survived five hundred years of Turkish domination because she had never given in. But Prince Paul's policy could only lead to capitulation. We [the British] were wrong to put our faith in this White Russian Prince. Paul was no hero and no leader. He had no following among the people. Of course, he was clever enough and was playing for time. But every concession he made to the Germans carried the moral disintegration of the country a stage further. 'The Prince,' said Djonovitch, 'is already an unconscious agent of the Germans. You will soon find him a conscious one.' (Amery, 174-5)

Đonović's assumption that Germany would carve Yugoslavia up to meet the territorial claims of Italy, Bulgaria and Hungary, whether Yugoslavia "fought or surrendered", should be evaluated in light of the reality that followed. Hitler asked Hungary and Bulgaria to cooperate in the liquidation of Yugoslavia - promising them slices of her territory – only **after** the military coup of 27 March (van Creveld, 147-8) – not before it. Hungary joined the Tripartite Pact on 20 November 1940, and Bulgaria on 1 March 1941 – long **after** Đonović talked with Amery. Without the coup of 27 March, the events which unfolded would have taken a different direction.

Amery continued:

> Djonovitch now told me that he had been in consultation with Birchanin for several days. They had examined every possible course of action and had come to a solemn but radical conclusion. The only way to save their country from capitulating to Hitler was to overthrow Prince Paul's regime by a military coup d'état. *Birchanin had taken sounding among his friends in the Army* and was satisfied that the job could be done. *Several senior officers*, indeed, were already pressing him to give a lead. (Amery, 176. Italics added.)

> Djonovitch, for his own part, had also discussed his analysis of the situation, *though not his conclusions,* with the chief men in the Opposition parties. They shared his views and would all be prepared to serve in a Government of National Unity. (Amery, 176. Italics added.)

Thus, according to baron Amery: Birčanin and some of his friends in the Army were in favor of a military coup;
    the political opposition leaders – with whom he talked - agreed with Đonović's analysis;
    however, he did not tell them of his radical conclusion – the need for a military coup – so they did not endorse the idea.

Amery proceeded :

> He [Đonović] wanted no material support from Britain for what was to be done in Yugoslavia. But he needed our moral support and wanted to know that we should treat the Revolutionary Government as friends. He would also need our help in Bulgaria. He and his friends could do little to organise the Opposition in Sofia while they were still in Opposition themselves. this, like the preparation of a revolt in Albania, would be a task for Britain. ... He asked me to come again next day at the same time when Birchanin would be with him. (Amery, 177)

The next day, Amery met Trifunović-Birčanin and later recorded:

> He and his friends were ready to do the job and *put a true Serb at the head of the Government*. All they wanted to know that, in our hearts, whatever we might say officially, we were with them. (Amery, 178. Italics added.)

Amery did not provide the dates of the meetings. However, as they followed George Taylor's secret visit to Belgrade in early April of 1940, the meetings likely took place in late April or early May. That was some time **before** the following events occurred:
    on 22 June 1940 - the Franco-German armistice was signed;
    on 17 September – the British realized that Germany's intended invasion of Britain had been postponed;
    on 27 September – the Tripartite Pact among Germany, Italy and Japan was signed;

on 28 October – Italy attacked Greece from Albania; German-Yugoslav negotiations began in November.

Therefore, none of these events could have inspired Đonović and Birčanin – which leads to the conclusion that internal domestic affairs and their personal agenda – and not the foreign policy issues - had motivated them for a military coup.

Furthermore, according to J. Amery: In order to execute the coup, they would have needed Britain's *moral support and friendly treatment of the ensuing Government, assurance that Britain was with them.* In other word: without such support and recognition - there would be no military coup.

**

And that was what actually happened: the coup was executed three days **after** Foreign Secretary Anthony Eden – on 24 March 1941 - instructed his Minister in Belgrade, Ronald Campbell: *"Any new Government formed as a result of these events and prepared to resist German demands would have our full support. You may secretly so inform any prospective leaders in whom you have confidence."* (Eden, 227)

How the *military coup d'état* was executed is examined in **Part Two**.

**

Now back to J. Amery's description of the events... After hearing the idea of the coup, the more he thought about it, the more he liked it.

> I could, indeed, see objections from a Yugoslav point of view. ... But from a British point of view, I could see only advantage. If Yugoslavia stood up to German, some, at least, of the pressure on Britain must be relieved an there was just a chance that Russia might be drawn into the war. ....
> (Amery, 177)

* **"D"-men's report to Minister Campbell**

Bailey – who replaced Hanau as the head of Section D in Belgrade - left Belgrade for a discussion with Gen. Wavell's headquarters, and was replaced by Glen. Amery and his Section D colleagues, Glen and John Bennett, discussed the Đonović-Birčanin's proposal.

> We accordingly told the Minister what was afoot. **(#)** He reported to the Foreign Office, but recommended that we should discourage Djonovitch and his friends from any action against Prince Paul. The Foreign Office reaction was less negative. They suggested that we should keep in touch with the conspirators and, while discouraging *immediate* action, try to form our own assessment of how much support Djonovitch and his friends could rely on. (Amery, 178. Italics added.)

**

In the meantime, on 22 July 1940, Section D was incorporated into the newly established, very secret Special Operations Executive (SOE), headed by Dr. Hugh Dalton, Minister of Economic Warfare. However, the "D"-men in Belgrade were automatically transferred to SOE, so their activities continued serving the same purpose, whether as the "D" or SOE agents.

**

(#) On 2 August 1940, Glen sent a letter to Bailey, then in Istanbul, informing him of developments since he left Belgrade, especially about the idea of a coup, stating that the details were "somewhat disjointed extracts from a memorandum to" His Majesty's Minister [supplied by Amery, Glen and Bennett]. "Disjointed" as they may have been, these excerpts supplement the information provided by Julian Amery in his book, thus confirming that the proposal for a coup d'état was indeed already made in 1940.

> The two intermediaries through whom information as to the proposed coup has been transmitted are Jovan DJONOVICH and Ilija TRIFUNOVICH. DJONOVICH has the reputation of being a sincere patriot and commands respect for his personal integrity and his balanced judgment. TRIFUNOVICH is known as a leader of men, as a soldier and as a patriot. He is believed to be absolutely trustworthy, and his great influence in all sections of Yugoslav life, combined with his

reputation as one of the best orators in the country, make his views worthy of the utmost attention.
...
In these circumstances it is argued that the present totalitarian trend must be reversed at once and that only a coup d'état can accomplish this. Certain elements in the country, particularly the patriotic groups controlled by Narodna Odbrana, and the Serbian Church, have stated that they are prepared to attempt this and simultaneously *to make joint cause with Great Britain*. They claim to enjoy strong support amongst the army, the Serbian Church and particularly the peasants. While in no way exaggerating their powers of resistance, they believe they can hold the country long enough to arm the civilian population, to expel the Italians from Albania and to effect a similar coup in Bulgaria. Most important, they believe that support for their cause in the army is strong enough to avoid any temporary period of disunity.

There is at present no independent estimate of the accuracy of the views of the organisations as to the support they may enjoy and the military programme they could achieve in the event of the coup being effected. ...

In addition to the Narodna Odbrana, it is known as a result of Berne telegram to the Foreign Office of 17 July 1940 that the Agrarian Party [SPP] are planning action along somewhat similar lines. As Milan GAVRILOVICH is the present Yugoslav Minister in Moscow, and as his Counsellor is working with him to bring about a pro-English-Russian Government in Yugoslavia, it would seem that the Agrarian Party could be used to further the policy of HMG [His Majesty's Government] to embroil Germany with the USSR [United Soviet Socialist Republic]. The strong liaison existing between the Agrarian Party and the Balkan organisation might be employed with effect towards this end.

The plan of Narodna Odbrana is believed to be as follows:
a. To create simultaneous coup d'état in Yugoslavia and Bulgaria.
b. In Yugoslavia the Regent would be removed, if necessary by violence, from political life, but the dynasty, with the young King, will certainly be maintained.
c. In Bulgaria, DJONOVICH is in close touch with the Bulgarian Agrarian Party, which is believed to comprise about 70% of the present population. The avowed aims of the Bulgarian Agrarian Party are to kill the King and to enter a Yugoslav Federation. The Agrarians have the support of the Velcheffists, through whom they believe the army could be secured.
d. To create a defensive and offensive alliance between Yugoslavia and Bulgaria, as a primary step to Federation. The Narodna Odbrana believe that this provisional Government would receive the support of the Croats if only because the entry of Bulgaria into Yugoslav Federation would offer an additional offset to Serb imperialism. It is certainly intended hat seats in the Government should be offered to the Croat leaders.
e. To provoke Italy into war by attacking Albania as well as creating a revolution in that country. Simultaneously *to declare common cause with Great Britain and endeavour to secure Russian armed support.*

In return the Narodna Odbrana require that *HMG will recognize at once the new Government*, will reciprocate the so far unilateral alliance, and will give whatever military and air support possible. In connection with the last, it is realised that *the timing of the revolt will have to be determined by HMG's supply and military position in the Middle East.* ...

(Great Britain, Special Operations Executive, 91087-10.V, Hoover Institution archives. Italics added.)

(Glen's opinion on the resistance in Old Serbia is shown in **Appendix E.**)

* **Foreign Office's reaction to a coup proposal :**
  Eventual success must not be endangered by premature action

London did not dismiss the idea of the coup out of hand, and replied on 30 July:

We cannot possibly give any support to these elements in Yugoslavia *for the moment* but we must be careful not to give them too much of a cold douche with the result that they do not come back to us *later when time is riper* for an attempt of the kind discussed here. (Onslow, 35. Italics added.)

Although London poured cold water on the notion of supporting a *coup d'état* in the summer, and again in the autumn of 1940 when the idea was mooted again by Serb dissidents, it was agreed that SOE's aim of setting up and equipping resistance to the anticipated German occupation should be implemented. (Onslow, 35)

In E. Barker's words:

> In July 1940 the first reactions of the Foreign Office to the plan, as reported by Campbell, were relatively favourable. [John] Nicholls minuted [on 27 July] that while [Lord Edward] Halifax [the Foreign Minister] thought it would be premature to encourage the movement *at present,* later on it "might be of first class importance to H.M.G.".
>
> [Hugh] Dalton, as Minister responsible for S.O.E., minuted: "we cannot afford to neglect any chance, however slim, of improving our prospect within a tolerable time". He suggested a slightly more encouraging reply to Belgrade than the Foreign Office were contemplating; the Chiefs of Staff agreed. So on 3 August a telegram went to Belgrade:
>> "you should *indicate orally* that this plan does not, *at present,* enjoy the support of H.M.G. ... You should also indicate that the main reason why H.M.G. adopt this attitude is that they regard the questions ... as of such importance that the eventual success of some such scheme must not be endangered by *premature action,* more especially at a moment when they are unable to give a guarantee of any support."
>
> H.M.G. would in any case not support violence to the Regent. (Barker, 86; 281n48; 281n49. Italics added.)

The Serbian Peasant Party's proposals

While Julian Amery and his "D"-colleagues were dealing with the Đonović-Birčanin group, Yugoslavia was establishing diplomatic relations with the Soviet Union. The announcement of these relations - made on 24 June 1940 (just two days after the capitulation of France, the only Great Power friendly to and politically supportive of Yugoslavia) – involved J. Amery also, who was by then a welcome and frequent guest at the home of Dr. Milan Gavrilović.

> One evening shortly after this had been announced, I received an urgent summons from Milan Gavrilovitch. He led me out into the garden and told me that Prince Paul had asked him to go to Moscow as the first Yugoslav Ambassador. Only the Soviets could still prevent Germany from taking over Yugoslavia. His whole inclination was to accept.... His mind, he repeated, was pretty well made up. But he wanted to know what the British Government thought before giving the Prince his final reply.
>
> I was back two days later with a positive message from London, ... I asked him, at one point, what would happen to Yugoslavia if no help came from Russia. The choice, he answered, lay between war and occupation without war. Of the two, he favoured war but knew that the defeat was inevitable. The real struggle would begin after the occupation had taken place, and would be waged by the peasants. (Amery, 173)

It should be noted that Gavrilović, like Đonović, expected the war **before** the events of September, October and November 1940 shaped history, and that Yugoslavia would be defeated. Then he proceeded to inform Amery that a guerrilla resistance could develop. "Serbia, he went on, would be the natural centre of Resistance for all the Balkans, and his Peasant Party, with its links with Bulgaria and Croatia, would be the natural spearhead." (Amery, 173) But he did not stop at that vision.

> Gavrilovitch now asked me whether we could help him build up the necessary organisation. He would need wireless sets to communicate with the British after occupation and clandestine presses to print propaganda. He might also need our help to build up caches of arms and explosives. If I was interested, and I assured him I was, he would arrange for me to meet his deputy, Milosh Tupanyanin, who would be in charge of the Party after he had gone to Moscow. Tupanyanin and I, he suggested, might draw up a plan and then we could meet together to settle details before he left for Moscow. (Amery, 173)

A day or two later Amery went, with Altmaier, to meet Tupanjanin. "Between us we drew up a plan. Phase One aimed at expanding the Peasant Party's activities while Yugoslavia was still neutral. ...Phase Two was concerned with the organisation of propaganda, sabotage and guerrilla warfare in the event of German occupation." (Amery, 173) "Bailey and I agreed a final version of this plan with Gavrilovitch and Tupanyanin two days before Gavrilovitch left for Moscow. ... [Gavrilovitch left for Moscow on 2 July 1940 via Istanbul and Odessa.] "After some weeks of telegraphic discussion, phase one of the plan was authorised." (Amery, 174)

This authorization included the decision to "subsidize" Gavrilović's Peasant Party with four thousand sterling pounds a month, starting in July 1940. (This "subsidy" is described in **Part Two.**)

**

It would be interesting and important to know how did Dr. Gavrilović envision the expected German occupation and its concequences for the entire country, and specifially for the Serbs.

* The Serbian Peasant Party's idea of a military coup in 1938

The 1940-vision of the German occupation was not the only reflection of the Serbian Peasant Party's profound dissatisfaction with the policies of the Regent Prince Paul. Some two years earlier, SPP was also seriously considering a military *coup d'état*. Responding to the questions by *The Institute for Historical Inquiries,* General Dušan Simović stated about this subject:

During the course of 1938, at the invitation of the late Jovan Jovanović «Pižon», he met three times with Jovanović and Milan Gavrilović in the home of Dr. Miloš Sekulić. (In 1938 Jovan Jovanović was the Pesident of SPP and Gavrilović his deputy, and Simović was the Chief of the General Staff.)
   They wished to inform Simović about the political situation, and about the developing negotiations among the opposition political parties, and about their striving for politial change.
   ((To me personally they made no proposal or demand. What were their combinations and what did they want, is unknown to me.))
   «Meni lčno nisu činili nikave predloge niti zahteve. Kakve su njihove kombinacije bile i šta su hteli, nije mi poznato.» (Simović(51), 4)

**

Captain, later Major, Dragiša N. Ristić, formerly Simović's aide and executive secretary, visited Washington, DC, in April 1956. On the 17th he met with Gavrilović and on the 18th with Vladko Maček, the former Vice Premier in the Cvetković Government. Ristić left notes about both meetings, which include Gavrilović's statement about the SPP-Simović meetings in 1938. According to these notes:
   Dissatisfied with what he considered to be the dictatorship of Prince Paul, Gavrilović felt that the foreign policy of Yugoslavia would move toward the Germans. That led him to the conclusion that something ought to be done. He looked to find a suitable and known military man with whom they would begin talking about it.
   Jovanović and Gavrilović chose General Dušan Simović to organize the *coup d'état* because of his popularity and because of his critical attitude toward General Petar Živković, who was still holding the Ministry of the Army and had a devoted Royal Guard.
   ((General Simović declined this proposal without giving any reasons; however, the secrecy of this talk was kept, and the relations between the General and two politicians remained correct.))
   "General Simović je odbio ovaj predlog ne davajući razloge za isto; ipak tajnost tog razgovora je sačuvana i odnosi između Generala i dva političara ostali su korektni." (Dragiša Ristić correspondence and interview, Gavrilović, Milan, 1956-1957, Box 2, Folder 2.18. Hoover Institution Archives.)

**

Gavrilović's statement from 1956 contradicts Simović's of 1951. Having met with the leaders of SPP three times, and yet not knowing what their combinations were and what they wanted – seems unlikely. Therefore, it seems that the idea of the dismissal of Price Paul Government dates from at least from 1938 – which is **before** the conclusion of the Serbo-Croats *Sporazum (Agreement)* on 26 August 1939.
   (General Bora Mirković – the chief executor of the military coup of 27 March 1941 – claimed that he had had the idea of a change of the Government since 1937.)

**

On the basis of the above-presented information if follows that the SPP's idea of a military coup was also motivated by internal Yugoslav affairs and personal / Party's agenda. Whether the idea was considered in 1937, in 1938, and in the summer of 1940, it was realized only **after** the British approved and authorized it on 24 March 1941.

Rumors of the substitution of the Government in Yugoslavia

[Hugh] Dalton, as Minister responsible for S.O.E., minuted: "we cannot afford to neglect any chance, however slim, of improving our prospect within a tolerable time". He suggested a slightly more encouraging reply to Belgrade than the Foreign Office were contemplating; the Chiefs of Staff agreed. So on 3 August a telegram went to Belgrade:

> "you should *indicate orally* that this plan does not, *at present,* enjoy the support of H.M.G. ... You should also indicate that the main reason why H.M.G. adopt this attitude is that they regard the questions ... as of such importance that the eventual success of some such scheme must not be endangered by *premature action,* more especially at a moment when they are unable to give a guarantee of any support."

H.M.G. would in any case not support violence to the Regent. (Barker, 86; 281n48; 281n49. Italics added.)

With German troops entering Rumania, the situation was becoming more complex and disquieting – particularly for the British – even prior to Italy's attack on Greece. "The missions entered Romania openly on 7 October, their ostensible purpose being to train the Romanian forces but their real task being to protect the Romanian oil and to prepare Romanian's facilities for use in future operations." (Hinsley *et al*, 249-50) That, in turn, affected British demands and pressure on Prince Paul Karađorđević, the Regent of Yugoslavia.

During this changing state of affairs, on 15 October 1940, the British Minister in Belgrade, Ronald Ian Campbell, reported that

> there were persistent rumors of "an imminent substitution for the present [Yugoslav] government of a strong military one which would cease the policy of concessions to the Axis"; there might be a "spontaneous movement" on the part of the army "and/or Serb elements" dissatisfied with the government's attitude towards Germany. *He asked whether a change of government would be in Britain's interest.* (Barker, 86; 281n50. Italics added.)

This report referred to contacts and collaboration of British agents from both **Section D** - of the Secret Intelligence Service (SIS) - and the **Special Operations Executive** (SOE), engaged with political parties, individuals, and various other entities in Belgrade, who were already opposed to the policies of the Prince Regent at that time, for various reasons. (Some of these domestic co-operators were "subsidized" by the British. This subject is examined **in Part Two.**)

On 24 October, the Foreign Office responded to Campbell, more cautiously than they had in July, saying *inter alia,* that they shared his own view that, in a crisis, Prince Paul "would be in a position to enforce a stand", though they regretted that no hope could be held out for any of Britain's material aid except *"naval pressure"***;** and, that the Yugoslav government's attitude remained of great importance to Britain regarding three things: resistance by force to Axis attack, refusal to make any territorial concessions, and, in particular, refusal to permit passage of Axis troops. (Barker, 86; 281n51)

However, events were developing fast, and E. Barker observed,

> If the British had stuck consistently to these three demands, there would have been no quarrel between them and Prince Paul. But the events of early 1941 moved the British to make further demands – in effect, *that Yugoslavia should abandon neutrality and enter the war.* It was this that opened their breach with the Prince. (Barker, 86-7. Italics added.)

Appendix E - The issue of resistance in old Serbia

Along with excerpts from Amery-Glenn-Bennett's report to Campbell dated 2 August, Glen added to Bailey his own comments on the military capabilities of the Yugoslav army and chances of resisting Germany. It is worth keeping his comments in mind when analyzing the actions and reasoning of the coup-wishers-and-plotters, and their justification for staging the coup.

> As you well know, lack of anti-aircraft and anti-tank guns places the Yugoslav army in no position to offer opposition to a German attack. Some talk of resistance from the hills of old Serbia, invoking gallant memories of a war that is past. That resistance too, I am convinced would be quickly broken for Yugoslavia has no air force to oppose what would be the systematic low level bombing and machine-gunning of every village and every road.
>
> Yugoslavia has at present one policy and one only, which, from our point of view, she must follow. That is to do nothing to invite German or Italian attack, but to maintain factual independence and to arm and prepare as rapidly as possible. This policy one might describe as "wriggling", and I believe they are carrying it out fairly successfully.
>
> In order to assist them to carry it out I am convinced we must be accommodating over matters which are in the long run trivial. ... In the more important ways the Yugoslavs are playing ball. The very excellent stream of information from Germany continues and *our own activities are not being interfered with unduly.*
>
> If the above estimate is true I believe our policy should be as follows. Internally we should build up a latent support for our cause through the medium of the Peasant Party. The monthly subsidy of £5,000 *[it was settled at £4,000]* is going to be of the greatest help in this. At the same time the shadow organisation to replace us in the event of our departure from the country must be constructed and the lines of communications with Istanbul opened. Small scale sabotage might then be begun.
>
> In Croatia a new organization is being built up and a new Slovene organisation is already working. (Great Britain, Special Operations Executive, 91087-10.V, Hoover Institution Archives. Italics added.)

**

These initial coup proposals, and the British Government's reactions to them, took place in the summer of 1940 - before Italy attacked Greece from Albania on 28 October 1940, and when HMG strove to maintain the status quo in the Balkans, and therefore was not encouraging an overthrow of Prince Paul's Government – for the time being. Onslow first quoted FO's minute of 30 July 1940:

> The Foreign Office in London temporised, equally intent on their policy of embroiling Germany and Russia in eventual conflict via the Balkans, and painfully aware of the paucity of British aid that could be offered to a Yugoslav war effort should such an abrupt change of government precipitate a German attack. 'It is by no means certain that the Chiefs of Staff would now recommend anything calculated to "set the Balkans ablaze".' But London did not dismiss the idea out of hand. (Onslow, 34)

In January 1941, when time was getting riper,

> Stalin had been carefully monitoring the strategic debate in London concerning British assistance to Greece. It did not escape him that on their own the British could not possibly reactivate the Balkans against the 'unemployed German army'. Eden, for instance, [on 22 January 1941] had been inciting [the Soviet Ambassador in London, Ivan] Mayski, warning that Yugoslavia's drift to Germany and 'the loss of Salonika would be a threat to the [Dardanelles] Straits, in the future of which Russia had historic interest.' Stalin therefore had become increasingly obsessed with what he conceived to be a British scheme to lead Russia into a premature confrontation with the Germans in the Balkans. (Gorodetsky, 139. 354n14)

Stalin continued to suspect "the British of trying to ensnare Russia in war. He was fully aware of Eden's efforts during his prolonged tour of the Middle East to form a defensive bloc of Turkey, Greece and Yugoslavia." (Gorodetsky, 141)

**

By March 1941, the situation had changed. What had been *premature* then, was *timely* now. The Balkan Front was the order of the day. . Now, after Eden's authorization of 24 March, Campbell could *secretly* assure Đonović, Birčanin, Tupanjanin, Mirković and other oppositionists - whom the SOE's George Taylor and Tom Masterson were urging for the coup - of *full* British moral and political support. The Minister was duty-bound to do so. He could do it through his Service Attachés and/or SOE network and/or other links. This promise of British support should be kept in mind during the examination of British contacts with the coup-plotters dating from 24 March 1941 onwards.

Indeed – as is shown in **Part Two**- in the pre-coup days in Belgrade, Birčanin was one of the major links between the Legation-SOE team and the physical executors of the coup. His *Narodna Odbrana* (the National Defense League) – described by Amery as a "powerful patriotic society, some two hundred thousand strong with branches in every town where there were Serbs" (p. 175) – had been by now "subsidized" by the British. So was Tupanjanin's Serbian Peasant Party – with the largest "subsidy" given to any of their co-operatives in Yugoslavia.

**

On 23 March 1941, George Taylor sent a telegram to London SOE pointing out to the coordinated operations between the Legation in Belgrade and SOE:

> C. I have seen Foreign Office telegram drawing attention to possibility of using organisation [SOE] for raising resistance to Government if Pact signed. Wish to assure you that Minister [Campbell] has made fullest use of SO2 and particularly of MASTERSON personally throughout the crisis.
> D. SO2 has undoubtedly made important contribution to the struggle to prevent signature both as source of information and contacts, above all by work through TUPANJANIN, who has been heart and soul of the resistance.
> (Great Britain, Special Operation Executive, 91087 – 10.V, Hoover Institution Archives)

Whatever Campbell's earlier dissatisfaction with the SOE operations might have been, from Taylor's arrival in Belgrade, on 27 February, the Legation personnel and SOE agents cooperated fully and with the complete knowledge and approval of Minister Campbell.

Appendix F - Yugoslavia's lack of military supplies

Campbell had good reason to request military supplies which would give the British *something with which to approach potential leaders directly.* Yugoslavia's military leaders were extremely aware of the inadequate armament of their military forces to resist Germany's Blitzkrieg-war machine. General Simović – the leader who would be approached directly twice on 26 March – wrote about his concern on this subject when he met Colonel W. Donovan on 24 January :

> ((Explaining to him the dangers of our situations and the insufficiency of our forces for a decisive defense, I insisted that America send us, promptly, help in armaments, especially in airplanes and arms for anti-aircraft and anti-tank defense.
> ((With [head] nodding and facial expression, Colonel Donovan was showing that he was agreeing with my explanation, but he made no proposals at all, he was not even trying. (Simović(51), 6-7)

Campbell also had to be aware of the British handling of Yugoslav requests. In February 1941,

> The Belgrade Military Attaché's [Charles Clarke] office reported that satisfactory and rapid mobilization of the Yugoslav army required the provision of some 12,000 tyres. The Ministry of Economic Warfare objected as rubber was a scarce commodity in Germany and was determined to deny this; however, as 'a political gesture' some 650 tyres were sanctioned for delivery (that is, sufficient for approximately 150 vehicles, or 5 per cent of the required consignment). (Onslow, 11-12)

On 4 February 1941, Campbell informed London that nearly 20,000 tires would be needed to retrofit the Army motor vehicles. On 26 February 1941 - the Ministry of Economic warfare finally authorized shipment of 12,126 tires on *SS Bosiljka* from New York. However, these tires did not reach Yugoslavia before the German attack of 6 April 1941. (Onslow, 11n26)

It is interesting that the authorization was given on 26 February – four days after the Anglo-Greek agreement on the defense of Greece was reached. One wonders whether this agreement altered the initial decision.

Similarly, in November 1940, the British Air Attaché in Belgrade [A.H.H. Macdonald],

> reported that the Yugoslav Air Force only had sufficient aviation fuel for a two-week conflict, and applied for provision from Britain's Middle East supply. The Petroleum Department were able to arrange for the supply of this oil, but the Ministry of Economic Warfare objected, arguing that Yugoslavia already had enough for its peacetime needs; and that it was dangerous to accumulate stocks in Salonika, given the vulnerability of the port to German attack. If war erupted, then Britain would review whether to provide additional fuel from the Middle East store. (Onslow, 12)

Thus, in the summer of 1940, Britain could not supply Yugoslavia with needed armament; in February 1941, the Ministry of Economic Warfare objected to supplying tires and aviation fuel. Campbell – the head of the Legation – had to know this. And which Minister objected? It was Dr. Hugh Dalton – the same man who was in charge of the Special Operations Executive and who sent his most capable operative, George Taylor, on the special mission to the Balkans, as has already been stated.

Although Dalton's Ministry finally authorized shipment of 12,126 tires, the initial reason for not sending them – that rubber was a scarce commodity in *Germany* - seems suspect, because the tires were to have been sent to Yugoslavia, not Germany. So why was *Germany* mentioned at all? One possibility:

In December 1939, John Shea, of the Military Intelligence "conducted an extensive survey into the capabilities and requirements of the Yugoslav Army" and thus "London possessed detailed knowledge of the shortcomings of the Yugoslav Army in terms of military personnel, armaments and strategic plans, etc." (Onslow, 11) Those deficiencies did not bode well for an extended resistance to Germany, in the case of war. Now, if Britain had sent 12,000 or 20,000 tires to Yugoslavia – all those tires would be confiscated by the occupier, Germany – where rubber was a scarce commodity – and that was unacceptable to Britain at that moment, and consequently the tires were not sent.

When one considers the report that showed that Yugoslavia's air force could not operate for more than two weeks, at the existing supply levels, then why send oil which might also be seized by Germany?

**

Putting it all together, it was expected that – in a war against Germany – Yugoslavia would quickly lose and would be occupied. With that expectation, a major task of the Special Operations Executive and their domestic co-operators was to organize the "post-occupational resistance".

But they did not ... they scurried out and only the sickly "Daddy" Trifunović stayed ... in a territory annexed by Italy.

Sources

* Notes regarding General Simović's and General Mirković's documents –

A - On 28 March 1941, after *the Thanksgiving service* for the young King Peter's accession to the throne, Simović delivered a long speech before the Holy Assembly of Bishops of the Serbian Orthodox Church about the coup of 27 March 1941 and his own role in it. His speech was recorded by two stenographers, in the presence of the Chief of the Central Press Bureau, Dr Milorad Radovanović. Patriarch Gavrilo [Dr Dožić] included the recorded text of the speech in his Memoirs, and Živan Knežević reprinted it in his book, *27 mart 1941* (pp. 361-70).

B - Mirković himself never published his memoirs, which were written in Cairo, dated and signed on 1 December 1941. In various newspaper articles he wrote and/or debated about specific subjects and/or events, but his overall account was published in Belgrade for the first time in 1995.

The typescript, *Istina o 27. martu 1941. godine* (*The truth about the 27th March 1941*), was brought to Belgrade after the conclusion of WWII. Given to the *Military-Historic Institute of the Yugoslav National Army* in Belgrade, the script was forwarded, for comments, to Gen. Simović – who in 1945 had returned from London to Belgrade. Mirković's text and Simović's comments were published by Nenad Stefanović in Belgrade's biweekly *Duga*, in March and April, 1995. Petar Bosnić then published the memoirs – and information on their itinerary – in a serial in Belgrade's daily *Politika*, in March and April 1996. The same year he also published them in book format. Translated data, appearing herein, are taken from that book.

However, these, Mirković's memoirs, were circulated in Great Britain. They served – among other purposes - as a source for an article titled, "March 27th. Day of Pride. Yugoslavia Thrice-armed", reportedly written (but not signed) "by one who was present on the day". The Hon. Rowland Winn advised Guy Wisdom to send it to Frank Betts, in London, to be published on or near the first anniversary of the coup. The article contained the following exchange between Mirković and British Air Attaché A. Hugh Macdonald:

> The day the pact was signed [25 March 1941] a British Embassy official called on General Mirkovitch in his office, to inform him of the fact.
> The General replied "That pact must be killed!"
> "But what is to be done?"
> "That is my responsibility. The pact must be killed."
> "And who can do it?"
> "I can." said the General, gravely.
>
> (Žarko Popović collection, Box 2, folder 2.21, Hoover Institution Archives)

C – Formed on that fateful day of 27 March, 1941, without a consensus political program, the Simović Government fell on 11 January 1942. On 9 July 1942 the General offered his military services to Prime Minister Churchill. "I took on the grave responsibility for the military defeat which was to be foreseen and inevitable, but which I was convinced would be of utmost value for the allied cause, …", wrote the General to the Prime Minister.

On 25 August 1942, Churchill responded, "with deep regret", that he was "not able to find any means by which it would be possible to take advantage of your generous offer to serve once more." (Dušan Simović file, Box 2, Hoover Institution Archives)

Only Simović knew how he had felt after this cool rejection. Without an official assignment, he turned to writing his memoirs, among other things.

In a lengthy document, dated 1 January 1944 in London-Barnet, the General described the events related to the coup in a 30-pages, single-spaced type-script with Latin letters. The account of the 27 March 1941 *coup d'état* Simović organized in three sections: Prethodni događaji; Događaji koji su prethodili 27. martu; and Pripreme za državni udar (Preceding events; Events which preceded to the 27th March; and Preparations for the *coup d'état*). Then he added one-page of changes and supplements, hand-written in Cyrillic. (Dušan T. Simović, Recollection of events surrounding coup of 3/27/41, Box 1, Hoover Institution Archives)

However, his associates transcribed only the first 20 pages of the original into a 41-page document with Cyrillic type, without incorporating the requested changes and supplements.

On the first page in the upper right-hand corner of the typescript – 41 pages long, double-spaced- there is a hand-written note, in Cyrillic: "Za Dr Mišu Simovića" (For Dr Miša Simović) [the General's brother Miloš].

On the last page there is a hand-written explanation, in Serbian: ((20 March 1944, Cairo. Compared and found that the transcription is true to the original.
/signed/ Colonel S. T. Živković
Colonel Žar. R. Popović
Dr. Miloš T. Simović))

For purposes of reference, this account is entitled herein "Simović(44)"

In Box 1, along with Simović's recollections there are comments on the document, addressed to the General by his devoted former adjutant, Captain Dragiša N. Ristić. Most of them suggested a need to rewrite or delete the General's phrasing of the role of Major Živan Knežević which - in Ristić's opinion – the self-promoting Major had not deserved at all. Ristić wrote that Major Knežević's influence among officers was non-existent, that the brothers Knežević were "morbidly ambitious", and that they had cashed in on the coup "to the utmost limits".

D - Ristić's book, *Yugoslavia's Revolution of 1941,* was published in 1966. In the Forward to the book, on 11 September 1959 Dušan T. Simović wrote: "I entrusted my archives to him for the sake of preservation and in order to set the record straight - the record of my endeavors and work." Ristić often quoted from *Simović's "Memoirs"* - and his own recollections and diary – but it is not clear which version of the General's recollections was he referring to: the updated ones, as suggested by Ristić, or the un-updated ones. At least in one scene – Simović's instruction to Mirković during their second meeting on 26 March – Ristić used his updated version.

E - As total British political, propaganda, and military support was behind the Communist-controlled Partisans in Yugoslavia, in March 1944 Simović also declared his support for the Partisans. In May 1945 he returned from London to Belgrade. The communist Government gave him a General's pension and the right to live in his pre-war home. Those were great benefits at the time: after all, the Putsch set in motion the events which ultimately led to Communist power in Yugoslavia. On 14 June 1951, *Institut za istorijska pitanja(The Institute for Historical Inquiries)* asked the General to comment on some political events in Yugoslavia, including the coup of 27 March 1941. Some of his responses and comments, dated July 1951,are summarized herein(translated), in a document referred to as «Simović(51)".

F - Troubled by claims and comments published, mostly abroad, about the Putsch of March 27, 1941, in 1956 General Simović wrote an explanation which he, allegedly, kept to himself for some five years, and decided - shortly before his death on 26 August 1962 - to send abroad for publication.
With an accompanying letter, dated 8 December 1961, he forwarded ((a handwritten text in which he explained the role of the participants in the coup d'état of 27 March, 1941)) to Ante Smith Pavelić. With another letter dated 22 March, 1962, Simović sent to Smith Pavelić ((some supplements and corrections of that text, with the instruction that these documents could be published in their entirety only after his death))
Smith Pavelić fulfilled Simović's wish. With a letter dated in Paris 24 September, 1962 – containing the above cited information – he sent the General's text to Jovan Kontić, the editor of *Glasnik (The Herald)* of the Serbian historical-cultural association "Njegoš", to be published. The editor did so in the issue No. 10, December 1962, under the title "Politički testament generala Dušana Simovića" ((Political testament of General Dušan Simović)), duly noting that Simović's letter was being published in its entirety. The document is herein referred to as «Simović(56)".

Sources and selected bibliography

Alexander, Field Marshal, Earl of Tunis   *The Alexander Memoirs 1940-1945,* Cassell, London, 1962
Amery, Julian   *Approach March: a Venture in Autobiography,* Hutchinson of London, 1973
Autty & Clogg(ed)   Autty, Phyllis and Clogg, Richard (eds) *British Policy Towards Wartime Resistance in Yugoslavia and Greece*   Barnes & Noble with S.S.E.E.S., 1975

Bailey *et al*   Bailey, Ronald H. *et al. Partisans and Guerrillas,* World War II Time-Life Books, Alexandria, Virginia, 1978
Balfour & Mackay   Balfour, Neal & Mackay, Sally *Paul of Yugoslavia, Britain's Maligned Friend,* Hamish Hamilton, London, 1980
Barker, Elisabeth   *British Policy in South-East Europe in the Second World War,* Macmillan, London, 1976
Barker(CE)   Barker, Elisabeth *Churchill and Eden at War,* St. Martins, New York, 1978
Batty, Peter   *Hoodwinking Churchill: Tito's Great Confidence Trick*   London, Shepheard-Walwyn, 2011
Beloff, Nora   *Tito's Flawed Legacy: Yugoslavia & the West 1939-84,* Victor Gollancz Ltd, London, 1985
Bennett, Ralph   *Ultra and Mediterranean Strategy,* William Morrow and Co, New York, 1989
Blake & Louis(eds)   Blake, Robert & Louis, Roger   *Churchill,*   W.W. Norton & Company, New York, London, 1993

Blau, George E. *Invasion Balkans! The German Campaign in the Balkans, Spring 1941,* Burd Street Press, Shippensburg, PA, 1997. First edition was published in November 1953.
Blum, John Morton *From The Morgenthau Diaries, Years of Urgency 1938-1941,* Houghton Mifflin Co. , Boston,1965
Bosnić(ed)   Mirković, Borivoje *Istina o 27. martu 1941. godine (The Truth about the 27th March 1941),* Prepared and edited by Petar Bosnić, Beograd, 1996
Bruce Lockhart, R.H.   *Comes the Reckoning,* Putnam, London, 1947

Carlton, David   *Anthony Eden A Biography,* Allen Lane, London, 1981
Cave Brown1   Cave Brown, Anthony *Bodyguard of Lies* Harper & Row, New York, 1975
Cave Brown, Anthony   *The Last Hero Wild Bill Donovan* Vintage Books, Random House, New York, 1984
Charmley, John   *Churchill: The End of Glory A Political Biography,* Harcourt Brace & Co., New York, San Diego, London, 1993

Churchill, Winston S. *The Second World War:*
Churchill(GS)   ---   *The Gathering Storm,* Houghton Mifflin Company, Boston, 1948
Churchill(FH)   ---   *Their Finest Hour,* Houghton Mifflin Company, Boston, 1949
Churchill(GA)   ---   *The Grand Alliance,* Houghton Mifflin Company, Boston, 1950
Churchill(HF)   ---   *The Hinge of Fate,* Houghton Mifflin Company, Boston, 1950
Churchill(CR)   ---   *Closing the Ring,* Houghton Mifflin Company, Boston, 1951
Churchill(TT)   ---   *Triumph and Tragedy,* Houghton Mifflin Company, Boston, 1953

Clissold, Stephen *Whirlwind : An Account of Marshal Tito's Rise to Power,* Philosophical Library, New York, 1949
Colville, John *The Fringes of Power, 10 Downing Street Diaries 1939-1955,* W.W. Norton & Co., New York, 1986

Dalton, High   *The Fateful Years   Memoirs 1939-1945,* Frederick Muller Ltd, London, 1957
Danchev(ed), Danchev, Alex   *Establishing the Anglo-American Alliance -   The Second World War Diaries of Brigadier Vivian Dykes,* Brassey's(UK), London, 1990
De Guingand, Major General Sir Francis   *Operation Victory,* Natraj Publishers, Dehra Dun, 2006 (First published in 1947)
Dilks(ed), Dilks, David   *Diaries of Sir Alexander Cadogan, O.M., 1938-1945,* G. P. Putman's Sons, New York, 1972

Dilks2(ed)   *Retreat from Power, Studies in Britain's Foreign Policy of the twentieth Century, Volume Two, After 1939,* M, 1981 (First published 1981 by The Macmillan Press Ltd.)
    * Dilks, David "Introduction"
    * Dilks, David "The Twilight War and the Fall of France: Chamberlain and Churchill in 1940"
    * The Late Lord Strang, "War and Foreign Policy: 1939-45"
    * Graham, Ross "Operation Bracelet: Churchill in Moscow, 1942"
    * Gowing, Margaret "Britain, America and the Bomb"
    * Gopal, Sarvepalli "Nehru and the Commonwealth"
    * Spiers, Edward "The British Nuclear Deterrent: Problems and Possibilities"

Dodds-Parker, Douglas *Setting Europe Ablaze Some Account of Ungentlemanly Warfare,* Springwood Books, 1984 (First printing 1983.)
Dunlop, Richard   *Donovan America's Master Spy,* Rand McNally & Company, Chicago   New York   San Francisco, 1982

Eden, Anthony (The Earl of Avon)   *Memoirs: The Reckoning,* Cassell, London, 1965

Five authors   *Churchill: Four Faces and the Man,* The Penguin Press, London, 1969
    * A.J.P. Taylor, The Statesman
    * Robert Rhodes James,   The Politician
    * J. H. Plumb, The Historian
    * Basil Liddell Hart, The Military Strategist*
    * Anthony Storr, The Man

Ford, Corey   *Donovan of OSS,* Little, Brown and Co., Boston, 1970

FRUS   *Foreign Relations of the United States Diplomatic Papers,* US Government Printing Office, Washington
FRUS1   ---   1941, Volume II,   Europe,   1959
FRUS2   ---   1942, Volume III , Europe,   1961
FRUS3   ---   1943, Volume II,   Europe,   1964
FRUS4   ---   1944, Volume II,   Europe,   1966
FRUS5   ---   1945, Volume V,   Europe,   1967
FRUS6   ---   1946, Volume VI, Eastern Europe, The Soviet Union, 1969

Glen, Alexander *Footholds Against a Whirlwind* Hutchinson of London, 1975
Glen(B)   Glen, Alexander with Bowen, Leighton   *Target Danube, A River Not Quite Too Far* The Book Guild Ltd., Susssex, England, 2002
Gorodetsky, Gabriel *Grand Delusion Stalin and the German Invasion of Russia,* Yale University Press, New Haven and London, 1999

Grol, Milan *Londonski dnevnik 1941-1945 (London's Diary 1941-1945)*, Filip Višnjić, Beograd, 1990

Hehn, Paul N. *A Low Dishonest Decade,* Continuum, New York, London, 2002
Hinsley et al   Hinsley, F.H., Thomas E.E., Ransom C.F.G., Knight R.C. *British Intelligence in the Second World War – Its Influence on Strategy and Operations,*   Volume One, Her Majesty's Stationery Office, London, 1979
Holmes, Richard *In the Footsteps of Churchill, A Study in Character*   Basic Books, New York, 2005
Hoptner, J.B. *Yugoslavia in Crisis 1934-1941* Columbia University Press, New York and London, 1962
Howard, Michael *The Mediterranean Strategy in the Second World War,* Frederick A. Prager, New York Washington, 1968
Howarth, Patrick *Undercover   The men and women of the Special Operations Executive,* Phoenix Press, London, 2000. (First published in 1980.)

Ismay, General Hastings L. *The Memoirs of General Lord Ismay,* The Viking Press, New York, 1960

Jacob, Sir John, in Wheeler-Bennett(ed)
Jukić, Ilija   *The Fall of Yugoslavia*, Translated by Dorian Cooke, Harcourt Brace Jovanovich, New York and London, 1974
Jukić(65)   Jukić, Ilija   *Pogledi na prošlost, sadašnjost I budućnost hrvatskog naroda (Views on the Past, Present and Future of the Croatian People)* Hrvatska politička knjižnica, London, 1965

Karapandžić(AB)   Karapandžić, Adam & Borivoje *Srbija – Zemlja prevrata, zavera, buna i pučeva(Serbia – The land of subversions, conspiracies, mutinies and putschs),*   Slobodna knjiga, Beograd, 2001
Keegan, John   *The Second World War*, Viking, 1989
Kennedy, Major-General Sir John   *The Business of War,* Wiliam Morrow and Co., New York, 1958 (First published in Great Britain in 1957.)
Knežević, Živan   *27. mart 1941.(March 27, 1941),*   Author's edition, New York, 1979
Kočović, Bogoljub   *Žrtve Drugog svetskog rata u Jugoslaviji*, Biblioteka Naše delo, London, 1985
Koliopoulos, John S.   «General Papagos and the Anglo-Greek Talks of February 1941», in the *Journal of Hellenic Diaspora,* Vol. VII, Nos. 3-4, Fall-Winter 1980, Pella Publishing Co., New York
Krylov,   Ivan   *Soviet Staff Officer,* Translated by Edward Fitzgerald,The Falcon Press, London 1951

Lamb, Richard   *Churchill as War Leader*, Carroll & Graff, New York, 1991
Langer & Gleason   Langer, William L. and Gleason, S. Everett,   *The Undeclared War 1940-1941,* Harper and Brothers, New York, 1953
Lawlor, Sheila *Churchill and the politics of war, 1940-1941*   Cambridge University Press, 1995 (First published in 1994)
Leary, William M. *Fueling the Fires of Resistance*, Army Air Forces Special Operations in the Balkans during World War II - Air Force History and Museums Program, 1995
Liddell Hart, Basil H.   *Defence of the West,* William Morrow & Co, New York, 1950
Liddell Hart, Basil H.   "The Military Strategist", in *Churchill: Four Faces and the Man*
Loewenheim et al [ed]   Loewenheim, Francis L., Langley, Harold D., Jonas, Manfred (eds) *Roosevelt and Churchill - Their Secret Wartime Correspondence,* Saturday Review Press / E.P. Dutton & Co, New York, 1975

Mackenzie, W.J.M. *The Secret History of SOE: The Special Operations Executive 1940-1945,* St. Ermin's Press, 2000
Maclean, Fitzroy   *Eastern Approaches* TIME-LIFE Books, New York, 1964
Maček, Vladko   *The Struggle for Freedom*, Translated by Elizabeth and Stjepan Gazi, The Pennsylvania State University Press, University Park and London, 1957
McClymont, W.G. *To Greece: Official History of New Zealand in the Second World War, 1939-45,* War History Branch, Department of Internal Affairs, Wellington, New Zealand, 1959
 (http://www.nzetc.org/tm/scholarly/tei-WH2Gree-c6-1.html   1/31/07)
Moran, Lord   *Churchill at War 1940-45*   Carroll & Graf Publishers, New York, 2003 (First published in 1966)

Onslow, Sue   "Britain and the Belgrade Coup of 27 March 1941 Revisited", *Electronic Journal of International History,* (March 2005)
Ostović, P.D. *The Truth about Yugoslavia,* Roy Publishers, New York, 1952

Pandurović, Gen. Dragiša *27. mart 1941. - Prilog za vojno-političku istoriju - (27th March 1941 - A controbution to the military-political history)* Oflag XIIIB, 18 December 1941
Parrott, Cecil   *The Tightrope,* Faber and Faber, London, 1975
Pearton, Maurice   «SOE in Romania», in Seaman(ed)
Petranović & Žutić   Petranović, Branko& Žutić, Nikola   *27.Mart 1941.   Tematska zbirka dokumenata (A thematic collection of documents),* NICOM, Beograd, 1990
Petrov, Vladimir   *A Study in Diplomacy: the Story of Arthur Bliss Lane,* Henry Regenry Co., Chicago, 1971
Pimlott(ed)   Pimlott, Ben *The Second World War Diary of Hugh Dalton 1940-45,* Jonathan Cape in Association with the Lonodon School of Economics and Political Science, 1986

Rhodes James, Robert   *Anthony Eden   A Biography,* McGraw-Hill Book Co, 1987. First published in 1986

Rhodes James, Robert "The Politician", in *Churchill: Four Faces and the Man*
Ristić, Dragiša N. *Yugoslavia's Revolution of 1941,* The Pennsylvania State University Press, University Park / London, 1966
Roberts, Walter R. *Tito, Mihailović and the Allies, 1941 – 1945,* Rutgers University Press, New Brunswick, New Jersey, 1973

St. John, Robert *From the Land of Silent People,* Doubleday, Doran & Co., Garden City, New York, 1942
Scanlan, John D. "Turkey's World War II Policy", Student Project for Amity among Nations, University of Minnesota, 1954

Seaman(ed)   Seaman, Mark, ed. *Special Operations Executive A new instrument of war,* Routledge, London and New York, 2006
* Seaman, Mark   "Introduction"
* Seaman, Mark   " 'A new instrument of war' : the origins of the Special Operations Executive"
* Cornish, Paul   "Weapons and equipment of the Special Operations Executive"
* Richard, Sir Brooks   "SOE and sea communications"
* Stafford, David   "Churchill and SOE"
* Charman, Terry   "Hugh Dalton, Poland and SOE, 1940-42"
* Kraglund, Ivar   "SOE and Milorg: 'Thieves on the same market' "
* Foot, M.R.D.   "SOE in Low Countries"
* Woods, Christopher   "SOE in Italy"
* Wheeler, Mark   "Resistance from abroad: Anglo-Soviet efforts to coordinate Yugoslav resistance, 1941-42"
* Pearton, Maurice   "SOE in Romania"
* Smith, Bradley F.   "SOE in Afghanistan"
* Clogo, Richard   " ' Negotiations of a complicated character' : Don Scott's 'adventures' in Athens, October-November 1943"
* Wylie, Neville   "SOE and neutrals"
* Bailey, Roderick   "SOE in Albania: the 'conspiracy theory' reassessed"
* Jespersen, Knud J.   "SOE in Denmark"
* O'Halpin, Eunan   " 'Hitler's Irish hideout': a case study of SOE's black propaganda battles"
* Stuart, Duncan   " 'Of historical interest only': the origins and vicissitudes of the SOE archive"

Seton-Watson(ER)   Seton-Watson, Hugh   *The East European Revolution,* Frederick A. Praeger, New York, 1951
Shoup, Paul   *Communism and the Yugoslav National Question,* Columbia University Press, New York and London, 1968

Simović(44)   Simović, Gen. Dušan,   Memoari (Memoirs),   Žarko Popović collection, Box 2, Folder 2.9, Hoover Institution Archives
Simović(51)   ---   "Simovićev testament" ("Simović's Testament") *Glasnik,* Vol. 21, June 1968, pp. 4-23
Simović(56)   ---   "Politički testament generala Simovića» ("Political Testament of General Simović") *Glasnik,* Vol. 10, December 1962, pp. 76-78.

Smith, Bradley F. *The Shadow Warriors* Basic Books, Inc., New York, 1983

Stafford(C)   Stafford, David *Churchill and Secret Service,* The Overlook Press, Woodstock & New York, 1998
Stafford(cp)   ---   "SOE and British Involvement in the Belgrade Coup d'Etat of March 1941", *Slavic Review,* Vol. 36, No. 3, September 1977
Stafford D.   ---   «Churchill and SOE», in Seaman(ed)
Stafford(so)   ---   *Britain and European Resistance, 1940 – 1945 : A Survey of the Special Operations Executive, with Documents,* M in association with St. Anthony's College, Oxford, 1980

Sulzberger, Cyrus Leo   *A Long Row of Candles, Memoirs and Diaries [1934-1954]* , The Macmillan Company, New York, 1969
Sweet-Escott, Bickham   *Baker Street Irregular,* Methuen & Co., London, 1965

Taylor, A.J.P. "The Statesman" in *Churchill: Four Faces and the Man*
Taylor, George Francis REPORT ON S. O. ORGANISATION AND PLANS IN THE BALKANS, MOST SECRET, Athens, 26th February 1941, The National Archives, HS5/166 275583
Thomas, Gordon *Secret Wars , One Hundred Years of British Intelligence Inside MI5 and MI6,* Thomas Bunne Books, New York, 2009
Troy, Thomas F. *Wild Bill and Intrepid - Donovan, Stephenson and the Origin of CIA,* Yale University Press, 1996

van Creveld, Martin L. *Hitler's Strategy 1940-1941   The Balkan Clue,* Cambridge University Press, 1973
van Creveld(G)   van Creveld, Martin L. "Prelude to Disaster: the British Decision to Aid Greece, 1940-41", *Journal of Contemporary History,* Vol. 9, No. 3 (Jul., 1974), pp. 65-92, Sage Publications, Ltd.
Vauhnik, Vladimir *Nevidljivi front Borba za očuvanje Jugoslavije (The invisible front The struggle for the preservation of Yugoslavia),* Minhen, 1984

Vodušek Starič, Jerca   *Slovenski špijoni in SOE 1938-1942 (Slovenian Spies and SOE 1938-1942)*,   Ljubljana, 2002
Wedemeyer, General Albert C.   *Wedemeyer Reports!*   Henry Holt & Co., New York, 1958

Wheeler-Bennett[ed], Wheeler-Bennett, Sir John   *Action This Day , Working with Churchill,* Macmillan, 1968:
    * Lord Normanbrook (Cabinet Secretariat 1941—46, Secretary to the Cabinet 1947-62)
    * John Colville (Assistant Private Secretary (1940-41, 1943-45, Parliamentary Private Secretary 1951-55)
    * Sir John Martin   (Private Secretary 1940-41, Principal Private Secretary 1941-45)
    * Sir Ian Jacob (Lt.-Gen, Military Assistant to War Cabinet 1939-45)
    * Lord Bridges   (Secretary to the Cabinet 1938-45)
    * Sir Leslie Rowan   (Private Secretary 1941-45, Principal Private Secretary 1945)

West(6)   West, Nigel *MI6 British Secret Intelligence Service Operations 1909-45,* Random House, New York, 1983
Williams, Heather   *Parachutes, Patriots, and Partisans: The Special Operations Executive and Yugoslavia, 194 –1945,*
           The University of Wisconsin Press, 2003
Winterbotham, F.W.   *The Ultra Secret* , Harper & Row, New York, Evanston, San Francisco, London 1974
Woodward(1), Woodward, Sir Llewellyn   *British Foreign Policy in the Second World War,* Volume 1, Her Majesty's
           Stationery Office, London, 1971

Index

Adriatic Sea..95
Aegean Sea 33, 45, 88, 125
Africa.........................26, 29, 32, 39, 45, 59, 65,
69 - 70, 73, 79, 92, 103, 124,
137 - 138, 159 - 160, 167 - 169,
171 - 172, 182, 185, 188, 205
Afrika Corps, or Africacorps................70, 79,169
Albania, or Albanians............................16 - 18,
29 - 30, 33 - 34, 36, 38 - 39,
43 - 46, 48 - 49, 51, 54, 59 - 60, 63,
72 - 75, 78 - 79, 93, 96 - 98,
100 - 101, 103, 127, 132, 135 - 137, 142,
145 - 147, 149 - 151, 153 - 156, 158, 166,
169 - 170, 189, 204, 214 - 218, 222, 230
Alexander, Field Marshal Harold....................166
Alexander, King of Yugoslavia.......................17,
131, 201, 215
Alexandria................................67, 176, 207, 227
Aliakmon line, or Aliakhmon line...............74, 77,
84, 89 - 92, 100, 153 - 154
Allied, or Allies ....33 - 34, 38, 42 - 43, 47,
54, 62, 75 - 76, 85, 97, 103, 107, 114,
116, 131, 135 - 137, 144 - 145, 150, 152 - 154,
176, 192 - 193, 195, 198, 200, 202, 216, 226
Alpine Violets, Operation...............................101
Altmaier, Dr. Jacob 15, 215, 219
America, Americans or United States.......25, 26,
38, 50, 51, 56 - 58, 61, 65,
68, 71, 74, 80, 87,
97 -98, 103, 112,
115 - 116, 120, 126, 129, 131,
135, 145, 166, 168, 171, 172,
183 - 193, 189, 190, 192 - 194,
197 - 201, 202 - 205, 207 - 209, 224, 228
Amery, Julian (later Baron) ...114, 116, 120, 129,
134, 136, 143, 175, 215, 217, 219, 223
Amery, Leopold-Leo...............110, 129, 137, 161
Ankara or Angora...................34, 44, 71, 75 - 76,
78, 82, 83, 86, 101, 131, 155, 203
Antic, Milan 44
Antwerp...37
Anzac troops...211
Argos..211
Arms Supplies, American for Balkan Front.....50,
189, 205
Arms Supplies, Britain for Balkan Front..........77,
92, 95, 101, 104, 121, 122,
124, 127, 135, 166 - 167, 187,
189 - 199, 201, 203, 209 - 210, 224
Arms Supplies, Italian for Balkan Front.........103,
127, 150
Asia...21
Athens.....................................20, 31, 38, 40, 42,
53, 60, 63 - 66, 68, 71, 73 - 74, 77 - 81,
83 - 87, 90 - 92, 95 - 96, 98, 100 - 103,
121, 131, 135, 142 - 143, 145, 154, 156,
161 - 163, 169, 171, 176 - 179, 186 - 191, 201,
203, 205, 209, 210 - 213, 230
Australia or Australians 15, 26,
91, 94, 124, 150, 163, 211
Austria 17, 25, 94, 123, 157, 160
Austria-Hungary 25, 94
Auty & Clogg 25, 181
Avalon Project, The 102, 126, 147
Axios (Vardar) River................................78, 135,
143, 151, 170, 209, 212, 213
Axis (Berlin-Rome), or Axis Powers 17,
19 - 20, 22, 26, 30 - 32, 34, 38, 40, 43, 46,
48 - 57, 61 - 62, 66, 69, 71, 79 - 80, 83,
85, 87 - 88, 92, 98, 101, 104, 125 - 126,
129, 131, 133, 136 - 137, 142 - 143,
151 -154, 170, 185, 187, 189,
191 - 192, 195, 201, 203, 209, 212, 221

Bačka 18
Bailey, Colonel William "Bill" S. 217, 219, *222*
Bailey, Ronald H....................................179, *227*
Baku..21, 88, 198
Balfour & Mackay 97, 98, 100,
103 - 104, 107, 118, 121,
124 - 125, 129, 131, 148, 191, 193, 227
Balfour, 'Jock,' Sir John 201
Balkan entente 58, *193*
Balkan Front......................................17, 78, 92, 93,
106, 116, 131, 145, 155, 158, 165,
166, 173, 187, 205, 206, 209, *222*, 223
Balkan Peninsula............................39, 145, 158
Balkans, or Balkan States ... 160 - 163, 167, 169,
171, 176, 177, 181, 185, 187, 188, 191,
195, 199, 201, 203 - 205, 207, 208, 211, 219
Baltic Sea 14, 186, 198
Baltic States 38
Banat..18, 147, 148
Bank of England..201
Banovina Croatia, or Banovina Hrvatska 18
Baranja...18
Barbarossa, Operation ....22, 37, 52 -53,
102, 105, 147 - 148, 169
Bardia...59
Barker, Elisabeth ....32, 33, 35 - 36,
42 - 43, 46 - 48, 50, 53, 55 - 56, 64,
66, 68, 79, 81, 87, 93 - 94, 96 - 97,
101 - 102, 104, 106 - 107, 111, 114, 116,
121 - 122, 124, 132 - 133, 136, 145,
150 - 151, 154 - 155, 161, 163, 165 - 166,177,
181, 206, 207, 212 - 213, 215, 219, 221, 227
Batum 21, 198
Beles 78
Belgium 25, 29
Belgrade .... 15 - 20,
22 - 24, 30 - 32, 40, 45 - 47, 49,
50, 52, 56, 58, 60, 64 - 66, 68,

        70, 76, 78 - 79, 81, 85, 87 - 89,
        91, 98 - 100, 102 - 117, 120,
        122 - 123, 126 - 139, 141 - 145,
        148, 150 - 155, 157 - 162, 165 - 167,
        170, 172, 174 - 175, 190 - 192,
        194 - 197, 199, 201 - 203, 206,
        209 - 217, 219, 221, 223 - 224,
        226 - 227, 229, 230
Beloff, journalist Nora............. 17, 19, 24, 25, *227*
Below, Major von 147
Belvedere Palace.. 126
Benghazi................................. 65, 69, 74, 89, 206
Bennett, John H. 15, 217
Berchtesgaden.. 87
Berghof 53, 87, 88
Berle, Adolf 50
Berlin..20, 61, 62, 83,
        88, 99, 124, 128, 146, 157
Berne 218
Bessarabia 38
Bibica-Rosetti.. 210
Birčanin, Ilija or Trifunović-Birčanin ("Daddy") 15,
        16, 68, 109 - 111, 120, 121, 123,
        124, 127, 129, 134, 138, 141, 142,
        143, 215 - 217, 219, 223, 225
Bitolj (Monastir) Gap 74, 103, 115, 158, 212
Black Sea...................... 32, 59, 98, 145, 155, 198
Bladon.. 28
Blake & Louis 19, 39, 45, 59, 94,
        126, 130, 167, 206, 227
Blau, George E. 18, 23, 45,
        51 - 53, 157, 162, 164, 167, 170, 228
Bletchley Cryptographers, or Bletchley Park 102,
        159, 167, 184
Bohlen, Charles "Chip"..................................... 14
Bor mines......................................148, 153, 200
Boris III, King of Bulgaria 150, 207
Bosnić, Petar................. 119, 126, 140, 226, *228*
Boughey, Peter 15
Brašić, General Ilija.. 213
Breadbasket, The Balkan............................... 194
Britain, British or England, United Kingdom.........
        14 - 15, 17 - 20, 22 - 61, 63 - 124,
        127 - 129, 131 - 146, 151 - 179,
        181 - 198, 200 - 219, 221 - 231
Britanova news agency............................ 77, 115
British Broadcasting Corporation, BBC or B.B.C.
        ....83, 110, 115, 116, 129, 137
British Empire, or Commonwealth 26, 27, *228*
British Expeditionary Force (BEF)................... 89
Brooke, General Sir Alan 167, 182
Broz, Josip or Tito ("Engineer Tomanek")........ 23,
        176, 177, 180, 202, 227, 228, 230
Bruce Lockhart, Sir Robert..................... 207, *228*
Bucharest...60, 83
Budapest.. 150
Budionny, Marshal Semyon 21
Budisavljević, Srđan....................................... 111
Bukhovina 38
Bulgaria, or Bulgarian .... 17 - 20,
        22, 25, 29 - 30, 32, 33, 35, 39,
        40, 43 - 46, 48 - 49, 51, 52, 59, 62,

        63, 65 - 71, 79, 82 - 83, 85 - 89,
        91, 99, 101, 104, 113, 115,
        117, 118, 125, 135, 141, 142,
        146 - 148, 150, 151, 155, 160, 170, 173,
        186 - 190, 193, 196 - 198, 203 - 207,
        211, 215, 216, 218, 219

Cadogan, Sir Alexander 15, 32, 36, 47,
        57, 60, 64 - 67, 69, 72, 80, 82 - 83,
        86, 91 - 93, 96, 100, 115 - 116, 118,
        123 - 124, 128, 131, 136, 158, 160, 213, 228
Cairo...39, 40, 42, 54, 55,
        63, 65, 71 - 74, 81, 84, 90,
        92 - 93, 98 - 99, 109, 113 - 115,
        117, 121 - 122, 124, 131, 158,
        165, 167, 169, 176, 181,
        186 - 188, 203 - 204,
        206 - 207, 211, 213, 226, 227
Campbell, Ronald Ian (later Sir) 15, 22,
        23, 46 - 48, 56 - 57, 63, 76 - 77, 79,
        85 - 86, 91, 94 - 96, 98, 100 - 102,
        104, 107 - 109, 112 - 117, 119,
        120 - 122, 124, 126, 128 - 129,
        132, 134 - 136, 138, 141, 146, 150,
        152 - 153, 156, 161, 166, 174 - 175,
        192, 212 - 213, 217, 219, 221 - 224
Campbell, Sir Ronald [Hugh].........................201
Camp X 208
Canada..26
Cape Matapan 151
Cape of Good Hope 72, 168
Carlton, David (Eden biographer).............53, 60,
        63, 67 - 68, 70, 74, 78 - 79, 82, 84, 92,
        106, 135, 165, 167, 204, 206, 209, 228
Carver, Field Marshal Lord Michael 167
casus belli..69, 82, 86,
        106, 113, 119, 155, 214
Cavalliero army group, Italian Army in Albania
       101
Cave Brown, journalist Anthony 184,
        186, 196, 228
Chakmak, Marshal Fevzi..........................81, 82
Chamberlain, Neville 59, 228
Charmley, Professor John...............73, 166, *228*
Chequers 60, 85, 86, 106, 129, 137, 174
Chicago 159, 192, *228*, 229
Chicago Daily News 192
Chief of Imperial General Staff (CIGS)............15,
        37, 41, 47, 52, 59, 63, 66, 68, 70 - 71,
        78, 80, 92, 136, 152, 161, 164, 166,
        169 - 170, 175 - 176 187,
        203, 204, 207, 219 - 222
Churchill, Randolph 177
Churchill, Winston S. (later Sir) 14,
        18 - 19, 22, 28, 32 - 42, 45 - 48,
        50 - 53, 55 - 60, 63 - 74, 78 - 94,
        96 - 101, 103, 106, 114, 116 - 118,
        122, 124, 128 - 129, 131 - 132,
        134 - 138, 140, 142 - 143, 145 - 150,
        153, 155 - 157, 159 - 167, 169,
        171 - 179, 181 - 188, 191 - 192, 198,

    202, 206 - 208, 215, 226 - 231
Churchill and the Balkan Front........................78,
    92-93, 106, 116, 131, 145,
    155, 165 - 166, 173, 187, 206
Churchill and Greece 22,
    46 - 48, 56 - 57, 63, 69, 85 - 86,
    91 - 94, 98, 100, 117, 122, 124
Churchill and Italy ....33 - 34,
    36, 38 - 42, 48, 51, 53, 56,
    60, 64, 67, 83, 86 - 87, 92, 94,
    96 - 97, 99 - 101, 103, 131 - 132,
    135 - 138, 145 - 149, 153, 161,
    169, 177 - 179, 182 - 183, 185,
    188, 192, 198, 206 - 207, 215
Churchill and SOE 32,
    35, 40, 47, 51, 58, 60,
    64 - 68, 71, 77 - 81, 83, 85,
    94, 96, 99, 102, 106 - 114, 118,
    120 - 124, 128 - 129, 132,
    136 - 138, 161, 174 - 175,
    179, 181, 184 - 185, 191,
    195, 202, 207 - 208,
    217 - 218, 229 - 231
Churchill and Turkey ....33 - 35,
    42, 46, 48, 50,
    59 - 60, 64 - 74, 90 - 94,
    98 - 101, 103, 106,
    116, 118, 123,
    145 - 148, 150, 155,
    159 - 160, 163, 166 - 168, 171,
    173, 186 - 188, 191 - 192,
    198, 206 - 208, 230,
Churchill and USA..38,
    38, 50, 51, 56 - 58, 65,
    68, 71, 74, 80, 87,
    97 -98, 103,
    116, 129, 131,
    135, 145, 166, 171 - 172,
    183 - 188, 192,
    202, 207 - 208, 228
Churchill and Yugoslavia 22,
    34 - 40, 42, 45 - 48,
    50 - 53, 55 - 60, 63 - 74,
    78 - 94, 96 - 101, 103,
    106, 110 - 138, 141 - 143,
    145 - 150, 179, 181 -183,
    185 - 186, 191 - 192, 198, 231
Ciano, Galeazzo 16, 39, 46, 49, 124, 125
Cincar-Marković, Aleksandar,
or Cinzar Merkovich ....45, 48 - 50,
    77, 85, 102, 105, 119,
    123 - 124, 139, 192
civil war 23, 163
Clarke, Col. Charles S. 15, 55, 121, 212, 224
Clissold, Stephen.............. 23, 137, 163, 177, *228*
Clogg, Professor Richard............................... 181
Code and Cypher School, Bletchley Park...... 184
Colonies 26
Colville, John "Jock"........................... 41, 46, 57,
    68, 70, 86, 90 - 91, 93, 112, 116,
    137, 151, 158 - 159, 161 - 164,
    167 - 168, 178, 207, 228, 231

Comintern.................................. 13 - 14, 23, 163
Communism, Communists 23, 47,
    176 - 179, 200, 207 - 208, 230
Communist Party of Yugoslavia (CPY) 13, 23,
    163, 176
Cooper, Duff...165
coup d'état in Belgrade, puč or the putsch 17,
    22, 32, 51, 55, 58, 60, 85, 102, 106,
    108 - 109, 113 - 115, 118, 120 - 123,
    125, 127 - 129, 131 - 143, 150,
    158 - 160, 172, 174 - 176, 194, 196,
    210, 213, 215 - 218, 220, 226 - 227
Cracow 22, 126, 130
Crete.................................. 20, 23, 34, 38- 40, 42,
    90, 164, 167, 171 - 173, 179, 211
Creveld, Professor Martin, van..................38, 41,
    43 - 46, 48 - 49, 51 - 53, 60 - 61,
    74 - 76, 83 - 85, 87 - 88, 98 - 99,
    101, 145, 148 - 150, 168 - 170,
    189, 204, 214, 216, 230
Creveld, Prof. and Greece........................38, 41,
    22 - 23, 25, 29, 32 - 36, 38 - 46,
    97 - 99, 101, 204, 230
Creveld, Prof. and Yugoslavia.........................38,
    43, 44, 48 - 49, 51 - 53, 60 - 61,
    74 - 76, 83 - 85, 87 - 88, 98 - 99,
    101, 148 - 150, 168 - 170,
    189, 214, 216, 230
Cripps, Sir Stafford 94, 118
Croatia, or Croats .... 17 - 18, 23,
    25, 30, 46, 94 - 95, 104, 113 - 115,
    139, 147 - 148, 151, 153, 161, 170,
    192 - 193, 212 - 213, 218, 220, 222
Croatian Peasant Party (CPP),
or Hrvatska Seljačka Stranka 16
    95, 104, 114, 152, 193
Crown Council (Yugoslav)...................85, 88, 99,
    104 - 105, 107, 110
Cunningham, Admiral Sir Andrew 73,
    88 - 90, 97, 164, 186
Cvetković, Dr. Dragiša,
or Cvetkovich, Tsvetkovich...................... 16, 49,
    62, 66, 77, 85, 102, 106 - 108,
    111 - 112, 116, 119, 123 - 125, 192,
    194, 199, 202, 209, 220
Cyprus 32, 106, 112, 113, 119, 123
Cyrenaica 74, 161, 167, 172, 182, 189
Čubrilović, Dr. Branko 111

Daily Telegraph, The 177
Dakar...73, 90, 166
Dalmatia 17, *18*
Dalton, Dr. Hugh................................35, 51, 60,
    66, 81, 85, 96, 106, 110,
    112, 115, 120 - 124, 127,
    132 - 134, 136 - 138,
    142 - 143, 146, 158, 160, 172,
    174 - 175, 207, 217, 219,
    221, 224, 228 - 230
Danchev, Alex .... 71, 186 - 191,
    193 - 194, 196 -197, 202, 204 - 207, 228

Danube, River 40, 47,
    68, 82 - 83, 108 - 109,127, 136,
    142, 148, 157 - 158, 194, 228
Dardanelles Strait 67, 166, 222
de Guingand, General Francis 54, 84, 90, 228
Deakin, historian William (later Sir) 176
Debar 154
Defence Committee 60, 63, 66, 72, 74,
    138, 143, 169, 174 - 175, 188, 203
Dekanozov, Vladimir 157
Democratic Party .... 16, 111, 139 - 141
Despard, Capt. Max 212
Dew, Armand 122, 194
Dilks, Professor David 33, 39, 47,
    57, 60, 63 - 67, 69, 72, 80, 82 - 83,
    86, 91 -94, 96, 100, 115, 118, 123 - 124,
    128, 131, 158, 161, 195, *228*
Dill, General Sir John .... 51, 54, 58 - 59,
    63, 69 - 81, 84, 90 - 92, 100, 103, 107,
    135, 145, 150- 154, 158, 160 - 161,
    165 - 169, 172, 182, 203 - 205, 213
Dios Mountains 148
Directive No. 18 45
Directive No. 20 .... 52, 107
Directive No. 21 53
Directive No. 22 101
Directive No. 25 .... 102, 148, 170
Dixon, Pearson (later Sir) 42, 46, 151,
    153, 165, 178, 212
Dodds-Parker, Sir Douglas 20, 208, *228*
Dodecanese Islands 179, 188
Doering, Otto C. 186
Dojran, Lake or Doran, Doiran 97,
    154, 159, 230
Dominions 33
Donovan, Col. William Joseph 19, 50,
    56 - 58, 61, 63, 65 - 66, 68 - 69,
    72 - 74, 79, 86, 100, 106, 152, 157,
    171, 183 - 208, 224, 228, 230
Dowding, Air Marshal Sir Hugh 37
Downing Street 56, 58, *228*
Dubrovnik 137
Duchess of Kent 24, 201
Duke and Duchess of Kent 30, 31
Dunkirk 19, 70, 73, 78,
    90, 95, 166, 171 - 172, 182
Dunlop, Richard 19, 58, 184,
    186 - 189, 191- 195, 206 - 207, 228
Dykes, Lt.-Col. Vivian..63, 65 - 66, 71, 186 - 191,
    193 - 197, 201 - 202, 204 - 207, 228
Đonović, Jovan also Djonovic. Djonovich, and
Djonovitch 47, 114, 120, 134,
    136, 138, 143 - 144, 175, 215 - 219, 223

Economist, The 182
E.A.M, or EAM 178
E.L.A.S., or ELAS 178, 179
Eden, Anthony (later The Earl of Avon) 22,
    23, 32, 34, 39 - 43,
    45, 51 - 54, 58 - 60,
    63 - 87, 89 - 100, 102 - 107,
    111 - 124, 126 - 129, 132,
    134 - 138, 145 - 146, 150 - 158,
    160 - 169, 171 - 172, 174 - 175,
    178 - 182, 186, 190, 202 - 209,
    211 - 213, 215, 217,
    222 - 223, 227, 228, 229
Eden and Campbell, ... 22,
    23, 46 - 48, 63, 76 - 77, 79,
    85 - 86, 91, 94 - 96, 98, 100,
    104, 107, 112 - 117, 119,
    124, 126, 128 - 129,
    134 - 136, 138, 146, 150,
    152 - 153, 156, 161, 166,
    174 - 175, 212 - 213, 217,
Eden and Greece .... 22 - 23,
    32, 34, 39 - 43,
    51 - 54, 58 - 60, 112 - 117,
    123 - 124, 126, 129,
    132, 134 - 136, 142, 145,
    178 - 182,
    186, 202 - 209,
    217, 222, 227, 229
Eden and Turkey .... 33 - 35,
    39, 43, 45, 52 - 54, 59,
    64 - 86, 90 - 94, 100, 103 - 104,
    111 - 113, 116, 118 - 120, 123,
    145 - 146, 150 - 151, 155,, 160,
    163, 171, 174 - 175, 186, 208, 222
Eden and Yugoslavia 22, 23
    34, 39, 44 - 45, 51 - 54,
    58 - 60, 63 - 87, 89 - 100,
    106 - 107, 217, 222 - 223, 227, 229
Edessa 78
Egypt .... 29, 32, 34, 40 - 42, 50, 60, 65,
    67, 76, 162 - 163, 167, 171, 186, 188, 203
Enigma coding machine 19, 22, 37,
    59, 67, 102, 184, 203, 204
Esher, Lord 100
Eton College 136, *193*
Europe .... 14, 18 - 19, 29,
    32- 33, 35, 39 - 40, 50,
    54, 59, 64, 67, 69, 81, 88, 98,
    163, 168, 171, 176, 179, 183 - 184,
    186, 190, 197 - 198, 202, 227 - 228

Fadden, Arthur W. 150
Fascist, or Fascism 16, 32, 43, 95, 96
Fiume 148
Florina 78, 151, 155
Forbes 201
Ford, Corey .... 58, 106, 186 - 187,
    194 - 195, 203, 207, 228
Foreign Office (FO) 186, 212
Foreign Office (FO) ...48, 50, 57, 63, 94, 96, 124,
    151, 187, 222
Fortier, Colonel Louis 192, 197, 199
France 17, 19, 23, 25, 29,
    33 - 35, 41, 48, 56 - 57, 90, 94, 120,
    164, 177, 183 - 184, 188, 200, 212, 219, 228
FRUS1 ....87, 107, 126, 228
Fulton, Missouri 14, 35

Fuschl 53

Garron, embassy second secretary 194
Gavrilović, Dr. Milan or Gavrilovic (Gavrilovitch)
.... 88, 94
120, 136, 175, 215, 219 - 220
George II, King of Greece 50, 74
George VI, King 81, 184
German Air Force (GAF), or Luftwaffe 19,
22, 36 - 37, 45, 55, 65,
89, 94, 102, 126, 157, 208
German Bombardment of Belgrade 159
German High Command 18, 21, 146, 157
German invasion of Greece 70, 158
German Invasion of Yugoslavia 158
German-Soviet Pact, or Nazi-Soviet Pact 23,
58, 198
Germany, or Germans .... 13, 15, 17 - 23,
25, 32, 34, 36 - 49, 51 - 56,
58 - 63, 65 - 68, 71 - 96,
98 - 104, 106 - 108, 110 - 113,
115 - 119, 121 - 122, 124 - 126, 128,
130, 132, 135 - 136, 145 - 146,
149 - 154, 157 - 165, 167 - 173,
177 - 178, 181 - 186, 188 - 211,
214 - 216, 218 - 222, 224 - 225
Germany and Bulgaria .... 17 - 20,
22, 25, 32, 39,
40, 43 - 46, 48 - 49, 51, 52,
59, 62, 63, 65 - 68, 71, 79, 82 - 83,
85 - 89, 91, 99, 101, 104, 113,
115, 117, 118, 125, 135,
146, 150, 151, 160, 170, 173,
186, 193, 196 - 198, 203 - 207,
211, 215, 216, 218, 219
Germany and Greece .... 15, 17, 19 - 20,
25, 32, 34, 38 - 46,
48, 51 - 56, 58 - 63, 65 - 68,
71 - 96, 98 - 99, 106 - 107, 110,
112, 115, 117, 124, 126, 132,
135 - 136, 145, 151, 153 - 154,
158 - 165, 167 - 173, 177 - 178,
185, 188 - 191, 195 - 196, 198,
202 - 211, 214, 217, 221 - 222, 224 - 225
Germany and Yugoslavia 13, 15,
17 - 23, 25, 32, 34,
36 - 40, 42 - 43, 44 - 49,
51 - 56, 58 - 63, 65 - 68,
71 - 96, 98 - 104, 106 - 108,
110 - 113, 115 - 119, 121 - 122,
124 - 126, 128, 130, 132,
135 - 136, 145 - 146,
149 - 154, 157 - 165,
167 - 173, 177, 186,
193, 196 - 198, 203 - 207,
211, 214 - 2215, 216, 218, 219
German-Yugoslav negotiations ... 44 - 46, 48 - 49,
52, 61, 87, 98, 217
Gezira 158
Gibraltar 185, 186, 207
Glanville, Trevor 132

Glasgow 57
Glasnik (The Herald) 227, 230
Gleason, historian S. Everett. 50, 51, 52, 65, 171,
185, 187, 189, 193 - 194, 197, 229
Glen, Alexander "Sandy", (later Sir) 15, 60,
68, 108 - 109, 128, 133, 143,
175 - 176, 201, 215, 217 - 218, 222, 228
Godfrey, Rear Admiral John 184
Göring (Goering), *Reichsmarschall* Herman ......
36 - 37, 62, 126, 146 - 147
Gorodetsky, Professor Gabriel 39,
61 - 62, 82, 88, 157, 169, 222, 228
Grand Alliance 79, 228
Grand, Colonel Laurence or Lawrence .. 201, 215
Graz 147, 148, 149
"Great Purge" in the USSR 21
Greece, or Greeks .... 15, 17, 19 - 20,
22 - 23, 25, 29, 32 - 36, 38 - 46,
48 - 55, 57 - 94, 97 - 99, 101 - 107,
110, 112 - 117, 123 - 124, 126, 129,
132, 134 - 136, 142, 145, 147,
151, 153 - 156, 158 - 173, 176 - 182,
185 - 191, 195 - 196, 198, 202 - 214,
217, 221, 222, 224, 227, 229, 230
Greek General Staff 33
Gregorić or Gregoric, Danilo 45, 61
Grol, Dr. Milan .... 140 - 141, 229
Gulf of Orphanos 97
Guzzoni, General Alfredo 149
Gypsies, or Roma 18, 23

Haining, Lt.-Gen. Sir Robert 73
Halder, General Franz 45, 83, 103, 105, 148
Halifax, Lord Edward 17, 36,
46 - 48, 112, 186, 204, 219
Hanau, Julius 30, 139, 174, 176, 215, 217
Harding, Lord John 182
Hargyropoulos, Former Greek Foreign Minister
.... 107
Heeren, Viktor von .... 45, 87 - 88, 98 - 99, 152
Hehn, Professor Paul N 62, 229
Henderson, Sir Neville 201
Hensinger, Colonel 147
Hewel, Ambassador Walther 147
Heywood, Major-General T. G. ...... 74, 190 - 191
Hinsley *et al* .... 19, 22, 36 - 40,
59, 67, 79 - 80, 102 - 103, 105,
108, 127, 134, 169, 188, 203 - 204, 221, 229
Hinsley, historian Sir Francis Harry 19, 39, 45,
126, 130, 134, 206
His Majesty's Government, H.M.G. 17, 42, 79,
81, 129, 134, 137, 218, 222
Hitler, Adolf, *der Führer, Fuehrer* 14,
17 - 23, 29, 32, 35 - 40, 43 - 46,
48 - 49, 51 - 53, 55 - 58, 61 - 62,
66, 69, 83, 85 - 89, 93 - 107,
116 - 118, 124, 126, 128 - 129,
131 - 133, 137, 146 - 150, 152 - 153, 157,
159 - 160, 162 - 163, 165 - 167,
170 - 172, 183 - 184, 191 - 199, 202,
206, 208, 210, 214, 216, 230

Hitler and *Barbarossa* ....22, 37, 52 -53,
102, 105, 147 - 148,
Hitler and Yugoslavia ....17 - 23
29, 32, 35 - 40, 43,
43 - 46, 48 - 49, 51 - 53,
55 - 58, 61 - 62,
66, 69, 83, 85 - 89,
93 - 107, 106 - 108, 116 - 118,
124, 126, 128 - 129,
131 - 133, 137,
146 - 150, 152 - 153, 157,
159 - 160, 162 - 163, 165 - 167,
170 - 172,183, 185, 191 - 199, 202,
206, 208, 210, 214, 216, 230
Holland.. 37
Holmes, historian Richard...................... 117, 182
Holt, Colonel, Brazilian Attache 149
Hoover Institution Archives 109, 111,
118, 132, 139 - 142, 144, 174,
197, 218, 220, 222 - 223, 226, 230
Hopkins, Harry ..56 - 57, 182, 187, 198, 202, 208
Hoptner, Dr. Jacob.............................. 35, 66, 97,
110, 129, 162, 169, 192, 229
House of Commons 159, 165
Howard, Michael 33, 44, 176, 229
Howarth, Patrick.. 50, 229
Hudson, Capt. Duane T. "Bill" 15
Hull, Cordell 68, 183, 186, 202
Humphreys, wing commander 37
Hun (slang, a German) 78
Hungary ....17 - 18, 29 - 30,
46, 49, 69, 99,
125, 147 - 148, 150,
160, 211, 215 - 216

Ilić, General Bogoljub.................... 140, 151, 153
Independent State of Croatia (ISC) or Nezavisna
Država Hrvatska (NDH) 18, 23, 161
Independent, The... 177
India 15, 26, 50, 129, 181, 198, 215
Inönü, Ismet, President of Turkey 43, 67, 145
Institut za istorijska pitanja 199, 227
Ismay, General Sir Hastings 41, 89,
90, 92 - 93, 98, 132, 143, 161,
164, 169, 176 - 177, 179, 229
Istanbul ....67 - 68, 77, 85,
142 - 143, 181, 217, 219, 222
Istria 94, 153
Italians, or Italy................................... 16 - 20, 25,
29 - 30, 32 - 34, 36, 38 - 46,
48 - 51, 53 - 54, 56, 60, 62, 64,
67, 83, 86 - 87, 92, 94, 96 - 97,
99 - 101, 103, 124 - 125, 131 - 132,
135 - 138, 145 - 149, 152 - 156, 161,
168 - 170, 177 - 180, 182 - 183,
185, 188 - 189, 192, 198, 205 - 207,
214 - 218, 221 - 222, 225, 230

Jacob, Sir Ian 159
Jajce... 149

Janković, General Miloje .... 153 - 155
Janković, General Radivoje, or Jankovitch ....
153, 154
Japan.............................19, 25, 38, 44, 124, 216
Jasenovac concentration camp......................23
Jebb, Gladwyn (later Lord) 60,
66 - 67, 123, 136, 160
Jews 18, 23
Jodl, General Alfred........................ 62, 146 - 147
Johnston, Tom...57
Joint Planning Staff, Cairo (JPS)....................89
Josimović, Colonel B. 153
Jovanović, Jovan "Pižon" 220
Jovanović, Professor Dragoljub....................113
Jovanović, Professor Slobodan........19, 113, 146
Jukić, Ilija............................ 46, 48 - 49, 68 - 69,
86, 88, 93, 96 - 97, 111 - 112,
124 - 125, 153, 182, 191, 200, 202, 210, 229
Julian Alps 149

Kajmakčalan, or Kajmakcalan 78, 115
Kalafatović, General Danilo...................162, 210
Karageorgevich, Prince Paul........................16,
22 - 24, 30 - 32, 36, 42, 46,
48 - 50, 56, 58, 61, 63 - 64, 66,
71, 76 - 77, 79, 81, 85 - 88, 91, 93,
96, 99 - 101, 103 - 104, 106 - 107,
111, 113 - 114, 116, 118, 120,
122, 124, 128 - 129, 133 - 138,
142, 150 - 152, 155, 157, 161, 163, 166,
172 - 173, 192, 193, 195, 197, 201 - 202,
205, 208, 212, 216 - 217, 219 - 222
Kavalla...43, 76, 97, 212
Kazan defile...142
Keegan, military historian John .... 32 - 33,
40, 70 - 71, 88 - 89, 94, 169 - 170, 229
Keitel, General Wilhelm................. 83, 146 - 147
Kennedy, General Sir John 41, 55, 59,
63 - 64, 66, 69 - 72,
75 - 76, 80, 84, 89, 91, 160,
162 - 166, 170, 207, 229
Kharkov..21
Kimball, Professor Warren F. 35
King Peter II .... 20, 22 - 24, 116,
133 - 134, 138, 159,
172, 195, 210, 226
Klagenfurt..147
Knatchbull-Hugessen, Sir Hughe 83
Knez Lazar...126, 129
Knežević, Major Živan-Žika or Knjevich, Jika.......
16, 139 - 142, 226 - 227, 229
Knežević, Radoje or Knjevich, Radne............16,
111, 121, 139 - 141, 176
Knox, Frank .... 56, 183 - 187,
189 - 190, 192, 196, 202, 205
Kočović, Bogoljub..229
Koliopoulos, Ioannis .... 33, 42 - 43,
51 - 53, 63 - 64, 74, 80, 84, 229
Konstantinović, Mihailo or Constantinovich....111
Kontić, Jovan...227
Koroshatz, Anton or Korošec 30, 49

Koryzis, Alexandros .... 67 - 68, 74 - 75, 214
Kosić, Dr. Mirko.................................... 140, 152
Kosić, General Petar..................... 192, 199, 212
Kosovo .... 17 - 18, 115, 126, 129
Košutić, August 95
Koviljača 158
Kremlin 21
Krnjević, Dr. Juraj... 95
Krylov, Capt. Ivan Nikitch 20, 21, 86, 229
Kukosi, Kukesi 154
Kulovec, Dr. Fran 16, 88

Lady Dobbie... 135, 175
Lamb, Richard 69, 80, 229
Lane, Arthur Bliss .... 56, 68 - 69, 87,
100, 107, 112, 152,
191 - 192, 195, 202, 208, 228, 229
Langer, historian William Leonard ...... 170 - 171,
185, 187, 189, 193 - 194, 197, 229
Larissa 78
Lawrence, Vice-Consul 191
Leary, William M. 43, 229
Leeper, Allen R.W. 178
Legation, American 205
Legation, British .... 15, 64 - 65,
84, 91, 94, 103, 107 - 108, 111,
116 - 117, 120 - 123, 126, 131 - 132,
137 - 138, 174, 187, 189 -191, 195,
197, 201, 203, 210, 215, 223 - 224
Lemnos 40
Lend-Lease .... 51, 103 - 104, 124, 189, 208
Lenin, Vladimir Ilich 14, 20
Lethbridge, Robert 201
Libya 60, 63, 89, 94, 158, 171, 185, 188, 203
Liddell-Hart, historian Basil Henry .... 65 - 67,
74, 98, 166, 171 - 172, 181, 228 -229
Loewenheim et al 14, 56, 135, 183, 229
London .... 24, 36 - 37, 41 - 42,
44, 50, 55 - 56, 58, 60, 63,
65 - 66, 70, 72, 74, 77, 78 - 81,
84 - 85, 90, 92, 94, 96, 98, 100, 102,
108, 110, 112, 116, 118 - 119,
121 - 122, 135 - 136, 138, 141 - 143,
150, 159 - 160, 162, 164 - 165, 171,
173 -175, 178, 181, 184 - 185,
202, 204, 207 - 208, 213,
218 - 219, 222 - 224, 226 - 231
Longmore, Air Vice-Marshal Sir Arthur 40,
63 - 64, 66, 73, 78, 188 - 189, 205
Los Angeles 159
Lothian, Lord Philip Kerr 185
Lovelt, Major 149
Low Countries 183, 230
Lowlor, Dr. Sheila 171, 229
Lustre operation 150
Luterotti, Contra-Admiral Julij 192
Luxemburg 183
Ljubljana 137, 139, 141, 231

Macdonald or MacDonald, Group Capt. A. Hugh, H. ....
15, 109 - 110, 118 - 121, 126 - 129,
133, 136- 137, 145 - 146, 150 - 151,
155, 176, 194, 201, 224, 226
Macedonia, or Macedonians .... 17 - 18,
68, 74, 76, 85, 90 - 91,
147 - 148, 160, 170, 189
Maček, Dr. Vladko 22, 49, 68, 88,
95, 100 - 111, 128, 152,
192 - 194, 202, 220, 229
Mackenzie, William J. 66, 68,
123, 158, 207, 229
Maclean, Brigadier Fitzroy 172,
176 - 177, 182, 229
MacVeagh, Lincoln .... 190 - 191, 203
Major Christian 147
Malta 32, 40, 131,
135, 145, 186, 207
Mapplebeck, Thomas .... 15, 109 - 110,
116 - 117, 121, 129, 176
Margesson, David (later Lord) 73, 90
Maribor 109
Marita, Operation .... 23, 52 - 53,
89, 103, 105, 147 - 148, 169
Marseille 17
Marshall-Cornwall, General Sir James 71, 188
Martin, John 37, 231
Masterson, Thomas 15, 81, 96,
106 - 107, 110, 121 - 122,
133, 139 - 141, 176, 223
Mayski, Ivan 222
McClymont, historian W. G. 34, 40,
64 - 66, 68, 79, 89, 93,
135, 153 - 155, 229
Mediterranean .... 32 - 35, 38 - 41,
45, 48 - 49, 56 - 60, 65, 74, 88 - 89,
94, 97, 101, 105, 135, 145, 160,
164 - 165, 171, 177, 179,
181, 185 - 187, 195 - 196,
204 - 205, 209 - 210, 227, 229
Menzies, Major-General Stewart 37, 184
Meštrović, Ivan .... 30 - 31, 95
Metaxas, General Ioannis .... 20, 33 - 34,
39, 42, 44 - 45, 48, 50, 53 - 54,
61, 63 - 68, 90, 103, 145, 154,
170, 189 - 190, 207, 214
Metohija 18
Mihailović, Col. Dragoljub-Draža (later General)
.... 15, 132, 163, 230
Military Intelligence (MI) .... 54 - 55, 67, 73,
102 - 103, 184, 224
Military Intelligence, Yugoslav 62
Miloševa street 140
Ministry of Economic Warfare (MEW) 224
Ministry of Political Warfare (MPW) 181, 207
Mirković, General Borivoje-Bora,
or Mirkovitch 55,
109 - 111, 116 - 121, 123 - 124,
126 - 129, 133 - 134, 136, 139 - 141,
192, 194, 200, 220, 223, 226 - 228
Mohilev 21

Molotov, Vyacheslav 62, 69
Montenegro 18, 25, 30
Montgomery, Field Marshal Bernard 54
Morris, Lelan B. 126
Morton, Major Desmond (later Sir) 70,
                                    136, 184, 228
Moscow .... 13 - 14, 16, 20 - 21, 23,
                    83, 86, 88, 91, 94, 118, 157, 163,
                   177 - 178, 180, 198, 218 - 219, 228
Mosul 198
Mussolini, Benito, *il Duce* .... 16 - 18,
             33 - 34, 38 - 39, 43 - 46, 48 - 49,
               55, 62, 69, 88, 94, 96, 98, 101,
             116, 147 - 149, 150, 166, 182, 183

Narodna Odbrana (The Defense League) 96,
                   109 - 110, 120 - 121, 133,
              142 - 143, 174 - 175, 218, 223
Nazis, or Nazism 18, 21, 35,
                  58, 134, 137, 187, 194
Nedić, General Milan 44
Nelson, Sir Frank 32, 51, 60,
                         66 - 68, 80, 85,
                 142 - 143, 161, 184, 207
Nemanjina Street 140
Nestos line 76, 78, 135
New York City 159
New York Times, The 65, 131
"New world order" 87
New Zealand, or New Zealanders 26, 91,
                  94, 124, 170, 211, 229
Newall, Sir Cyril 37
Newmarket 50
Nicholls, John 219
Nikolić, General Milutin 153
Nikšić or Niksic 211
Nile Delta 162
Ninčić, Dr. Momčilo 16, 152
Niš or Nish 68, 109, 191
North Africa 39
Norway .... 29, 72 - 73, 90, 149, 166
Nuremberg Trial 126

Obradović, Capt. Obrad 210
Odessa 147, 219
Office of Strategic Services (OSS) 170,
                    194, 197, 208, 228
Official Gazette, The 128
Olympus Mountain 78, 155, 214
Onslow, Dr. Sue .... 17 - 18, 32,
                70 - 71, 81, 91, 108, 111 - 113,
                119 - 120, 122, 134, 137 - 138,
                  146, 165, 203 - 204, 208,
                 212 - 213, 218, 222, 224, 229
Onslow and the coup 17,
                  102, 106, 108 - 109, 113,
                  120, 122, 134, 213, 218
Onslow and Greece 17
                     70 - 71, 81, 91, 112,
                    117, 134, 145, 147,
                151, 153 - 156, 165, 203 - 204,
             208, 212 - 213, 218, 222, 224, 229
Onslow and Yugoslavia 17
               32, 70 - 71, 81, 91, 108, 111 - 113,
                119 - 120, 122, 134, 137 - 138,
                  146, 165, 203 - 204, 208,
                212 - 213, 218, 222, 224, 229
Opposition (parties) 23, 81, 89, 96,
                108, 110 - 112, 114 - 115, 121,
                133, 136 - 137, 142, 174, 195,
                209, 211, 216, 220, 223
Ostović, Pavle D. 22, 95, 229
Oxford University 24, 71, 100,
                         136, 193, 201, 230

Palairet, Sir Michael 38, 40, 42,
                    63, 189 - 190, 212 - 213
Palestine 29, 186
Pandurović, General Dragiša 126, 229
Papagos, General Alexandros 16,
             64 - 65, 75 - 76, 78, 84, 90 - 92,
              97, 115, 145, 153 - 155, 167,
            170, 189 - 190, 212 - 214, 229
Pappas, Greek journalist .... 116, 209 - 211
Parrott, Sir Cecil 24, 138, 172, 201, 229
Part Two 40, 51, 58, 60, 64,
              68, 81, 89, 96, 109 - 110, 114,
             116, 126 - 127, 129, 133 - 134,
          139, 141, 152, 212, 217, 220, 223
Partisans .... 176 - 177, 202, 208, 227, 231
Passport Control Officer (PCO) 187, 201, 202
Patriarch Gavrilo, Dr. Dožić 226
Pavelić, Ante Smith 227
Pavelić, Dr. Ante, Poglavnik 18
Pearton, Maurice 38, 67, 229, 230
Peloponnesus peninsula 172, 211
Perišić, Major Milisav or L.R. (Last Ray) Hope
                     ...... 96 - 98, 101, 104, 107
Pešić, General Petar 126, 192, *199*
Petković, Colonel Vasa 153
Petranović & Žutić 66, 91, 107, 108, 112, 113,
                                   156, 229
Petric 159
Petrograd 21
Petrov, Vladimir 44, 66, 89,
                 187, 189 - 192, 203, 229
Petrović, General Milorad 126
Peyton, Colonel 149
Pimlott, historian Ben 60, 127,
           133 - 134, 136, 143, 155, 158, 160, 229
Pirie, Ian 68
Planica 200
Plevlje 210
Ploesti 40
Podgorica 154
Poland 22, 29, 33, 35, 41, 56, 164, 183, 230
Polish brigade 161
Politika 128, 226
Popović, Colonel Branko 153
Popović, Colonel Žarko .. 16, 111, 226 - 227, 230
Portugal 25, 29

Prague 17
President (Roosevelt) 14, 29, 32, 35,
    46, 50, 56 - 58, 68 - 69, 72, 93,
    98, 100 - 101, 104, 106, 113, 117,
    132, 135, 137, 145, 159, 176, 183,
    186 - 187, 191 - 194, 196 - 197,
    199, 202 - 204, 207, 229
Princess Olga..36
Prisoners of war (POW)..................... 18, 23, 170
Proclamation, Royal..............................140 - 142
propaganda..........................18, 25, 51, 81, 89,
    106, 112, 116 - 117, 122 - 123,
    131 - 132, 137, 139 - 142, 144,
    156, 161, 173, 175 - 176, 184,
    197, 207, 209 - 211, 219, 227, 230
Punishment, Operation ....157 - 158, 161, 172
Puttkamer, Commander Konstantin von 147

Radovanović, Dr. Milorad..............................226
Rapp, Sir Terence................................15, 31, 95
Ravna Gora..163
Red Guards...21
Reich, Third German.......................................21
Rhodes James, historian Robert..............40 - 41,
    60, 80, 95, 100, 102, 134,
    159, 165, *228*, 229, 230
Ribbentrop, Joachim von 45, 48,
    50, 53, 61 - 62, 87, 99,
    110, 124 - 126, 146
Rintelen, Gen.-Maj. von 147
Ristić, Capt. Dragiša N......................19, 38 - 39,
    44 - 45, 87, 99, 103, 105, 125 - 126,
    128, 140, 152, 162, 210, 220, 227, 230
Rogatchev...21
Romania, or Romanian.....................36 - 40, 55,
    59, 67, 115, 126, 142, 157,
    177, 188, 205, 221, 229, 230
Rome 46, 49, 61
Rommel...70, 94
Roumania...66, 86
Royal Air Force, R.A.F.......36, 90, 161, 184, 211
Royal Navy..36, 90, 164
Rumania, or Rumanians 129, 147
Rupel Pass...159
Russia ....13, 14, 19 - 23,
    25, 29, 33, 37 - 39, 43, 45,
    48, 51, 58, 60, 87, 88, 94 - 95, 98,
    100, 102, 111, 147 - 148, 159,
    167, 169 - 170, 172, 177, 178,
    198, 199, 206, 217, 219, 222, 228

Salonika 20, 30, 32, 41,
    43 - 49, 51 - 53, 59 - 61, 63 - 67,
    72 - 76, 78 - 79, 81, 83, 85 - 88, 91, 93,
    97 - 98, 100, 106, 112 - 113, 117, 119,
    125, 135, 145 - 146, 148, 150 - 155,
    158, 160, 178, 188, 190 - 191,
    204 - 205, 212, 214, 222, 224
Salter, Sir Arthur 185
Saracoglu, Sükrü 16, 106

Sarajevo 174, 211
Sargent...60
Sargent, Orme..181, 213
Scanlan, John D. 60
Scherff, Lt.-Col. Walter...................................147
Schmidt, Colonel 147
Schmidt, Dr. Paul 45, 61
Schmundt, Colonel Rudolf..............................147
Scobie, Lt.-Gen. Ronald 178
Sea Lion, Operation .... 19, 36 - 38,
    182, 185 - 186, 190, 205
Seaman, Mark 38, 67, 85, 229, 230
Secret Intelligence Service (SIS), or MI6 17,
    39 - 40, 67, 79, 108, 127,
    137 - 138, 184, 187, 191, 194,
    201 - 202, 215, 221, 230, 231
Section D of SIS 15, 17, 40, 47,
    68, 136, 179, 181, 191,
    194, 201, 215, 217, 221
Sekulić, Dr. Miloš..220
Selborne, Roundell Palmer 3rd Earl................15
Serb, Serbs or Serbian....................12, 16, 18, 23,
    25, 30, 47, 55, 61, 78, 81, 85, 89, 96,
    99, 108 - 111, 113 - 116, 120 - 121, 129,
    132 - 134, 136 - 137, 140, 142 - 143,
    147, 152, 161, 170, 174 - 175,
    192 - 194, 209, 211 - 213,
    215 - 216, 218 - 221, 223, 226 - 227
Serbian Orthodox Church.......................215, 226
Serbian Peasant Party (SPP) or Serb Peasant
Party 16,
    108 - 111, 120, 133 - 134, 136,
    142 - 143, 174 - 175, 215, 218 - 220, 223
Seymour, Horace 161
Shaposhnikov, Marshal Boris..........................21
Shea, General John 224
Shearer, Brigadier Eric J. 73
Shirer, William L. 146
Shkodra 154
Shone, Terence.... 103 - 104, 107, 111, 118, 201
Shoup, Paul...23, 230
Siberia 21
Sieverth, Lt.-Col..147
Simović Memoirs .... 226 - 227
Simović, Dr. Miloš-Miša........................ 226 - 227
Simović, General Dušan...........................16, 58,
    89, 109, 120 - 121, 123 - 129,
    131, 133 - 134, 136 - 141, 145 - 146,
    150 - 153, 155 - 158, 161 - 162,
    174 - 175, 192, 194 - 202, 206,
    209 - 211, 214, 220, 224, 226 - 227, 230
Skoplje, or Skopje 68, 137, 147,
    149, 159, 174, 191, 213
Slavs, the......................................24, 84, 160, 215
Slovakia..88
Slovenia, or Slovenes.........................18, 25, 46,
    94 - 95, 147, 151, 153, 193, 200, 213
Smith, Maj.-Gen. Arthur..................... 84, 97 - 98
Smith, Professor Bradley F. .... 56 - 58,
    79, 173, 182, 184 - 187,
    190 - 192, 195 - 197, 202 - 208, 230
Smith-Ross, Alec..201

Smuts, General Ian Christian................... 92 - 93
Smyrna.. 67
Sofia.................................... 66, 142, 147 - 148,
    150, 190 - 191, 201 - 203, 216
'Sophocles'.. 88
Southern Department of FO........... 146, 165, 212
Southern Serbia, or Old Serbia....... 46, 160, 212,
    213, 214, 222
Soviet Union, or U.S.S.R. .... 13 - 14, 16,
    19 - 23, 33, 36 - 38, 47, 51 - 52,
    62, 69, 71, 87 - 88, 94, 102,
    111 - 112, 118, 120, 126, 146 - 147,
    149, 157, 159 -160, 169, 176 - 177,
    179, 192, 194, 198 - 200, 206,
    218 - 219, 222, 228, 229, 230
Spain............................. 29, 48, 90, 92, 120, 185
Special Operations Executive (SOE), S.O.2... 15,
    17, 30, 32, 35, 40, 47, 51, 58, 60,
    64 - 68, 71, 77 - 81, 83, 85, 94, 96,
    99, 102, 106 - 112, 115 - 118,
    120 - 124, 127 - 130, 132 - 134,
    136 - 144, 158, 161, 174 - 175,
    179, 181, 184 - 185, 191, 194,
    195, 202, 204, 207 - 208,
    217 - 218, 221 - 225, 229, 230, 231
Split...................................... 31, 137, 149
Sporazum (Serbo-Croat).............................. 220
SS Bosiljka.. 224
St. John, correspondent Robert.................... 159,
    172 - 173, 209 - 211, 230
Stafford, Professor David....................... 32, 35,
    51, 60, 85, 94, 106 - 111,
    113 - 115, 118, 120, 122, 126, 129,
    131, 134, 137 - 138, 174, 179, 213, 230
Stafford and the coup 32,
    51, 60, 85, 106,
    108 - 109, 113 - 115, 118, 120, 122,
    129, 131, 134, 137 - 138, 174, 213
Stafford and SOE............................. 32, 51, 60,
    85, 106, 108 - 109, 115, 118,
    120, 122, 129, 134,
    137 - 138, 174
Stalin, Joseph Vissarionovich 13, 14,
    20, 22, 62, 88, 157, 171,
    176 - 177, 179, 206, 222, 228
State Department, US.......................... 100, 112,
    191 - 192, 203, 208
Stephenson, William 198, 230
Stimson, Henry L. 185, 186
Stip, or Štip 159
Stoyadinovitch or Stojadinović, Dr. Milan........ 30,
    147
Straight of Otranto... 36
Strang, Lord William............... 57, 166, 173, 228
Struga 154
Struma River........................... 78, 151, 152, 154
Stukas dive bombers 78
Suda Bay 40
Sudan... 137, 204
Suez Canal 40
Sulzberger, Cyrus Leo 65, 110, 128, 230
Sušak, or Susak.. 137

Sweet-Escott, Bickham 47, 51, 60,
    65, 132 - 133,
    136, 181, 230

Tatoi Conference........................ 74, 81, 143, 168
Taylor, George Francis........................ 15, 51, 58,
    60, 64, 66 - 68, 70, 77, 78, 80 - 81,
    85, 96, 102, 106 - 109, 115,
    117 - 119, 121 - 123, 132 - 133, 138,
    142 - 143, 158, 161, 174 - 176,
    184 - 185, 194, 215 - 216, 223, 224
Taylor, historian Alan John Percival (A.J.P.) ...33,
    35, 98, 100, 166, 173, 228, 230
Teheran 14, 176
Teheran Conference 176
Teleki, Count Pal 160
Thomas, Gordon 230
Thompson, George 182
Thrace, or Thracia .... 67, 75 - 76,
    84, 91, 103, 149, 160
Tiflis... 21
Tobruk 63, 68, 158, 188
Treaty of London, 1915 94
Trepča mines.. 15
Trieste 14
Tripartite Treaty of Mutual Assistance, Anglo-
French-Turkish Pact .... 19 - 22,
    34, 38, 44 - 45, 51 - 52, 55, 61 - 62,
    83, 85, 87 - 88, 91, 94, 96, 98 - 99,
    101 - 102, 104 - 105, 107 - 108, 110,
    112, 114, 118, 122, 124 - 126, 128,
    134, 146, 150 - 152, 160, 212, 216
Tripoli.. 67, 69 - 70,
    73, 169, 172
Troy, Professor Thomas F.................... 184 - 187,
    197, 201 - 202, 204, 230
Tupanjanin, Dr. Miloš, or "Uncle"............ 15 - 16,
    108 - 111, 120, 138,
    176, 212, 215, 219, 223
Turkey, or Turks .... 16, 25, 29 - 30,
    33 - 35, 38 - 39, 42 - 46, 48, 50,
    52 - 54, 59 - 61, 64 - 86, 90 - 94,
    98 - 101, 103 - 104, 106,
    111 - 113, 116, 118 - 120, 123,
    145 - 148, 150 - 151, 155,
    159 - 160, 163, 166 - 168, 171, 173,
    186 - 189, 191 - 192, 194,
    197 - 198, 200, 203 - 208, 222, 230
Tyrol 156

Ukraine, or Ukrainians .... 20 - 21, 88, 95, 198
"Ultra" messages 73
United States, America or Americans 25, 26,
    38, 50, 51, 56 - 58, 61, 65,
    68, 71, 74, 80, 87,
    97 -98, 103, 112,
    115 - 116, 120, 126, 129, 131,
    135, 145, 166, 168, 171, 172,
    183 - 193, 189, 190, 192 - 194,
    197 - 201, 202 - 205, 207 - 209, 224, 228

Uman 21
"ungentlemanly warfare" 60
Ustaše, the .... 17 - 18
Užice 158

Valjevo 163
Valona 60, 206
Vauhnik. Colonel Vladimir 44, 88, 149, 230
Veles 109
Veria 78
Vichy France 92, 120
Vienna .... 110, 123 - 124, 126, 152, 195
Vodušek Starič, historian Jerca .... 30 - 31,
110, 130, 141, 143, 191, 231
Vojvodina 17
Vrnjačka Banja 161
Vucinich, Professor Wayne S. 19
Vyshinsky, Andrei 118

Waldan, Gen.- Maj. von 147
War Cabinet 14, 57, 71, 75,
80, 84, 99, 122, 159, 165
War Office 69, 73,
139 - 141, 151, 184, 189, 212
Washington, D. C. .... 56 - 58, 68,
83, 91, 106, 112, 152, 185,
187, 189 - 190, 195, 200,
205, 206, 208, 220, 228, 229
Washington, George 200
Wavell, General Sir Archibald (later Field
Marshal Earl Wavell) ....
40 - 41, 45, 47, 54, 59, 60, 63 - 66,
68 - 70, 72 -74, 76 - 78, 80 - 81, 84,
89 - 92, 94, 97, 100, 103, 158,
161 - 162, 164 - 165, 168, 170,
188 - 191, 204 - 205, 213, 217
Wedemeyer, General Albert C. 57, 104, 231
West, Nigel 231
Western Europe 190
Wheeler-Bennett 14, 41, 57, 159, 229, 231
Whitehall .... 38, 102 - 103,
133 - 134, 169, 203
Williams, historian Heather 116
Wilson, Dr. Charles - Lord Moran 33
Wilson, General Sir Henry Maitland (later Field
Marshal Lord Wilson) ....
70, 81, 89, 97, 135, 145,
152 - 154, 161, 178, 213
Winterbotham, Frederick William 36, 37, 231
Woodhouse, Christopher Montague 181
World War One, or WWI 25, 27
World War Two, or WWII 26, 27, 36, 226

Yalta 14
Yugoslav Air Force 85, 140, 148,
157, 194, 197, 224
Yugoslavia, or Yugoslavs (also Yugo-Slavia,
Jugoslavia, Jug, Jugs, Juggery) ....
13, 15 - 32, 34 - 40, 42 - 43, 44 - 104,
106 - 108, 110 - 138, 141 - 143,
145 - 177, 179, 181 -183, 185 - 186,
188 - 212, 214 - 227, 229, 230, 231

Zagreb .... 15, 18, 22 - 23,
30, 95, 104, 114, 132,
137 - 138, 161, 174
Zemun .... 139, 141, 194 - 195, 197, 202
Živković, General Petar 220, 227

www.ingramcontent.com/pod-product-compliance
Lightning Source LLC
Chambersburg PA
CBHW081220170426
43198CB00017B/2670